Roman Political Thought and the Modern Theoretical Imagination

Oklahoma Series in Classical Culture

Roman Political Thought and the Modern Theoretical Imagination

Dean Hammer

University of Oklahoma Press : Norman

Also by Dean Hammer

The Puritan Tradition in Revolutionary, Federalist, and Whig Political Theory: A Rhetoric of Origins (New York, 1998)
The Iliad *as Politics: The Performance of Political Thought* (Norman, 2002)

Library of Congress Cataloging-in-Publication Data
Hammer, Dean, 1959–
Roman political thought and the modern theoretical imagination / Dean Hammer.
p. cm. — (Oklahoma series in classical culture ; v. 34)
Includes bibliographical references and index.
ISBN 978-0-8061-3927-2 (hardcover : alk. paper) 1. Political science—Rome—History. 2. Political science—Cross-cultural studies. I. Title.
JC83.H36 2008
320.092′237—dc22 2007049488

Roman Political Thought and the Modern Theoretical Imagination is Volume 34 in the Oklahoma Series in Classical Culture.

The paper in this book meets the guidelines for permanence and durability of the Committee on Production Guidelines for Book Longevity of the Council on Library Resources. ∞

1 2 3 4 5 6 7 8 9 10

Para nos compadres Denis y Maria Beatriz,
nos ahijado Juan Pablo y nos amigos
Salvadoreños

Contents

Acknowledgments		ix
Abbreviations		xi
Introduction		3
1	The Romans in Political Thought	13
2	Cicero, Arendt, and the Cultivation of the Political World: Reading the *Tusculan Disputations* Politically	38
3	Livy, Machiavelli, and the Recovery of Felt Meanings	78
4	Tacitus, Montesquieu, and the Malady of Despotism	132
5	Seneca and Foucault: Restoring the Jurisdiction of the Political	180
Epilogue		223
Notes		229
Bibliography		283
Index of Classical Passages Cited		339
General Index		351

Acknowledgments

This project began innocently enough on a tennis court when a colleague and playing partner of mine asked whatever happened to the Romans in political thought. Admittedly, that is an odd question in that setting, but such conversations had always been (and continue to be) part of the game. I planned initially only to write the article on Hannah Arendt and the Romans that appeared in *Political Theory*. Little did I know that the question would occupy the next half decade of my scholarship, leading me into a world far removed (in almost every conceivable way) from my earlier work on Homer and archaic Greece.

A number of people have been essential in the development of this project. Tom Banks, Ted Lendon, Kurt Raaflaub, Kerry Whiteside, Tony Woodman, and two reviewers for the University of Oklahoma Press provided invaluable guidance on the manuscript. Their comments have been particularly helpful in forcing me to communicate my ideas to both classicists and political theorists. I worked closely with Marina Lutova, one of my students, on the first chapter. Other students who have provided needed assistance include Amy Miller,

Michael Kicey, Jeremy Stump, Craig Harris, Dominique Martella, Lauren Neal, Laura Selway, and Ben Wilson. I want to thank the Hackman Scholars Program for providing funding for student research for both Marina Lutova and Jeremy Stump. And I want to thank Duke University for showing me such hospitality while I was there as a visiting scholar.

Abbreviations

MODERN TEXTS

BPF	Hannah Arendt, *Between Past and Future*
C	Montesquieu, *Considerations on the Causes of the Greatness of the Romans and Their Decline*
CS	Michel Foucault, *The Care of the Self* (vol. 3 of *The History of Sexuality*)
D	Machiavelli, *The Discourses*
EC	Montesquieu, "An Essay on the Causes that may Affect Men's Minds and Characters"
HC	Hannah Arendt, *The Human Condition*
LM	Hannah Arendt, *The Life of the Mind*
MDT	Hannah Arendt, *Men in Dark Times*
OR	Hannah Arendt, *On Revolution*
OT	Hannah Arendt, *The Origins of Totalitarianism*
P	Machiavelli, *The Prince*
S	Montesquieu, *The Spirit of Laws*
UP	Michel Foucault, *The Use of Pleasure* (vol. 2 of *The History of Sexuality*)
WP	Hannah Arendt, *Was ist Politik?*

CLASSICAL TEXTS

Aristotle

De An.	*De Anima* (*On the Soul*)

Celsus

De Med.	*De Medicina (On Medicine)*

Cicero

Acad.	*Academica* (*Academics*)
Amic.	*De Amicitia* (*On Friendship*)
Attic.	*Epistulae ad Atticum* (*Letters to Atticus*)
De Orat.	*De Oratore* (*On the Orator*)
Div.	*De Divinatione* (*On Divination)*
Fam.	*Epistulae ad Familiares* (*Letters to Friends*)
Fin.	*De Finibus* (*On Ends*)
Leg.	*De Legibus* (*On Laws*)
Nat.	*De Natura Deorum* (*On the Nature of the Gods*)
Offic.	*De Officiis* (*On Duties*)
Orat.	*Orator* (*Orator*)
Q. Fr.	*Epistulae ad Q. Fratrem* (*Letters to his Brother Quintus*)
Rep.	*De Re Publica* (*On the Republic)*
Tusc.	*Tusculanae Disputationes* (*Tusculan Disputations*)

Galen

De Plac.	*De Placitis Hippocratis et Platonis (On Precepts of Hippocrates and Plato)*

Ovid

M.	*Metamorphoses*

Plutarch

Cato Mai.	*Cato Maior*

Quintilian

Inst.	*Institutio Oratoria*

Sallust

Jug.	*Bellum Jugurthinum* (*The War with Jugurtha*)

Seneca

Cons. Helv.	*De Consolatione ad Helviam* (*To Helvia on Consolation*)
De Ben.	*De Beneficiis* (*On Benefits*)
De Ot.	*De Otio* (*On Leisure*)
Ep.	*Epistulae* (*The Epistles*)
De Tranq. An.	*De Tranquillitate Animi* (*On Tranquillity of Mind*)
Natl. Quest.	*Naturales Quaestiones* (*Natural Questions*)

Tacitus

Agric.	*Agricola*
Ann.	*Annales* (*The Annals*)
Dial.	*Dialogus* (*A Dialogue on Oratory*)
Germ.	*Germania*
Hist.	*Historiarum* (*The Histories*)

Virgil

Aen.	*Aeneid*
Ec.	*Eclogues*
G.	*Georgics*

Roman Political Thought and the Modern Theoretical Imagination

Introduction

No worse a fate can befall a political thinker than to appear boring. But that is precisely what happened to the Romans. Part of the blame certainly lies with the Romans, who seemed unable to shed the crusty image of Cato the Elder, famous for among other things banning the philosophers from Rome. Even Virgil, who sought to duplicate Homer's feat by creating a Roman epic, describes how Rome's greatest contribution was not in its art, or its discoveries, or its eloquence, but in its "rule" over others (*Aen.* 6.851).[1] Part of the blame may also be placed on the Romantics, who saw the Romans as bound to the finite and uninspired expression of the "actual world" rather than displaying the creativity and spiritual idealism of the Greeks.[2] Even in the Roman lamentations about the corruption of the republic and the growing decadence of imperial politics, they, as Schiller writes, failed to transform or express this loss "in an ideal sense."[3] And some general trends, such as the decline of exposure to Latin in public schools in the twentieth century, further explain the decreased interest in the Romans. But it is in the professionalization of the academy that Roman thought suffered its cruelest fate: classical scholars removed theory from their Roman accounts at the same time that theorists omitted the Romans from their theoretical accounts.

Simply put, the Romans have ceased to be central to political thought. A brief survey of the scholarly landscape reveals how rarely visited our Roman artifacts have become. Since the founding of the journal *Political Theory* in 1973, only a handful of articles have addressed the Romans.[4] From 1980 to 1990, the British journal *History of Political Thought* published just four articles that dealt with ancient Rome. More surprising, only five articles on ancient Rome were even submitted to the journal.[5] There is no commercially available reader devoted to Roman political thought. The closest a Roman comes to appearing in *Classics of Moral and Political Theory* is in the selections from Epictetus, a Greek philosopher raised as a slave in Rome. Klosko subsumes Roman political thought under Hellenistic Political Theory. Thiele's *Thinking Politics*, which aims to "integrate the insights of ancient, modern, and postmodern political thought," contains two references to the Romans: one brief quotation by Cicero and the term *res publica*.[6] The *Blackwell Encyclopaedia of Political Thought* describes the "principal interest of Roman political thought" as lying "in the fact that its exponents were for the most part actively engaged in public life and made sustained efforts to relate what they knew of Greek Political Thought to their perceptions of the Roman political process."[7] And Cicero's works appear in the *Encyclopaedia* as a "revival of the intellectual activity in the Greek world under Roman rule, on a vast scale, if not of great originality."[8] What has become most noteworthy about the Romans is their striking unoriginality.

So complete is the disappearance of the Romans as original thinkers that we do not even notice that they are gone. And, ironically, we do not notice how often they appear in other guises. For although scholars may no longer view the Romans as central to the activity of political thinking, theorists who are invoked frequently did. I am speaking about theorists as diverse as Machiavelli, Montesquieu, Arendt, and Foucault. More than an irony, this poses an interpretative problem. Our conception of the Romans obscures our understanding of how they could contribute to the political thinking of the past or present. My interest is to revisit this connection by asking, by way of Machiavelli, Montesquieu, Arendt, and Foucault, whether there is anything worth retrieving from this Roman past—things that might excite the contemporary political imagination. In bringing these theorists into conversation with Romans who inspired them—Cicero with Arendt, Livy with Machiavelli, Tacitus with Montesquieu, and Seneca with Foucault—I argue that each of these modern theorists saw in the Romans an exploration of the ways in which politics and its loss are experienced. Moreover, reversing the conclusion of the Romantics, I suggest that the Romans translate this loss into a conception of the role that political thought can play in the recovery of political meaning.

TERRA RECOGNITA

From Cicero's death to Tacitus's birth is a century, yet during this time Rome passed, by way of decades of turmoil, bloodshed, and civil war, from a republic to an increasingly cruel and corrupt imperial monarchy. These events provide the backdrop to an overwhelming sense of loss, a "looming awareness," as Joy Connolly writes, "that the living web of communal virtue" is "being torn apart by human vice and mortality; that the basis for legitimacy is slowly eroding; that the citizen and the state must die together."[9] We can attribute this sense, at least in part, to the Romans' own conservatism in which politics always operated in the shadow of the *mos maiorum*, ancient and venerated norms. This sense may also be simply an aspect of the human tendency to romanticize better times, even if those times were not so great. But one would be hard pressed to explain why Machiavelli, Montesquieu, Arendt, and Foucault—hardly romantics—would find intellectual sustenance in a Roman desire to return to some Golden Age.

It is certainly the case that Machiavelli, Montesquieu, Arendt, and Foucault were (like the Romans) wrestling with what Arendt points to as a loss of bearings, whether of the political fragmentation of Machiavelli's Italy, the shadow of despotism for Montesquieu, the dark times of totalitarianism for Hannah Arendt, or an imperial society that, for Foucault, is both expansive and isolating. There is a shared nostalgia among these modern and Roman authors, but it is a nostalgia that plays a critical and interpretive role in their respective writings. The nostalgic sense that something has been lost reveals that there was, quite simply, something to lose. That "something" is more than power and position; it connects to a whole series of affective associations that orient the person in the political world. Rather than simply yearning for some other world, the recollection of these affective associations by Cicero, Livy, Seneca, and Tacitus is read by these modern theorists as performing a task akin to Plato's: they are engaged in constructing a vision of the political world. But where Plato starts with the nowhere of a canvas wiped clean, the Romans begin with the somewhere of the political world that they saw themselves as inhabiting. The Roman question that underlies my reading, and the one that I believe attracts these modern thinkers to the Romans, is not "How do we create anew?" but "Where do we go from here?" Rather than a *utopia*—a perfect nowhere—the Roman task can be better understood as reconstituting a *terra recognita*—an attempt to know again, to recognize, the world that we inhabit. Roman political thought becomes world-building, not as an "architectonic vision" where, as Sheldon Wolin argues, one imagines a better world that exists outside the existing order, but as an attempt to restore our experience of the world and the contours of the political terrain.[10]

The starting point for this *terra recognita* is the mental map by which individuals orient themselves politically. Much of the tradition of political thought has sought to construct this map according to theories that, as Wolin writes approvingly, endeavor to "mould the totality of political phenomena to accord with some vision of the Good that lies outside the political order."[11] Such a political vision might proceed by way of reasoned argument, such as the Socratic *elenctic* method that attempts through questioning to strip away prejudices and ungrounded opinion. Or such a map of community life might be organized by a notion of Truth like one encounters in Augustine or Aquinas. Or one can posit historical laws, such as Hegel's unfolding of *Geist* or Marx's historical materialism. Or one can wrap oneself in a veil of ignorance and proceed, like Rawls, to rationally construct a community.

To political theorists steeped in reason and abstraction, the Roman map seems almost embarrassingly affective and tangible: it is filled with recollections of laws and institutions, names and places, and events and traditions. To read the Romans is to immediately enter this world. But in such attachments we can locate the conceptual core of Roman political thought. As Kaster notes, "we do better to conceive the Romans' emotional life as being concerned not with questions of high existential drama" but with the question of "enjoying the sort of communal life worth living."[12] Their attention to tradition, their building of institutions, their mechanical and architectural contributions, and their love of talking about all of these things reveal a fundamental ontology: we are what we build.[13] Or to state it with a bit more nuance, the human artifacts that surround us provide a foundation, like Livy's *ab urbe condita*, by which we relate not just to those things, but also to each other.

Cicero, Livy, Seneca, and Tacitus speak to the loss of particular aspects of this mental map. Their point is neither that these markers change, nor that there is detachment (as there is in all ages) of signifiers from the signified. Meanings are always in transition, and there is always a gap between forms (such as laws) and the concepts represented by the forms (such as justice). Their point is that in the wake of tumultuous violence, naked self-interest, hypocrisy, corruption, and terror, the markers lose both their objectivity and their salience. By objectivity, I mean the sense, born of history and experience, that these markers have an existence and meaningfulness apart from the individual. They lose their objectivity as their outlines become indistinct from one's own interests, desires, inclinations, and fears. At that point, they become less and less helpful in guiding conduct, clarifying goals, distinguishing best from worst, or even demarcating the terms of debate. And these markers lose their salience, their ability to attract us and speak to us, when they no longer accord with a set of experiences that are lived each day. Collective meanings stop being seen by individuals as belonging to them. The Romans do not respond to this loss of objectivity and salience, though, by taking us to a place outside this world to imagine some better realm; rather, each of these Roman thinkers attempts to reanimate one's relationship to a political world that may have been forgotten or perhaps never have been known.

We begin this journey with Cicero, who at first lifts us from this world in the dream of Scipio and then retreats from the world in the *Tusculan Disputations*. As a response to personal loss, the *Tusculans* appears as a philosophic meditation on how one can shore up oneself against the vicissitudes of life by recognizing that true happiness lies in a virtuous soul. But the *Tusculans* never reaches this note of reconciliation. Like Scipio's dream in *The Republic*, the *Tusculans* continually and fondly recalls a world that one knows through its tangibility: its monuments, buildings, art, literature, festivals, laws, and institutions. Arendt associates this desire to cultivate and care for our tangible world with "culture" and traces its fullest elaboration back to Cicero. These artifacts have an illuminating quality to them, to use an image employed by both Cicero and Arendt, not only giving testimony to the past but also providing durable markers by which we orient ourselves both temporally (to past and future) and spatially (to others inside and outside the community). But these artifacts, captured in Cicero's image of the republic as a once beautiful painting, have now faded from neglect because the current age values the immediacy of wealth, power, and pleasure. In bringing together Arendt and Cicero, I am suggesting, in short, that we can read the *Tusculans* politically: not as a break from but as a deepened reflection on the role of culture in the recovery of the durable markers by which we orient ourselves in the political world.

Livy picks up where Cicero leaves off, placing before his audience the monuments of the past that no longer inspire or convey the living history of the Roman people. It has frequently been suggested, following Walsh, that Livy provides us with a "psychological history" as he attempts to take us inside his historical characters—partly for entertainment, partly for instruction—to convey their thoughts, emotions, and reactions. I return to this idea of a psychological history to give it a more conceptual twist by suggesting that Livy provides a way of thinking about politics in which political concepts become comprehensible as *felt meanings*: accumulated over time, woven into the emotions, and made salient by memory. Felt meanings, as the term suggests, are ultimately phenomenal rather than philosophical; they are given coherence more by experience than logic. And suggestive of the difference between *utopia* and *terra recognita,* Livy emphasizes the role of vision as the most powerful political sense, not because we can gaze into the sky and imagine a better world, but because through sight our experience of the world is most vividly imprinted and recalled. For Machiavelli, Livy's "psychological history" appears as an alternative to Plato's theory of philosopher-kings, Aristotle's model of *phronesis*, and Christian moralism, each of which ultimately looks to reason as the mechanism by which communities can be made to endure. For Machiavelli, Livy's psychological history traces how political concepts such as liberty are born of affective associations. Moreover, by way of Livy, Machiavelli charts how corruption is nurtured by abstracted emotions: a form of political blindness in which meanings are no longer animated by collective experience. Ultimately, Machiavelli looks to Livy's historical method as a way of constituting or reconstituting felt meanings through the sensory act of perception, simulated in the mind's eye, that invokes shared impressions, reactions, and conclusions.

Both Cicero and Livy hold out some hope of rekindling the vague flickering of a republican past. I turn to Tacitus next because, while writing later than Seneca, he provides an analysis in the *Annals* of the early principate. Although Tacitus spends considerable time chronicling the intrigues of the imperial court, his discussion of the principate suggests that something far more enduring had penetrated into Roman political life. By way of Montesquieu, with his emphasis on the invisible impressions, recollections, and arrangements of experiences that serve as the impetus for collective action, we can read Tacitus as exploring less the personality of the tyrant or the institutional forms of imperial Rome and more the political psychology of despotism. Despotism functions by slowly breaking down the public and private cues by which people can orient their action. The true cost of despotism that emerges by way of Tacitus and Montesquieu is not the dead bodies but the lifeless souls of individuals who are consigned to navigate through a political netherworld in which nothing, including one's own expression of experience, has any measure of authenticity. The role of the political thinker is first and foremost to address the numbness of political life by connecting the individual back to experience: prodding, provoking, agitating, and ultimately animating the reader.

I turn finally to Seneca, who provides something of a case study of the disorienting effects of despotism. Rather than reading the *Epistles* as hypocritical self-justification or as a retreat from the political world, I argue by way of Foucault that the *Epistles* emerge as an analysis of the ways in which individuals become entrapped in the political discourse of despotism, making withdrawal from the political world as problematic as involvement. Ultimately, I suggest that Seneca seeks to establish the ground, or jurisdiction, by which individuals, absent any durable political markers, are able to reorient themselves. Foucault locates this orientation in the care of oneself by which one begins to fashion oneself as a work of art. I think we can only take this image so far—less far, perhaps, than Foucault does. But the notion of the self as a work of art serves as a starting point by which one can begin to bring into view the contours of a political self so that one can recognize oneself again, and thus begin to define one's responsibilities and duties in a broader social, political, and civic realm.

The Roman texts that I use are guided in large part by the choices of each of the modern thinkers. To that extent, I am not attempting to offer an exhaustive analysis of Roman political thought, nor even of any one thinker. My goal instead is to speak to two groups—classicists and political theorists—who have something to offer to each other, but who do not always have a common vocabulary with which to do it. To that end each chapter proceeds in two ways. First, I use these modern theorists as a starting point for thinking about how each of these Roman texts can be read as a form of political thinking. In working through these texts, I suggest that these Roman writers depart most fundamentally from both a Platonic and Aristotelian philosophical tradition that emphasizes the role of reason in defining a vision of collective action. What emerges, instead, is an attempt to articulate a political vision that is organized around affective associations; an attempt to reanimate one's own sense of the meaningfulness of the markers of the political terrain. I then return to these modern theorists to explore how the Romans are played out in the modern theoretical imagination. In neglecting the Roman dimension of modern thought we risk detaching political concepts from the experiences that animated them so that, as Arendt writes, we get "caught in a maze of abstractions, metaphors, and figures of speech in which everything can be taken and mistaken for something else" (*BPF* 136).

Arendt's warning is particularly apt in our contemporary age in which democracy risks becoming an abstraction: exported as an ideal while barely lived as an experience at home. By that I mean that however intact may be particular formal democratic processes like voting, two forces are at work that privatize our passions: global economic markets that are publicly unaccountable but answer to our private desires; and an expansive and increasingly secret imperial society in which quiescence accompanies fear. What these modern writers, by way of the Romans, recall and explore for us are the ways in which the experience of politics is formed and lost. Certainly formalized processes remain important, but more than that are the complex array of sentiments that make our public world collectively recognizable, accountable, and changeable. These works do not suggest that unbridled passions provide political answers; rather, they explore how sentiments form a conceptual part of our political experience. Taking Arendt's point seriously, I seek to explore how political theory can return thought to the world.

1

The Romans in Political Thought

We "march on Roman highways of law," Basil Gildersleeve wrote, sounding a common refrain about the Roman contribution to political thought.[1] Gildersleeve's language is revealing. Whatever was seen as Rome's contribution to the West, they were builders more than creators. And while on Roman legal ground we trod, in Greek literary and philosophic skies we soar. The story did not have to be this way. How we have come to interpret the past has as much to do with how we understand ourselves—what we choose to emphasize and ignore, what resonates with us, and what has been passed down to us—as it does with anything that resides in the past. In this chapter, I trace how and why the Romans came to all but disappear in twentieth century discussions of political thought. This outcome has a great deal to do with the paths taken by political theorists, on the one hand, and classicists, on the other, as they formed themselves into disciplines with distinct methodologies. For political theorists, the Romans failed to inspire new ways to think conceptually about politics. And for classicists, theory encumbered the philological and historiographic recovery of the Roman past.

The lines between political philosophy and classical inquiry were not always so stark. To the generations of scholars steeped in the political thought of Spencer, Comte, and the neo-Hegelians, the Romans were part of a philosophical and historical discourse that viewed the state as an organic entity that grew and decayed and whose constitutional and legal structures revealed the unfolding and realization of the human spirit, reason, or mind.[2] Bluntschli, whose widely read Hegelian discussion of the state appeared in English translation in 1885, saw the state as a "moral organism and not the product of mere cold Logic." Bluntschli rejected both "arid formulas" that disregarded "the facts of actual political society" and an empirical approach that "holds to the mere outward form."[3] He argued, instead, for a "philosophic-historical method" that "recognises, explains, and interprets the inner connection between Past and Present, the organic development of national life and the *moral idea* as revealed in its history." For Bluntschli these historical developments were revelatory of "the spirit of man in history."[4] In this context, the Romans were praised for their "genius for Law and Politics" that was most fully realized in Western constitutionalism.[5]

This idealist conception of a Western tradition saw the world as organized by eternal essences, linked the past with the present, envisioned a progressive conception of historical development, and provided a moral foundation to contemporary conceptions of the state. Although the language of progress would linger in the academy, these *a priori* philosophic assumptions that guided historical and political inquiry fell out of favor in both classics and political science, especially in the United States and Britain. An important impetus for this transformation was the professionalization of the academy, reflected in the formation of professional associations and corresponding struggles to stake out distinctive disciplinary identities. With these identities were also established norms of scholarly practice, including the types of questions asked and the techniques for answering them.

In classics one of the earliest of these organizations was the American Philological Association, founded in 1869, followed by the publication of the inaugural issue of the *American Journal of Philology* in 1880. Gildersleeve, the first editor of the journal and a critical figure in introducing a German philological tradition to American classical scholarship, clearly drew the disciplinary battle lines when he pointed out that "a country which boasts a Journal of Speculative Philosophy" does not have "even a solitary periodical devoted to a science which counts its professed votaries by hundreds, if not by thousands."[6] Classics was not about philosophy, but about history, language, and (especially in England) prose- and verse-making. This focus on language study and composition was further confirmed by the formation of the Classical Association in 1903 to address the decline of language instruction in British schools. Four regional associations of the Classical Association were organized in the United States over the next decade and the first issue of *Classical Philology* was published in 1906.[7]

Classicists, more in Germany and the United States than in England (where classical study was still seen as training to be a gentleman rather than a scholar), envisioned an expansive notion of *Altertumswissenschaft*, or science of antiquity. Articulated influentially by Wilamowitz, *Altertumswissenschaft* encompassed traditional philology (deciphering and reconstructing original texts), archaeology, art history, and ancient history, and was aimed at personal cultivation and national education.[8] A more expansive notion of philology, which for Wilamowitz was synonymous with *Altertumswissenschaft,* was now conceived as a "science" and joined to an investigation of the ancient past that provided a rigorous method by which "advance in the definiteness and certainty of knowledge" could be obtained.[9] Leopold von Ranke's dictum that the role of historiography was to discern the past *wie es eigentlich gewesen*, or "how it actually was," sent scholars to the archives to examine the data of history, most significantly, inscriptions and papyri.[10] Notably, Mommsen departed from the German philhellenic, aestheticizing tradition of Goethe, Herder, and Humboldt and grounded inquiry in a critical examination of historical data and sources. In his attempt to identify and systematize the unwritten constitutional arrangements of Roman politics, Mommsen set the terms by which the Roman political past would be understood for decades to come. Others, notably Ulrich Wilcken, Max Weber, Ludwig Mitteis, Josef Partsch, and (later) Michael Rostovtzeff, extended the interest in law and administration to study both regional administration and agrarian history.[11] Source criticisms, commentaries, and collections of inscriptions abounded. In reflecting on these dramatic changes in methodological orientation, Gildersleeve commented in 1917 that it seemed almost like "an ancient of days" when in fact it was "comparatively recent" that classical scholars "walked humbly on the lines of the Hegelian logic."[12]

There were concurrent developments in the formation of distinct venues for political scientists. As with classics, political science was seen as an essential aspect of the education of a democratic citizenry. Similarly, as well, political scientists saw history as important to their inquiry. Munroe Smith, in introducing the *Political Science Quarterly* in 1886, delineated the centrality of "historical investigation" to the task of political science.[13] Through this historical investigation one could make comparisons and identify the general tendencies in the "processes" of the "evolution of the state" and the "deeper substantial identities" that defined the essential nature of the state.[14] But Smith's language already outlined a disciplinary focus that was not solely historical, but was also theoretical (in identifying generalizations and principles).

Indicative of this departure from strictly historical approaches, the American Political Science Association was formed in 1903 out of the American Historical Association and the American Economic Association.[15] The Association was established in large part to provide an outlet for scholars interested in policy oriented and practical political concerns. Although the application of scientific methods to the study of politics had been a part of political science at least since Bluntschli and Burgess, the creation of the American Political Science Association seemed to focus much more attention on what it meant to be a "science." In his address to the American Political Science Association and the American Historical Association, James Bryce argued that "in calling Politics a Science we mean . . . that there is a constancy and uniformity in the tendencies of humans which enable us to regard the acts of men at one time as due to the same causes which have governed their acts at previous times." Thus political science may be defined, he claimed, as the "data of political history"; that is, acts of men "reclassified and explained as the result of certain general principles."[16]

The heightened emphasis on the study of politics as a science applied to contemporary affairs had implications for political theory. In several pages of pedantic prose, Bryce lectured theorists on how they should avoid the "methods of metaphysics" and should focus on concrete "facts."[17] Others, though, notably W.W. Willoughby, who (with Charles Merriam and William Dunning) served on the initial APSA Political Theory committee, defended the abstractions and speculations in the "philosophical systems" of such theorists as Plato.[18] Although theory should in no way lose its grounding in historical fact, it should not simply serve as "guidance of practical politics."[19] In a 1904 article describing the founding of the APSA, Willoughby provided a more formalized definition of political theory. Political theory, he suggested, should be concerned with "the analysis and exact definition of the concepts employed in political thinking, and which thus includes the consideration of the essential nature of the state, its right to be, its ends, its proper functions and its relation to its own citizens, and the nature of law."[20] Most influentially, Dunning, who maintained his close affiliation with history, created the paradigm in the United States for the study of political theory at the turn of the century. In his 1902 work, *A History of Political Theories*, Dunning organized political theory by theorist rather than as a thematic inquiry into the nature of the state. And he instilled in several generations of theorists, both through his scholarship and as a professor at Columbia, a historicism in which political ideas were understood as responses to social questions and events of the time.[21] The importance of the study of the history of political theories for Dunning was to examine the relationship between ideas and "political fact" or "institutional development" and to some extent to shed light on the origins of the contemporary practice of political theory, political science, and political organization.[22]

Although classics and political science were developing their distinct methodological orientations, discussions about Rome coalesced around its contribution to the development of the constitutional state. This shared interest was informed by a strong tradition of jurisprudence that developed alongside (and in many ways bridged) both classics and political science and encompassed United States, British, and Continental scholarship. Whether Mommsen or Gildersleeve in classics, Dunning in political science, or Pollock in jurisprudence, scholars at the turn of the century characterized with striking consistency the Roman contribution to Western thought. Even a quick perusal of book reviews in these early journals reveals the focus on Roman law.[23] The evaluation of that contribution certainly varied. Willoughby, like Dunning, saw the importance of the Romans as laying in their creation of the first secular organization of the state.[24] Sir Frederick Pollock acknowledged that the Romans were "great as rulers and administrators and they created systematic law" but were not capable of "invention in politics," contributed "nothing worth mentioning" to political science, and were utterly derivative (even in law) of the genius of the Greeks.[25] And for Gildersleeve, the Romans came to us as toilers, able to build but never able to achieve the conceptual genius of the Greeks.

CHALLENGES TO DEMOCRACY

The interwar years presented a challenge to classicists and political theorists on both sides of the Atlantic. Simply put, the question raised was to what extent the ancients could speak to the turbulence of world war, economic crises, revolution, communism, and fascism. These events did not create the question of the relevance of the past to the present, but gave more urgency to the answer. Some, for example, attributed England's lack of technical preparedness for World War I to the nation's focus on the humanities rather than the sciences.[26] Economic depression pulled students into more practical studies, such as the social sciences.[27] New pedagogies were emphasizing the role of education in acculturating students to their social heritage rather than training them rigorously in classical language.[28] And questions were raised about the application of the study of the ancient world to the "real problems of modern society," not the least were threats to democracy.[29] Dewey saw the ancient past as an unhelpful model of education for citizens in a liberal democratic and industrial state because it characterized vocational and practical education as "the training of a servile class."[30] Even more dire, Arnold described how "the eye looks upon a shattered civilization" as "the black clouds of war lift from the surface of the Continents of Europe and Nearer Asia."[31]

The first principles that guided Western scholars in their

confident judgments about the progress of civilization were now cast into doubt. Shorn of its idealistic metaphysics that had always placed inquiry in service to the perfection of humanity, the value-free methodologies employed by classicists and political scientists could only describe but not advocate. Moreoever, advocacy had become indistinguishable from propaganda. One could not help but be shaken, for example, by how Germany, which had been the preeminent model of disciplinary rigor and the basis of scholarly focus on the nature of the state, had placed learning in service to a nationalist and militarist culture.[32] As Merriam noted, the preceding years had demonstrated that "political theory" could easily be a "pawn or piece in the larger game of military, pecuniary, or other group advantage."[33] Suggestive of this dwindling status, political theory was dropped as a category for books and articles in the *American Political Science Review* from 1914–1916, and then placed in Miscellaneous until 1944. Put starkly, what distinguished political thought from propaganda and historical investigation from antiquarian escapism? What tied explorations of the ancient past to concerns of the contemporary world?

Classical scholars and political theorists found themselves with similar options for responding. One option was a humanistic counteroffensive. Political theorists pointed to the need to stake out ethical positions and to more consciously undertake its role in educating a people for political democracy. The debate only intensified with the mounting chaos of the Weimar years and became part of intellectual discourse in the United States and Britain with the immigration of German intellectuals. For example, Waldemar Gurian, a Catholic émigré, helped to establish *The Review of Politics* in 1939 to bring an Aristotelian and Christian ethical perspective to political events.[34] Classicists, too, claimed to be making ethical contributions, not by developing specific moral philosophies but through exposure to advanced language study. The study of the ancient world constituted a "development toward the 'humane' which reaches its fulfillment only in philological understanding and education."[35] Ironically enough given the reaction against Germany, the claim had its roots in German idealism, whether that of Wilamowitz before or Jaeger during the interwar years. The role of classical study was the creation of a cultivated class that could resist (variously) the rise of the "mechanical state," capitalist instrumentality, democratic populism, "cliques and fashions," and the loss of human values in the wake of economic depression.[36] Industry, Granger argued, with "science for its guide," had destroyed the beauty of human surroundings and the capacity for human expression. The romantic and religious undertones of the redemptive promise of classics rang through Granger's answer to this plight: "the Spirit comes often by way of the Word."[37] The study of ancient language, accessible to only a few, held the key to the recovery of human spirituality. Such language, though, could not help but seem out of step with science, industry, and the egalitarian sentiments of democracy.

Responding to the risk of becoming irrelevant, a second group of classicists and political theorists attempted to demonstrate their ongoing cachet in an age of science and industry. The model of science was so powerful precisely because its methodological rigor yielded results that could be applied. Classicists, whose German heritage had always understood philology as a *Wissenschaft*, opposed the exclusive appropriation of the term "science" by the technical and natural sciences. Although *Wissenschaft* meant nothing more than a systematic field of inquiry, in translation its meaning often slipped into comparisons with the natural sciences. An editorial for the *Classical Journal*, for example, noted that "linguistic science and literary science" involved principles of "observation, experiment, and proof" similar to the sciences.[38] Perhaps most trenchant was Housman's critique of the "nonsense" of textual criticism and the need, like the physical sciences, to rigorously apply rules of grammar, meter, and prosody to the reconstruction of manuscripts.[39] Classicists also claimed a role in providing crucial professional preparation for business leadership, a point made at the 1917 Princeton Classical Conference composed of classicists, scientists, doctors, engineers, journalists, economists, and architects.[40]

Political theorists, too, sought to place their inquiry in the context of increasing interest by political scientists in adopting "modern methods of inquiry and investigation."[41] By drawing on scientific practices of "measuring and comparing and standardizing," Merriam hoped that political scientists would be able to establish a sound basis in knowledge for reaching conclusions about the operation of politics.[42] And Catlin, who was influential in the direction of both English and American political science, sought to construct a "science of social relations and formations," rather than theories of the state, by which power could be directed toward the achievement of particular values.[43] The role of political thought was to analyze and articulate these values.

If the Romans had a role to play in this inquiry, it was by way of their practical contributions to law, jurisprudence, and constitutionalism. Less important was the attempt to place law in an overarching framework of right, grounded in reason, that expressed itself in the historical development of the state. The emergent view was that law was derived from social, cultural, and even personal practices. The legal scholar, thus, sought to identify the specific practices and understand the development of these practices by grounding them in their specific historical environment.[44] The extent of scholarship was breathtaking, encompassing the discovery of new fragments, the compilation of sources, and exhaustive interpretations of all facets of Roman law.[45] The accumulating volumes seemed to confirm a view of the Romans as detailed and technical (even plodding) practioners more than as theoretical or scientific visionaries. Merriam, for example, described the Romans as a "marvel of political prudence and sagacity" though they "did not advance beyond the Greeks" in the "scientific study of government."[46] McIlwain, whose course on the history of constitutional development was taken by almost all Harvard undergraduates in political science, provided a highly influential reading of the linkage between Rome and the development of Western constitutions.[47] McIlwain wrote, "in the general development of political thought the importance of Rome is very great but this importance results from no striking originality, nor from any considerable new Roman contribution to the world's stock of political ideas, it is owing almost wholly to the great practical part that Rome played in laying the legal and political foundations of the western world, and in her transmission of ideas learned from Greece."[48] Where Greek political philosophy was the work of "exceptional individuals," the Roman contribution to constitutional thinking was the result of the "working system of capable people."[49]

It was difficult to distinguish what was, in fact, McIlwain's praise of the Romans from more negative assessments. The Carlyles, in their magisterial account of medieval political thought, connected modern with ancient thought by way of a legal (and contractual) tradition that began with Roman lawyers such as Ulpian and Gaius. The lawyers were not philosophers but "intelligent and able men" who engaged in the "practical work of interpretation and application of law to the changing conditions of Roman Society."[50] Cicero suffered the same fate with the Caryles as with Mommsen: discussed as a person of interest because he "summed up the commonplaces of the political theory of his time," but judged as a thinker who did not possess "any great originality of mind, or any great power of political analysis."[51] Seneca faired no better. He was described as not a "very profound philosopher" and one who "often mistakes rhetorical sentiment for profound ethical emotion."[52]

The most influential incorporation of the Romans into political thought was by Sabine, who, in his widely used *History of Political Theory*, suggested that the "greatest political theories" were important both in their "analysis of a present situation and in suggestiveness for other situations."[53] Sabine (like McIlwain) read the Romans as contributing to a Western notion of law and jurisprudence. In an earlier essay on Cicero, which appeared in his translation with Smith of *On the Commonwealth*, Sabine and Smith concluded that Cicero's work "denotes an advance in political thinking" because of the "noble insistence that it is the duty of all men to serve their country," the "inculcation of the principles of justice and fair-dealing," and the "recognition of the universal society, founded upon reason and including all rational beings within its ambit."[54] In his *History*, Sabine extended this claim, suggesting that the great contribution of Cicero and the Roman lawyers was in the development of "legalism," or "the presumption that the state is a creature of law and is to be discussed not in terms of sociological fact or ethical good but in terms of legal competence and rights."[55] It was an aspect of theory that "hardly existed in Greek thought."[56] The Stoics, too, contributed to these legal foundations of Western law by showing how law was rooted in universal notions of equality (thus serving as the intellectual predecessors of natural law approaches). And Sabine depicted Seneca as exemplifying the newly constructed theological approach to politics and as a predecessor to the "Christian Fathers." In language echoed later by Wolin, Sabine closed the story of the Romans on a note of pessimism: where Cicero had the "illusion that the great day" of the Roman Republic might be "recaptured," for Seneca "the illusion has passed." As an advisor to Nero, Seneca saw clearly that Rome had "fallen into senility, corruption is everywhere, and despotism is inevitable." Seneca, suggested Sabine, "already shows much of the despondency and pessimism that overshadows the Latin literature of the second Christian century."[57]

Sabine's language is suggestive of a final response to the crises of the interwar years. Rather than reading the Romans in order to recover lost moral principles or to restore faith in Western constitutionalism, scholars viewed the past through the sobering realities of the present. Some attempted to read the ancient world by way of a set of modern problems, such as unemployment or machine politics, or by way of modern experiences of practical politics.[58] There were "lessons for the American democracy," Haskell wrote, "in the disintegration of what was called the Roman Republic."[59] Economic, social, and cultural history, as well as a new interest in propaganda, also became more prominent as ways to explain political action.[60]

Perhaps most influential was the emergence of group power approaches that departed from the study of constitutional forms. Matthias Gelzer and Friedrich Münzer pioneered the methodology of prosopography: a painstaking, often empirical, compilation of family names, careers, and relationships. The point was to study the "formation, duration, and dissolution" of influential families and groups that comprised the governing elite.[61] Part of its allure for the historian was its focus on gathering facts rather than generating broader explanations of historical development. Building on prosopography, Anton von Premerstein viewed Roman politics as comprised of extralegal and extrainstitutional relations or transactions that were organized by social power: the ability to influence (through wealth, patronage, and position) and the ability to coerce (through fear). That framework resonated with similar debates within political science and sociology between the pluralist school developed in the works of Arthur Bentley, David Truman, and Robert Dahl, on the one hand, and elite power approaches, reflected in the pioneering work of the Lynds in the 1920s and 1930s and articulated, theoretically, by Gaetano Mosco, Vilfredo Pareto, and Robert Michels, on the other hand. How one appraised group influence, whether oligarchic or democratic, depended to a large extent on whether the informal relations were seen as open, fluid, competitive, or transparent. Probably most influential was Syme's study of the transformation of the Roman state and society into an oligarchy, a work that was as much about the rise of totalitarianism in Europe as it was about the hidden ways in which political freedom in Roman society was abolished. These approaches provided an answer to the question of how lessons from the past could be applied to the concerns of the present. The study of the past could puncture political ideologies and propaganda through a careful, empirical examination of the evidence that revealed the "realities of power."[62]

POST-WAR CHALLENGES: METHODS AND MORALS

Sabine, in his 1939 article, "What is a Political Theory?", addressed an issue that would perplex both political theorists and classicists in the decades to come. Sabine asked, by what standard can we judge political theories as truthful, valid, or useful since they contain both causal and evaluative statements?[63] Classicists had sought to strip the evaluative elements from historiography and philology, only to watch helplessly as fascism and communism gained political hold. And theorists, particularly in their historicism, seemed to have fulfilled Merriam's fear that they could not articulate a set of values that could be distinguished from propaganda. It was unclear how the study of the past could be useful in establishing principles for political action. Hammond, for example, provided a warning to contemporary theorists when he argued that the failure of ancient political theory was its inability to update itself when historical circumstances changed from the democratic city-state to the imperial state.[64] This, too, might be the fate of contemporary political thought. As Mary White wrote in introducing the first issue of *Phoenix*, "One of the reasons for the present neglect of classical studies, and the consequent all too imperfect understanding of that portion of our cultural heritage which derives from Graeco-Roman civilization, is the failure to emphasize the constant interpenetration of the classical and the modern."[65] The looming question was: Does political thought have anything to say to the contemporary age?

This question took on particular urgency, and a renewed German (and decidedly Hellenistic) shape, as it was influenced by a wave of émigrés who were among the leading intellectuals in political theory and classics. Critiques of modernity, mass society, liberalism, and technology were articulated prominently by Hannah Arendt, Leo Strauss, Eric Voegelin, Herbert Marcuse, Max Horkheimer, Theodor Adorno, Hans Jonas, and Hans Morgenthau. Classics saw the immigration of such prominent scholars as Hermann Fränkel, Paul Friedländer, Herbert Bloch, Kurt von Fritz, and Werner Jaeger.[66]

The failure of German liberal democracy served for many as a renewed warning about a perceived ethical, religious, and philosophical vacuum of a modern, technological society. For Voegelin, who viewed the political order as related to the order of being, the Romans were important only as they contained glimpses of the origin of theology and early experiences of

Christianity. What was lacking in the Romans was any insight into the divine ground of human existence. Cicero, suggested Voegelin, "not only is not an original thinker, but he expressly refuses to be one." His mixed attitude of respect and "amused contempt" for Greek philosophy "indicates that the truth of theory, while sensed as an enlargement of the intellectual and moral horizon, could have no existential meaning for a Roman."[67] Hallowell, who was strongly influenced by Voegelin, read Roman ideas, particularly the later Stoics, from the perspective of Christianity.[68] And for Strauss, "The crisis of modernity reveals itself in the fact, or consists in the fact, that modern western man no longer knows what he wants—that he no longer believes that he can know what is good and bad, what is right and wrong."[69] The Roman historians, though, provided examples more than they illuminated ideas. And Cicero, as Holton wrote in Strauss and Cropsey's *History of Political Philosophy*, "diluted [Greek philosophy] to meet the needs of the practical or political life" of the Romans.[70]

Such excursions into the moral foundation of human action did little to alter the trajectories of the mainstreams of political science and classics. In methodological rigor was disciplinary credibility, a judgment reinforced by rankings of research universities and requirements for tenure. The methods, though, led political scientists and classicists to dramatically divergent conceptions—in fact, a severing—of the relationship between history and theory.

In classics McDonald pointed to the sharpening of the methods by which "strict analysis and reconstruction of the evidence" could be achieved.[71] Epigraphic, numismatic, textual, architectural, and artistic evidence were marshalled to reconstruct the cultural, social, economic, and ideological factors that figured into Roman political life.[72] The study of the political past by classicists remained not just agnostic about theory, but resolutely anti-theoretical. Granted, theory did make incursions into the study of the ancient world. New Criticism (and the related approaches of French *explication de texte* and Russian Formalism), for example, focused on the formal aspects of the text, looking for tensions, ambiguities, and paradoxes, in isolation from the historical and biographical context of its production. Classicists were aware, as well, of some of the methodological debates that challenged fundamental assumptions about how all acts of interpretation were theory-laden. But these new conceptual approaches became more the province of literary criticism than history. As Finley noted, "It is generally agreed that Ancient historians rarely discuss questions of method," other than questions of technique.[73]

There seemed to be little to discuss; the historian's task was the "reconstruction of past actuality."[74] Scholarship that employed contemporary theoretical perspectives or was motivated by present concerns was seen as lying "on, or close to, the lunatic fringe of scholarship" and was rightfully "weeded out [as] trash."[75] Historical generalizations and developmental laws were not only untestable but also born of the "perversity of human nature" that arose when the historian had not exhibited as carefully "the selection and arrangement of his facts."[76] One could understand politics and the "conceptual world of a society in the past," as Millar wrote, by "subordinat[ing]" oneself "to the evidence" and by avoiding using concepts that would have "contaminated the presentation of the evidence."[77] Gruen, seeking to cleanse his argument of "underlying causes," attributed the decline of the Roman Republic to "accident and irrationality, stubbornness and miscalculations" among the elite.[78] Even the assumptions about human behavior were self-evident. As Badian stated in his opening to *Roman Imperialism*, the longing for power is so rooted in what we are as humans that it "does not call for explanation."[79] The classical past appeared impervious to theory, whether as examinations of methodological assumptions, as the introduction of new perspectives and concerns, as explorations of the ways in which the past speaks to the present, or even as attempts—as Momigliano pointed out—to understand the expression of common aspirations, principles, beliefs, and human yearnings in the political past.[80]

Political scientists also adopted increasingly empirical methods. David Easton famously announced the "impoverishment" of political theory and suggested that it could have a place in political science when it abandoned its "historical approach" and sought instead to provide "generalizations" that would allow the ordering of political data.[81] The "behavioral revolution" in political science shed the institutional, historical, philosophic, and legal context from the study of politics and replaced it with empirically testable hypotheses about aggregate behavior. The *Annales* school, which began in the interwar years, provided additional scientific impetus in its fusing of thought and history. *Annales* scholars drew on new techniques of quantification and measurement in sociology, demography, psychology, geography, cultural ecology, linguistics, and economics to create an "anonymous history": an uncovering of the "social realities" of civilizations, discernable as mentalities (or deeply imbedded habits of thought), vast historical trends, and structural constraints like climate, geography, and technology.[82] Expressing much of the enthusiasm of the era for making social science into a true science, and intoxicated by new computer technologies that allowed for computation of complex data, Ladurie concluded, "history that is not quantifiable cannot claim to be scientific."[83]

Caught between the Skylla of speculative irrelevance and the Charybdis of historicist relativism, theorists attempted to navigate a route by which theory could be defended on methodological grounds. Ebenstein, for example, sought to place political theory in the context of scientific methodology. His influential survey, *Great Political Thinkers*, was framed by the opening section on Plato in which he declared that the Greeks "were the first to develop—going beyond observation and knowledge—the *scientific attitude*, a new approach to the world that constitutes to this day one of the distinctive elements of western life."[84] Guided by new concerns with methodology, Ebenstein emphasized "original sources" as the best way to understand the importance of the ideas of these writers.[85] This use of original texts brought with it another change in the presentation of political theory. Each chapter was not a historical narrative woven together by names and themes but, in Ebenstein's words, dealt "with only one writer."[86] This placed a premium on identifying single writers who could convey, in these selections, important ideas. From the cast of characters that paraded through Sabine's and McIlwain's histories, Ebenstein chose four representatives of the Roman period: Polybius, Cicero, Epictetus, and Marcus Aurelius. Each expressed a particular set of ideas: Polybius with the mixed constitution, Cicero on law and duty, and the two Stoics as originators of natural law. Interestingly, each of the choices also became associated with particular methodological contributions: Polybius was "the first to apply the institutional method to the study of politics"; Cicero appeared as something like an early jurist; and the Stoics began "the tradition of thinking according to natural law."[87]

Not surprisingly, the appraisal of Roman political thought—its ability to articulate a vision of political life—suffered in the face of these intellectual trends. If at mid-century one were to ask, "What vision of politics can be retrieved from the Roman past?" one would hear from classicists, in their embrace of philology and the building of "true history," a resolute rejection of the relevance of the question.[88] The task of the classicist was to reassemble the linguistic and material artifacts that could be recovered and understand the past in its own terms. Political theorists, as they were guided by concerns with methods, on the one hand, and morals, on the other, would say that there was little to recover. The Romans were at best practical, at worst derivative. Even their contributions to Western constitutionalism now seemed more like antecedents to oligarchy. As Ebenstein noted, "there is not much formal political theory in the Roman heritage that compares with the brilliant masterpieces of Greek philosophers. The only Roman political writer who has had an enduring influence throughout the ages is Cicero." And that contribution was reducible to "law and administration."[89] In Ebenstein's *Political Thought in Perspective*, Plato received forty-nine pages of treatment and Aristotle received thirty-six. Cicero could muster only six pages—less attention than was allotted to Dante, Luther, Calvin, Bodin, Jefferson, or Owen. Regardless of the broader efforts to bring together the traditional historiographic emphasis on compiling facts with the social scientific use of propositions, what was most striking was how political theorists and classicists had moved in such different directions that they found themselves with less and less to say to, or learn from, each other.[90]

POLITICS AND CULTURE

It can hardly be said that classicists and political theorists each spoke in their respective, unified voices. There had always been different challenges to the assumptions and methods of these disciplinary fields. But the 1960s and 1970s, with their political turmoil, new social concerns, and changing pedagogies, saw the splintering of approaches to the classical past. The Romans, though, seemed to fair no better. The different perspectives tended to exaggerate even more the received views of Roman political thought as derivative, as lacking conceptual form, or as hypocritical and corrupt.

One set of voices that emerged sought to restore the normative dimension of political theory, but with a sense of the limits to speculative philosophy.[91] Credit is frequently (and rightly) given to John Rawls for reopening this path of inquiry. Other theorists, including Jürgen Habermas, Richard Rorty, Alasdair MacIntyre, William Connolly, Michael Walzer, and Charles Taylor, each laid claim to ways in which we could conceive of ourselves as democratic citizens and form judgments in a global context. These theorists appropriated the ideas of past thinkers. Galston, in his exhaustive survey of this scholarship, named Aristotle, Hobbes, Locke, Rousseau, Hegel, Wollstonecraft, Mill, Nietzsche, and Kant as among the influences.[92] But no Roman made the list.

A second set of approaches to political thought coalesced around attempts to ground thought more explicitly in its historical and material context. Political thought, particularly as it grew out of earlier work on material and cultural history, was seen as an aspect of social history. That is, the study of political thought was the examination of the ideas and ideologies that emerged as social groups responded to each other and to larger structural issues and events, such as demographic changes, famines, debt, and war.[93] Material approaches to political thought also found expression in Marxian scholarship that focused less on how societies cohered and more on the conflicts that inhered in the economic relations of society. Marxian perspectives asserted themselves most prominently in discussions of ideology, used in Roman studies to explain how elites were able to perpetuate their rule.[94]

A third voice was a form of intellectual history, updated with a new interest in language. Most prominent was what became known as the "Cambridge School," led by Quentin Skinner and J. G. A. Pocock. The Cambridge School took aim at the license that theorists were exercising in reading and interpreting political thought without regard to the historical, social, or linguistic environment in which the texts were created, or without a sense of how these ideas were communicated and translated over time.[95] The Cambridge School sought to trace the history of ideas as a history of "language and discourse."[96] "There is the text," Pocock writes, "and there is the language, visible at more than one moment and in more than one culture; they are material vehicles for the bearing of encoded messages, and we cannot prejudge the question whether they transmit messages from one point or moment to another. If they do this to any extent whatever, then to that extent the text or language is an agent in determining its own translation and to structuring the situation in which it is to be interpreted."[97] The Romans, particularly Cicero, were important to these readings, though they were placed in service to a larger tradition of civic republicanism that stretched back to the Greeks, and forward, by way of Machiavelli most importantly, to the American founding.[98]

A fourth voice, developed influentially by Wolin in his book *Politics and Vision*, provided a challenging, nuanced, and devastating account of the Romans.[99] Wolin's project was in large part an answer to both the forces of methodism and moralism by conceiving of political philosophy as constituting "reflections on matters that concern the community as a whole."[100] Political theory appeared neither as social history, as it did for Sabine, nor as a hidden dialogue that purported to provide insights into truth, as it did for Strauss, but as a lost dialogue about the vision of the political: "Political theory is not so much interested in political practices, or how they operate, but in their meaning."[101] Imagination, more than methodology, was the means by which theorists strove to "transcend history" and present the "totality of political phenomena."[102]

The difficulty that confronted the Romans, suggested Wolin, was that the spatial dimension of politics had changed from the city-state to an expansive empire. Yet, the Romans were unable to modify their own categories of thought to rediscover the meaning of the political in this new institutional setting. Wolin acknowledged that one should not "ignore Roman political thought."[103] But the negative formulation of this injunction provided only a hint of the searing indictment of the Romans as political thinkers that followed. Of Roman thinking in general, Wolin noted that "the student of political ideas must deal with a period notoriously lacking in great political thinkers."[104] The "little there was in the way of systematic theory proves on closer analysis to be more often Greek than Roman in origin."[105] Roman politics had become "abstract," or a "politics from a distance, where men were informed about public actions which bore little or no resemblance to the economy of the household."[106] The Epicureans "opened the way to a radical individualism grounded in self-interest."[107] The Stoics sought to create a "universal society" of "non-communing members" that was grounded in nature rather than politics.[108] A political ethic of duty and responsibility degenerated into a "joyless bureaucratic morality."[109] With Polybius's "pragmatic form of knowledge," a vision of the political was replaced by contentment "to report the drift of events rather than to master them, and to resign itself to a world ultimately unconquerable."[110] Cicero defined a set of Roman principles that diminished politics to "nothing but the pursuit of interests."[111] The philosophy of Seneca was reduced to "groveling helplessness" in the face of absolutism.[112] And Wolin concluded his characterization of the Roman period by suggesting that political philosophy had "exchanged its political element for a vapid moralism."[113] In a new politics of meaning, the Romans possessed neither the vision nor the conceptual power to address the ontological questions of political being. To students who later encountered and were influenced by Wolin's book, he provided a reason—in fact, several reasons—to ignore the Romans.

A final response was a new emphasis on culture. In effect, it was an embracing of historicism that viewed the artifacts of the past as cultural (primarily elite) productions used to maintain power relations. This approach was inspired variously by cultural anthropology (e.g., Victor Turner), sociology (e.g., Erving Goffman), semiotics (e.g., Mikhail Bakhtin), linguistics (e.g., J. L. Austin), phenomenology (e.g., Hannah Arendt), philosophy (e.g., Nietzsche), literary analytic approaches of New Historicism and cultural poetics (e.g., Stephen Greenblatt), feminist theory (e.g., Judith Butler), and post-structuralism (e.g., Michel Foucault and Pierre Bourdieu). Rather than viewing culture as narrowly synonymous with art and subordinate to history, cultural studies focused on the role of culture both in the "production of meaning" and, as Habinek and Schiesaro note in their reappraisal of Syme's *Roman Revolution*, as "constraining in that it defines limits beyond which a person, activity, or belief is marginalized or even excluded from the community in question."[114]

These cultural approaches have done much to breathe new life into Roman studies. They have broadened the scope of what counts as political beyond a community's formal arrangements, processes, and groups. They have blended theoretical insight with literary interpretation and historical context. And they have given contemporary relevance to the Roman past by exploring how scholarly discourse is involved (often complicitly) in the production of elite power relations.[115] But these approaches often embarked on a relentless stripping away of meaning that derived, as Ricoeur writes, from a "demystifying and reductive hermeneutics, stemming more from suspicion than from reminiscence."[116] Habinek, for example, calls for a "contrapuntal reading" of the past that questions the "European bourgeois subject's need to absolve himself/herself of responsibility for conquest while enjoying its benefits."[117]

This interrogation of the past has compounded the cruel fate of Rome's legacy in political thought. The Romans were choked of life by the arid prose of legalism and constitutionalism. They vanished into the lofty heights of moralism. And now they appear only to be excoriated for their (and our) hypocrisy and corruption. The turn to the past, as I am arguing here, need not be interpreted only as an activity of distortion and unveiling; reminiscence may also be productive of symbolic forms that make political power and possibility comprehensible, meaningful, and communicable.[118] I am suggesting a reading of Roman political thought in which the Romans articulated with some emotion what it meant to lose one's political bearings and how political thought might help to recover those bearings. In an age when politics illuminates less and less, the Romans may summon us to think about what has been lost.

2

Cicero, Arendt, and the Cultivation of the Political World

Reading the *Tusculan Disputations* Politically

Writing in 51 BCE on the eve of civil war, as Rome's political future lay more and more in the hands of avaricious and opportunistic leaders, Cicero sounds a note of despair in the fifth book of *On the Republic* (*De Re Publica*). The Roman Republic had been passed down like an extraordinary painting whose colors were "already fading because of age." But the current generation had neglected to renew (*renovare neglexit*) the "original colors" or even to have taken care to preserve its form or outermost outlines (*Rep.* 5.1.2).[1] The once vibrant republican practices had so fallen into obsolescence that they were no longer even known, much less practiced (*Rep.* 5.1.2).

Cicero speaks to a quite modern concern: the loss of traditions by which individuals orient themselves in the world. As Wallace-Hadrill notes, Cicero "is not talking about the fall of the Republic as a political system, but the collapse of a whole way of life," of "social confusion and the abandonment of tradition."[2] In Rome, whatever vestige of the republic remained after the Social War, the proscriptions, the Sullan constitutional reforms, and escalating urban violence was giving way to a bloody scramble for power by "military dynasts."[3] Violence and economic exploitation had become the political weapon of choice.[4] Sallust describes how "the nobles began to abuse their position and the people their liberty, and every man for himself robbed, pillaged, and plundered" (*Jug.* 41.5; trans. Rolf). Cicero's own political fortunes, let alone his legacy, were in free fall. Cicero speaks frequently, for example, of the "billows and storms" of political life, as well as the humiliation and sorrow that followed from his exile.[5] But even Cicero's sense of loss was tempered by the hope that he might again return to a life of politics.[6]

Just a few years later, Cicero wrote the *Tusculan Disputations* with no such hope. In the years following his completion of the *Republic,* Cicero described to his childhood friend, Atticus, the sense of unbearable loss he felt as he scanned the political landscape (*Attic.* 9.10.2). In fact, his divorce from his wife and the death of his only daughter, Tullia, in childbirth only deepened his despair. Viewed as a response to suffering, scholars characterize the *Tusculan Disputations* as marking a departure from his earlier political writings and as an escape from the political world into an inner life. Douglas observes, "it is while writing the *Tusculans* that in political matters at least Cicero reached his lowest ebb. He now turns inwards, to personal problems," looking to philosophy to provide solace for his grief.[7] Narducci suggests that by "withdrawing into the shrine of conscience, the wise man celebrates his victory over the outside world and his exalted independence from every form of submission."[8] Cicero, according to Narducci, reverses his earlier sense of despair arising from his political exile: "The *res publica,* the ideal of one's country and of the *civis* who within it fulfills himself, loses substance and meaning, while the alternative model of a *déraciné* cosmopolitanism takes on a dignity which was previously unthinkable."[9] And Wood describes Cicero's philosophic writings as "a mode of mental therapy" that he undertook with his retirement from politics.[10] And that is the good news. Douglas, in an earlier essay of his, passes over the *Tusculans* in his survey of Cicero's philosophic contributions, damning it with the unphilosophic moniker, "popular."[11] And Schofield observes that the modern reader will no doubt express "surprise" or "dismay" that Cicero places so much emphasis on the *Tusculans* in his catalogue of philosophic works in *On Divination* (*De Divinatione*).[12]

My interest in this chapter is to suggest that there is something both searching and political in the *Tusculan Disputations* that complements and deepens Cicero's earlier discussion in the *Republic*. The *Tusculans* shares with the *Republic* a struggle with loss, a mingling of Cicero's different experiences of political and personal agony and sorrow (*Tusc.* 5.1.1; 5.41.121).[13] The searching nature of the *Tusculans* is suggested when one interlocutor confesses that his sense of agreement about the immortality of the soul derived from logic and argument slips away when reflecting on his own experience (*Tusc.* 1.11.24; also *Tusc.* 5.1.3).[14] However much Cicero in the *Republic*, through Scipio, warns against any attachment to things of this world, Cicero, nonetheless, expresses in the *Tusculans* the rather un-Stoic perspective that he has been "robbed of the consolations of family life and the distinctions of a public career" (*Tusc.* 1.34.84).[15] The sense of loss conveyed in the *Tusculans* is reinforced by the frequency, as MacKendrick points out, of the appearance of the verb *carere*, which means "to feel a lack" or "to be without."[16] Cicero similarly defined himself by his surroundings in his letter to Atticus to describe his exile: It is not only property or friends that I miss, but myself (*Attic.* 3.15).[17]

The problem of loss, as Cicero's letter implies, raises the

corollary problem of worth: what is it that I miss, and why should I miss it? Cicero's struggle with the question of the worth of the world is interesting precisely because he finds himself at the crossroads of two contending philosophic schools: he rejects recourse to Epicurean pleasures of the body but calls into question through his own experiences the attainability of Stoic grieflessness (*indolentiae*) (*Tusc.* 3.17.36–18.43; *Tusc.* 3.6.12).[18] Cicero takes his cue from the Stoics in looking to philosophy as *animi medicina,* the art of healing the soul.[19] Philosophy becomes a way of teaching endurance so that one can fortify oneself against the vicissitudes of earthly life. But Cicero is only partially effective in relieving his distress, and the reason for the incompleteness of the solution lies in the worth he assigns both to his daughter and to the political world. My suggestion is that Cicero, in seeking to address his sense of loss, raises the larger issue of one's relationship to the tangible manifestations of the world.

My point of departure is Hannah Arendt, who locates in Cicero two different paths of philosophic thought. Arendt suggests in *The Life of the Mind* that "philosophy had found a kind of foster home in Rome during the last century before Christ, and in that thoroughly political society it had first of all to prove that it was good for something" (*LM* 1:158). One such path of usefulness, written against a sense of a disintegrating public realm, was that philosophy could "teach men how to cure their despairing minds by escaping from the world through thinking" (*LM* 1:152). Philosophy becomes the *animi medicina,* as Cicero writes in the *Tusculan Disputations,* the art of healing the soul (*Tusc.* 3.3.6).[20] Philosophy, as articulated by Cicero and in turn adopted by such a thinker as Hegel, appears not as a response to "reason's need" but "has an existential root in unhappiness" (*LM* 1:153). The "disintegration of reality" and the corresponding "*dis*-unity of man and the world" create a "need for another world, more harmonious and more meaningful" (*LM* 1:153). Cicero, Arendt argues, discovers "the thought-trains by which one could take one's way out of the world" (*LM* 1:157).

The second path that Arendt identifies in Cicero is the way in which philosophy, as *cultura animi,* a cultivation of the soul, may also return us to the world. Cicero, Arendt suggests, is the first to extend the metaphor of cultivating nature to "matters of spirit and mind" (*BPF* 212). She points, for example, to Cicero's claim, "Just as a field, however good the ground, cannot be productive without cultivation (*cultura*), so the soul (*anima*) cannot be productive without teaching" (*BPF* 212; *Tusc.* 2.4.13).[21] Arendt associates the Roman notion of cultivation with culture, suggesting a disposition of care for the things of the world that humans have made: monuments, buildings, works of art, political institutions, and laws. The cultivation of the soul, thus, directs us back to, and instills a particular attitude toward, the tangibility of the world. Building on Arendt's insight, I am suggesting, in short, that we can read the *Tusculans* politically: not as a break from, but as a deepened reflection on, the disposition of care that is necessary for the recovery of the durable markers by which we orient ourselves in the political world.

THE DREAM

Cicero wrote *On the Republic* in the years following the renewal of the first triumvirate of Caesar, Crassus, and Pompey in 56 BCE when he was effectively deprived of a political voice even though he had returned from exile. *On the Republic* can be read, at least in part, as a reflection on the rewards of public service. The dialogue is set in 129 BCE, a time (like Cicero's own) of extraordinary political and cultural upheaval in the tribunate of Tiberius Gracchus, of strife over land redistribution, of growing discontent in the provinces, and of the beginning of social and civil conflict that would last for decades.[22] The trials of political leadership receive their greatest metaphorical expression in "Scipio's Dream" ("Somnium Scipionis"). In the final book of the *Republic*, Cicero relates a dream by Scipio Aemilianus, a Roman political and military leader. In the dream, his grandfather by adoption, Scipio Africanus, the statesman and military hero who defeated Hannibal, prophesizes that his grandson will destroy Carthage (which he does in 146 BCE). Then, Africanus continues, after a series of other military and political successes, Scipio Aemilianus will find Rome in disarray. Rome would be shaken by the crisis between Tiberius Gracchus, who pushed through land reform, and the senate, which sought to violently stop the reform. In the dream, Scipio Aemilianus is to go to Rome as dictator to restore the republic if he can "escape the wicked hands of [his] kinsmen," ostensibly the Gracchi, against whom Scipio Aemilianus had spoken (*Rep.* 6.12.12). But Scipio is found dead in his bedroom before he can return to Rome (though who killed him remains a mystery).

In calling for Scipio Aemilianus to return to Rome, Scipio Africanus reminds him that the highest place in the heavens is reserved for those "who have preserved, aided, or enlarged" (*conservaverint, adiuverint, auxerint*) the homeland (*Rep.* 6.13.13). As Cicero writes, "For nothing of all that is done on earth is more pleasing to the supreme God who rules the whole universe than the assemblies and gatherings of men associated in justice, which are called States. Their rulers and preservers come from that place, and to that place they return" (*Rep.* 6.13.13; also *LM* 1:159). Humans are given life, Cicero continues, so that they might inhabit earth and perform their duty to the community (*Rep.* 6.14.15). Indeed, nature has implanted in humans "a desire to defend the common safety" and to make human life better (*Rep.* 1.1.1; 1.2.3).

Through nature, as Cicero writes in *On Duties* (*De Officiis*), we are given the way to reconcile our affections and put them to use (*Offic.* 2.5.17).[23]

Although the gods favor a devotion to things of the earth, no commensurate human reward can make up for the toil and suffering. "For what fame can you gain from the speech of men," asks Africanus the Elder, "or what glory that is worth the seeking" (*Rep.* 6.19.20)? As Scipio Africanus lifts Scipio Aemilianus into the air, they look back toward the ever-shrinking earth. Through a process of what Arendt refers to as "relativization," Cicero shows how the earth itself and the things of the earth (such as fame and glory, life and death, and the passage of time) now appear insignificant and quite fleeting in their place in the cosmos (*LM* 1:160). For Arendt, Cicero provides "perhaps the first recorded [example] in intellectual history" of how "thinking means following a sequence of reasoning that will lift you to a viewpoint outside the world of appearances as well as outside your own life" (*LM* 1:160).[24]

We might be surprised that Arendt associates this form of thinking with Cicero rather than Plato. But Arendt sees Plato as addressing "invisibles that are present in the visible world" rather than, as does Cicero, adopting a stance that lifts us out of this world (*LM* 1:151). The comparison to Plato is apt since Cicero is styling "Scipio's Dream" after Plato's "Myth of Er," which ends Plato's *Republic*.[25] Although both myths attempt to show the ultimate rewards of striving for the earthly perfection of one's soul, Cicero's "Dream" leaves us in a different place than does Plato's "Myth." Perfection, for Plato, lies in the pursuit of the philosophic life that accords a decidedly secondary status to politics. Cicero reverses the hierarchy: the statesman not only most resembles the divine in his ability to make a world, but the political life is superior to the philosophic because it affects more people (*Rep.* 1.7.12; 1.2.3). Not by accident is Scipio Aemilianus, unlike Er, a statesman (and, at least in Cicero's mind, one of the first Romans to embrace Greek philosophic teachings).[26] And, significantly, Scipio is directed back to the toils of earthly life where, with his knowledge of the movement of the universe, he is told that care (*cura*) for the country's health is the best exercise of one's eternal spirit (*Rep.* 6.26.29).

"Scipio's Dream" is read most frequently as Cicero's call for a strong leader, even a Stoic sage, who can restore order to the republic.[27] But of more interest to us here is the ambivalence that accompanies Scipio's return to earth. Our detachment from our body and our contemplation of what "lies outside" us may prepare us for our ascent upon our death. But what is less clear is how the philosophic life prepares us for this political return (*Rep.* 6.26.29).[28] Scipio Aemilianus is instructed to scorn the earthly allure of honor and fame (*Rep.* 6.19.20). Viewed against the backdrop of the eternal movement of the universe and the divinity of the soul, to be concerned with the testimony of others is to embrace that which is mortal and, consequently, fleeting in our earthly life (*Rep.* 6.19.20; 6.21.23). Furthermore, to vest oneself in earthly things is to relinquish one's happiness to unpredictable and uncontrollable fortune. Even as one heeds Africanus's injunction, "Know, then, that you are a god," what awaits any political leader is toil that is so thankless that it appears to some as madness (*Rep.* 6.24.26; see *Rep.* 1.1.1; *Rep.* 1.3.4). Philosophy seems important in preparing us for this labor by instilling *fortitudo*: the ability to patiently endure suffering (see *Rep.* 1.2.2).

Cicero had thought about casting himself as Scipio (*Q. Fr.* 3.5.1–2). Fortunately for Cicero's intellectual legacy and the elegance of the "Dream," the explicitly autobiographical and self-serving moments appear confined to the first book of the *Republic* where Cicero describes the "anxiety and vexation that resulted from the injustice done to me" (*Rep.* 1.4.7). These personal comments only deepen the perplexity that attends political life. If Cicero acted solely from a begrudging sense of obligation, then he might appear more as one of Plato's philosophers who had to be dragged back into the darkness of the cave.[29] Quite on the contrary, Cicero had to be forced into exile from what he characterized as "the light" of the political world (*Fam.* 2.12.2). If Cicero had only contempt for Roman politics then he, like Plato, might wish to wipe the canvas clean and start anew. But Cicero, instead, invokes the contrasting aesthetic image of the "beautiful painting" of the republic, one that once was renewed and now has been neglected by succeeding generations (*Rep.* 5.1.2). Cicero's language of care, beauty, and loss speaks to a deep and abiding attachment to the political realm that leaves us at the end of the *Republic* with a series of questions: How is one to exercise both care and contempt? What is beautiful about political toil? And what is lost with the passing of the republic?

ANIMI MEDICINA

Despite the obvious differences, the *Tusculans* shares a similar trajectory with "Scipio's Dream." Both have as their starting point a sense of loss, a sense made all the more poignant in the *Tusculans* by Cicero's nearly inconsolable grief for the death of his beloved daughter, Tullia.[30] Cicero reveals in a series of letters to Atticus his unrelieved (even unmanly) grief following the death of Tullia, a sorrow unmitigated by what in Cicero's mind are cold Stoic syllogisms.[31] Cicero recounts how his burning sadness remains, despite his efforts to resist (*Attic.* 12.13.1). A day later, Cicero explains, "Nothing has been written by any author on the alleviation of grief which I did not read in your house. But my sorrow (*dolor*) is stronger than any consolation" (*Attic.* 12.14.3). Again, Cicero describes the uncontrollable "fits of weeping" that interrupt his writing, unable to "escape the memories which pain (*dolorem*) me" (*Attic.* 12.15; 12.18.1; trans. modified). Cicero even sounds a defiant, anti-Stoic note: "As to my literary consolation of myself, I am not dissatisfied with what it achieved. I reduced the outward show of grief (*dolorem*); grief itself I could not reduce, and would not if I could" (*Attic.* 12.28.2).

Only after three months and the composition of his *Consolatio* does Cicero return to his villa at Tusculum where Tullia had died. Cicero admits that he had wished, while writing the *Consolatio,* to leave the world (*Tusc.* 1.31.76). In the *Tusculan Disputations,* though, Cicero turns to philosophy as therapy: "Assuredly there is an art of healing the soul (*animi medicina*)—I mean philosophy, whose aid must be sought not, as in bodily diseases, outside ourselves, and we must use our utmost endeavor, with all our resources and strength, to have the power to be ourselves our own physicians" (*Tusc.* 3.3.6; see also *Nat.* 1.4.9). The proper treatment for such longing, a remedy that Cicero seeks in (and through the writing of) the *Tusculans,* is to realize "how trivial, contemptible and absolutely insignificant is the object of his desire, how easily it can either be secured from elsewhere or in another way, or else wholly put out of mind" (*Tusc.* 4.35.74; also 4.38.83).[32]

Like "Scipio's Dream," philosophy lifts us outside our bodies so that we may see the insignificance of the things we cling to. Through philosophy, we are able to "embrace the whole earth in our survey, its situation, shape, and circumference, as well as both the districts that are habitable and those again that are left wholly uncultivated because of the violence of cold or heat" (*Tusc.* 1.20.45). In our separation from our body, we finally experience the happiness of the soul freed from envy and desire (*Tusc.* 1.19.14). Philosophy awakens the slumbering soul, empowering us with the foremost virtue, *fortitudo*, which will compel us to assume a spirit "that will make you despise and count as nothing all that can fall to the lot of men" (*Tusc.* 3.17.36). The *Tusculans* becomes Cicero's therapeutic exercise, his attempt to free himself from earthly longing.

But like in "Scipio's Dream," the original flight from earth through reflection, where the mind and spirit comes to know themselves and "feel [their] union with the divine mind," seems ultimately to direct us back to human affairs (*Tusc.* 5.25.70; compare to *Rep.* 6.24.26; 6.26.28).[33] "As the wise man is gazing upon this spectacle and looks upward or rather looks round upon all the parts and regions of the universe, with what calmness of soul he turns again to reflect upon what is in man and touches him more nearly" (*Tusc.* 5.25.71). In the practice of virtue, the perfection of that which is nearest to us, we are returned to the earth. Far from now "undervalu[ing]" the *civitas*, as Narducci suggests, Cicero contends that the wise man is happiest who passes over to the care *(tuendam)* of the public realm (*res publicae*) (*Tusc.* 5.25.72; also *Tusc.* 1.14.32; 4.23.51). Although Cicero finds solace in what he interprets as Socrates' claim to be a citizen of the world, Socrates' greatest contribution is that he called "philosophy down from the heavens" to "set her in the cities of men" (*Tusc.* 5.37.108; 5.4.10).[34]

In his return to the world, Cicero, as Graver contends, "makes himself an advocate for the Stoic ideal of impassivity (*apatheia*)": the complete absence of passions.[35] But in the passage referred to by Graver, Cicero takes up the position of Crantor, an early member of the Academy (c. 335–275 BCE). Crantor's position in *On Grief*, that a certain amount of grief may serve a useful and natural purpose, seems considerably more ambiguous than suggested by Graver. Cicero seems to express some sympathy toward the opinion that the wise man is susceptible to distress: "we are not sprung from rock, but our souls have a strain of tenderness and sensitivity of a kind to be shaken by distress as by a storm" (*Tusc.* 3.6.12). Although not totally affirming Crantor's position, Cicero does allow that it is "not absurd" for Crantor to reject "that sort of griefllessness" (*indolentiae*) that would leave us without the "capacity for feeling" (*Tusc.* 3.6.12; trans. modified). Indeed, in *On Friendship* (*De Amicitia*), composed the following year and set a few days after the death of Scipio Aemilianus, Cicero rejects the Stoic ideal of *securitas*, or "freedom from care" (*Amic.* 13.47). "In appearance it is indeed an alluring thing," but, as Cicero continues, "in reality often to be shunned" (*Amic.* 13.47). But one can feel Cicero's struggle to reconcile philosophically the sense of sorrow and loss that he has experienced personally. Cicero warns against using our human capacity for feeling to "flatter the infirmity of our nature," even ending on the Stoic mantra that the soul will be wretched unless cured of its emotions (*Tusc.* 3.6.13). Even when one "lop[s] the branches of wretchedness" and "tear[s] out all the fibres of its roots," Cicero concedes, there will "perhaps, be some left" (*Tusc.* 3.6.13). If we are to follow Cicero's metaphorical language, we can perhaps understand why some emotions would remain. We can remove distress, as Cicero writes in *On Friendship*, only if "human sympathy has been rooted out of the heart" (*Amic.* 13.48).

Cicero's qualification of Stoic cures may be attributed as much to personal experience as to the built-in skepticism of the New Academy. Cicero writes in the final book of the *Tusculans*, "For my part, when I consider with myself the hazards in which fortune has tried me so severely, there are moments when I begin to lose confidence in this opinion of yours and feel exceeding fear of the weakness and frailty of mankind" (*Tusc.* 5.1.3). The unalloyed personal sorrow can be read in Cicero's rejection of Stoicism's benign universe. "Nature," as Cicero addresses his friend, M. Junius Brutus, has given us "feeble bodies, with which she has combined both incurable diseases and unendurable pains, has also given us souls that both share in the suffering of physical pain and, apart from this, have their own entanglement of anguish and trouble" (*Tusc.* 5.1.3; trans. modified). Moreover, and in another departure from Stoicism, Cicero claims that feelings of loss are not the results of "any process of reasoning or instruction" but from "the promptings of nature" (*Tusc.* 1.13.30). That is to say, emotions may not be (as they are for the Stoics) irrational judgments.

One prompting of nature that seems to underlie this sense of loss is a concern for the future: a "deeply rooted presentiment of future ages" that is felt most strongly "in men of the greatest genius and loftiest spirit" (*Tusc.* 1.14.33). Such a presentiment arises because our immortal soul directs us to a future beyond our death (*Tusc.* 1.14.31). The soul's prompting is played out politically as one undertakes great deeds on behalf of the commonwealth in the hope of achieving some earthly immortality (*Tusc.* 1.15.32).[36] And such a prompting is characteristic of intimate relationships, as well, which project "the bright ray of hope into the future" (*Amic.* 7.23). But this presentiment, while driving men toward greatness, also becomes the basis of longing when we desire what we do not have, and anxiety when we fear the loss of what we do have. Cicero describes the "tender recollection and the deep longing" that remains among friends, even when separated by death (*Amic.* 7.23). We can read a similar longing in Cicero's desire to immortalize Tullia by building a shrine whose "sanctity" would be "respected by posterity" (*Attic.* 12.36.1).[37] And politically, we long not just for our own glory, but also for the continued health of our country even after we have departed earth. As Cicero asks rhetorically, "Why then should Camillus have felt pain (*doleret*), had he thought that some 350 years after his lifetime the present troubles would come, and why should I feel pain (*doleam*) if I should think that some nation would get possession of our city at a date 10,000 years hence" (*Tusc.* 1.37.90)? Cicero answers his own question: "Because so great is love of country that we measure it" by "the salvation of our country itself" (*Tusc.* 1.37.90; also *Amic.* 12.43).[38]

Cicero does stake out a Stoic explanation for this sense of longing. Stated simply, nature implants in us a desire for virtue, which leads us to cultivate our own virtue (the basis of wisdom), to be attracted to virtue in others (the basis of friendship), and to develop the conditions for the full enjoyment of virtue (the basis of politics).[39] Directed by a desire for virtue, we love that which is unchangeable and eternal. In fact, metaphysically we are never separated from that which is eternal (*Amic.* 9.32; 27.102). Thus, we can alleviate our grief by knowing that in the passing of earthly things, nothing unexpected has happened, nothing evil has occurred, and nothing eternal has been lost (*Tusc.* 3.23.55; 3.29.72; 3.32.77; 4.28.60).

As tidy as this solution may be, and as frequently as Cicero repeats the claim that distress is inconsistent with virtue and that the solution to such distress is found in reason, there is little that is resolved by the end of *Tusculans*.[40] If we are forever connected to that which is eternal, then what is it that we long for when those who are dear to us have departed? If on our death we may ascend quickly to our "proper home and permanent abode," then what is it that we fear will be lost with the disintegration of the commonwealth (*Rep.* 6.26.29)? However much Cicero may seek recourse in the desire for the eternal, at the heart of love is loss. The desire and, indeed, the joy of love derive precisely from the frailty and fleeting nature of our existence (*Amic.* 27.102). We become connected to something—the eternal—that is more than us, but the eternal for Cicero is fostered in the tangibility and particularity of the things we have come to know. Although not eternal, these artifacts become the earthly expressions of the spirit's longing for immortality: the ability, as Arendt writes, to see oneself as connected in this life by a "thread of tradition" that ties us to both a past and a future (*BPF* 204).

We can read the importance of tangibility in Cicero's frequent references to the power of memory. In his own personal grief, Cicero struggles to "escape the memories" of Tullia, a struggle that underlies Cicero's more general observation that distress arises not just because of the abruptness of the event but because the "impression is still fresh" (*Attic.* 12.18.1; *Tusc.* 3.23.56). One may attempt to mitigate the force of this impression, so Cicero writes, by recalling instances of others who have lost children; yet, such stories do not seem to be able to touch us in the same way (*Tusc.* 3.24.58). Although we share a fundamental humanity with all people, our attachments are strengthened through "our proximity to each other" (*Amic.* 5.19). We can get some sense of the nature of this intimacy in Cicero's discussion of the discourse between friends: "What is sweeter than to have someone with whom you may dare discuss anything as if you were communing with yourself? How could your enjoyment in times of prosperity be so great if you did not have someone whose joy in them would be equal to your own? Adversity would indeed be hard to bear, without him to whom the burden would be heavier than even to yourself" (*Amic.* 6.22; also *Tusc.* 5.22.63). With the death of Tullia, Cicero all but abandons the possibility of self-mastery, admitting that the alleviation of his suffering will come neither through abstractions (death is not an evil) nor generalizations (others, too, have lost loved ones), but through his friend, Atticus (*Attic.* 12.14.3; 12.16).

Life itself becomes worthwhile as it is woven into the lives of ancestors through memory of the past, memories that are closely connected to place (*Orator* 120). As Cicero has Atticus say in *On Laws* (*De Legibus*), a dialogue that is as much a meditation on place as on law, "we are affected in some mysterious way by places about which cluster memories of those whom we love and admire" (*Leg.* 2.2.4). In these recollections, Cicero points us to the tangible artifacts of earthly life. Odysseus himself, as Cicero recalls, foregoes the promise of divinity so that he may "see" Ithaca once more (*Leg.* 2.1.3). Quintus, on returning to the island of Fibrenus, points to his house that was "rebuilt and extended by my father's care" (*Leg.* 2.1.3). Dotting the landscape are memorials of one's ancestors as well, linking past to present (*Leg.* 2.1.3). Atticus comments that in his visits to Athens he delights not only in the buildings and the art, but also in the tombs of other great men where he can gaze and imagine the conversations that occurred (*Leg.* 2.2.4). Cicero also writes to Atticus of being carried away in his enchantment with certain statues to decorate his villa (*Attic.* 1.8.2). We might recall Arendt's own reference to the ability of cultural objects to "grasp and move" the spectator (*BPF* 203).

Cicero's works are themselves testimonies to the enduring importance of the tangible artifacts of a culture that, as Arendt writes, attest to a community's past, lending to our fleeting time on earth some sense of permanence and immortality (*BPF* 202).[41] Oratory, as it gives life to recollection, can, in Cicero's words, be entrusted with history's "immortality" (*De Orat.* 2.9.36). Cicero's orations become a veritable map of Roman culture: at once a representation and interpretation of the places, monuments, and institutions that would be familiar to his audience.[42] Through the selection of characters, setting, and time, Cicero's writings serve as a "memorial" to the men, events, and deeds of the past.[43] Cicero immortalized others through his dedications in his books and was not above desiring that his own life be similarly immortalized.[44] Cicero even envisioned his philosophic writings as setting before his Roman audience the neglected tradition of Greek philosophy

(*Tusc.* 1.3.5). He consciously casts his writings before a "wider public," decrying those who compose only for themselves or for a small circle of friends (*Tusc.* 1.3.6).

My point is not to suggest that Cicero's already questionable originality and capability as a philosopher lapses into disingenuousness when placed against his own vanity, interests, and political aspirations. That argument has already been made quite ably by Mommsen, following Drumann.[45] Rather, I want to suggest that in the *Tusculans* Cicero's invocation of the cultural world emerges as the flipside to his sense of loss. However internally directed might be the use of philosophy as therapy for the soul, Cicero's own inability to discount as worthless the things of this world lends the *Tusculans* its political cast. Ultimately, the *Tusculans* seeks in philosophy an answer to the question: How should one care for the things of this world?

CULTURA ANIMI

Hannah Arendt points out that culture as "word and concept, is Roman in origin" (*BPF* 211). "Culture" comes from *colere*—"to cultivate, to dwell, to take care, to tend and preserve"—and refers, at least initially, to the "intercourse of man with nature in the sense of cultivating and tending nature until it becomes fit for habitation" (*BPF* 211–12). Cicero makes clear the relationship of cultivation to habitation when he imagines that if we were to see the whole earth from afar, we would see those regions that are "habitable" and that are "wholly uncultivated" (*omni cultu . . . vacantes*) (*Tusc.* 1.20.45; also *Tusc.* 1.25.62; 1.28.68, 69). By contrast, as Arendt argues, the Greeks saw their relationship to nature as violent, where they sought to tame and rule the wildness of the earth (*BPF* 212–13). The Roman idea of preserving and tending to things expands beyond its immediate agricultural context, though never leaving the association far behind. Cicero speaks of Greek ideas as being "cultivated" (*culta*) in Rome from its founding and of himself as tending to Greek philosophy through his writings (*Tusc.* 4.1.2; 3.1.1). Cicero also compares how the wise will "sow the seed of laws, regulations and public policy" just as the farmer will "sow trees, no berry of which his eyes will ever see" (*Tusc.* 1.14.31). And Cicero famously applies the idea of cultivation to matters of the mind, comparing the soul to a field, and defining philosophy as the cultivation of the soul (*cultura animi*) (*Tusc.* 2.5.13).

What is it that philosophy cultivates? Certainly reason, which yields consistency of belief and judgment. But philosophy, more suggestively, sharpens the soul's perception of the "true nature" of things, a nature that cannot, itself, be comprehended fully in its earthly state because it is "fenced in with a compound of earthly particles" (*Tusc.* 1.20.47). The true nature of things can be recognized, though, by its beauty (*Tusc.* 1.20.47; 1.28.68; 4.13.31). With philosophy, "darkness" is dispersed "from the eyes as it were of the mind, so that we saw all things above, below, things first and last and in between" (*Tusc.* 1.26.64). For the Stoics such an apprehension of nature's order and ends is removed from the senses and from this world, denying any reality or ethical significance to practical activity.[46] For Cicero, however, the wonder of the soul, its ability to discover and understand, is continually expressed as a set of earthly accomplishments. To demonstrate the power of the soul, Cicero traces the course of human discovery and progress: the "great men" who first cultivated the earth to provide "an ordered way of life" (*cultum vitae*), those who, under "civilizing and refining (*exculti*) guidance," developed the "finer arts," those who discovered how to combine musical sounds, those who inquired into the movement of the heavens, those who composed poetry, and those who established justice (*Tusc.* 1.25.62).[47] Cicero writes, as well, of how the "genius" of the Roman people shows up in the establishment through laws and usage of the "direction and organization" of the commonwealth, including the political assemblies, the court system, and the council (*Tusc.* 4.1.1). Even Cicero's ode to philosophy celebrates the earthly accomplishments of the soul: "Thou hast given birth to cities, thou hast called scattered human beings into the bond of social life, thou hast united them first of all in joint habitations, next in wedlock, then in the ties of common literature and speech, thou hast discovered law, thou hast been the teacher of morality and order" (*Tusc.* 5.2.5). Cicero's city is not the Platonic "city in speech," but a city made beautiful by its tangibility.[48]

If philosophy for the Stoics is a preparation for death that teaches us impassivity toward things of this world, then for Cicero philosophy seems more like a preparation for life that heightens our delight of the world. The philosophic life—that is, the life in "communion with the Muses"—is itself a part of broad learning that contributes to a life of cultured refinement, or *humanitas* (a word of Cicero's creation) (*Tusc.* 5.23.66).[49] What could be more delightful than a life devoted to literature in which we acquire knowledge not only of infinite nature but, as Cicero continues, of "this actual world of ours, of the sky, the lands, the seas" (*Tusc.* 5.36.105)? In this political role of philosophy, we can understand as well how the leisure associated with the philosophic life can fulfill the political duties of the statesman, an equation captured in the well-known phrase *cum dignitate otium*.[50]

Such refinement, Arendt suggests, "is suggestive of something like taste and, generally, sensitivity to beauty" (*BPF* 213).[51] For Cicero, an appreciation of beauty derives from an understanding of how that object fits into a more universal order of reasons and causes.[52] One might discern beauty in objects that fulfill a function or purpose: the functional interdependence of the human body, for example. The sensation of beauty can be an organic part of the item: the delight we feel at the smell of a rose. And beauty can lie in objects that represent order, whether that order is created by nature (e.g., the planets) or, importantly for our discussion, purposively developed by humans (e.g., agriculture).[53]

Of interest to us here is that recognition of beauty for both Cicero and Arendt suggests a mode of intercourse with the world. Furthermore, it is a mode of intercourse that is located in the spectator rather than the artist. As Cicero writes in *On the Orator* (*De Oratore*), in a passage that Arendt quotes, "Everybody is able to discriminate between what is right and what is wrong in matters of art and proportion by a sort of subconscious instinct, without having any theory of art or proportion of their own" (*De Orat.* 3.50.195; Arendt *LK* 63). Such a discriminating sense occurs not only for "pictures and statues," but also "in judging the rhythms and pronunciations of words, because these are rooted deep in the general sensibility" (*communibus sensibus*), a term that Arendt translates as "common sense" (*De Orat.* 3.50.195; Arendt *LK* 63). In such a sensibility Arendt locates the faculty of political judgment. As Arendt writes, "could it be that this right love of beauty, the proper kind of intercourse with beautiful things—the *cultura animi* which makes men fit to take care of the things of the world and which Cicero, in contradistinction to the Greeks, ascribed to philosophy—has something to do with politics" (*BPF* 215)? Judgment does not admit of formal rules, as McClure writes, in drawing out these Ciceronian links to Arendt, but rests "on the sort of tacit knowledge that characterizes one's participation in ongoing cultural practices."[54] I would qualify McClure's statement in two important ways: first, for Cicero beauty may be tacit, but it is also innate (*De Orat.* 3.50.195; 3.51.197); and second, common sense is a product of ongoing cultural practices only if we understand these cultural practices, as does Cicero, as expressions of nature's purpose. Thus, Cicero writes that "the name of beauty" is given to impartiality and consistency of beliefs and judgments that follow from virtue (*Tusc.* 4.13.31).

I am sympathetic to critics who argue that taste is an inadequate basis for political judgment since taste tells us very little about right and wrong, true and false, or just and unjust.[55] But I think Cicero's discussion of beauty plays a role for Arendt other than as a criteria for judgment. The sensitivity to beauty that is cultivated through philosophic training itself plays a part in creating "culture": the "mode of our intercourse" with our worldly products (*BPF* 218). The "products" of politics, words and deeds, share with art the "need of some public space where they can appear and be seen" (*BPF* 218). Both politics and art similarly face a futility in which their products "if left to themselves, come and go without leaving any trace in the world" (*BPF* 218). What gives the traces of words and deeds some permanence is beauty. To recall Cicero, beauty becomes the manifestation of the true nature of things, the trace of things that would otherwise be invisible to us. For Arendt, such beauty also appears as the trace of words and deeds that otherwise disappear the moment they occur. Culture indicates a public attitude of sensitivity and care for these traces—a recognition and love of beauty—that allows for the enduring greatness of human action and the survival of politics. For Cicero, as well, the role of culture in bestowing beauty and permanence to the fleeting greatness of humankind can be seen in the ancestors' use of poems and songs to praise the deeds of virtuous men (*Tusc.* 4.2.3).

We can begin to understand the broader relevance of Cicero's depiction of the Roman Republic as a beautiful painting, and in turn, the political role of philosophic thought. The comparison of the republic to a painting is a statement both of its perishability and of the need for those who can see and care for its beauty. Cicero invokes similar imagery in the *Tusculans* to describe an age where people no longer strive after a distinctive likeness of virtue, one that is formed like a statue from a solid substance, but are attracted instead to a vague outline (*Tusc.* 3.2.3).[56] People "are blinded" by their inability to distinguish true glory from "a copy" (*Tusc.* 3.2.4). The copy, the desire for public reputation, is a "counterfeit" that "mars the fair beauty of true honour" (*Tusc.* 3.2.4). People not only choose the wrong thing to admire, but are so driven by the desire for gain and lust for pleasure that they value nothing other than satisfying their own limitless emotions (*Tusc.* 3.2.4).[57] Cicero does not have to look far to see the effect of such attitudes: the ransacking of provinces and allies, the corruption of courts, and even the plundering of one's own citizens.[58]

Scipio, to recall the "Dream," is told to care (*curare*) for Rome, a term that ties together the agricultural meaning of tending to the earth with a corresponding anxiety that comes from loving something (*Rep.* 6.26.29). In the *Tusculans*, Cicero describes the happiest life as one devoted "to the care (*tuendam*) of the public realm" (*Tusc.* 5.25.72; trans. modified; also *Tusc.* 4.23.51). *Tueri* means "to look at" or watch over with the purpose of protecting the object.[59] Perhaps most revealing of this attitude of care is Cicero's story, referred to by Arendt, of how Pythagoras, when asked how philosophers differ from the rest of the world, compares the "life of man" to the magnificent Olympic festivals celebrated by all of Greece (*Tusc.* 5.3.9; *BPF* 218–19). At the festival are athletes who seek glory in victory and vendors who see the games as an opportunity for financial gain. A third group of people, "the best type of free-born men," seek neither "applause nor gain, but came for the sake of the spectacle and closely watched what was done and how it was done" (*Tusc.* 5.3.9).

Several aspects of this story are worth pointing out. First, the philosopher occupies a public space, drawn to the worldly spectacle and delighting in the appearance of things. Second, the spectacle of the games necessarily requires nonphilosophers: those who compete and those who sell. Third, the philosopher seems to have an important, even if unnoticed, role as a spectator. The philosopher's role is not to quash the different motivations of the participants but to cherish what others might see as the byproduct—certainly a product unintended by the participants—of the activities of the games. Fourth, to play that role the philosopher's own partial interests (in gain, in who will win, etc.) must be suspended. Finally, the ability to admire something like the games even though one does not have a self-interest in that thing suggests a broader ability and desire to admire the things of this world without regard to one's self.

We can perhaps better answer Schofield's question as to why Cicero in *On Divination* might see the *Tusculan Disputations* as the "centrepiece" of his philosophic account.[60] Cicero stresses in *On Divination* that philosophy becomes particularly important in a time when *mores* no longer educate the youth (*Div.* 2.2.4). Cicero's language might invite a narrowly ethical interpretation: moral laxity can be checked and individuals can be directed "in the right way" through ethical instruction (*Div.* 2.2.4). But philosophy plays a more broadly ethical role, if we understand ethics as an *ethos* or attitude toward one's relationship to the world. Philosophy is not just a body of knowledge; it is a practice of discernment by which we learn how to care for this world.

Cicero's concluding discussion in the *Tusculans* points suggestively toward how the *Tusculans* might contribute to this care of the world. Although the immediate topic is the happiness that attends life, even when denied obvious comforts (like sight or hearing), Cicero describes how Homer, though blind, can make us see. Cicero (following Simonides) says of

Homer, "it is his painting (*picturam*) not his poetry that we see; what district, what shore, what spot in Greece, what aspect or form of combat, what marshalling of battle, what tugging at the oar, what movements of men, of animals has he not depicted so vividly that he has made us see, as we read, the things which he himself did not see" (*Tusc.* 5.39.114)? Cicero might add, "and the things we might not otherwise have seen." The *Tusculans* is not a quiet meditation. In speaking to his cruel sorrows in a popularizing philosophic language, the *Tusculans* emerges as a practice of culture—a mode of intercourse with the artifacts of the surrounding world—that records Cicero's own struggle to cultivate a spirit that can love without longing and care without desiring.

WORLDLESSNESS

I have thus far used Arendt to look back at Cicero. But to fully appreciate the conceptual contributions of Cicero, we might also read Cicero forward to understand what role he plays in Arendt's thought. Such a reading is particularly warranted since controversy about Arendt's debt to the ancients has most often been fought on the terrain of Athens, to the exclusion of the Roman experience. Macauley, for example, notes an instance when "Arendt seems to prize the Roman perspective over the Greek," adding parenthetically, "somewhat untypically."[61] O'Sullivan suggests that though Rome "stands high" in Arendt's "estimation," it is "the life of the Greek polis (as theorized by Aristotle), which constitutes the focal point of all her thought."[62] Kateb speaks only of the "philosophical incapacity of the Romans" which makes it "extremely arduous to rescue the original meaning of political action."[63] Villa, in his wide-ranging collection of essays, takes note of "Arendt's beloved Greeks" but makes no mention of the Romans.[64] And indicative of the desire to Hellenize not just Arendt, but a Western philosophic tradition, Springborg omits any influence of the Romans on Arendt. She places Arendt in a tradition that includes Machiavelli and Montesquieu, whom she describes, in a surprising claim, as guided by the "desire to legitimise the Western nation-state as heir to the political institutions of Athens."[65] This requires ignoring not just the essays and passages in Arendt where she talks about the distinctive contributions of Rome, but (as we will see in subsequent chapters) both Machiavelli's and Montesquieu's stated and demonstrable elevation of Rome over Greece. Even when scholars note Arendt's mention of the Romans—most notably her discussion of Roman notions of tradition, authority, and culture—they are reluctant to assign conceptual form to Roman thinking and, related to this, to explore the significance of their influence on Arendt's thought.[66] The Romans, instead, are painted in the broadest of strokes: lumped together with the Greeks, seen as indicative of Arendt's conservatism or elitism, or categorized as a "neo-Roman" phase in Arendt's thought.[67]

But this focus on the Greek experience limits our understanding of one of the central themes of Arendt's work: "worldlessness." Although difficult to define precisely, "worldlessness" can be understood generally as Arendt's diagnosis that the "human artifice," which comprises our home in the world, is no longer seen as shared, secure, familiar, or enduring (*HC* 173).[68] This artifice, the work of humans as fabricators, includes tangible artifacts (such as monuments and buildings), works of literature, art, laws, and institutions. The problem that Arendt confronts is how we can recover our world as a home when the ways by which this human artifice is transmitted—or what Arendt refers to as the "Roman trinity" of tradition, religion, and authority—no longer exist (*BPF* 128; *OR* 117). "What has been lost," Arendt writes, "is the continuity of the past as it seemed to be handed down from generation to generation, developing in the process its own consistency." Arendt continues, "What we then are left with is still the past, but a *fragmented* past, which has lost its certainty of evaluation" (*LM* 1:212).

Inspired by the Athenian *polis*, commentators on Arendt locate the recovery of this world, as Villa emphatically notes, in "political action, and *only* political action."[69] This model of action is seen (whether favorably or unfavorably) as a celebration of agonistic display in which individuals, in competitively appearing before others like Homeric warriors on the battlefield, "endow the world *with* meaning" and "give it a significance and beauty it would otherwise lack."[70] In this model, action must be strictly demarcated from the "boundless instrumentalization that converts everything into a means for some subjectively posited end," a mentality associated with what Arendt describes as fabrication.[71] Arendt is most concerned with how politics has been placed in service to these forces of instrumentalization, both because it caters to economic interests that turn everything into a commodity, and because it imagines itself as forming (as with fascism and communism) a new type of citizen. Arendt's politics, which emphasizes the spontaneity and unpredictability of human affairs, is seen as "smash[ing]" the idea of politics as a "plastic art" that shapes and molds the world.[72] Fabrication's role is generally limited to providing a space (a home) where action can occur and the means (art) by which it can be remembered.[73]

The problem is this: not only do images of fabrication abound in Arendt's discussion of politics, but worldlessness is itself a problem of our attitude toward the things of this world.[74] There is no doubt that action is the hero of Arendt's political thought. But the attitude toward the world that Arendt hopes to recover is one that she associates with culture and the Romans. In paying closer attention to Arendt's discussion of the Romans, we can give a little more depth to the role of a lesser character, *homo faber,* in the story that Arendt tells. The issue is not whether fabrication is complementary to action. It is the way that fabrication may play a part in the recovery of thought and action.[75] In understanding this role (or roles) of fabrication, we might gain a better sense of the different ways in which, as Arendt writes, "the human capacity for building, preserving, and caring for a world" can find expression in contemporary politics (*BPF* 95).

Arendt's diagnosis of the causes of worldlessness is most fully developed in the final section of *The Human Condition.* What is striking about the discussion, and revealing of the dimensions of our alienation, is its shared trajectory with Scipio's ascent in which he, like us in our modern age, assumes a location in the heavens by which he may view the earth. Two developments that stand at the threshold of modernity for Arendt mark this ascent: the exploration of the earth and the invention of the telescope. The exploration and the mapping of the earth allow us to take "full possession" of our "mortal dwelling place" and gather "the infinite horizons" (*HC* 250). The shrinkage of the earth that Scipio sees as he is lifted into the heavens is experienced in the modern age of globalization through the shrinking of distance by the invention of ever quicker forms of transportation and communication. More significantly for Arendt, this shrinkage occurs by the condensing of the earth to scales of human comprehension: numbers, symbols, and models exemplified by bringing the globe into our "living rooms to be touched by our hands and swirled before our eyes" (*HC* 251). Through the "shrinking of the globe," we achieve what would seem to be the Stoic ideal of universal citizenship: "each man is as much an inhabitant of the earth as he is an inhabitant of his country" (*HC* 250). Arendt's statement is intentionally ironic because in a fundamental sense we may be as much inhabitants of the earth as of a country, but we are similarly alienated from both. Where Scipio is directed back to the earth to care for his native land, in our modern world "the nature of the human surveying capacity separates us from the earth." This surveying capacity, as Arendt writes, "can function only if man disentangles himself from all involvement in and concern with the close at hand and withdraws himself to a distance from everything near him" (*Rep.* 6.26.29; *HC* 251).[76]

The invention of the telescope makes possible the realization of Archimedes' dream of occupying a place outside earth. While certainly not anticipated in the first centuries of the modern age, the abolition of the "dichotomy between earth and sky" and the "unification of the universe" so changes our view of the earth that "from then on nothing occurring in earthly nature was viewed as a mere earthly happening" (*HC* 262–63). The invention of the telescope, though initially functioning as an extension of the senses, confirms the fear that our senses, "our very organs for the reception of reality, might betray us" (*HC* 262). As Scipio rises into the heavens he encounters a magnified sensuality: rushes of sounds that human ears cannot hear because they have become dulled (*Rep.* 6.18.18–19). But in our modern world, science subsumes the earth into universal laws and processes that are "valid beyond the reach of human sense experience (even of the sense experiences made with the help of the finest instruments), valid beyond the reach of human memory and the appearance of mankind on earth, valid even beyond the coming into existence of organic life and the earth herself" (*HC* 263). With mathematics, "all that man is not" can be reduced and translated "into patterns which are identical with human mental structures" (*HC* 266). From this Archimedean point, all human activities, like all other natural phenomena, come to appear as questions of processes: of *how* things come into being, change, and are destroyed (see *HC* 296, 322).

What we encounter on our return to earth is not a world of things, as does Scipio, but processes. The modern unleashing of the economic forces of production and wealth, as Arendt argues, can be maintained "only as long as all worldly things, all end products of the production process, are fed back into it at an ever-increasing speed" (*HC* 256). Even the focus of fabrication changes, from an emphasis on creating durable products to an interest in the process of production itself (*HC* 296–97). With the shift in emphasis from "what" to "how," and thus the transformation of *homo faber* from a maker of products to a fashioner of tools and instruments, *homo faber* is "deprived of those permanent measures that precede and outlast the fabrication process and form an authentic and reliable absolute with respect to the fabricating activity" (*HC* 307). More than anything, what is lost is an audience. *Homo faber*'s products no longer have reference to a public realm where they are valued and beheld (as beautiful, as creative, as unique, as bold) but have reference only to measures of efficiency and the private pleasures of the consumer, discarded when they no longer bring that pleasure (*HC* 307–8). Our relationship to the fabricated world is defined by two sorts of people: the consumer, who judges items by the gratification they bring when consumed, and the philistine, who judges items in terms of the "immediate usefulness" and "material values" (*BPF* 201). This philistinism bears directly on Arendt's more weighty characterization in *The Origins of Totalitarianism* of Himmler as a "philistine." Himmler, who was " 'more normal,' that is, more of a philistine, than any of the original leaders of the Nazi movement," defined the "new type of man" as one "who under no circumstance will ever do 'a thing for its own sake' " (*OT* 338, 322; also *BPF* 215).

Arendt, like Cicero, is speaking to a more general loss of

any claims of the past—the obsolescence of old products, the inefficiency of old production methods, the irrelevance of tradition, the loss of common standards of value and their replacement with individual measures of immediate gratification—so that it is as though we are "living and struggling with a Protean universe where everything at any moment can become almost anything else" (*BPF* 95). Lacking any stable markers by which we know and share the world, we look for certainty in introspection, the "sheer cognitive concern of consciousness with its own content" (*HC* 280). As Arendt writes, "Man, in other words, carries his certainty, the certainty of his existence, within himself; the sheer functioning of consciousness, though it cannot possibly assure a worldly reality given to the senses and to reason, confirms beyond doubt the reality of sensations and of reasoning, that is, the reality of processes which go on in the mind" (*HC* 280). Arendt's analysis in *The Human Condition* resonates with her earlier discussion of Rahel Varnhagen, a Jewess born in the eighteenth century, who seeks to anchor her sense of reality in her dreams, sorrows, and fears. The danger is that we, like Rahel Varnhagen for Arendt and Cicero in the aftermath of Tullia's death, can become lost in the dark and formless interiors of our moods.[77]

Worldlessness is also manifest in our theoretical ventures in which the "living force" of our political concepts gives way to empty formalisms (*BPF* 26). In a particularly instructive passage, Arendt draws a contrast between how we have "faithfully preserved and further articulated until they became empty platitudes" the different Greek images of authority—"such as the statesman as healer and physician, as expert, as helmsman, as the master who knows, as educator, as the wise man"—but have "entirely lost and forgotten" the Roman experience "which brought authority as word, concept, and reality into our history" (*BPF* 136). We have so emptied our concepts of any connection to experience that, as Arendt writes in a passage that parallels her description of our Protean world, "we have no reality, either in history or in everyday experience, to which we can unanimously appeal" (*BPF* 137). No less lost than Varnhagen in mood is Heidegger in the abstractness of thought.[78]

THE RECOVERY OF THE WORLD

Recourse to the Greek experience of action can only take us so far in this recovery of the world. The focus on the "politics of personal display," as Waldron argues, "tells us very little about what is necessary for politics as *inter*-action, the politics that involves debate, deliberation, and the making of decision."[79] What lies between us, for Arendt, is precisely our cultural world: a world of artificial things that we have endowed with meaning. Villa, sounding a note of celebration at the collapse of any claims of the past, suggests that the elementary problems that face humanity can finally be addressed.[80] But one of the central problems facing humanity for Arendt is that since we inhabit such a world without stable markers, there is little that we share or can talk about. Curtis, though sensitive to the role of culture and context, seems almost to replace the cultural world of things with the imagination. In Arendt's account of judging, for example, Curtis notes, "we see the importance of the sheer force of our imagination as it holds our world in common by giving it a certain durability and spatiality. And this we must of course do over and over again."[81] Through this account of the imagination, Curtis sees Arendt as going "a good way toward substantiating her claim" that even with the loss of worldly permanence and stability we retain the capacity for building and caring for the world.[82] As important as the imagination is for Arendt, though, it cannot create a world that endures.

If we are to look for an example of the task of recovering the world from a past that presents itself only in fragments, we might better take our cue from Arendt's discussion of the Romans. Arendt writes in an uncompleted manuscript she was preparing for Piper, *Was ist Politik?*, that the Romans (in certain legends) are able to rebuild their community from the annihilating fires of the Trojan war (*WP* 105). The Romans do not see themselves as establishing a new foundation from something unprecedented but as forming a renewed foundation (*erneute Gründung*) from something old (*WP* 102). By conceiving of foundations as "reconstructions" the past can be rescued and made into something new (*OR* 211).[83] As Arendt quotes Cicero's *Republic*, "For there is really no other occupation in which human virtue approaches more closely the august function of the gods than that of founding (*condere*) new States or preserving (*conservare*) those already in existence" (*OR* 201; *Rep.* 1.7.12). *Condere* means to fashion, found, establish, or produce and is used to describe different types of human fabrication: the construction of buildings and walls (Virg. *Aen.* 1.276–77; Livy 1.7.11), the composition of written works (Virg. *Ec.* 6.7; *Rep.* 4.10.12), the founding of cities (*Rep.* 1.7.12), and carries with it the idea of carefulness, as of putting something somewhere for it to be cared for or preserved.[84] In this care of beautiful things, we should be reminded of Cicero's comparison of the republic to a beautiful painting, one that the current generations have failed to maintain (*tenere*), preserve (*retinere*), or renovate (*renovare*) (*Rep.* 1.1.1–2).

Such an image of fabrication might, at first glance, recall Arendt's critique of Plato and Aristotle who, as Arendt writes, "elevated lawmaking and city-building to the highest rank in political life" because in such activities "men 'act like craftsmen': the result of their action is a tangible product, and its process has a clearly recognizable end" (*HC* 195). There is, in fact, an affinity between Greek philosophy and this image of the political actor as an architect, which is that both act from an ideal: an already formed model to which politics is fashioned to conform. The problem is that such an image deprives politics of the openness, uncertainty, and spontaneity that is the centerpiece of human freedom (*HC* 307). In employing the image of politics as craft, Plato and Aristotle, as Arendt argues, turn "against politics and against action" by transforming politics into a form of making (*poiêsis*) (*HC* 195).

In describing Roman political action, Wolin argues that the Romans similarly conceive of politics as an activity that had to conform to preestablished institutions.[85] Canovan characterizes "the Roman experience of foundation" as "a once-for-all affair that establishes a political world and leaves successive generations to carry it on rather than to repeat the experience of action."[86] But less frequently acknowledged—in fact, almost never mentioned—is that Arendt is making a comparison to Roman political thought and experience, a comparison that is not favorable to Greece.[87] As Arendt points out, Plato's and Aristotle's transformation of politics into a form of making "does not indicate that they enlarged the fundamental Greek experiences of action and politics to comprehend what later turned out to be the political genius of Rome: legislation and foundation" (*HC* 195).

Arendt does not provide much more than this brief formulation in *The Human Condition*. But in *Was ist Politik?*, which she was writing at about this same time, Arendt provides a fuller explanation. The Greeks, according to Arendt, conceive of the founder as an architect who is called upon to set up the institutional structures of the state (the laws and constitution) but (like their own artisans) are not an actual part of the community (*WP* 109). Law is similarly conceived as "pre-political" because it is understood as originating (like the Greek conception of fabrication) in violence, from outside the community, as it is derived from the lawgiver (*WP* 111–12). The Roman conception of founding is distinctive, though, and in fact points to a significant departure from a Greek conception precisely because founding is not seen as a "once-for-all affair." Founding appears much more as an incremental process, which, as Cicero writes, occurs over "a longer period of several centuries and many ages of men" (*Rep.* 2.1.2). Roman founding is "not the work of single men," as Arendt notes, but of "agreement" (*der Vertrag*) between two groups in conflict, the patricians and plebeians (*WP* 110).[88] We will need to interpret "agreement" very broadly, and it is certainly more useful in explaining later parts of the process of community formation and consolidation. The point is, though, that preserving and renovating appear as forms of political action that do not follow from foundation but are ongoing aspects of founding.

Law, similarly, is understood as a form of action established in settlement and agreement (*WP* 109). The power of law exists not as a boundary handed down by the lawgiver that defines the space of politics, but as a "perpetual bond" (*dauernde Bindung*) forged in speech and argument, in which people continually bind themselves together (*WP* 109). While fabrication creates boundaries, we are mistaken to apply the Athenian definition of a political space to the Romans.[89] Through law Athens, according to Arendt, creates the space in which political activity can occur, itself limiting the ability of political freedom to be extended beyond the confines of the *polis*. For the Romans, though, the boundaries of political community can continually be expanded and negotiated as political acts, including the incorporation of previous enemies (*WP* 99, 111, 108).

The Roman revision of the Greek boundaries of fabrication and action appears, as well, in the overlapping relationship of what are seen by Arendt as the respective realms for these activities: the private realm of the *oikos* and the public sphere of the *polis*. Brunkhorst, for example, in grouping together the Greeks and Romans, emphasizes the "stable hierarchy" between the "lower" realm with its emphasis on instrumental action and the "higher" realm where men (specifically) experience freedom and achieve glory.[90] But for Arendt the Romans establish a greater balance between the public and private realm, one that emerges in the Roman revision of the Greek conception of glory and immortality. As Arendt writes, the Greek hero, born in the image of Achilles, can achieve greatness only by sacrificing his private attachments. Glory is the celebration of the great individual and the great deed (*WP* 101). But for the Romans, born in the image of Hektor, the guarantee of earthly immortality (*die Garantie für irdische Unsterblichkeit*) is tied to the defense of the household and "the care for the continuation of the family and its glory" (*die Sorge um den Fortbestand des Geschlechts und seinen Ruhm*) (*WP* 103). The interpenetration of the republican Roman household and politics is seen in a variety of contexts: the public courtyards for Roman houses, the prominent display of ancestor masks in the house, which serves both private and public functions, and the public celebration of household deities.[91]

Even Arendt's "elitism," which is seen as descending from her use of the Greeks and Romans, stands in need of revision.[92] Canovan is correct in characterizing Arendt's conception of politics as "assimilated to high culture."[93] I do not think, though, that we can go as far as Wolin, who claims that Arendt "restricts 'high culture' to the few."[94] In fact, by being attentive to the Ciceronian source of this idea of culture, quite the opposite emerges: taste, which Arendt associates with the faculty of political judgment, must necessarily be public and broadly shared.[95] Arendt, in her discussion of Cicero, describes taste as "the discriminating, discerning, judging elements of an active love of beauty," a sensibility, as both Cicero and Arendt claim, that everybody shares (*BPF* 219). Furthermore, the stance occupied by those exercising taste, as Cicero's example of the philosopher attending the games suggests, is that of the spectator who "is not involved in the act" but is "always involved with fellow spectators" (*LK* 63). Cicero, as we have seen, places his own work before the "wider public," disagreeing with those who write only for themselves and their small group (*Tusc.* 1.3.6). As Nederman notes, for Cicero statesmen are expected to put their arguments before citizens who "are deemed to be competent to judge between competing arguments within the public arena and to choose in accordance with the best and most persuasive (that is, the wisest) case that they hear."[96]

Cicero's sense of loss of the republic as a work of art has less to do with the Platonic loss of the conformity of politics to an ideal and more with a change of attitude that extends to all groups of society and has implications for how we think and act. As such, fabrication is a category that, ironically enough, extends beyond its boundaries. Its appearance as art is "the most intensely worldly of all tangible things" because its durability is not worn out in use (*HC* 167). In its durability, it stands as a "premonition" of "something immortal achieved by mortal hands" that becomes "tangibly present, to shine and to be seen, to sound and to be heard, to speak and to be read" (*HC* 168). Works of art are also "thought things," inspired by "thought" which, for Arendt, "has neither an end nor an aim outside itself" and is not reducible to a use (*HC* 169–70). Art transforms the "mute and inarticulate despondency" of feeling and introspection into something public and communicable (*HC* 168).[97] It transforms the futility of words and deeds, which would be lost the moment they are performed, into something that lasts (*HC* 173). Its "living spirit," what gave it life, must be continually renewed through its contact with, and rebirth in, subsequent generations (*HC* 169). And this "living spirit" is made possible by its "condensation" of thought and experience, giving it a "closeness to living recollection" that allows the work of art to be transmitted, remembered, and recalled (*HC* 169). As Arendt writes, "no remembrance remains secure unless it is condensed and distilled into a framework of conceptual notions within which it can further exercise itself" (*OR* 220).

POLITICAL THOUGHT AS CULTIVATION

The importance of the Romans as a model of action does not lie in the sense that a Roman world can be (or should be) reclaimed. But what this model points to are some less explored, more modernized, versions of the role of fabrication in the recovery of thought and action. One figure that comes to mind is Walter Benjamin, who originally began to collect books for his library but then turned his attention to collecting quotations. Cicero, too, was an avid book collector and stood at the beginning of an age of collectors. The collector, Arendt suggests, is both a destroyer and creator. He becomes a destroyer as he wrenches the item out of its context, a destructiveness that Arendt finds as contrary to the intentions of the collector but strangely in keeping with the age (*MDT* 193). There is, for Arendt, a "close affinity between the break in tradition and the seemingly whimsical figure of the collector who gathers his fragments and scraps from the debris of the past" (*MDT* 201). On the one hand, the collector may have nothing to do with the public realm as he takes possession of these things from the past, withdrawing from the public "into the privacy of his four walls" and taking "with him all kinds of treasures that once were public property to decorate them" (*MDT* 198). On the other hand, as Arendt suggests, "collecting is the redemption of things which is to complement the redemption of man" (*MDT* 197). Benjamin, drawing on a theologically laden idea, sees himself as bringing something into existence (an attribute of action, for Arendt) by "naming rather than speaking" (*MDT* 203–4). Moreover, by "tearing fragments out of their context and arranging them afresh," Benjamin is careful "not to ruin everything with explanations that seek to provide a causal or systematic connection" (*MDT* 202). That is, the fabricator, ironically, in reconstituting the past, frees the past from causal processes. So, too, Arendt approvingly cites Harrington's advice to "ransack the archives of ancient prudence," making political founders and legislators into types of collectors.[98]

Arendt's use of Benjamin is instructive because Benjamin, too, is concerned with an aesthetic, associated with fascism, that presses into use the mechanical reproduction of modern media technologies, namely film, for "the production of ritual values."[99] Benjamin's concern is played out in a distinction that Arendt poses between "culture," which "relates to objects and is a phenomenon of the world," and "entertainment," which "relates to people and is a phenomenon of life" (*BPF* 208). For Arendt, as for Benjamin, the cultural technologies of modernity transform cultural production into something that is easily "rewritten, condensed, reduced to kitsch in reproduction, or in preparation for the movies" (*BPF* 207). Cultural production, like the political processes that support it, aims not at contemplation, nor even duration, but distraction.

If the fabricator stands as a figure who threatens to turn the entire world into an object of use, then the fabricator is also the one who can give durability to the world, can give expression to thought, and can give permanence to words and deeds. What mediates between thought, action, and fabrication is *cultura animi*, the cultivated spirit that gives tangibility to thought and care to action. It may be possible, Arendt suggests, to persuade *homo faber* of a "change of attitude," to step back from and take pleasure in his creation (*HC* 304). This change would not be a "radical turnabout" since, as Arendt suggests, the fabricator would only have to be convinced to "let his arms drop" and prolong the act of beholding the "excellence and beauty" of the model "he had formerly wanted to imitate" (*HC* 304). Scipio, in much the same way, is directed to return to earth where he is told that happiness lies in the ability to contemplate that which lies outside one's body, not as a disavowal of the earth but as a rejection of the devouring impulses of gratification (*Rep.* 6.26.29). With the absence of such care, the mark of human permanence on earth faces "oblivion," erased from earth and from memory (*Rep.* 5.1.2).

But the model that emerges from Arendt's account is different from the Platonic *eidos*. Arendt's discussion of Isak Dineson shows the two different ways that fabrication can relate to action. One way, which is akin to the Platonic model of "making," marks Dineson's youth when she attempts to live her life as a story (see *MDT* 105–6). The attempt to conform her life to a blueprint cannot prepare her for her "complete 'failure' ": her loss "of what constituted her life, her home in Africa and her lover" (*MDT* 98). As Arendt writes of Dineson, "the earlier part of her life had taught her that, while you can tell stories or write poems about life, you cannot make life poetic, living it as though it were a work of art (as Goethe had done) or use it for the realization of an 'idea' " (*MDT* 109).[100] Only when Dineson returns home to Rungstedlund "with nothing in her hands except grief and sorrow and memories, did she become the artist and the 'success' she never would have become otherwise" (*MDT* 98). Cicero, too, conveys not just the contradiction and loss that inhere in human life but also the necessary openness by which future generations must continually shape and give color to their cultural past. In much this same sense, Arendt writes that each generation must "discover and ploddingly pave anew the path of thought" (*LM* 1:210).

Arendt's contribution to political thought, like what Cicero conveyed to Montesquieu, is to instill a feel for what it means to cultivate the world.[101] She does not formalize "theories and concepts" but seeks to identify the "uncertain, flickering, and often weak light" that illuminates the concepts that have been lost (*MDT* ix). And her work, like Cicero's, is an engagement in the activity of judgment and discrimination as she attempts to locate in the past the "elemental quality" of human artifacts that "grasp and move the reader" (*BPF* 203). Arendt looks to the past not to romanticize it but, like Cicero, to paint a world so vividly that we might see it again (see *Tusc.* 5.39.114). By seeing and hearing, the political thinker seeks to restore (like Scipio in the heavens) our sensitivity to the movement of thought and judgment in our world.

3

Livy, Machiavelli, and the Recovery of Felt Meanings

Livy began the writing of his history of Rome on the other side of the civil war from Cicero. Where Cicero witnessed the gathering storm of private armies, heightened aristocratic rivalries, mounting armed and mob conflict, and the rise of Caesar, Livy's writing was informed by the next decade of strife: the assassination of Caesar, violent reprisals by a new triumvirate comprised of Lepidus, Octavian, and Antony, and ultimately a bloody struggle for supremacy between Octavian and Antony that spanned the Roman world. Livy's Preface sounds an expectedly plaintive note. Although his readers might want to delight in the spectacle of modern times, Livy finds some joy in escaping to the Roman past. As Livy writes, "I myself, on the contrary, shall seek in this an additional reward for my toil, that I may avert my gaze from the troubles which our age has been witnessing for so many years, so long at least as I am absorbed in the recollection of the brave days of old, free from every care which, even if it could not divert the historian's mind from the truth, might nevertheless cause it anxiety" (pref. 5).[1]

When Livy describes the disorders of Rome, he draws upon what would have been familiar images of illness.[2] For Livy, the "gradual relaxation of discipline" (*labente . . . paulatim disci-*

plina) had bred an unhealthy disposition, and thus a disorder (*vitium*) of the soul that Rome could no longer endure (pref. 9).[3] The disorders that Livy identifies, which had reached their most alarming expression in the civil wars in Rome,[4] were of "excessive pleasures" that had brought a "longing to carry wantonness and license to the point of ruin for oneself (*pereundi*) and of universal destruction (*perdendi*)" (pref. 12). This intemperance echoes Livy's earlier use of *festinare*, suggesting a dangerous hastiness, to describe how contemporary readers will hurry past the old parts because they "will offer little pleasure" (pref. 4).[5] And Livy holds out the possibility of the study of history as healthful (*salubris*) because it allows us to behold "the lessons of every kind of experience set forth as on a conspicuous monument" (pref. 10).

Whatever were the reactions of Livy's ancient readers, and the evidence seems to suggest that his *History* may have been a critical but not a popular success, for the political theorist today there seems to be little to recover from Livy.[6] We will be frustrated if we look for a unified historical narrative because of the influence of an annalist tradition in which the listing of names, dates, and events rather than theme often "dictates the presentation."[7] We will be disappointed as well if we hold Livy to today's standards of historical investigation and accuracy. Not only is verifiable evidence from much of Roman history, particularly the early republican era, absent, but the influence of a Hellenistic historiographic tradition leads Livy to embellish the past by creating dramatic encounters between characters, inventing speeches, and inferring emotions.[8] Burck sees Livy as adapting the dramatic techniques of tragedy to engage and instruct the audience.[9] And Walsh, following Burck, characterizes Livy's approach as a "preeminently psychological history" because of its emphasis on vividly portraying the "mental and emotional experiences felt" by the historical actors.[10] But in constructing these narratives, Livy is sometimes seen as more interested in glorifying than critically analyzing Roman political development, including the rise of Augustus.[11] As one political theorist comments, Livy substitutes analytic insight with "melodrama," content to see Roman grandeur as springing from a natural Roman character.[12] Collingwood, too, pronounces, "From the beginning" of Livy's history "Rome is ready-made and complete. To the end of the narrative she has undergone no spiritual change."[13] And Wiedemann, in his survey of Latin historical writing, makes the sober assessment that "political theory is absent from the surviving thirty-five books of Livy's history."[14]

More flattering interpretations are offered by a number of scholars who seek to tease conceptual substance out of Livy's "psychological history." For Moles, history, as a visual monument of the past, is meant to evoke both an emotional and moral response.[15] Feldherr argues that "the ability to reconstruct the emotional experiences of the spectators" makes Livy's audience into participants in the structures of religious and political authority that connect past with present.[16] Vividness becomes a legitimating device that, like Augustus's establishment of the visual monuments of his reign, attests to Livy's own *auctoritas* as an historian.[17] Livy's *History*, thus, emerges as a form of political action that mirrors and prepares the Roman citizen for a changing relationship with "the collective authority of the state."[18] Kraus and Woodman suggest that in making us " 'see' the events in our mind's eye," Livy helps us "feel the emotions and understand the thoughts and motives of the actors from inside."[19] The vividness of Livy's narrative serves in turn as a "medicine for the state" by transforming the reader into an actor who "evaluates, judges, and acts according to the lessons of the past."[20] And for Matthes, each lesson from history, or *exemplum*, "encapsulate[s] a theory" that the reader learns by becoming a participant in the story.[21]

Matthes's language is revealing of the attempt by many political theorists to salvage the conceptual elements of Livy's *History*: dramatic stories serve as a transmission device, a way of packaging theory. But the case is considerably more complex. As Chaplin has noted, Livy's *exempla* are not fixed in time—they are not encapsulated theories—but "surface, flourish, and pass away over the course of the narrative."[22] Chaplin provides us with a tantalizing suggestion, one that opens Livy's *History* to the interpretation of different audiences at different times facing different circumstances. But the more we extend the work beyond its own time, the farther we seem to move from understanding the conceptual coherence or contribution of Livy's *History*. What holds it together if not specific lessons? What does it have to say about the nature of politics not just to Livy's generation but also to future generations? On what basis can Livy be justified in hoping that his work will be remembered? And what keeps our return to Livy's *History* from being an exercise in little more than antiquarianism or puzzle-solving?

We find perhaps the greatest appreciation and fullest elaboration of Livy's contribution to political thought in Machiavelli's *Discourses*. Taking his cue from Livy's claim that historiography is like a "conspicuous monument" by which "you behold the lessons (*exempla*) of every kind of experience," Machiavelli depicts the monuments of the past as quite literally the fragments of ancient statues now desired as collector's items (*D* 1.preface).[23] Similarly, the history of great deeds is more "admired than imitated," read only for the pleasure it brings as it relates the "variety of accidents" (*D* 1.preface).[24] The monuments of the past have lost their life; no trace (*segno*) or sense (*senso*) of the ancient *virtù* that gave rise to these monuments remains (*D* 1.preface).

Machiavelli's task, then, appears as an attempt to restore this *sense* so that the *virtù* of the past may be seen and imitated.[25]

When Machiavelli claims that the *Discourses* are aimed at the spirits (*anime*) of the youth, he is providing some insight into the psychological underpinnings of his argument (*D* 2.preface). However significant may be our faculty of reason, individuals are ultimately beings who are moved as much by affections and feelings as by reasoned argument. Returning to Livy's *History* is central to Machiavelli's task of exciting the minds, not because Livy's *exempla* serve as repositories of political wisdom, timeless examples, authoritative accounts, or the empirical basis for a systematic study of politics (the usual suspects), but because Livy's method reveals a way of thinking about politics in which political concepts become comprehensible as *felt meanings*.

The term is meant to connect the psychological to the conceptual. Felt meanings, as the term suggests, are ultimately phenomenal more than philosophical. They acquire conceptual form through the association of experiences rather than the logic of argument. And the primary way in which meaning is experienced is as a form of vision, which, for both Livy and Machiavelli, is the most powerful of political senses since through sight our experience of the world is most vividly imprinted and recalled. In short, we are what we see. In the psychology that informs both writers, which I take up in the first section of this chapter, what we see and experience leaves an impression on the mind that we compare with other impressions. Whether influenced by innate dispositions or habituation, we come to form beliefs about how to act based on favorable and unfavorable emotions that we associate with a succession of experiences and that we extend in turn to other experiences. Meaning, in short, becomes an association of experiences by their effect on us. This effect can be something as seemingly mundane as what we imagine when we hear the word "blue," as emotionally charged as when we hear the word "terrorist," or as multivalent as a term like "liberty" or "authority." What is called to mind is not reducible to a formula or even able to be fixed as an image once and for all. Rather, the image is itself affected by context, by potential application, and by previous experiences. Concepts, thus, emerge through a process of assimilating different experiences into a composite image that guides us in turn in how we see and respond to other situations. Along these same lines Raymond Williams describes the "structures of feeling" as containing interlocking relations of "impulse, restraint, and tone." These feelings are not defined in opposition to thought; rather, they are "affective elements of consciousness" in which thought is felt. These affective elements have implications for the mental map by which one orients oneself politically. Thought acquires salience — it is seen as belonging to oneself — to the extent that it is felt.[26] And thought acquires objectivity or meaningfulness beyond oneself when one has a sense that these sensations are aspects of shared experience.[27]

Livy's "psychological history," thus, entails more than the construction of dramatic personae. It appears to Machiavelli as an alternative to Plato's philosopher-king, to Aristotle's model of *phronesis*, and to Christian moralism, each of which ultimately looks to reason as the mechanism by which communities can be made to endure.[28] Machiavelli's alternative, indeed, his originality, is most frequently seen as his privileging of appearance as the mechanism by which leaders (cynically or realistically, depending on one's evaluation) can and must manipulate appearance to survive. The use of Livy, though, suggests some very different implications for this privileging of appearance. At the very least, gone is the philosopher, or even the leader, who can stand outside time and history and craft appearance. Although there may be differences in innate dispositions to understand and respond to situations, the way in which elites and masses make sense of the world is essentially the same. We are beings animated by impulse. The emphasis on appearance also suggests shared vulnerabilities. Corruption is not the failure of reason (as it is for Plato); it is the failure of vision, which, more than anything else, is the inability to see beyond our own fears, pleasures, interests, or even generalizations.

But the most dramatic implication to this notion of felt meanings that Machiavelli takes from Livy's psychological history is that elites, no matter how important they may be (or may want to be) in crafting appearances, are never able to completely define those meanings for the populace. They are never able to fix interpretations. The people, as Livy's *History* makes all so clear, are continually and vigorously engaged in acts of interpretation that derive as much from their own experiences and conditions as from anything the elite might contrive.[29] Whether begrudgingly recognizing this or not, Livy's psychological history traces the animating role of popular vision in the emergence of liberty and the effects of political blindness by both elites and masses in the corruption of the community. The trajectory of the first ten books of Livy's *Ab urbe condita*, the focus of Machiavelli's *Discourses*, is toward the increasing openness of Roman politics, not out of a principled belief in rights but because the health of the community depends on the shared, though not necessarily harmonious or identical, ability to see.

THE ANIMATION OF POLITICAL CHARACTER

The affinity between Machiavelli and Livy can be traced, at least in part, to the shared medical and psychological underpinnings of their arguments. We, of course, must be careful in talking about "psychology" since the term is unknown before the seventeenth century. I use the language as shorthand for how both Livy and Machiavelli understand the processes of perception, decision, and action, processes that are traceable to the motions of the soul and are consistent with the earliest definitions of psychology.[30] In exploring these assumptions, we end up with a clearer sense of the close connection between perception and conception that lies at the heart of Livy's contribution to political thought.

Scholars, most prominently Anthony Parel, have explored some of the psychological underpinnings of Machiavelli's thought.[31] The psychological assumptions informing Livy's thought, though, are less clear, and less well established in scholarship. It is at least likely that Livy thought about these issues (or at least was not ignorant of them), given his study and work in rhetoric and philosophy that likely preceded his writing of his history.[32] Furthermore, medical knowledge, which included the study of internal (what is now called "psychological") disorders, was not the province of particular experts but had become a part of intellectual culture.[33] Medical analogies that compared the task of the philosopher to the task of the physician in healing the diseases of the soul, for example, were already well established in Roman discourse, shared by the Stoics, Epicureans, and, to some extent, the Skeptics.[34]

Pinning down Livy to a particular philosophic school, or ascribing to Livy a specialized, technical vocabulary, is unlikely to be successful. Walsh, for example, attempts to demonstrate Stoic influences on Livy.[35] But Livy seems rather un-Stoic in his continued appeal to the emotions in his historiography. This resort to the emotions has led some scholars to suggest an Aristotelian influence. Although the actual texts of Aristotle were probably not widely read in Rome, his ideas (and the ideas of the Peripatetics who followed Aristotle) on the arousal of the emotions through vivid description "filtered into wider culture" through a rhetorical and historiographic tradition, transmitted most prominently by Polybius and Cicero.[36] But Livy is also seen as influenced by the New Academy, including Posidonius and Cicero, which drew on Platonic strands.[37] Given what we know of the intellectual climate, we can reasonably posit a general diffusion of these different intellectual currents in Roman culture and an ability to incorporate peripheral ideas into any particular approach.[38] My primary interest is to demonstrate how, given this general diffusion of medical knowledge, the appeal to the emotions is more than just dramatic, as is often seen as the importance of an Aristotelian influence on Livy, but is integral to history as *remedia*. Cicero and the skeptical Academy provide an important and suggestive bridge between the therapeutic task of the philosopher and the historian. Drawing on Stoic analogies of sickness, Cicero, as we saw in the previous chapter, criticizes both Stoic claims to the certainty of knowledge and the Stoic inability to employ rhetoric to change minds.[39] Underlying Livy's *History* is a sense of how the rhetorical formulation of history—the ways in which the past is depicted—can change minds.

To understand how historiography can effect such change, we need to look to the Hippocratic tradition, in which Machiavelli and Livy wrote, that viewed the human body and soul as comprised of *pneuma*, a material substance made up of air and water that moved continually through the body. One part of the *pneuma* is the *psuchê* (= *animus*/ *anima*), which is the animating source of life responsible for our drives, perceptions, and cognitive actions.[40] The "command center" (*to hêgemonikon* = *mens*) of the *psuchê* is connected throughout the body to the sense organs (though its location was debated). Stimulated by external data (the *pneuma* flowing from the sensed object), the senses transmit a "presentation" (*phantasia* = *visum* [also *species*]) or an image to the command center.[41] All sensory stimuli are not presentations, though, but only those that make an "imprint" or "impression."[42] The most important presentations are those that lead to a "grasp" or "apprehension" (*katalêpsis*), which Sandbach refers to as a "cognitive presentation" and Frede calls a "thought."[43] The process of grasping a presentation involves combining information about the present object with stored images, including our memory of past experiences, our reaction to and evaluation of these experiences, and our ability to "make inferences and form concepts" from those images.[44] A presentation includes, as well, an image of whether something is good or bad and should or should not be pursued. As Frede writes, "the soul calculates through images and thoughts 'as if seeing.' "[45]

Although our control over our *phantasiai*—that is, how the world appears to us—is somewhat limited, we do have control over our "assent" (*synkatathesis* = *adsensio*) to these images. Through assent, we affirm the validity of the presentation; namely, whether we have assessed the situation and responded to the situation properly. From this assent arises an "impulse" (*hormê* = *impetus*) to "pursue or avoid the external thing causing the stimulation of the sense organs."[46] Although the soul does not animate the structure of the body, "it can literally govern the body because it can decide what description and value to give to its present, past or future bodily states."[47]

The property associated with *pneuma* is tension (*tonos*).[48] Proper "tensional movement" of the *pneuma* allows data to be clearly transmitted and in turn evaluated. But imbalances can affect the functioning of the imagination by altering what we see and how we respond. Drawing a comparison to diseases and disorders of the body, Cicero writes, "the disturbing effect of corrupt beliefs warring (*pravarum opinionum conturbatio*) against one another" creates "troubled movement . . . in the soul" (*motus in animo turbidus*) (*Tusc.* 4.10.23; 3.10.23). Sicknesses (*aegrotationes)*, or more generally "defects" (*vitia*), arise when, through repeated association of desire and pleasure with a particular object, we come to value an object as good that is not good (*Tusc.* 4.10.23–11.27).[49] Likewise, aversions (*offensiones*) arise when we associate fear with an object that is in fact good. Over time, as Graver notes, "when an agent has, on several different occasions, assented to the same evaluation of some particular object-type, he begins to form a more extensive system of beliefs linking that positive or negative evaluation to numerous other opinions he happens to hold."[50]

So too Pico della Mirandola writes in one of the most important Renaissance works on the imagination, just as "the bodily eye experiences illusions through tinted, particoloured lenses," so diseased humors—the organic substances of the body—change and deceive "the spiritual eye of the soul, the intellect."[51] From imbalances in the humors emerge "all the deception of phantasies."[52] Diseases of the humors can also affect our decisions to act. Imbalances can either make the imagination "prone to slip" so that it cannot "retain the appearances of things as conceived" or make the imagination "more fixed than is necessary, and holds so fast to the same spot that only with difficulty can it pass from one likeness to another."[53] Thus, in action we become prone to "leap over the proper bounds" or become dragged down in "excessive delay when action is needed."[54] In this same vein Machiavelli writes of the "confusion" of the mind that can overtake one at the point of decision, leading people to "do that which you ought not" (*D* 3.6).

Although one cannot change the nature of an individual, one's dispositions are developed both in good and bad ways by habituation.[55] Like the exercise of a body, habituation trains the soul. Posidonius poses the possibility that two people may have similar weaknesses and both receive a similar "presentation" (*phantasia*) of good and evil, yet one will be emotionally moved and the other not (Gal. *De Plac.* F. 164.41–50).[56] He suggests that "the more unused a man is to a situation, the more affected he is in circumstances of fear, distress, desire and pleasure; and the more vicious, the more speedily seized by emotions" (Gal. *De Plac.* F 164.48–50). Cicero uses the example of the artist who through training learns to see things "in shadows and in the foreground which we do not see" (*Acad.* 2.7.20; also *Tusc.* 2.23.56). Likewise, Livy, as Jaeger suggests, seeks through the construction of scenes to train our senses by moving us from partial and hasty assessments of a situation through one set of eyes to a more complete, careful, and patient assessment of the situation through a different set of eyes.[57] Machiavelli, too, seems to hold out the possibility that experience and practice can influence human disposition. Human tendencies "gain form" through what Mirandola calls "our manner of living" or what Machiavelli calls a "mode of life."[58]

So what is the remedy for a disordered soul? In the best of all philosophic worlds, reason. But the individual with the disordered soul is in no position to do that since, as Cicero notes, the soul would have to pass "judgment upon its own condition at a moment when the actual instrument of judgment is sick" (*Tusc.* 3.1.2). Furthermore, as Posidonius notes, one cannot move the "irrational rationally" (Gal. *De Plac.* F 163.8): "I think that you have noticed for long enough how we may be rationally convinced that an evil is within us or approaching, and yet we are neither afraid nor distressed, but we are so when we get an image presentation (*phantasias*) of the evils themselves" (Gal. *De Plac.* F. 162.4–8). For Machiavelli, as well, the individual is not guided by reason but "conducts himself according to his disposition and his imagination (*fantasia*)."[59]

As beings animated by impulse, sometimes the only way to correct our imagination is to "thrust before" the emotions "a vivid mental picture similar to one you can see."[60] "Truth," as Moles suggests in his discussion of Livy, "is a matter of sight."[61]

We might add that action is a matter of sight, as well, for it is through our assent to an image of a future good or bad that we are moved to act.[62] The problem with the diseased soul is that its mix of inconsistent opinions renders it unable to feel the distinguishing effect of different presentations, and thus to recognize what is similar or dissimilar. The laxness of the soul cannot be addressed through reason nor cured by precepts. Rather, Livy directs the attention (*intendit animum*) of each reader by *thrusting* before his audience a vivid picture of the experiences of the past (pref. 9–10), seeking to train the soul by condensing the historical accumulation of felt meanings.[63]

This training takes several forms, elements of which have been thoughtfully explored in scholarship. First, Livy's *History* addresses errors of direction. The problem of hastiness, as diagnosed by Livy, is more an error of giving assent to improper means than an error in choosing ends. That is, one chooses the correct goal but the wrong way to get there. As Arnold writes, hastiness occurs when one gives "assent to a picture which is not really clear."[64] Such hastiness corresponds to "lax psychic tension."[65] Addressing this problem requires restoring tension to the soul so that it is able to withhold assent to a presentation until it is sure that the presentation is a true one.[66] Such patience requires that we exercise the soul to teach it endurance and, to the extent possible, that we cultivate our senses through practice. Patience and sensory discrimination are related. Although we may not be able to control the initial presentation—how something immediately looks to us—the mind is able to direct the senses to look again, or look more closely, or look from a different angle, to better perceive the object (Cic. *Acad.* 2.10.30).[67] Likewise, Livy moves us from partial and hasty assessments of situations to more complete and careful assessments. Such examples appear frequently with military commanders sizing up the strategic situation, but also, as we will see, with the detection of corruption. Livy's approach here is captured at least in part in Jaeger's metaphor of the labyrinth in which those making their way through the maze must continually struggle to be attentive to detail: to identify clues, assess the situation, see opportunity, and sort through confusion.[68]

For Livy the Roman people have succumbed not just to errors of hastiness, but errors of purpose. The love of Rome once oriented individual dispositions toward a common purpose. But such a common orientation has given way to faction as newly incorporated populations no longer share a civic identity and individuals become animated by their separate lusts for power, luxury, and gratification.[69] Sallust points to how the community was "torn to pieces" by contending factions following the destruction of Carthage because there was no longer an enemy to fear (*Jug.* 41.5). "Thus," Sallust writes, "by the side of power, greed arose, unlimited and unrestrained, violated and devastated everything, respected nothing, and held nothing sacred, until it finally brought about its own downfall" (*Jug.* 41.9). Such "blindness of the mind" (*mentis caecitas*), as Cicero describes it, results in a disarray of the community, not unlike the disarray of the soul, in which its parts are pulled in separate directions (*Tusc.* 3.5.11; also 3.2.4). Since errors of vision are errors of belief, what must be changed is a sense that power and luxury bring about pleasure.[70] Reason alone cannot tell the lustful man that lust does not bring pleasure. Only the vivid illustration of the outcomes of indulgence can counter the disorder of the soul.[71] "Experience," Cicero writes, "teaches the lesson which reason should have taught before" (*Tusc.* 3.22.54). Livy's *History* is filled with such examples of misdirected purpose, not the least of which are events leading to the sacking of Rome by the Gauls. Livy provides his audience with a double perspective on this experience: the perspective of time allows the audience to witness the enactment of indulgence while knowing its outcomes.

The individual must be taught not only the disadvantage or displeasure of error, but must also develop an impulse toward civic virtue. That impulse is more than a copy of past examples; it is the basis of a creative response to new situations. The focus of this chapter is on how Livy's *History* traces the ways in which impulses are formed into concepts, not as philosophic precepts but, following Cicero, as presentations that are united "into systems by their mutual resemblances" (*Acad.* 2.30). The diseased soul, with its mix of inconsistent opinions, is unable to properly feel the distinguishing effect of different presentations, and thus to recognize what is similar or dissimilar. When one "chooses" (*capit*) what presentations to imitate and what to avoid according to what is "shameful in the conception and shameful in the result" (pref. 10), one ratifies one's assent to an image. That is, we come to associate negative emotions with improper ends (and positive emotions with proper ends). Through this ratification, that image becomes the basis of comprehension (*katalêpsis* = *comprehensio*), grasped with greater certainty, stored in memory, and able to be combined with other similar images to form concepts.[72] In seeking to inspire by casting our gaze to the past, Livy points to how concepts are born in time and animated by experience.[73] Through the telling of history as a record of deeds that are "worthy of memory" (7.2.2), what is not just portrayed but also felt are the animating forces of politics: the beliefs, ideas, habits, and principles that move people to act.

FOUNDING

Livy begins his history with "poetic legends" that even he admits are fanciful (pref. 6).[74] Such founding legends, as Livy reminds his audience, are designed "to add dignity to the beginnings of cities" (pref. 7). But by any measure the founding of Rome in fratricide and rape appears as something of an embarrassment, even to Roman writers.[75] Cicero glosses over the issue in *On the Republic* (*Rep.* 2.2.4). In *On Duties*, Cicero calls Romulus's murder of Remus a crime (*Offic.* 3.10.41). Horace, writing in 30 BCE, portrays the violence of civil war as the legacy of Rome's founding in crime (Horace *Epode* 7). Lucan also attributes civil war to Rome's origin in fratricide (Lucan 1.95). So embarrassing is the legend that Strasburger suggests, though perhaps implausibly, that it may have been a Greek imposition created as a response to the expansion and aggressiveness by Rome.[76] Only Machiavelli does not seem shocked.

Murder frequently lurks behind legends of ancient foundings.[77] But Livy's recounting of Rome's founding contrasts most dramatically with Plato's account in *The Republic* of a visionary founder who wipes the slate clean, establishes a community governed by reason, and creates a myth in which the people spring from the earth.[78] Livy explicitly contrasts these autochthonous myths of a pure people born from the earth with how Rome is populated by "an obscure and lowly" multitude: untutored rustics, on the one hand, and a disordered (*turba*) mob who flock to Rome on the promise of asylum, on the other (1.8.5; 1.8.2; 1.8.6). The founders are themselves born of desire: Romulus and Remus are suckled in the wild and gain both strength of body and resolution of spirit by hunting in the wilds, preying not only on wild beasts but on wild men—bandits (1.4.9). The decision of founding is one in which the desire seized (*cupido cepit*) the twins to locate the city where they had been raised (1.6.3). The establishment of Romulus as the city's founder occurs as he kills his brother in anger (1.7.2). And the continuation of Rome is secured by the abduction of the Sabines.[79]

For Machiavelli, the question that emerges from Livy's account in contrast to Plato's is not how, standing outside time, one constructs a state anew, but how from the array of traditions, habits, and desires one can forge order from disorder.[80] Such order, as it turns out, has its origins in affection. In talking about the beginnings of our sense of justice, for example, Machiavelli emphasizes how the experience of "seeing" one's benefactor harmed "aroused" (*veniva*), in turn, sentiments of love for the benefactor and hatred toward the villain (*D* 1.2, trans. modified). From this experience "arose the knowledge (*cognizione*) of things honest and good, differing from the pernicious and bad" (*D* 1.2). Imagining (*pensando*) that a similar wrong may come to them, the people established laws and punishments. From this, as Machiavelli writes, arose the concept of justice (*D* 1.2).[81] So, too, Livy traces the success of the Roman founding to the "affection," nurtured by slow growth, which unites the aspirations of the community (2.1.5). The answer to how one creates order from disorder for both Livy and Machiavelli is necessarily a temporal and phenomenal one, depending initially on "successive founders" who are able to guide vision and direct the animating spirit of the people toward a common goal (Livy 2.1.2; *D* 1.19).

A starting point for uniting a diverse people into a "single body politic," as Livy points out, is the rule of law (1.8.1). But authority, as a concept, is fairly abstract, requiring an ability by people to direct their assent toward something that is invisible. This is a particular problem when the new community is populated by a rabble that lacks the discipline to control their impulses. People never willingly adopt reforms, as Machiavelli suggests, unless the need for change is "shown" (*D* 1.2). Even more of a problem for establishing a community is that people without experience are easily "taken in by appearance and the issue of the event" (*P* 18; also *D* 2.22). The early founders, thus, have to craft appearance, guiding in some sense the *phantasia* (and thus response) of friends and foes alike. Persuaded that laws alone will not appear binding to the rural people, Romulus makes his authority visible, most fundamentally by cloaking himself in regal vestments and by surrounding himself with twelve lictors who, as they are armed to execute his orders, embody the power and force of law (Livy 1.8.3; *D* 1.9).

If foundings are to go beyond the moment of violence, they must shape a common animating spirit and affection from newly incorporated (and not necessarily willing) groups.[82] Livy's construction of the abduction of the Sabines, an abduction carried out by Romulus's ability to control what others see, is interpreted frequently and not incorrectly as demonstrating the violence of founding.[83] But Livy also traces the transformation of affections: from a begrudged acceptance compelled by visible reminders of strength to a reconciliation that arises from recognition of affective ties.[84] The initial indignation and resentment of the women, not unlike the "burning anger" of the men of Caenina (one group affected by the abduction), is "ineffectual . . . without strength" (1.9.14; 1.10.1; 1.10.3–4). Romulus teaches this lesson by routing the Caeninenses, fashioning a frame to display the body of the commander in the march back to the city, establishing Rome's first temple (the temple to Jupiter) on the site where he deposited the body, and marking off an area within the bounds of the temple where only the spoils of the killed kings and commanders of the enemy can be dedicated (1.10.5–6). The destruction of a second army, that of the Antemnates, lead Romulus's wife, Hersilia, on behalf of the captured women, to a more resigned appeal "to forgive their parents and receive them into the state" (1.11.2). By doing this, Rome would "gain in strength by harmony" (*concordia*): the surrounding territories could be integrated through colonization and by allowing people from the outlying territories to move to Rome (1.11.2; 1.11.4).

Acquiescence, though, is still an artifact of strength that dissipates when strength is not visible. The Sabines prove to be the most illusive enemy, less moved by displays of Rome's power and more patient than the other aggrieved tribes (1.10.2). The Sabines thus plot through the deception and the treachery of the Sabine women their seizure of the citadel (1.11.6). Although strong, the Roman army is not far removed from its origins as a mob. Thus, when Hostius Hostilius falls the Romans "gave way at once and fled" (1.12.3). Even Romulus "was swept along in the crowd of the fugitives" (*turba fugientium*) until he is finally able to direct, as though speaking with a voice from the heavens, the disordered mob to stand their ground (1.12.4; 1.12.7). The Romans now gain the advantage until the Sabine women dare to rush into battle to separate the armies, pleading that the opposing armies are now related through marriage so that the women's husbands and sons are facing their parents (1.13.2). This plea for reconciliation, born of a felt connection between the groups, moves both the multitude and leaders, creating a "stillness" and "sudden hush" (1.13.4). In this stillness the leaders agree to a truce that "made one people out of the two" (1.13.4). The institutional forms of this early state reflect the transfer of affections. Romulus divides the people into thirty *curiae* and, recognizing how the women had become "endeared" to both their husbands and parents, names these political units after the women (1.13.6). Resentment, disorder, and instability give way to a common spirit, affection, and sense of purpose.

Rome's founding demonstrates not only the way that felt meanings give form to inchoate desire, but parallels the process by which these felt meanings must be continually shaped through imitation, innovation, and reenactment. Romulus is a renovator, recovering (*reciperando*) the land of his grandfather, Numitor (a descendant of Aeneas and king of the Latins), who had been overthrown by Amulius (1.15.6).[85] He is an innovator "in founding the City" (1.15.6). And he reenacts his own precedents when he renews the treaty to preserve peace with the Laurentians (1.14.3). But Romulus, as Machiavelli notes, does not get it completely right: a still-savage Roman spirit leaves Rome ill-prepared for either liberty or empire (*D* 1.2; 1.11).[86] Numa, who follows Romulus (after an interregnum), appears in turn as a successive founder. Imbued with a disposition that "tempered his soul" and trained in the strict discipline of the ancient Sabines, Numa both imitates Romulus in consulting the augural omens (1.18.6) and innovates by giving to Rome, which had been established by arms, a "new foundation in law, statutes, and observances" (1.18.4; 1.19.1). Numa simultaneously softens the animating spirit of men that grows wild in war and instills into their hearts a fear of the heavens so that, lacking military discipline, they do not lapse into extravagance and idleness (1.19.2, 4–5). The establishment of religious authority by Numa, as Machiavelli notes, allows him to move people to act when the reasons might not be easily seen (*D* 1.11).[87] Furthermore, Numa's actions direct the thoughts of the people away from arms and toward the gods (Livy 1.21.1). The people, in imitating the character of Numa as their "unique exemplar," come to live by promises and oaths rather than the fear of laws and punishments (Livy 1.21.1–2). Later, Ancus visually imprints this example by ordering the pontifex to copy the religious commentaries of Numa and "display them in public on a whitened tablet" (Livy 1.32.2).

Founding appears as the most extraordinary act, not because it creates anew, but because it shapes a common animating spirit from the disordered wildness of the soul. As important as is Livy's *History* in shaping Rome's own sense of its origins is his contribution to a notion of founding, discerned by Machiavelli, that stands as an alternative to the Greeks. The contrasts could not be starker. Plato's politics is founded in reason, which transcends history. For Machiavelli, politics is founded in passion that requires history—the accumulation and balancing of experiences—to direct a people toward common ends. Plato paints on a clean canvas. For Machiavelli, the founder is like the sculptor who does not have the ease of honing a perfect statue from an unblemished block of marble but must make a beautiful sculpture out of a statue "badly blocked out by another" (*D* 1.11). And if the corruption of the political world makes Plato's founder reluctant to enter it, then it is precisely that corruption that inspires Machiavelli's founders to reform it. Machiavelli, in one extended and dramatic passage, seeks to transport the potential prince back to Roman times. As the prince imagines himself in a corrupted Rome, he will see "so many civil wars, so many external ones; Italy afflicted and full of new misfortunes, its cities ruined and sacked. He will see Rome burning, the Capitol taken down by its own citizens, the ancient temples desolate, ceremonies corrupt, the cities full of adulterers. He will see the sea full of exiles, the shores full of blood" (*D* 1.10). And with these sights, "he will be terrified away from every imitation of wicked times and will be inflamed with an immense desire to follow the good" (*D* 1.10). Livy's notion of founding speaks to an age when there are no longer deserts and wildernesses out of which may be formed new communities but only the rubble of the past: populations divided in their loyalties, born of different historical experiences, and oriented toward different and opposing ends.

THE TARQUINS: INCITING LIBERTY

The importance of the early kings lies in their success in directing the animating spirit of a disordered mob, at first moving people by the compulsions of fear and awe until the principles of authority, law, discipline, and vigor are internalized. As important as the kings were, they did not and could not provide for the experience of liberty. Not only did the kings fail to establish institutions most essential for liberty, but kingship itself posed a threat to the cultivation and maintenance of liberty (*D* 1.2). The danger of kingship, as Machiavelli writes, is that the community can be easily exposed to ruin through "weak" or "malevolent" kings without the people having the institutional resources or the experiences to resist them (*D* 1.19; 1.20). And this is, in fact, precisely what happens in Rome. Tarquinius Superbus, the seventh Roman king, deprives the senate of its authority, diverts funds from public projects to the building of his palace, and makes slaves of his own people (*D* 3.5). Himself ruled by youthful ambition, inspired by his wife Tullia's frenzy, and seizing power through murder, Tarquinius governs neither by senatorial sanction nor by the affection of the people (*caritate civium*) but by fear (*metu*) (Livy 1.47.6–7; 1.49.4). In a description that could as easily be made of the late republic dictatorships of Sulla and the Second Triumvirate, Livy writes: "To inspire terror therefore in many persons" he tried all capital cases himself and thus "was able to inflict death, exile, and forfeiture of property, not only upon persons whom he suspected and disliked, but also in cases where he could have nothing to gain but plunder" (1.49.5). Under the terror of Tarquinius Superbus, the spirit of the Roman people was suppressed (1.51.1).[88]

Tarquinius's concentration of all power into his hands might at first glance appear as an imitation of Romulus's actions. There is a replay of Romulus's incorporation of the Sabines into Rome when Tarquinius, unwilling to allow the Latins to have "their own leaders, or a separate command, or their own standards," therefore mixes Latins with Romans, placing them ultimately under his command (1.52.6). Tarquinius also displays Romulus's military prowess, extending control over the surrounding territories. And the abduction of the Sabines bears some resemblance to Sextus Tarquinius's rape of Lucretia in the sexual violence that it initiates.[89]

The salient differences between tyranny and kingship, as developed in this episode, cannot be identified by any one observable feature but for Livy coalesce around its felt effects. Tyranny achieves its ends by terror. Through visual demonstrations (*documenta*) of the futility and danger of opposition, the tyrant creates one will; but it is one directed toward the lustful desires of the tyrant and not toward the lawful maintenance of the state (1.52.4).[90] Any intimation of a contrary will, thus, is suppressed. So Tarquinius, angered by the Arician king, Turnus, stages a plot to accuse Turnus, refuses to allow him to plead his case, and (seemingly flouting the memory of the horrifying punishment of Mettius [1.23.11]) invents a new form of death in which Turnus is placed in a wicker crate and drowned in the Ferentine Water (1.51.9). Tarquinius's youngest son, Sextus Tarquinius, extends his father's reign over the Gabii, killing those who might threaten him and bribing through spoils others so that "in the sweetness of private gain men lost their feeling for the wrongs of the nation" (*dulcedine privati commodi sensus malorum publicorum adimi*) (1.54.10). And Sextus, "burning with passion" and driven by lust, seeks to conquer Lucretia (1.58.2, 5).

The tyrant, as portrayed by Livy, inflicts a disorder on the soul, rewarding timidity (rather than vigor) and private interest (rather than public good). What brings down tyranny, as Livy seems to indicate, is not force per se (though that is certainly necessary) but resoluteness: a decision no longer to acquiesce.[91] The problem is that acquiescence occurs so incrementally and in such a hidden way that citizens cannot perceive themselves becoming slaves. The greatness of Brutus, for example, is that he is able to survive but not succumb by making himself politically invisible (1.56.7; 1.56.8).[92] And the exemplary character of Lucretia is that her soul, too, can not be moved by the tyrannical will (see 1.58.4). Her political significance is that she, in her death, is "thrust before" the Roman populace, etching a "vivid mental picture" of a resolute soul: a lifeless body that reminds the Romans of what they once were (1.59.3; 1.59.4).[93] Lucretia produces a "shock of *recognition,*" to use Raymond Williams' phrase, when she becomes a "semantic figure" that articulates a widely held experience.[94]

Before the gathering crowd Brutus recreates in words the vivid image of Lucretia's death: the violence and lust of Sextus Tarquinius, the defilement of Lucretia, and the sorrow of the father (1.59.8). Brutus articulates, as well, the meaning of tyranny by recalling a set of experiences: how the king made slaves of the people, made warriors into artisans, murdered Tullius (the previous king), and how Tullia (the wife of Tarquinius and daughter of Tullius) drove over the body of her father. He recalls the misery of the plebs who were made to toil in ditches and sewers (1.59.9). After recounting these outrages, made still more vivid by the freshness of the death of Lucretia, Brutus moves the "inflamed crowd" (*incensam multitudinem*) from lament and complaint to action until they abrogate the king's authority and exile the Tarquins (1.59.11; trans. modified; also 1.59.4).[95] However terrifying may be the raw power of the tyrant, its strength, whether Sextus's "victorious lust" or his father's reign, rests on the acquiescence of the soul (1.58.5).

Ultimately, liberty acquires conceptual substance in memory. Machiavelli may not have been far off in suggesting that the story of Lucretia is not by itself the cause, but the catalyst, for the Romans to establish a republic (*D* 3.5).[96] The point is that concepts are not born in a moment, but are formed through a succession of events that we come to recognize as similar. Brutus, in identifying the mark of tyranny, summons a collective set of experiences. Lucretia's body, as Brutus reminds the people, is the culmination of how tyranny enslaves not just the body but the will by subjecting it to another will that is both arbitrary and unbounded. From the experience of subjugation to the arbitrary will of another, the principle of liberty, in which "laws [are] superior in authority to men," arises (Livy 2.1.1).[97]

LIBERTY AS ANIMATING MEMORY

Livy's account plays out in important, though not always appreciated, ways in Machiavelli's understanding of liberty. Most influentially, the Cambridge School, led prominently by Pocock and Skinner, places Machiavelli's notion of liberty in a broader, civic republican tradition. Viroli, for example, points to the "recovered Roman liberty after the expulsion of the kings as consisting in the fact that the laws were more powerful than men."[98] Liberty is secured by equality before the law, the ability to participate in public deliberations, and the allowance for the free expression of ideas.[99] McCormick has recently critiqued the Cambridge School for extracting from Machiavelli an "abstract 'concept' of liberty" that emphasizes the desire of the populace to be free from interference and from the fear of interference in their persons and property.[100] McCormick suggests that one needs to look at the specific institutional mechanisms discussed by Machiavelli to secure this liberty. What appears to be a "passive"—or at least well-heeled—political disposition of the populace "in the abstract turns out to be a quite animated one in the concrete."[101]

McCormick perhaps understates the extent to which the Cambridge School recognizes the importance of tumult in the maintenance of liberty.[102] But of greater concern here, McCormick, like many other commentators, seems to salvage the more original and democratic implications of Machiavelli's notion of liberty by distancing it from Livy.[103] That distancing is unfortunate because through Livy Machiavelli both echoes some of Livy's concerns with the political blindness of the people — thus tempering some of McCormick's conclusions — and, more importantly, sees the emergence of liberty as a series of institutional responses that are animated and united by the memory of felt oppression: the oppression of the tyrant initially, and the oppression of the elite eventually.[104]

Liberty first takes form as a replacement of the king with two elected consuls (rather than a diminution in the power of the office) and a limit on the consuls' terms to one year (Livy 2.1.7). The number of lictors that the consuls can have is also limited so that "the terror they inspired should not be doubled by permitting both to have the rods" (2.1.8). The senate is restored. Sacrificial ceremonies performed by the king are transferred to a new office. And the people (*populum*), who were vehement about their new liberty (*avidum novae libertatis*), swear an oath to never allow a king in Rome again (1.2.9). For both Livy and Machiavelli these first moves toward liberty occur cautiously and, as Machiavelli writes, within "the shadow of its ancient modes" so as not to further "alter the minds" (*menti*) (or what might be translated as the "memories") of the people through too much innovation (*D* 1.25; see also Livy 2.1.3–6).

Liberty does not just parade as a form of protection from oppression or as acclamation of elite ideas but finds its earliest expression as *initiation*: the people demand that Brutus, to his astonishment, exile the Tarquin family, including a current consul (Livy 2.2.7).[105] Later, after the death of Brutus, the people begin to suspect that Publius Valerius, who is building his house on the highest part of the Velia, is aspiring to be king. The power of the people is evidently strong enough to initiate concern by Valerius who, in appearing before the people, acknowledges that "the people's majesty and power were superior to the consul's" (2.7.7). And he agrees not only to bring his house down from the hill, but to place it "under the hill" so that "you may live above me" (2.7.11). Nor do the masses forget the experience of tyranny when faced with the first test of liberty: Porsenna, the king of Clusium who had been harboring the exiled family, leads an attempt to restore the Tarquins to Rome. But, as Machiavelli writes, the "memory (*memoria*) of the kings by whom they had been vilified and injured in many modes, was fresh" (*fresca*) and leads the people to unite with the senators, endure the hardships of war, and defeat the attack (*D* 1.32). Although Livy notes that the people's loyalty is in a sense purchased, he nonetheless concludes that kingship was not more horrible to the highest as to the lowest ranks of society (2.9.7). The point is that liberty, as a felt meaning, emerges as both an animated and animating concept. It is born of the horror of oppression, but serves as a stimulant to action as new experiences are interpreted through these meanings. But memories fade, animosities reappear, and the cause of liberty will be newly contested and dramatically expanded.

THE *DECEMVIRI*: POLITICS, VISIBILITY, AND CORRUPTION

However much Livy praises the "civic virtue of *concordia*" as a moderation of spirit, Machiavelli is not misreading Livy when he sees in his *History* a close relationship between discord and concord that underlies the emergence of liberty in the Roman state.[106] As Livy notes, in a passage that Machiavelli cites, "So difficult is it to be moderate in the defence of liberty, since everyone, while pretending to seek fair-play, so raises himself as to press another down; while insuring themselves against fear, men actually render themselves fearful to others; and having defended ourselves from an injury, we proceed—as though it were necessary either to do or suffer wrong—to inflict injury upon our neighbour" (Livy 3.65.11; also *D* 1.46). Drawing his lesson from Livy, Machiavelli observes that nothing renders a republic more stable than an ability to vent the "humors that agitate it" (*umori che l'agitano*) (*D* 1.7).[107]

In part publicness is protective of liberty because the desires of free people, as Machiavelli notes, "arise either from being oppressed or from suspicion that they may be oppressed" (*D* 1.4). To allow felt oppressions to fester in the people's imagination is to invite faction and discord. But there is another reason for publicness, and one that counters the tendency of a newly freed people, "used to living" under the government of others, "not knowing" (*non sapiendo*) how to discuss public affairs, and "neither knowing (*non conoscendo*) princes nor known by them," easily to slip back into servility (*D* 1.16). This ignorance appears in Machiavelli's writing as a form of political blindness in which people do not have sufficient experiences that give them knowledge of how to act, judge, or govern themselves. The people are prone to delusion because their imaginations conjure what is not real and neglect what is. The publicness of Roman politics—both in the role of the assemblies and in the faculty of public accusation—makes visible through words the aspirations and motivations of others in the community so that judgments can be formed.[108] This goal is not unrelated to the medical venting of the humors because the problem of delusion arises when there are unhealthy balances in the humors; when one's ability to see is distorted by anger, distrust, or the desire for vengeance. We should not read the restoration of health as a Polybian equilibrium between different groups within society, each differently disposed but similarly myopic, as is frequently assumed. Rather, treating the "maladies" of the community requires venting the excessive humors that distort the imagination and animating the dormant humors through an attention to the particulars of political experience that help the imagination see (*D* 1.pref., trans. modified).

The danger is that even the best people can become blinded to the realities of political life, deceived, for example, by treachery or seduced by the prospect of personal benefit. Such blindness alters the experiential source that animates political character. Absent political sight, we lack the ability to resist corruption, both within ourselves because we take pleasure in using public institutions for private ends and from others because we are unable to detect the visible traces by which motivations and actions can be judged. Corrupt individuals can attempt to disguise their motivations so that their private goals appear as public ends. An uncorrupted people, attentive to the particular actions of the ambitious few, can generally detect the peril posed to the community. But even a previously uncorrupted people can lose, however momentarily, their ability to see how actions can affect the public good. These cases are particularly perilous because a tyrant can use this confusion to seize power (see *D* 1.58) and through the transformation of the political environment, dispose individuals to act by license or fear rather than *virtù*.

Private Ambition Detected

To illustrate how private ambition can be detected, Machiavelli employs Livy's story of Spurius Maelius, who offers to use his private grain supplies to feed the people during a famine and gather support from them (*D* 3.28; also Livy 4.13.3). Concerned that Maelius wanted nothing less than to be king, but unable to punish him because he has the right to appeal to the people, the senate appoints a dictator. Spurius, when called to appear before the dictator, is killed while fleeing.

The seeming abruptness of the reaction by the senate and the dictator, though, points, for Machiavelli, to a fundamental distinction that all republics must draw between public and private means by which citizens acquire influence. Public means are when a citizen acquires reputation "by counseling well, by working better in the common benefit" (*D* 3.28). One ought "to open (*aprire*) to citizens the way to this honor" (*D* 3.28). On the other hand, private means of acquiring influence occur by "doing benefit to this and to that other private individual—by lending him money, marrying his daughters for him, defending him from the magistrates, and doing for him similar private favors that make men partisans to oneself" (*D* 3.28). Where a publicly acquired reputation will never be dangerous to the state, private means encourage those favored to "corrupt the public and to breach the laws" (*D* 3.28). The concern with rewarding public ends, as Machiavelli writes, can be seen in Rome's establishment of triumphs and other public honors for those who served the state, and the bringing of accusations against those aiming to "make themselves great by private ways" (*D* 3.28). But even public accusation may not work if the people, as in this case, are "blinded (*acceccato*) by a species of false good" (*D* 3.28). In that case, a dictator may be necessary to return the people "to the true way" from which they stray (*D* 3.28).[109]

A second case, that of Spurius Manlius, illustrates how the greed for rule can cancel the *virtù d'animo e di corpo*, or the qualities of spirit and body of both himself and the community (*D* 3.8). Where Manlius earlier displays such *virtù* through his love of and service to the country, his mind becomes so blinded (*tanta cecita di mente*) by his jealousy of the honors given to Camillus that he seeks to bring turmoil to the institutions of the city. Manlius calls into question the trustworthiness of the people's sight by claiming that Camillus and other private citizens had kept the ransom that was to be paid to the

Gauls. Manlius is thus summoned before the people where he is told to "disclose from their hidden plunder (*praeda clandestina*) those men" whom he accuses of stealing from the people (6.15.5; trans. modified). Manlius responds by playing on the idea of sight: "The more you bid us expose (*argui*) your sleight-of-hand (*praestigias*), the more I fear you may have robbed even our eyes (*oculos*), while we were watching (*observantibus*) you" (6.15.13; trans. modified).

Despite arrest and later release, Manlius's popularity grows as he calls for a leveling of dictatorship and consulship so that "the Roman plebs may be enabled to lift its head" (6.18.14). When the senate and tribunes meet to decide how to stop Manlius so as not to turn the conflict into a war, the tribunes of the plebs suggest a trial: "Nothing is less popular than kingly power. As soon as the populace will have seen (*viderint*) that our quarrel is not with them, they will change from supporters into judges, and see that the prosecutors are plebeians, the defendant a patrician, and the accusation that of seeking to set up a kingdom, they will not favour any man at the expense of their own liberty" (6.19.7; trans. modified). At first it appears that Manlius will not be convicted since the trial occurs in the Campus Martius, where Manlius is able to fix the people's eyes on the Capitol and Citadel, calling to mind their gratitude for his defense of the city. The tribunes realize that "unless they could also emancipate men's eyes (*oculos*) from the associations of so glorious a deed," no judgment will be possible (6.20.10). So the trial is moved out of sight of the Capitol where "men steeled their hearts" and pronounced judgment (6.20.11).[110]

Where Manlius goes wrong, Machiavelli suggests in a language that would be right at home in Livy's *History*, is in deceiving himself about the "city's mode of life" (*modo del vivere della città*) and not recognizing that its "matter" had not yet received "bad form" (*trista forma*) (*D* 3.8; trans. modified).

The language is suggestive of the psychological underpinnings of both Livy's and Machiavelli's arguments: beliefs and dispositions are formed by the imprinting of sensations on the mind. A weak imprint can be easily erased. But because of "the goodness of its matter" (*la bontà della materia sua*), the city does not succumb to the corruption (*D* 3.8; trans. modified). The nobility does not support Manlius, the tribunes bring charges against him, and the people judge him and condemn him to death. As Machiavelli writes, if the "matter" (*materia*) of the city had already been corrupt, then Manlius would have been able "to impress" (*imprimere*) on the city "the form of his ambition" (*la forma dell' ambizione*) (*D* 3.8). But at this time the people's love of country—the felt meanings that orient action—override all other considerations, and thus they are able to look at the present threat rather than Manlius's past accomplishments. In condemning him to death, the people, as Machiavelli notes, are able to set themselves free (*D* 3.8).

Political Blindness

Transgressions, if not punished, can quickly ruin the republic since it is only with difficulty that transgressors can be "brought back on the true way" (*D* 3.28). The problem arises when neither the nobility nor the people are able or willing to distinguish between public and private ends. Livy's discussion of the *decemviri* becomes a case study of corruption as a form of political blindness. My interest in particular is to use this episode to explore how the dissipation of the animating spirit of a community—the constellation of felt meanings—brings about political blindness, and how sight in turn can reanimate these meanings.

The backdrop to the rise of the *decemviri* was the fragmentation of the shared aspirations that inspired plebs and patricians to cast off kingship. The immediate dangers to the republic had receded and old hatreds had returned. The patricians were driven to harshness by their hatred of the plebs and were themselves divided by private interests that undermined public deliberation (2.29.9; 2.30.2).[111] The minds of the plebs were affected, as well, by a "spirit of license" because of "plenty and idleness" (2.52.2). The tribunes in turn used these occasions to rouse the plebs "to madness" with the "poison" of land legislation (Livy 2.52.3; see also *D* 1.37). Answering to the growing turmoil and threats to the state, in which the tribunes exacted concessions by obstructing the raising of troops, both sides agreed to send a delegation to Athens to copy the laws of Solon and learn about the customs, laws, and institutions of other Greek cities (3.31.8). The Romans then transferred all authority to the *decemviri,* a Board of Ten who would codify the laws of Rome.[112]

Although the beginning of the *decemviri* was by all appearances promising enough—and both Machiavelli and Livy point to the publicness by which the *decemviri* operated in the first year—the Board, when reappointed with Appius as the head, degenerated into tyranny.[113] The marks of tyranny were ignored, as Machiavelli indicates, because each side was "blinded" by the excessive desire to destroy the other (*D* 1.40). The aristocracy was happy to have the tribunes silenced. And the treatment of the plebs by the consuls over the last several decades had replaced one memory with another, leading the plebeians to hate the consuls as much as the kings and thus to favor a continuation of the *decemviri* (3.34.8). The seeds of demagoguery that Brutus feared would agitate the people at the inception of the republic had taken root (2.1.4; 2.1.9). The perverse way in which tyranny asserts itself into the political realm is suggested by Livy's portrayal of Appius's rise as the inversion of Brutus's. Where Brutus took off his mask to overthrow the Tarquins, as Livy comments, Appius "now threw off the mask he had been wearing," a mask of humility and support for the plebs, and began to act according to his true nature (3.36.1; also *D* 1.40).[114]

Tyranny asserts itself by eliminating any publicly shared meanings. There are several ways in which tyranny accomplishes this task. In part, tyranny works by instilling fear. Upon officially taking office, the *decemviri* fashioned the mark of their rule by a terrible threat: all ten *decemviri* retained their twelve lictors. As Livy describes the scene, 120 lictors crowded into the Forum, carrying axes bound up with the rods and making clear that there was no right of appeal (Livy 3.36.4). Like the terror inspired by Romulus against Roman foes and the terror in turn enacted by the Tarquins, "the terror inspired" by the *decemviri* was like that of "ten kings" (1.14.9; 1.49.4; 1.51.1; 3.36.5). Moved by fear (*metui*), neither the people nor senators dared to "pronounce a word in praise of liberty" (3.36.6). Tyranny also operates by making political decisions private. The *decemviri* "concocted their judgments in private, and pronounced them in the Forum" (3.36.8). Tyranny, furthermore, thrives by fostering division, playing in this case upon the distrust and hatred of the patricians toward the plebs. As Livy notes, when the people now looked to the patricians for help, the patricians, though hating the *decemviri*, had "no desire to help those who in their greedy rush for liberty had fallen upon servitude, preferring that their wrongs should even be multiplied, that disgust at the actual situation might in the end arouse a longing for the two consuls and the former state of affairs" (3.37.3). And tyranny functions by rewarding private interest. Thus, the *decemviri* soon attracted young patricians who freely plundered the plebs: "Corrupted by these wages, the young nobles not only made no stand against wrong-doing, but frankly showed that they preferred license for themselves to liberty for all" (3.37.8).

Livy is in part employing the stock image of the tyrant who

bases decisions on personal favor rather than law, makes judgments in private, holds power perpetually, and recognizes no boundaries on the exercise of power (3.38.1; 3.36.7–9; 3.37.8).[115] But Livy is also describing how tyranny alters the animating dispositions of the community. The people "had lost heart" (*desponderant animos*) (3.38.2). And the senators withdrew to their farms, disregarding public affairs in the belief that they would be safe from the *decemviri* (3.38.11). Livy emphasizes how the abandonment of civic engagement further dissipated the shared felt meaning of Roman political liberty. When a crier finally summoned the senators because of the need to declare war, "it was like an innovation, so long had they disregarded the custom of consulting the senate" (3.38.8). These felt meanings are given spatial form when we, like the plebs, encounter the stark emptiness of the political space: "Men looked about in every corner of the Forum to discover a senator, and seldom recognized one anywhere; then their glances rested on the Curia and the decemvirs sitting there alone" (3.38.10). When summoned again, additional senators attended but seemed more to gesture toward, than embrace, the memory of political liberty. Marcus Horatius Barbatus, for example, called the *decemviri* "ten Tarquinii" and reminded them that his family and the family of Lucius Valerius had been leaders in overthrowing the kings (3.39.3). He even recalled the reasons for the overthrow of the kings: the pride and violence that men had come to hate (3.39.4). But "liberty went no further than speech" (3.41.4). Fearful of the plebs and resentful of the tribunes, the senators acceded to the wishes of the *decemviri* (*D* 1.40).

If the story of the *decemviri* is one of the dissipation of the animating spirit of the community as tyranny operates out of sight, then the attempted abduction and death of Verginia reverses the trajectory, showing the role of sight in reanimating the political spirit. Where Appius Claudius is able to corrupt the young nobles through the promise of spoils, he is unable "to seduce" Verginia with money and promises (3.44.4). So, unlike Sextus who intrudes into the bedroom to fulfill his lusts, Appius Claudius carries out a legal abduction. Taking advantage of her father's absence, Appius plans for Marcus Claudius, his client, to claim Verginia as his slave. When the cries of her nurse alert the crowd, Marcus Claudius seeks to calm the excitement of the people, telling them "he was proceeding lawfully, not by force" (3.44.8). Marcus Claudius, thus, brings Verginia before the tribunal of Appius, the inventor of the plot.

The legal proceedings staged before the people are in fact "a fiction" (*fabula*): a public forum used to execute one's private desires (3.44.9; trans. modified). Livy traces the gradual disclosure of these desires and the resultant response of the people. At first, the crowd "murmured" their disapproval, but no one "dared to stand out" until Icilius, Verginia's fiancé, arrives (3.45.4). Icilius then speaks to the hiddenness of tyrannical desire and connects the personal grievance to the broader loss of public appeal when the *decemviri* take away the assistance of the tribunes and the right of appeal, "two citadels for the defence of liberty" (3.45.8). Icilius's excited words, like Brutus's before, agitate (*concitant*) the crowd from its earlier diffuse murmurs to near conflict (3.46.1). Appius, in response, mimicks past senatorial remonstrations by accusing Icilius of being "a turbulent fellow" (*inquietum hominem*) who breaths "the spirit of the tribunate" and who seeks only to stir up strife (3.46.2). But the abduction is postponed for the time, giving Verginius the opportunity to return to the city from battle.

On the day of the trial, the people assemble in expectation in the Forum. Verginius and then Icilius plead with the people, but the attending women seem better able to summon the felt experiences of tyranny. As Livy writes, emphasizing the emotions of the moment, the women "were more moving, as they wept in silence, than any words" (*plus tacito fletu quam ulla vox movebat*) (3.47.4). But ultimately it is the sight of Verginia's body, stabbed in desperation by Verginius and held up for the crowd to see, that recalls the animating spirit of liberty that had been dissipated by faction and, consequently, receded in memory.[116] The men now speak of the loss of the power of the tribunes, of the right of appeal, and "of their resentment at the nation's wrongs" (3.48.9). As Machiavelli writes, the people come to recognize their own servility to the private desires of a few (*D* 1.40). "The wildest excitement prevailed amongst the people," Livy notes, "occasioned in part by the atrocity of the crime, in part by the hope of improving the opportunity to regain their liberty" (3.49.1). The *populus* and leaders of the *populus* now join together, forcing back the lictors, and drowning out with noise Appius's voice. Valerius, to whom the crowd listens, commands, "as though vested with authority," that the lictors withdraw (3.49.5). Appius, now "broken in spirit," sneaks out of the Forum (3.49.6).

As with Brutus, and suggestive of the historian's task, Verginius in turn arouses those who were not present by telling of the event. Covered in gore, Verginius "drew the attention" of his fellow soldiers back in camp and "aroused greater commotion" than in the city (3.50.2–3). There he warns them that "the lust of Appius Claudius had not been extinguished" and that the calamity should be a warning (*documentum*) to protect against "similar wrongs" (3.50.7). The crowd responds with shouts that they will not fail his suffering or his liberty (3.50.10). Even then, those who came with Verginius go about to the crowd and tell them how much worse the event would have appeared (*visa*) if they could have seen (*potuerint videri*) it instead of just hearing about it (3.50.10). In response, the men arm themselves, abandon the camp, and march on the city to reclaim their liberty (3.50.13; *D* 1.40).

Machiavelli provides two interesting postscripts to his recounting of the *decemviral* affair. First, Machiavelli observes that the Roman armies, which had been "always accustomed to be victorious" under the consuls, now "always lost" under the *decemviri* (*D* 1.43). Although the armies had the same courage, they did not have "the same disposition" (*disposizione*) (*D* 1.43). Having to fight for another's ambition, the soldiers lacked the necessary resolve to risk death. But, with the overthrow of the *decemviri*, the armies returned to their ancient spirit (*animo*) and customs and began, once again, to win (*D* 1.43). Second, as is the tradition of Roman law, Verginius makes a public accusation against Appius. Appius appears, surrounded by nobles, and demands his right to appeal to the people (*D* 1.45). But Verginius argues that Appius is unworthy of such a right and can make no appeal to the people. Appius is imprisoned and, before his trial, commits suicide. For Machiavelli, the denial of a public appeal, even when earlier appeals to the people had endangered the republic, runs contrary to liberty and invites precisely the hiddenness that allows rumors, resentments, and recriminations to go unchecked. The *decemviri* affair becomes a case study in the critical role of publicness in the maintenance of felt meanings. The *decemviri* do not create faction; they give it private recourse by transforming public institutions into instruments of private desire. The result—and that result plays itself out in the end of the republic— is the dissipation of the animating spirit of the community.

CAMILLUS: REANIMATING POLITICAL VISION

Livy closes Book 5 by telling of the siege of Rome by the Gauls. The story—and Livy admits that it depends on an untrustworthy oral tradition (6.1.2)—reveals not only the visual dimension of corruption but also how historiography might restore health by training and reanimating political vision.[117] Employing a common view of the Gauls at the time, Livy constructs what Kraus (following François Hartog) describes as an "ethnographical mirror," showing how the Gauls had become like Romans and the Romans like Gauls.[118]

Livy attributes the Gauls' savagery, unpreparedness, and lack of adaptability to their damp and cold climate (see 5.33.11; 5.48.3).[119] He portrays the Gauls as powerless to control their anger, as marching toward Rome "in rapid motion," as moving hastily and noisily, and as filling the air with "wild songs" and "discordant shouts" since they are a race "naturally given to vainglorious outbursts" (5.37.4–5, 8). That this intemperate disposition had been bred over generations makes starker the encounter between the Romans and the Gauls, not because the Gauls appeared as a fearsome enemy but because the Romans had become so corrupt that they began to resemble the Gauls. The reversal of the Gauls and Romans is known well enough: the Gauls display the strategic acumen of the Romans and the Romans become as impatient, rash, and careless as the Gauls once were.[120] What I want to focus on is what this episode suggests about the psychological processes by which the political soul can be reanimated.

Ogilvie notes how Livy gives the occupation of Rome "an original treatment by stressing not so much the events as the impression of the participants."[121] The spectacle of the Gauls ransacking the city seizes the attention of the Romans who watch from the Citadel. The impression, though, is one formed by a mind in disarray, at least initially. So "confusing and frightening" is the assault to their eyes and ears, Livy writes, that the Romans are able neither to grasp (*concipere*) nor to "stand fast" (*constare*) (5.42.3).[122] Livy conveys some sense of the disorder: "Wherever there was shouting of the invaders, the lamentations of the women and children, the crackling of the flames, and the crash of falling buildings drew their attention, trembling at each sound, they turned their thoughts and their gaze that way, as though Fortune had placed them there to witness the pageant of their dying country" (5.42.4). But why Fortune? Because the grandeur of Rome has become so conflated with possessions, glory with greed, and discipline with wantonness, that the only way to restore Rome is to reduce it to liberty in its most elemental and visual form: a hill, "however small and naked" (5.42.8). The occurrence of the same events each day, causing the spectators to avert their eyes at first in one place and then another, though, conditions the soul so that, "like men grown used to grief, they ceased to feel their own misfortunes" and begin, with resolve, to look to their weapons as "their only remaining hope" (5.42.8).

In this exercise of endurance that accompanies the blockade by the Gauls, we see the reversal of trajectories as the Romans, reanimated by the sight of plunder, begin to remember their strength and resolve.[123] The Gauls had become "careless" with their success, not unlike the Romans before (5.44.6). The Romans, who had been "wanderers" since the capture of the city, begin to reassemble at Veii, gathering strength in the process (5.46.5). Furthermore, "the place itself reminded men of Camillus," recalling Romulus's own love of place and pointing to a reversal of their thanklessness for Camillus's past services (5.46.6; 5.44.2). Seeking now "a head," the men at Veii consent to recall Camillus from exile, and he arrives just as the Romans are about to ransom their lives (5.46.5). Directing their eyes to the temples, families, native soil, and "the hideous marks of war," which recall their earlier gaze as they watched the city burn, Camillus calls upon them "to defend, recover, or avenge" their loss (5.49.3).

As ominous as any external threat is the looming internal

division that threatens to leave Rome without inhabitants. Not by accident are Camillus's antagonists at the end of Book 5 the tribunes. For Book 5 opens with the tribunes decrying the decision by the Roman generals to erect winter quarters to continue a siege on Veii. The tribunes, seeking to agitate, "hurried" before the assembly and "set to work upon the passions of the commons" (5.2.2). The tribunes denounce the action as a way of enslaving the commons, claiming at one point (in what will become a horrible irony as Rome is placed under siege by the Gauls) that the Veientes, even having chosen a king, are freer under siege because they get to stay with their families (5.2.6–8). Appius Claudius's comments, in response to the tribunes, similarly foreshadow the coming trial of Roman character. It is important, the grandson of the *decemvir* argues, that "our soldiers become accustomed" not only to victory but to learn to "put up with the tedium and await the outcome of their hopes, however long-deferred," in a protracted war (5.6.2; also 5.6.8). Such "manly endurance" is part of the Roman soul that must protect against "softness and idleness" (5.6.5). But victory only increases division. The plebs, desirous of the wealth of Veii, begin to think about migrating to the conquered city.[124]

After the defeat of the Gauls, Camillus has to turn his attention to persuading the plebs to remain in Rome rather than migrate to Veii. Camillus's role as a "second founder" points to the possibility, and indeed the process, by which the historian also acts as a founder (5.49.7). Having known only civil war, Livy, like Camillus, seeks to create order from disorder by training and reanimating political vision. This vision is constituted by felt meanings, which are tied most obviously to traditions that lend some familiarity and an affective relationship to the recollections of places, spaces, objects, legends, institutions, beliefs, individuals, and families. As Viroli writes, in describing Roman patriotism, love of country "is an attachment not to abstract institutions and rights, but to the institutions and the rights that citizens feel as being theirs because they preserve and enjoy them through their service."[125] If Rome were only a place, then the community could as easily migrate to Veii. But Rome is more than a place: it is something formed on sacred foundations (5.51.4) and handed down and reaffirmed through state and family rituals that are tied to the place (5.52.2–3, 7, 8). Playing upon a Roman sense of military renown, Camillus further reminds the people that deserting Rome would accomplish what no enemy has been able to do: leave Rome empty and the enemy city full (5.51.3; 5.53.5). Camillus, furthermore, taps into a deeper set of felt meanings that have been overshadowed by interest. Why was Rome defended (5.51.3)? Why were sacred rites observed (5.52.12)? Can you "stomach" the outrage of our enemies inhabiting Rome (5.53.7)?

The city had been made into a wilderness, Camillus observed (5.53.1). But it is a wilderness that recalls the original founding. "Our ancestors, refugees and herdsmen, at a time when there was nothing in this region but forests and marshes, built quickly a new City," Camillus reminds his audience (5.53.9). Thus, Camillus summons to his audience's mind the land that is "familiar" to their "eyes," moving them in their own affection toward the city (5.54.3; also 5.55.1).[126] Like Camillus, Livy relentlessly casts his audience's gaze outward—to the bodies of Lucretia and Verginia, to the vacant Forum, and to the ruins of Rome. In the recollection of loss, one may initially react by thinking about one's own private grievances and interests. But individual loss can give way to a greater sense of collective loss as these images summon a set of affections that bind oneself to the city: to the strands of meaning woven into the fabric of the city. Felt meanings, most of all, have the power to animate: to overturn tyranny, to establish liberty, to resist corruption, and, like Camillus, to build a city again.

POLITICAL THOUGHT AS REMEDY

We are now in a better position to reassess the conceptual role that Livy plays in Machiavelli's political thought, a role that is not always appreciated in scholarship. On the one side are those who emphasize the indeterminacy that arises from Machiavelli's approach. Hanna Pitkin, for example, claims that "the 'particulars' to which he turns become the general observation that no one policy, even prudence itself, can successfully guide action in all situations. Prudence teaches its own insufficiency."[127] This formulation appears more as a riddle than a solution, though, for what Pitkin seems to suggest is that what is to be learned from history is the inability of imitation. Livy, from this perspective, appears as a source of stories, to be sure, but not a source of thought. Pitkin's conclusions have much in common today with poststructural approaches that depict Machiavelli's desire to establish a stable political language by which one can assert power on the world as dissolving in its own contradictions.[128]

On the other side are those who seek to formulate what is to be imitated. But they, too, do so by according a decidedly secondary status to Livy. Rubinstein emphasizes the importance of Aristotle for the revival of Italian political thought in the thirteenth and fourteenth centuries.[129] Garver Hellenizes Machiavelli, framing Machiavelli's discussion of prudence by way of Aristotle, Socrates, and the Sophists.[130] Machiavelli's most Roman of writings, the *Discourses*, in fact, appears to Garver as "an especially undramatic representation of actual political argument" that destroys any sense of deliberation.[131]

And for Hulliung, Machiavelli's interest in the Romans rather than the Greeks "accounts for his intellectual weaknesses as a political analyst."[132] The "brilliance" of the Greeks was first "diluted" and then debased in the hands of the Romans.[133] To understand Machiavelli's appeal and contribution to political thinking, suggests Hulliung, one must "search elsewhere" than the Romans.[134]

On a more flattering note, Straussians return to Livy's *History*. But they do so for reasons of comparison to show how Machiavelli's omissions or revisions of Livy point to additional meanings in the *Discourses*.[135] Moreover, as Strauss notes, as a historian Livy "supplies" Machiavelli only "with matter, with examples," but provides neither "the light which illumines the matter" nor "the reasoning which leads up to the causes of the events."[136] Machiavelli's methodological distance from Livy is evidenced, as well, by their respective uses of stories. Where "historians are inclined to regard as most worthy of being remembered that which is miraculous or spectacular," the political theorist sheds these extraneous elements, focusing on that which reveals natural order and truth.[137] Spectacle has little to do with political truth.

Where Strauss' exercise is consciously ahistorical, as he seeks to extract models of "ancient virtue" that can be imitated in modern times,[138] other scholars less deliberately flatten out the contours of Roman history by seeing in this past general rules of political action that can be applied to recurring events.[139] Cassirer notes how Machiavelli "was interested in the statics, not in the dynamics of historical life."[140] Although historical events occur at a specific time and place, this "static view of human history" means "that all historical events are interchangeable."[141] Parel, following Olschki, describes Machiavelli as the "Galileo of politics" who develops a science of politics premised on the uniformity of human nature and derived from empirical observation.[142] Generalizations emerge that can be "used as rules of practical conduct."[143] For Wolin, by looking to ancient history, particularly that of the Romans, Machiavelli locates a "timeless body of examples" that forms a "body of knowledge" by which political actors can learn "what to do in appropriate circumstances."[144]

In one noteworthy attempt to reconcile the seemingly contradictory directions of Machiavelli's work, Felix Gilbert separates the *Discourses* into a narrative and an analytic part. The first part of the *Discourses*, which corresponds for Gilbert to the original intention of Machiavelli, provides a traditional, humanistic commentary on Livy in an attempt to "rediscover the laws the ancients had known and followed."[145] The second part corresponds to a later developing intention to present a "systematic treatise on politics."[146] Although neither Machiavelli nor his contemporaries seem to have been aware of this division, Gilbert nonetheless argues that the "true significance" of Machiavelli's new method, carried out in the *Discourses*, was an "inductive" approach in which a "theoretical statement arises from an analysis of the empirical facts of history."[147]

Viewing the examples in the *Discourses* as the raw data of theory is bound to be disappointing, if for no other reason than, as Gilbert writes in a later book, Machiavelli "took to the technique of designing examples to fit his purposes."[148] As Coby quite rightly asks, "But if getting the facts straight is the starting point of true knowledge, why does Machiavelli choose those books of Livy which most resemble historical fiction, in which knowing for certain who did what to whom, when and how, is all but impossible?"[149] Coby's answer is that in using Livy, Machiavelli "is more poet than historian."[150] Coby then goes on to separate in Machiavelli's writing the poetic aspects that "inspire" and the more instructive aspects that train select readers in the "art of prudence."[151]

But I think in this delineation of the poetic and the prudential we miss the close relationship that Machiavelli (and Livy) see between narration (*narrazione*) and careful reflection (*grande considerazione*) (see *D* 1.40). In saying this, I find myself sympathetic to recent scholarly interpretations of Machiavelli's works as rhetorical.[152] Rhetoric is a dimension in understanding Machiavelli's ideological inheritance (as described by the Cambridge School) and in viewing aspects of Machiavelli's work as "written fraud" designed to influence others by disguising his true intentions (as characterized by Mansfield). I am referring more to the ways in which rhetoric is integral to the conceptual form Machiavelli's political thought takes.[153] For Kahn, Machiavelli deepens our understanding of the "rhetoric *of* political theory" by modeling through his own rhetoric how successful political action requires invention as a response to contingency.[154] Most suggestively, Kahn points to how Machiavelli "stages or dramatizes" his argument, both to point to the lack of "conceptual stability" of such notions as *virtù* and to recreate for the reader the experience of necessity that "led the Romans to form true opinions" and "taught them what to praise and blame, what to imitate and avoid."[155] Somewhat surprisingly, though, she characterizes the *Discourses* as offering a "systematic reduction of ancient history to a compendium of useful examples."[156]

Departing from the view of rhetoric as primarily a mechanism to transmit bits of political wisdom, Hörnqvist seeks to identify how Machiavelli (especially in *The Prince*) adapts his rhetoric and draws on a rhetorical tradition to control "the reaction of its implied audience."[157] Hörnqvist, though, emphasizes too much the "rhetorical duality" between the philosophic components (aimed at our reason) and the rhetorical components (which manipulate the audience's reception of the argument through the use of *ethos* and *pathos*). As a result, he understates how concepts are themselves constructed rhetorically.[158] Closing the gap between rhetoric and judgment,

Matthes suggests that Machiavelli's writing "both imitates the classical Roman tradition and is meant itself to stimulate imitation; as a theorist, he is himself both spectator and spectacle."[159] The examples that Machiavelli employs are "not merely illustrations of a theory or a principle but are themselves calls for judgment."[160] As Machiavelli constructs a "spectacle of the past," he "invites the reader to witness how he makes a judgment" and to learn in turn "how to think."[161]

I think Matthes is correct, but there is a danger in importing an Aristotelian notion of *phronesis* into Machiavelli so that individual judgment is seen, as Matthes writes, as ruled by "practical wisdom."[162] Machiavelli's method aims not at the intellective soul, in which reason rules spirit, but at the imagination, which animates action.[163] The problem of the imagination, as Minogue points out, is that it "is subject to a certain hardening and rigidity which is analogous to the natural processes of the body."[164] The imagination risks becoming lax for any number of reasons. Christianity, which teaches humility and quiet contemplation, makes individuals feeble and causes them to become susceptible to those with evil designs (*D* 2.2). The prolongation of kingship risks making people "weak and of no value" as they are never able to develop or exercise habits of liberty (*D* 1.17). Without the fear of an enemy, people can lose their apprehension—a form of agitated imagination—and become so comfortable that they choose as leaders those who will entertain them (*D* 1.18). Victory in battle can give people "false hope" which, when it "enters the breasts of men, makes them pass beyond the mark and most often lose the opportunity of having a certain good through hoping to have an uncertain better" (*D* 2.27). Traditional historical methods risk doing little more than foster these illusions, exaggerating the accomplishments and concealing the misdeeds of the past so that they no longer "offend you and do not give you cause to envy them" (*D* 2.preface). Even "considering [things] in general" creates mental laziness as individuals become content with drawing conclusions without seeing the problem (*D* 1.47).

Writing when Florence is beset by corruption and the Florentine republic has collapsed, Machiavelli looks to Livy for a method of political thinking that might reanimate political vision.[165] Machiavelli, as I have sought to demonstrate, locates political understanding not in general statements about political affairs, or even in timeless examples that can be used by political actors, but in the immersion of his audience into the particulars of human experience. "True knowledge" cannot be learned through abstractions but, like political character, must be forged in particular experiences acquired over time (*D* 1.preface). The problem of corruption is precisely that it renders one blind to the reasons or possible solutions to the problems of political affairs. One can "open the eyes of peoples" (*aprire gli occhi a' popoli*), Machiavelli observes, by establishing a mode in which they have "to descend to particulars" (*discendere a' particulari*).[166] The "knowledge (*cognizione*) of particular things" removes from the people's mind "that deception (*inganno*) that had been presupposed in considering them generally" (*D* 1.47). Machiavelli cites case after case that points to the possibility of people modifying their own initial inclinations and forming sound judgments when able to see the facts of particular cases. But political communities cannot long maintain themselves if the experience of judging particulars is not generalized into something more enduring; namely, the formation of political character.

MACHIAVELLI AND POLITICAL CHARACTER

To what extent can character be changed and the forces of corruption reversed? Pocock, for example, in placing

Machiavelli in a tradition of civic republicanism, argues that the experience of civic life (*vivere civile*) can change one's original nature (*prima forma*). Whereas the prince can only change one's "second nature" by imposing new customs, participation in republics "develop[s] irreversibly" the "original nature" of man as "a citizen or political animal."[167] Whatever may be Machiavelli's affinities with civic republicanism, textual evidence that Machiavelli goes so far as to assert that one can "change men's natures" is simply lacking.[168] In fact, Pocock's textual references at these critical junctures do not support the claim. In talking about how Numa implants religion in the "natures of the Romans," he refers only to *Discourses* 1.11 "generally," but one will find no statement by Machiavelli—or Livy—of how one's original nature is changed.[169]

Others have pointed to the invariant character of human dispositions. Fischer, for example, argues that one's primary nature cannot be changed through civic action. Not only is human nature in general ruled by ambition, but the people in particular can never hope to acquire the character necessary for political success because of their innate deficiencies of mind. When Machiavelli says that "men are apt to deceive themselves upon general matters, but not so much so when they come to particulars," Fischer interprets it to mean that for Machiavelli "the many" or "the common people" are deceived about abstract ideas whereas the "good leaders" are not.[170] As Fischer argues, "the multitude's grasp of reality is poor" because "their imagination is limited to the immediate consequences of actions."[171] The people are easily deluded so that they end up pursuing false aims or using improper means. For these reasons, the people are not able "to make good laws or to govern effectively."[172] The most that can be achieved is that people, under the direction of a leader and the rule of law, can internalize the costs of disobedience through the "dread of punishment" until they become used to "acting without thinking."[173] Or, stated slightly differently, a well-ordered regime is one in which the people become habituated to following the law "without calculating the associated costs and benefits."[174] Fischer later drops the phrase "unthinking imitation" from his characterization of habits, though this association remains when he describes how "citizens cease to obey the laws unthinkingly."[175]

There are several issues that need to be untangled here. First, Machiavelli is making a larger point about the importance of judging from particulars rather than judging from abstractions. Thus, Machiavelli refers more generally to men (*uomini*) than to the people (*popolo*) when describing a human tendency to be deceived by general claims. For good reason one will find very little abstract philosophizing by Machiavelli in the *Discourses*. In fact, it may be precisely the simultaneous need for flexibility and the reality of the "inescapable constancy of character" that leads Machiavelli to favor republics that rely on the psychological diversity of different humans over the rule of a few or of one.[176] Second, if Fischer means that no one from "the many" is capable of such leadership, then the claim runs contrary to Machiavelli who emphasizes, by Fischer's own admission, that Rome's success requires not only the involvement of the people through the assemblies (*D* 1.4) but also that the highest leadership position, the consul, be accorded all citizens, based only on merit (*D* 1.60).[177]

Finally, I agree with Fischer that for Machiavelli a mode of living cannot change our primary nature. This is particularly the case because of Machiavelli's rejection of the centerpiece of civic republicanism, an intellective soul that guides human behavior. But in elevating the imagination over reason, Machiavelli does not in turn limit human possibility to natural dispositions that can be curbed only by the internalization of utility calculations. Machiavelli, for example, in echoing

Livy's felt meanings, talks about how individuals are (and should be) "moved" by the sentiment of love of country over any other consideration (*D* 3.47; see 3.8, 3.41). Furthermore, Machiavelli refers to the role of "memory" in guiding people to resist kingship (*D* 1.32), to the importance of the Roman's ancient spirit in animating the army to fight (*D* 1.43), to the possibility of the people displaying the same goodness as the kings when regulated by law (*D* 1.58), to the "nature" (*natura*) of princes and the people that must be properly controlled (*D* 1.58), to the people who are capable of governing with stability, prudence, and gratitude (*D* 1.58), to the Roman people who have been a "lover" of the "glory and common good" of their country (*D* 1.58), to how education and religion makes men feeble rather than energetic (*D* 2.3), and to how discipline and exercise can offset the softness induced by climate and make soldiers better than what nature produces (*D* 1.1). All of this suggests not that one's primary nature can be changed, but that the specific public expression and orientation of this nature can be directed toward common ends.

The notion of political thought I am developing here allows us to reconcile Machiavelli's claim that only by "necessity" can humans be made to act well with his description of Camillus, who acts well regardless of the circumstances. Necessity is often interpreted as fear that counters the human tendency toward self-interest, envy, and viciousness (see *D* 1.3).[178] But Camillus maintains a "firm spirit" (*animo fermo*), even when exiled wrongly and then appointed as dictator (*D* 3.31; also Livy 6.7.5). Camillus is not simply an exception. Rather, we can make sense of this paradox by understanding that necessity refers to more than fear. Necessity is related to Machiavelli's view of humans as animated beings, who are disposed to act and react in response to felt experiences. Fear is one such response, but so is love and hatred, as Machiavelli makes clear in his discussion of the origins of justice. Furthermore, human dispositions are continually being shaped and modified as new experiences are encountered, recent experiences remembered, and past experiences forgotten. The question for Machiavelli is not whether some people are moved by compulsion and others not, but how compulsion can be translated into political character.

No doubt, fear plays a part in disposing people to act in ways that they might not otherwise choose. Machiavelli relates the case in which the Samnites, having been routed previously by the Romans, seek to make one last stand. But when asked to take a religious oath that they would fight to the death and kill all those who fled, some of the soldiers hesitate, and are instantly executed.[179] The "spectacle" so terrifies the people that the rest of the soldiers immediately take the oath (*D* 1.15). But fear is neither the only, nor the strongest, disposition. As Machiavelli continues, the Roman general Papirius seeks to "weaken the opinion his soldiers had of the enemy" by saying that "the oath [the Samnites] had taken represented their fear (*timore*) and not their strength" (*fortezza*) (*D* 1.15).[180] Fear can inspire, as Machiavelli notes, but it cannot necessarily overcome memory—in this case, the memory by the Samnites of their previous defeats at the hands of the Romans and the memory by the Romans of their own valor (*D* 1.15).

The difference between the Samnites and the Romans is not that one acts by necessity and the other does not, but that the compulsion to act with valor has become woven into Roman character through memory and experience. As Hörnqvist points out, the greatness of the Roman Republic for Machiavelli "consisted in part in its civic institutions, in part in its territorial expansion, but above all in its ability to engender and to foster this type of character."[181] Livy, too, would suggest that the advantage of Rome over the singular greatness of Alexander lay in the ability of Rome to continually produce soldiers and commanders with ability and valor (9.17.3). In part this character is borne of an aversion to something that will so possess a people that they persist in this disposition (*D* 1.58). So, the Roman people "held the kingly name so much in hatred that no obligation to any of its citizens who might try for that name could enable him to escape the proper penalties" (*D* 1.58). Disposed by this aversion to kingship, regulated by good laws, and given a public forum by which the movements of men are made visible, the character of the Roman people maintains a love of their country for 400 years (*D* 1.58). The people certainly waiver in their actions and judgments, but momentary lapses can be remedied by recalling their animating dispositions. Machiavelli quotes from Livy when Camillus, sensing some apprehension among his troops, tells them, "What anyone has learned or is accustomed to, he will do" (*D* 3.31; also Livy 6.7.6). For Machiavelli, Camillus's ability to reanimate his men is possible only because they are "ordered and trained both in peace and in war" (*D* 3.31). Through constant training and opportunities, the Roman people "both in particular and in public" are able "to make experiment both of their virtue and of the power of fortune" so that they are able to display valor regardless of the situation (*D* 3.31). Training must be reinforced, in turn, by experiences of victory (*D* 3.33). Over time, these experiences are woven into character, creating a lasting disposition of courage, discipline, confidence, and affection for Rome that cannot be extinguished by momentary disorders, slight setbacks, and vain ideas (*D* 3.33).[182]

Machiavelli's historiographic method reveals the possibility, the extent, and method by which change can occur. Whatever may be Livy's biases, the attractiveness of his historiographic method for Machiavelli is that it contains a certain ecumenical touch: there are no philosopher-kings; felt meanings are not abstractions but are accessible, and in fact need to be accessible, to all; everyone seems susceptible to the loss of vision that underlies corruption; and everyone seems capable, at least to some degree, of modifying their inclinations. From this perspective, Machiavelli's emphasis on appearance is much less cynical and much less manipulative than we see in *The Prince.* The writing of history becomes an act of constituting or reconstituting felt meanings through the sensory act of perception, simulated in the mind's eye, that invokes impressions, reactions, and conclusions. In contrast with Plato's ascent, Livy and Machiavelli continually summon us to descend into a world of particulars. Machiavelli's *Discourses,* like the words of Quintius to his army, are meant to stir the impulses so that "a tumultuously and badly ordered" body can be animated to act for the good of the community (*D* 3.14).

4

Tacitus, Montesquieu, and the Malady of Despotism

If Livy, writing while Augustus was at least making gestures toward the republican past, could imagine the possibility of reanimating a Roman republican spirit, then Tacitus, looking back at the reigns of Tiberius, Caligula, Claudius, and Nero, and having lived under the equally terrible Domitian, could convey no such hope. A "new factor," as Martin suggests, had imposed itself on the structure of historiography: "the reign of the individual emperor."[1] The theme that Martin, speaking on behalf of a long tradition of scholarship, sees as guiding Tacitus's *Annals* is the figure of the tyrant. The first six books of the *Annals*, the most complete extant portion of the work, appear to be organized around the question, "How was it that a man who till his mid-fifties had been 'excellent in both achievement and reputation' became at the end a cruel tyrant and licentious recluse?"[2] The answer, according to Martin, is that the "true Tiberius was there from the start, but hidden; progressively the veneer of virtue and civility wore off."[3]

Yet, even though the emperors were important, Tacitus's pessimism does not seem to stem solely from the character of the tyrant. Rome had known tyrants before. In fact, Tacitus opens the *Annals* with an account of the different experiences—all of them temporary—of power concentrated in the hands of individuals: kings ruled until the consulship was created; dictatorships were established "only on occasion";[4] *decemviral* power did not last beyond two years;[5] the consular authority of the military tribunes was not long-lived;[6] neither Cinna nor Sulla created "lengthy domination"; Pompey's and Crassus's power passed quickly; and Lepidus and Antony ruled an empire exhausted by civil war (*Ann.* 1.1.1).[7] Tacitus, furthermore, does not suggest that Augustus was more depraved than Appius Claudius, nor that Tiberius, particularly in the beginning of his reign, was crueler than Sulla.[8] Tiberius seems genuinely interested, even by Tacitus's account, in tempering the aristocratic excesses of the age and evinces little of the venality or extravagance that would characterize the reigns of later tyrants. What marks the difference between these earlier experiences of tyranny and the emergence of the principate is what Eder describes as "the eerie silence" that accompanies its rise.[9] Why would the aristocracy, who if not always virtuous was at least prideful, so continuously degrade itself? And why would the people, who built a hard earned reputation in Roman history for raucousness, become so compliant, except for some punctuated moments of frenzy? These perplexities lead Tacitus to a diagnosis that something more enduring had penetrated into Roman political life.

There is perhaps no political thinker who better appreciated Tacitus's insight into this new political phenomenon than Montesquieu. Interpretations of Tacitus had made periodic appearances in earlier political discussions. Leading up to Montesquieu, Tacitus was introduced as a civic humanist by Bruni, largely neglected until taken up again by Machiavelli (in whose spirit Botero would later employ Tacitus against Spanish tyranny), and then used by Guicciardini as a form of consolation and reconciliation to tyranny. Tacitus, particularly given the political experience that he brought to his historical writings, also figured prominently in Bodin's discussion of comparative jurisprudence.[10] Montaigne saw in Tacitus the figure of a person who did not avoid political responsibility but was also able to maintain his own detachment as a political thinker.[11] He was also used to introduce new discussions that extended the perspective of war as a relationship between states into conflict within civil society. Drawing on Tacitus's account of how Rome emerged through civil strife, these Tacitists saw that "all politics" was now at least potentially like civil war, and "our fellow citizens were no different from enemies with whom we lived in uneasy peace."[12]

Montesquieu draws on these various elements: on comparative jurisprudence, on the analysis of formal institutional arrangements of communities, on Tacitus's insights as a politician, and on the experience of civil war and despotism. But Tacitus plays his largest role in Montesquieu's analysis of the collective impressions, recollections, and arrangements of experiences—what he characterizes as the spirit of the community—that serve as the impetus for collective action (see EC 149; *S* 3.1). Particularly significant is Montesquieu's conceptualization of despotism, which he traces not to the corrupt nature of the tyrant, as had Aristotle, but to a more far-reaching alteration in the political impulses of the people.[13] Montesquieu's portrait of Rome's slide into "gentle servitude," a spirit that preceded the particular leaders and remained even with the overthrow of successive leaders, reveals a much more complex dynamic by which despotism operates (see *S* 3.3). The tyrant can change laws and institutions, but despotism requires a much slower and more complex transformation in the habits and mores of a people. Montesquieu evocatively conveys this transformation in the opening of his chapter on Tiberius: "As a river slowly and silently undermines the dikes erected against it and finally," using a term to describe both natural and political processes, "overthrows (*renverser*) them in a moment, flooding the countryside they protected, so in the same way the sovereign power that acted insensibly under Augustus overthrew things violently under Tiberius" (*C* 129; also *S* 3.9). We can hear in this description echoes of Tacitus's characterization of the *Annals* as *parva forsitan et levia memoratu*, "little things perhaps, and things petty to remember" out of which "movements of vast changes often take their rise" (*Ann.* 4.32.2, my translation). Montesquieu, following Tacitus, locates in Tiberius's reign the culmination of a set of political changes that result not just in the appearance of another tyrant, but also in the sustainability of a new despotic order.

If much of scholarship seeks to reconstruct the political world of the early principate, it does so by lending a certain normalcy to imperial political life. With some frequency scholars identify the formal structures of power, the operation of laws and institutions, the seemingly normal material interests that continue to motivate individuals, and the belief in the authority and legitimacy of imperial rule. Scholars then use this data to point to the exaggerations and biases in Tacitus's account. But I think when Tacitus views the principate from the experience of Domitian, like Montesquieu reading Tacitus from the experience of Louis XIV (and, I might add, like Syme turning to Tacitus as the specter of totalitarianism began to cast its shadow over the world), they are referencing a far less visible, far more experiential way in which despotism alters the cues by which individuals and groups develop their political attitudes, dispositions, and aspirations. Wirszubski suggests some of the distinctiveness of Tacitus's approach when he writes, "Perhaps the most striking feature of Tacitus's attitude to the Principate and to liberty is the fact that his estimate of the former and his idea of the latter are not determined solely, nor even primarily, by constitutional considerations."[14]

Institutions are important, of course, as they are transformed into instruments of the despot's will. But more than that, Montesquieu suggests that for despotism to work it must be able to "beat down" self-esteem, courage, and political ambition (*S* 3.9). Montesquieu, thus, directs us to a psychological component: how the impetus for political action is itself transformed. By "psychological" I do not mean it as a synonym for "character," as it is frequently used.[15] I am more sympathetic to Luce's attempt to shift scholarly focus from what he describes as the "almost exclusive concentration on the constancy of character" to what he calls "behavior": the ways in which an individual "acts and reacts" in response to the circumstances in which one finds oneself.[16] For Luce, Tacitus presents us with "discrete episodes" that emphasize the "anomaly, inconcinnity, and complexity" of a particular situation at a particular time so that we may "judge the merits of the individuals who pass before us, however difficult the judging may be."[17] I depart from Luce in my suggestion that Tacitus's approach leads to more than judgments about the merits of individuals; it tells us something about the effects of circumstances, both past and present, on how individuals understand and navigate through a despotic world. In this regard, Tacitus's psychology is as much political as it is individual as he is engaged in an exploration of the consequences of the gradual perversion and disintegration of the stable cues by which individuals orient themselves politically.[18]

We can perhaps better contextualize Tacitus's political psychology by comparing it to Celsus, who is credited with compiling one of the most important and comprehensive medical treatises of the early imperial era, *De Medicina*. Given the materialist understanding of the soul (that we see with Livy, as well), the art of medicine consisted of an examination of physical as well as psychological disturbances. And these disturbances could be set into motion by a whole range of geographic, climatic, and cultural conditions. Events, as Foucault would note, could "induce morbid effects in the body" (*CS* 101). In fact, for Celsus, medicine had become necessary for the Romans because of the growing complexity of diseases brought about by apathy and luxury (Cels. *De Med.* pro. 4). But medicine had also changed its methods, from a form of philosophy to a study of the causes and treatment of disease. Describing the method of medicine, Celsus writes that one needs "to lay open the bodies of the dead and to scrutinize" the innards to obtain "a knowledge of hidden causes involving diseases" so that one can know how to care for them (Cels. pro. 23, 14).

So Tacitus also performs a vivisection of the political body to understand the malady of despotism. What emerges is a description of the motions (*motus*) of history that correspond to the almost imperceptible alterations of the collective spirit (*Ann.* 4.32.2; 1.2.1).[19] Despotism appears as something akin to a wasting disease (*tabes*), or to what Celsus and the Greeks call *atrophia*.[20] Striking for our interpretation of Tacitus is that *atrophia* has two contradictory causes, both of which seem operative in the political body that has succumbed to despotism. *Atrophia*, according to Celsus, is brought about by excessive desire (*aviditate nimia*) in which the patient consumes more than he ought, or by excessive dread (*nimio timore*) in which the patient consumes less (Cels. 3.22.1). Combined, these forces set the political body against itself, leading to the gradual exhaustion of the animating impulses of Roman political life.

Tacitus is talking about the loss of political bearings: one's sense of the clarity by which institutions and norms transmit expectations, channel ambition, and recognize accomplishments. To recall the introduction, we are talking about how these markers lose their objectivity as they become increasingly indistinguishable from the emperor's will. With the progress of despotism, every marker—whether distinctions of legal and illegal, honorable and dishonorable, or trustworthy and untrustworthy—can mean its opposite. As Tacitus takes us inside the individual while the individual attempts to navigate through this unknowable and unreliable realm, we see the consequences of the transformation of the political landscape when ambition is channeled into melancholy, delirium, and servility. Tacitus's diagnostic starting point, which we turn to first, is the primitive societies of the Germans and Britons where the markers by which one navigated through public were in their most uncorrupted forms.

PRIMITIVE SOCIETIES AND POLITICAL BEARINGS

When Montesquieu describes humankind as a "feeling creature" (*S* 1.1) and life as a "series of passions" (EC 145), he is not describing the emotions as we would understand them today, but the more general operation by which perceptions, ideas, and memories have their origins in sensations.[21] Sentiments are the associations of pain or pleasure with particular external objects that are felt through the senses (EC 141; see also *Pensées* 549 [30]). This pain or pleasure causes the spirit (like the *pneuma* we saw in the previous chapter) to move in a particular path through what Montesquieu likens to the fibers of a web (EC 144, *OC* 489). So perception is an ability to correctly associate a movement with the external object. Memory is an ability to store in the mind the particular movement of the spirit associated with that object. And an idea is an ability to recall that sensation by the soul through an act of will, which causes the spirits to move in a path similar to the original sensation (see EC 141). Experiences multiply these paths. Education creates associations between these paths. And training and habituation repeat these movements until the fibers "seem to move by themselves and to depend not at all upon the will" (EC 159, fn. 15).

Montesquieu's sensualist psychology has a political component: the principles of government consist of the "human passions that set it in motion" (*S* 1.3). What animates a community is what animates individuals: feelings (*sentiments*) that inspire (*S* 5.1; see *S* 19.12). But the flow is two-way. Common sentiments derive from a general education that creates common paths by which the spirit moves. Communities provide an arrangement of experiences, and judgments about those experiences, from which individuals take their cue. Societies provide collective memories that precede the life of the individual. Societies also establish laws, customs, and institutions that prescribe and proscribe conduct, creating habits that connect succeeding generations. And societies transmit ideas that provide linkages between different experiences (see EC 157). A collective spirit, thus, is shaped through an "infinite" chain of causes that ultimately becomes decisive in their cumulation (*De la politique* 173).[22]

To understand the operation of human sentiments in their most basic form, Montesquieu looks to Tacitus's account of the Germans and Britons. As Montesquieu exclaims, "it is the work of Tacitus who summarized everything because he saw everything" (*S* 30.2).[23] In primitive societies, Montesquieu writes, individuals are governed by the "laws of nature," those laws that "derive uniquely from the constitution of our being" (*S* 1.2; see also *S* 14.3). Living "without arts, without education, almost with laws," these primitive northern tribes had "only the good sense connected with the coarse fibers of these climates" (*S* 14.3).[24] They were sober, rugged, and strong (*S* 14.14). But they also had a "wisdom" of sorts that allowed them to maintain themselves "against the Roman power until they came out of their forests to destroy it" (*S* 14.3). Although lacking the general social education that trains and develops the mind, these people still had basic "ideas" about "subjects related to their self preservation" (EC 147; see also *S* 1.2). Out of these ideas arose a primitive republic, one characterized most of all by transparency in the norms and expectations of community life.[25] As a profile of political psychology, these primitive tribes serve as a psychological starting point for tracing the course of despotism as it breaks down the categories—and thus disorients the sentiments—by which individuals orient themselves politically.

That Tacitus's earlier writings on the Germans and Britons have some bearing on his later discussion of the malady of despotism is suggested by a digression in the third book of the *Annals* that refers back to primitive societies.[26] In describing how Rome is now afflicted by "the infinite number and variety of laws" (*multitudinem infinitam ac varietatem legum*) of his time, Tacitus's language, as Woodman and Martin point out, parallels Seneca's characterization of medical treatments as simpler in earlier societies until "by degrees it reached its present stage of complicated variety" (*paulatim . . . in hanc pervenit tam multiplicem varietatem*) (*Ann.* 3.25.2; Sen. *Ep.* 95.15; also Cels. pro. 5).[27] Tacitus's claims also recall Celsus, who reports, as we earlier saw, that "complex" forms of medicine were not needed in primitive times because individuals were not spoiled by indolence or luxury (Cels. pro. 5).[28] Now, as Seneca writes, as did Celsus before, defenses need to be established that are all the more powerful because of the greater violence that attacks us (Sen. *Ep.* 95.14–15; also Cels. pro. 5).

The fundamental difference between the Germans and the Romans lies in the clarity of the mental map by which individuals could navigate through political life.[29] The Germans knew what the community expected and the types of actions that yielded rewards or punishments. Thus, both Montesquieu and Tacitus emphasize the norms of reciprocity and equal exchange (*Germ.* 21.1; *S* 30.18; also *S* 24.17), the clarity of the criteria for selection of kings and military leaders (*Germ.* 7.1; *S* 31.4), and the ability of commanders to lead by example (*Germ.* 7.1; 13.3–4; *S* 30.16). Important matters were brought before a public assembly, deliberation occurred when people were "incapable of pretence," and decisions were made when people were free from "illusion" (*Germ.* 22.4). The incentive to courage lay in the proximity of one's kin both in the organization of the squadrons and in the proximity of loved ones to battle so that the soldier could hear "the wailing voice of woman and the child's cry" and be seen and praised by those he "covets most" (*Germ.* 7.3–4). Punishments were proportionate to the crime (*Germ.* 12.2; also 21.1). Shame was still operative (*Germ.* 6.6). And in social life there was "no arena with its seductions, no dinner-tables with their provocations to corrupt them. Of the exchange of secret letters men and women alike are innocent; adulteries are very few for the number of the people" (*Germ.* 19.1). In striking contrast to the interactions in imperial Rome, people spoke "without craft and cunning, and expose in the freedom of the occasion the heart's previous secrets" (*Germ.* 22.4). As Montesquieu writes about the Germanic tribes, in quoting Tacitus, "vices are not subject to ridicule there; to corrupt or to be corrupted is not called a usage or a way of life" (*S* 18.25; *Germ.* 19; see also *Agric.* 21.2).

Employing an explanation common to the ancients, Tacitus writes that when the seeds of luxury are planted, modesty and decency give way to ambition and violence, and despotisms (*dominationes*) spring up (*Ann.* 3.26.2; see *C* 40, 44).[30] But why is despotism the result? In part, the release of constraints on the appetites removes any limits on ambition, giving rise to leaders who plunder the state for their own interests. More dangerously, though, because it permeates the political body, luxury distorts the perceptions of rewards and punishments, leading individuals to trade freedom for pleasure under the guise of progress (see *Agric.* 11.4). Such was the lot of the Britons who, under the corrosive influence of the Romans, called this luxury "culture" (*humanitas*) when it was really servitude (*Agric.* 21.2).

For some communities despotism "remained permanently" (*Ann.* 3.26.2). For other communities there was the establishment of laws, either immediately after the appearance of despotism or, as in Rome, after a period of kingship that devolved into despotism.[31] But laws themselves point in no better direction. At first aimed at protecting liberty and maintaining *concordia*, laws, in an increasingly tumultuous environment, become the forceful way of advancing one's perverted (*prava*) ends (*Ann.* 3.27.1).[32] Tacitus portrays the increasing disorganization of the political markers of Roman society: senators using laws to banish the virtuous and to acquire office, tribunes who "bribed by hope" and cheated with their actions, and contradictory (*diversa*) legislation that was not even interrupted by war (*Ann.* 3.27.2). Even the momentary calm under Sulla, who severely curtailed the power of the tribunes, was broken by Lepidus and the country was once again thrown into disorder (*turbidis*) (*Ann.* 3.27.2).[33] As Tacitus observes, "with the infection in the state at its peak, the number of laws was at its greatest" (*Ann.* 3.27.3).

The underlying motif of Tacitus's description of the final decades of the republic, a description that corresponds to his diagnosis of a larger collective malady, is of the healer as purveyor of sickness. We see in this description of the healer an indication of the perversion of the norms by which individuals orient themselves. Pompey, for example, chosen as the healer (*corrigendis*), was more burdensome (*gravior*) in his remedies (*remediis*) than the aliment itself (*Ann.* 3.28.1).[34] As sole consul, he established a new court and proceedings (the *lex Pompeia de vi*), ostensibly to prosecute swiftly individuals responsible for recent disturbances (such as the murder of Clodius, the burning of the senate house, and the ensuing riots), but in reality to eliminate Milo, a political rival.[35] Pompey also established the *lex de ambitu*, a law that retroactively as well as prospectively punished electoral corruption, especially bribery. But the use of the courts to advance one's own political interests served only to highlight the continued degeneration of the community.[36] With civil war, neither law (*ius*) nor custom (*mos*) remained, returning Rome to a now corrupt form of primitive society (*Ann.* 3.28.1).[37] In place of habits of honor was a jumbling of norms: "all acts of the basest nature passed with impunity, and many of honesty led to extermination" (*Ann.* 3.28.1). The legal system, as Tacitus observes, had become one "disrupted" (*turbabantur*) by force and fraud; it could offer itself only as a means of frail (*invalido*) protection to the people (*Ann.* 1.2.2). As Montesquieu writes similarly in a language descriptive of an unhealthy soul, the "torn (*déchirée*) city no longer formed a complete whole" but one plunged into frenzy (*fereur*) (*C* 93, 101; trans. modified).

The rule of one man in the figure of Octavian, at least in the eyes of some, appeared as the new *remedium* for the "disaffected fatherland," bringing about *quies*, or calm, to the disordered community (*Ann.* 1.9.4–5). Tacitus's language recalls the task of a physician who aims, as Celsus writes, toward the quiet of the spirit (*ad quietem animi*) of a disturbed patient (see Cels. 3.18.5). For Tacitus, though, the *quies* that Augustus creates recalls a less than healthy calm that gradually spreads (*gliscit*) throughout the community (*Ann.* 1.1.2).[38] Augustus, for example, restored the rule of law by reappointing an urban praetor, he invalidated illegal acts of the triumvirate, he reestablished the "collegiate character of the consulate," and he reduced (from the bloated roles) and then ratified membership in the senate.[39] He addressed the material needs of the populace, as Nicolet concludes.[40] And, as Galinsky argues, he spoke to the "revitalization of the mores of the *res publica*."[41] Tacitus, though, is not so generous. In Tacitus's account, Augustus mollified the people with cheap corn, a purchase of tyranny, to recall Livy, which Spurius Maelius had attempted unsuccessfully in the republic (*Ann.* 1.2.1; Livy 4.15.6). Augustus calmed the army through gifts (likely the promise of land upon discharge) (*Ann.* 1.2.1).[42] And he seduced the world with the false allure of peace (*Ann.* 1.2.1), gradually (*paulatim*) concentrating the functions of the senate, magistracy, and legislature into his own person (*Ann.* 1.2.1).[43] The most outspoken were silenced, either on the battlefield or through proscription lists.[44] The rest of the nobility accepted slavery, preferring safety to the danger of the old order (*Ann.* 1.2.1). Perhaps the most telling quiet from Tacitus's perspective is the silence and falsification of history that occurred as historians became enfeebled, whether because of the growth of *adulatio*, cringing flattery (said of Oriental despotism in Livy), or *metus* (dread) (*Ann.* 1.1.2).[45]

From a psychological perspective, the temper of the quiet that comes over the Roman citizenry seems more like political paralysis than tranquility. Like paralysis, in which, as Celsus writes, individuals "drag out a miserable existence, their memory lost also" (*miserum spiritum trahunt, memoria quoque amissa*), so no living memories of the republic remained. Few were left "who had seen the Republic" (Cels. 3.27.1A; *Ann.* 1.3.7). Gone with these memories was a republican disposition of equality that combined vigor and restraint (*Ann.* 1.4.1).[46] In the place of equality was the vigor of Augustus's body to which, in its prime, everyone looked (*Ann.* 1.4.1). The state, in fact, became legally the "parent of everyone," inheriting the property of childless households (*Ann.* 3.28.3) and formalized in Augustus receiving the title *pater patriae* in 2 BCE.[47]

Woodman and Martin point out that the state, as the inheritor of a household's wealth, would actually be the child.[48] But Tacitus's language, as it manipulates the image of the benevolence of the Augustan age, recalls a notion that has its origin in Aristotle: the emperor as *dominus*, the despotic head of the household.[49] As Tacitus insinuates through the murmurings of those opposed to Augustus's rule, "devotion to his parent" was merely the pretext "in a desire for dominion" (*cupidine dominandi*) (*Ann.* 1.10.1). Suggestive of the psychological power that the sovereign held, only when the body of the *princeps* was worn out by sickness did a few begin to speak idly of freedom (*Ann.* 1.4.2). "More panicked about war (others desired it)" but most simply exchanged rumors about their future masters (*dominos*) (*Ann.* 1.4.2). By the time of Tiberius, as Tacitus implies, the spirit of despotism had set in: there "was a rush into servitude" (*ruere in servitium*) by consuls, senators, and knights (*Ann.* 1.7.1). The hastiness and ruin denoted by *ruere* contrasts sharply with, and occurs under the guise of, quiet, justifying Tacitus's own aim to look beneath the surface (*introspicere*) of events not just to highlight the hypocrisy of the era but to diagnose the malady of despotism (*Ann.* 4.32.2).[50]

What lies beneath the surface is, simply put, madness that results from the loss of stable markers by which one can navigate through the political realm. These markers are of two types: institutions to which individuals can appeal, and cultural norms by which individual ambition is channeled and achievement recognized. As these markers become progressively subsumed under the will of the sovereign (as the political father), there are two primary choices that people who must navigate through this realm face. Both choices result in forms of madness. The first choice, which is played out in the mutinies that open the *Annals*, is to rage like a madman against the arbitrary decisions, the cruelties, and the disingenuousness of the sovereign until one ultimately collapses from exhaustion. The second choice is servility. The path to power, recognition, and status (and often survival) lies in the ability to cater to the whims of the emperor. Since those whims are themselves unstable and unknowable, servility fosters its own form of insanity in which what one says and how one acts becomes increasingly disconnected from any communication of meaning or feeling. It is in the institutionalization of terror, though, that the sentiments of honor, friendship, and liberty—the central animating impulses of Roman political life— are finally dissolved.

UNMEDIATED POLITICS

Tacitus, though unrelenting in his criticism of Tiberius, seems to recognize the ambiguities that inhered in Tiberius's reign. Tiberius spoke on behalf of the rule of law (*Ann.* 3.69.2–6), he at least gave lip service to ancient liberties (*Ann.* 1.7.3; 4.6), he often referred public matters to the senate (see, for example, *Ann.* 4.6.2), he rejected extravagance, even his own (*Ann.* 3.52–54), and he seemed genuinely frustrated with the willing subservience of the nobility (see *Ann.* 2.38.1; 3.35.1; 3.65.3).[51] Tiberius "handed out honors," as Tacitus notes, "by paying regard to the nobility of ancestors, brilliancy of soldiering, and illustrious qualities at home" (*Ann.* 4.6.2). But Tiberius's actions were fraught with paradox. His attempt to encourage debate in a senate where no one would speak his mind made more poignant, as Tacitus observes, the "traces of dying freedom" (*Ann.* 1.74.5; also 3.35.2; 4.6.1; 4.7.1). When Tiberius declared that he would vote in the prosecution of Granius Marcellus, hoping to instill equity in judgments, Gnaeus Piso asked in what order the emperor would vote: "If first, I shall have something to follow; if after everyone else, I am afraid lest I dissent improvidently" (*Ann.* 1.74.5).

However much Piso may have regretted his outburst, he expressed the anxiety— more than any tangible fear, as of yet—of navigating through public institutions and processes that appear incoherent and insincere.[52] Eder, in pointing to continuities between the republic and the early principate, suggests that one can understand the principate as "the formation of a social and political power based on personal relationships and dependencies," relationships that had always been central to the politics of republican Rome but were now "carried to extremes."[53] In fact, what makes these relationships so extreme is that they are no longer mediated through meaningful institutional forms. Although the imperial powers maintain a constitutional form, they are organized around, and subordinated to, the will of the sovereign.[54] As Rudich notes, "In appearance, Augustus preserved all traditional institutions intact, but transformed them by and large into channels of personal power while building up alongside them a centralized officialdom of his own."[55]

A quick review of the changes under Augustus—the institutional components of Augustus's assumption of political parentage—may be helpful to the reader unfamiliar with this period and will suggest the extent to which the cues by which individuals orient their political behavior came to be located in the emperor. As holder of a vast *imperium proconsulare,* Augustus placed almost all the military forces under the command of his legates, who operated, in turn, by his authority.[56] Endowed with *tribunica potestas,* Augustus assumed not only the formal power to veto senatorial action, but the more encompassing authority to speak on behalf of the people.[57] Augustus was also granted the right to judge appeals for capital cases, which under the republic had been appeals to the people (*provocatio ad populum*).[58] The senate had become, in Tacitus's words, an *imago antiquitatis,* a mere shadow of the past (see *Ann.* 3.60.1).[59] It continued to adhere to its procedures and traditions even as it was stripped, whether because of its own incompetence or because of the desire for imperial power, of its oversight of financial affairs, and military and foreign policy.[60] Their most visible new role in the early principate, issuing honors to the emperor and members of the family, demonstrated all the more clearly how closely their role had been organized around promoting imperial history and ideology.[61]

The tribunate, now chosen by the senate (with the approval of the emperor), had no connection to the plebs and little interest in or ability to exercise its traditional powers: vetoing, introducing legislation, and representing plebeian claims.[62] Augustus sought to sever the informal relationships of people to their aristocratic patrons and bind the people directly to him by taking on the responsibility of providing relief, establishing low interest loans, providing access to baths and games, and increasing recipients of the dole.[63] The assemblies of the urban plebs also lost their independence, becoming the site for "ceremonials of consensus."[64] Selection and election to office were largely contingent on imperial favor.[65] The equestrian order, depleted through heavy capital levies and banned from politics in the final years of the republic, was for Tacitus simply purchased by giving them a role in the military and administration.[66] The knights lacked sufficient identity or mechanisms, though, for articulating their interests.[67] The army, no longer citizen soldiers but professionalized under Augustus through set terms of service and year-long deployments in the field, and paid for from the treasury, owed its allegiance to the *princeps* more than to the senate and the state.[68] Military oaths of loyalty were sworn to each new emperor, replacing oaths that had once been made to commanders and (before that) to the *res publica*.[69] *Imperator* acclamations multiplied and were directed exclusively toward the emperor and imperial household rather than being spontaneous acclamations by the troops toward the commander.[70] And the praetorian guard was formed as an elite and well-paid corps whose primary responsibility was to protect the emperor.[71] By the time of Tiberius, as Asinius Gallus made clear in his appeal to Tiberius in the early days of the *princeps*' accession to office, "the body of the state was one and needed to be ruled by the mind of one individual" (*Ann.* 1.12.3).[72]

The result of this association of the political body with the body of the emperor is not the powerlessness of other groups but a lack of gradations in the ability to express power. Groups can affirm and groups can vent, but there are few other avenues that they can, or might want to, take. There is, as Montesquieu notes, "no tempering, modification, accommodation, terms, alternatives, negotiations, remonstrances, nothing as good or better can be proposed" (*S* 3.10). As Fontana observes, in words that would have made Montesquieu proud, "The principate has reduced political life and social life into one vast monolithic wasteland, where all political plurality and social differentiation no longer provided the basis for the life of the state."[73]

However much one might object to the gradations in access to wealth and power that defined Roman society, some sort of differentiation, as Montesquieu notes, is essential for the maintenance of liberty. One must "combine powers, regulate them, temper them, make them act," which requires not only particular institutional forms and boundaries but the inculcation and reinforcement of habits and mores that give those institutions life (*S* 5.14). If there are elections, then there must be a willingness to subscribe to the peaceful transfer of power. If military success is desired, then recognition and rewards must be given to the best strategists and fighters. If there are courts, then there must be judges and juries willing to subscribe to the law.

In the case of Rome, as we will see, Tacitus points to the

transfer over time, and in turn the perversion, of the social and political mechanisms by which the highest rewards of wealth, honor, and status are defined and earned. In sharp contrast to the German tribes where the rules, expectations, and enforcement of those expectations are transparent, in despotism one encounters, as Montesquieu writes, the "shadow" of laws and the "color" of justice (*C* 130).[74] In this political dreamscape, public categories of true and false, right and wrong, just and unjust, protected and unprotected, legal and illegal, and honorable and dishonorable have no reality apart from the emperor's will, making it impossible for individuals to know, understand, make inferences about, or predict the boundaries of political conduct.

I have suggested how Rome's institutional forms change as they lose their mediating function. Accompanying this change is the transfer of the mechanisms of political recognition and power to the will of the sovereign. But to fully understand the way in which despotism makes itself felt, Tacitus directs our attention to the disorienting effects of the loss of these institutional and cultural forms of mediation. Two different, seemingly contradictory, responses occur: frenzied and unsustainable outcry, and enfeebled and corrupted servility. Both responses are, in fact, two sides of the same coin. If the scenes of the armies abroad portray the madness of outcry, then the scenes at home point to the enfeebling of the elite. In both cases, everyone ends up mixed together in a political form that appears radically egalitarian because, as Montesquieu suggests, despotism transforms "man" into "a creature that obeys a creature that wants" (*S* 3.10). For Tacitus, this egalitarianism appears as a form of perverse political theater. Beneath the carefully maintained hierarchies of status, Tacitus, as we will see, will expose this radical, leveling quality of despotism in the primary language available to him: as the willingness of the elites to take on the attributes of mass behavior. Like the Roman theater, however much politics retains the forms of a status hierarchy, it becomes the most raucous and the most servile of forums.

The Mutinies: Outcry and Exhaustion

To understand the dynamics of this unmediated politics, I begin with the mutinies in Pannonia and Germany, which have drawn considerable scholarly attention. Seeking to revise a long tradition that sees the episodes as meant to contrast the heroic Germanicus to the villainous Tiberius, Ross argues that the episodes, in fact, highlight the degeneration of *libertas* into *licentia*, a lack of restraint that is often associated with popular leaders (like Germanicus) who cater to the mob.[75] The episodes, thus, according to Ross, rule out Germanicus as an alternative to Tiberius. Woodman, too, follows Ross in seeing these episodes as more critical of Germanicus than is often assumed, but broadens his diagnosis of the extent of the turmoil. In drawing on a Roman historiographic tradition of brothers fighting on behalf of Rome, Tacitus announces that something is amiss: rather than successfully integrating new territory into Rome, as do Tiberius Nero and Claudius Drusus at the end of Livy's *History*, Drusus and Germanicus "are obliged to combat mutiny in their own ranks."[76] The mutinies, Woodman argues, appear as "detailed and comprehensive case studies of collective madness" that require drastic forms of leadership.[77]

Rowe, quite in contrast, portrays the Pannonian and German mutinies as a form of political interaction in which the soldiers employed the "formal tools their political culture provided": they assembled, began constructing a *tribunal*, engaged in "oratory and response," selected ambassadors, made collective decisions, and issued their demands.[78] Rowe observes, "From a disinterested perspective, the same mutinies appear remarkable for their orderliness. Soldiers deliberated in assemblies, made moderate demands, and demonstrated a keen grasp of the political system to which they belonged."[79] Speaking generally about the soldiers as an imperial constituency, Rowe concludes, the military camps appear "like poleis" and the soldiers, perhaps unique in imperial Rome, develop a "participatory political culture centered on the *contio*."[80]

I am sympathetic with Rowe's attempt to tease political sanity out of the episode, but I tend to side with Woodman that the language of the mutinies connotes forms of madness. But where Woodman and Ross focus primarily on leadership responses to the mutinies, I want to suggest that Tacitus is using the episodes to identify a more widespread madness that results from an unmediated politics. In these episodes, political forms appear as stage props designed to give some order to a political world that is increasingly devoid of institutional mechanisms for mediation. The result, not surprisingly, is a distrust of these forms—indeed, often a reaction against them—with nothing to fall back on. We see, thus, a political realm with extraordinary volatility that ebbs and flows with the passions of the crowd and the ability of leaders to inflame or subdue this fervor. If we can borrow from, and substantially revise, the image of politics as performance, then politics becomes theatrical in the same way that theater in Rome became political: as an unstable and largely undifferentiated forum in which real and unreal, true and false, and trustworthy and untrustworthy become indistinguishable.[81]

Intimations of this perverse theatricality can be discerned immediately when Tacitus describes the instigator of the mutiny among the Pannonian legions, Percennius, as a "leader of a theatrical claque" in his early years whose experience of stage rivalries had taught him how to stir up (*miscere*) an audience (*Ann.* 1.16.3). The soldiers do indeed, as Rowe argues, employ a series of political forms, but they are forms, as Tacitus is careful to note, that are constructed in a state of madness (*furoris*) (*Ann.* 1.18.2). Blaesus, the commander, pleads with the soldiers to give up the sedition since "it was not through mutiny and disruption (*seditionem et turbas*) that soldiers' requirements should be conveyed to Caesar" (*Ann.* 1.19.2). Better, he insists, to name deputies and provide them with instructions. Although Blaesus brings momentary calm, he cannot establish long-term, procedural resolution: the decision, affirmed through a shout, to choose Blaesus's son as an envoy only demonstrated to the soldiers that "necessity had extracted what they would not have achieved through moderation" (*Ann.* 1.19.5).

What emerges through Tacitus's account is the sheer instability of these political interactions. The mutiny reignites when some soldiers, previously dispatched on work detail, hear of the disturbance and, looting on the way, return to camp. Blaesus orders the worst of the bunch jailed, transforming the political forum into the site of recrimination and abuse of the leaders until the crowd, aroused variously by odium, sympathy, alarm, and indignation, rises up, and frees the deserters and criminals condemned for capital offenses. The freed prisoners then mix (*miscent*) almost immediately with the crowd (*Ann.* 1.21.3). *Miscere* is a suggestive word here, meaning to mix or mingle, sometimes for good (like marriage) but often denoting an unnatural confusion.[82] In this case, the confusion is compared to a fever that burned hotter (*flagrantior . . . vis*) as the mutiny found new leaders to address the turbulent crowd, "agitated (*turbatos*) as they were" (*Ann.* 1.22.1).[83] Vibulenus, a common soldier, now becomes a leader, further inflaming the crowd through the most corrupt forms of rhetoric: he lies about the death of his brother, weeps and strikes his face and breast, and then fawns at the feet of each man until he "provoked so much consternation and resentment that some of the soldiers bound the gladiators who were among Blaesus' slaves, some the rest of his establishment, while others poured out to look for the body" (*Ann.* 1.23.1).

But there is nothing sustainable, and little that is trustworthy or predictable by either side, in this outcry. Tiberius sends Drusus to the camp, but with "no particularly fixed instructions" since there is no way of knowing what will greet him (*Ann.* 1.24.1). What Drusus encounters are images of disarray: not a camp "glittering with insignia but disfigured by filth and, despite their semblance of sorrowfulness, with looks approaching truculence" (*Ann.* 1.24.3). Turmoil, more than traditional dignity and order, mar the *adlocutio*, the formal imperial address to the troops.[84] Soldiers are unkempt, the military standards are not displayed, and the crowd greets Drusus with an angry roar. As Drusus calls for silence, the men variously look back at the multitude of men and roar and then look at Caesar and tremble: "There would be an indistinct growl, a frightening roar and suddenly quiet; in accordance with their different emotions they were panicked and terrifying" (*Ann.* 1.25.2).

As terrified as the troops are of Drusus, his suggestion that there are proper institutional mechanisms that obligate both the emperor and the troops for addressing the grievances provokes outcry.[85] At the point at which Drusus appeals to the jurisdiction (*arbitrium*) of the senate and his father, an assertion that such mechanisms exist, he is interrupted with a tumultuous shout (*clamore turbatur*) (*Ann.* 1.26.1). The soldiers exclaim (not inaccurately), "It was obviously a novelty that the Commander should refer only the benefits of soldiers to the senate: was the same senate therefore to be consulted each time reprisals or battles were declared" (*Ann.* 1.26.3)? Tensions again mount until an eclipse leads the troops to believe that the gods are against them. What is striking, though, is how Drusus chooses to take advantage of this chance event by sending popular officers to the tents of the soldiers to make them "mutually suspicious" so that the collectivity, once united in its outcry, would be separated again: recruit from veteran, legion from legion (*Ann.* 1.28.6). In division is safety, a maxim of despotic rule.

The German mutinies are portrayed in similarly tumultuous terms: fury (*Ann.* 1.31.1), delirium (1.31.3), frenzy (1.32.1), and paroxysms of rage (1.32.1). The anger again unifies the men, only absent mechanisms for collective expression the unity once again appears more as a disordered mixing. When Germanicus returns to address the troops, they "seemed thoroughly disorganized" (*permixta*) (*Ann.* 1.34.3; also 1.18.2). They are separated neither by company nor rank. And, just as the Pannonian troops respond to Drusus's letter from Tiberius as a farce, even though the letter is real, the German troops detect that the letter given to them promising the resolution of the grievances is a forgery and demand, instead, immediate action (*Ann.* 1.37.1). The actual difference between a real letter and a forgery, as it turns out, is of little consequence, particularly since, as Tacitus later observes, Tiberius will simply cancel any promises that had been made (*Ann.* 1.78.2). But Tacitus poses a striking juxtaposition in passing and one to which we will return. Against the backdrop of rebellious troops are the senate and commons, feeble and helpless (*invalida et inermia*) (*Ann.* 1.46.1). Tacitus concludes that it was time to apply some sedative (*fomenta*) to the passions of the soldiers, just as "sufficient provision" had already been made for Rome's servitude (*Ann.* 1.46.3).

Back at Home: Fostering Servility

Such madness is not an attribute only of the army. There are moments in which the urban plebs, too, express themselves collectively.[86] Absent formal institutions of political expression, the site of such outbursts was often the theater where, as Tacitus comments, "the common people have the greatest license" (*Hist.* 1.72; also *Ann.* 3.36.1).[87] This license is distinguished by, among other things, a leveling quality as distinctions (and recognition) of rank and status give way to rancor. Just as the murmurings of the soldiers crescendo into mutiny in Pannonia and Germany, so at about the same time in Rome the disorderliness of the theater (*theatri licentia*) "erupted more seriously now," leading soldiers, including members of the praetorian guard, to repress the insults made against the magistracy and the dissension of the people (*Ann.* 1.77.1). In subsequent events Lepida excites the audience attending the games, who "shouted savage execrations" against Quirinius (*Ann.* 3.23.1). Quirinius had accused Lepida of, among other things, attempting to poison him. The theatrical factions at another point whip up the people to a pitch of "outrage and violence" (*Ann.* 4.14.3). High corn prices nearly end in rioting with demands made by the populace in the theater for several days "with more license against the Commander than was customary" (*Ann.* 6.13.1). And Claudius reprimands the insolence of the crowd for mocking individuals of rank, including a consular (*Ann.* 11.13.1).

These collective bodies are not powerless.[88] The number of times that emperors address the troops suggests the importance of such appearances to both gauge opinion and establish a personal and imperial relationship with the army.[89] If Roman history demonstrates anything, it is that the army has options: Tiberius is quite rightly concerned that Germanicus's relationship to the troops could imperil his own rule (see, for example, *Ann.* 1.31.1; 1.35.3; 1.52.1).[90] The people, too, are able to bring pressure on imperial rule (see *Ann.* 2.87.1; 5.4.2). Tiberius, always bothered by the crowds (*Ann.* 6.13.1), struggles to find ways to effectively limit popular displays, both in the street (*Ann.* 1.8.5–6) and in the theater (*Ann.* 1.77;

4.14.3). And other members of the imperial family bask in the collective (and similarly undifferentiated) affirmations of imperial authority: Germanicus's son, Nero (*Ann.* 3.29), Nero and Agrippina (*Ann.* 5.4), Claudius (*Ann.* 12.7.1), the young Nero (*Ann.* 11.11.2), and Agrippina (*Ann.* 14.61).

But such outbursts become the rare collective expressions of the community. Tacitus more frequently shows how this unmediated politics, in which political reality is defined by the wants and desires of the despot, creates a disjointed and enfeebled public discourse.[91] Tacitus's description of the public reception of Tiberius's words upon assuming the throne reveals how disconnected discourse has become from expressions of purpose or meaning. Where Livy recounts the great words of someone like Camillus, who is able to twice save Rome, once through command of an army and then by convincing the people to return to the city, Tacitus depicts a public realm bereft not just of greatness, but also of the language by which people communicate understanding. Tacitus writes, "Tiberius' words, even on matters which he was not for concealing, were —whether by nature or habit—always weighed and obscure; but on that occasion, when he was striving to hide his feelings deep down, their extra complication led to uncertainty and ambiguity" (*Ann.* 1.11.2; trans. modified). Although there is not much that is credible in Tiberius's words, the senators, "whose one dread (*metus*) was that they seemed to understand," respond with "complaints, tears, and vows" (*Ann.* 1.11.3). In a despotic world where liberty is feared and flattery detested, words, facial expressions, and gestures have to be adjusted to betray no trace of one's thought (*Ann.* 2.87.1; also *Ann.* 3.65.2). Thus, one's expression (*vultus*), like the ramblings of an insane person, conveys nonsense: tears mixed with delight, complaints with adulation (*lacrimas, gaudium, questus, adulationem, miscebant*) (*Ann.* 1.7.1; see Cels. 3.18.2).[92] Only the dead, through books written as make-believe wills, could speak truthfully (*Ann.* 14.50.1).

Whether talking about the outbreak of mutiny or the sycophancy of the aristocracy, Tacitus continually conveys the mutual suspicion and anxiety that animates public interactions. Anything said, as Syme notes, "evaded verification and tended to be discredited."[93] Political discourse and debate, consequently, are replaced by rumors that are born of fear, hate, and distrust (see *Ann.* 1.4.2; 1.25.2; 3.19.2; 4.11.2; 13.26.1). Public orations, the way in which the elite constituted themselves as free citizens, are replaced by inconsequential private recitations that render speech "cold and lifeless."[94] One speaks only at great risk, and then without much effect, lending to Roman politics the continued guise of tranquility.[95] The populace can only give itself "permission for concealed utterances against the princeps or for suspicious silence" (*Ann.* 3.11.2; see also 3.19.2). And the senate demonstrates a continual unwillingness to debate, decide, initiate, and take responsibility, until "trained to love" vice, they make crimes into "eminent virtues" (*Hist.* 1.5; also *Ann.* 14.14; 14.60.1).[96] Even as flattery becomes the public discourse of choice, the coerced insincerity of praise only heightens the emperor's insecurity and deepens his contempt for the elite. As Tacitus remarks, in language that ironically plays on the imbalances that contribute to disease, the absence (*nulla*) or excess (*nimia*) of sycophancy in a corrupt society is equally dangerous (*Ann.* 4.17.1; also *Hist.* 1.85; see for example Cels. 1.3.2).

Tacitus is making an argument about the two primary responses that groups may take in this form of unmediated politics in which individuals lack appeal, recourse, or protection. One can join the voices of protest, which, as we have seen, is hardly sustainable as a form of collective expression and not particularly viable as a means of individual expression.[97] Or one can join in affirmations of the emperor's will, a will marked by increasing depravity. For good reason the path to power in imperial Rome lay in becoming part of the court: a personal retainer or advisor who, like Sejanus, can come to know and cater to the urges of the emperor.[98] As Marcus Terentius recalls when accused of his friendship with Sejanus, "intimacy with Sejanus meant an effective claim on Caesar's friendship; but those to whom he was hostile were constantly belabored by the dread of tatters" (*Ann.* 6.8.2). What is left is not to ask why the emperor elevates one person and not another, or why the emperor makes a particular decision. The gods, as Terentius continues, "have given [to the emperor] the supreme judgment of affairs; to us is left the glory of compliance" (*obsequii gloria*) (*Ann.* 6.8.4). The attributes of Sejanus point the way for others who might want to rise in imperial society: at once cringing and insolent, outwardly modest but possessed by "a lust for acquiring supremacy," and skilled at concealing himself (*Ann.* 4.1.3). Virtue, honor, and glory stand as the true obstacles to advancement; indeed, to one's longevity.[99] The administrators of the empire become, in Montesquieu's words, the slaves "chosen by his master to tyrannize over the other slaves" who have "no other felicity than that of sating the arrogance, desires, and voluptuousness of each day" (*S* 7.4).

There is, in short, security in baseness. For the people, as Montesquieu comments, the emperors were "prodigal of all the riches of the empire" that were acquired first through conquest and then by despoiling the nobility (*C* 137). The vilest of the emperors "wildly loved what the people loved, and contributed with all their power and even their persons to the people's pleasures" (*C* 137). Montesquieu is echoing Tacitus's own description of the crowd's delight in Nero's hunger, like theirs, for pleasure (*Ann.* 14.14.2).[100] The aristocracy, too, reveled in its corruption. When faced with proposals to limit luxuries (in an attempt to keep what remained of the aristocracy from bankrupting itself), Asinius Gallus explains to a willing audience that the enjoyments of luxury are proper compensation for the responsibilities and burdens of office, responsibilities that had grown with the expansion of the empire (*Ann.* 2.33; see also *S* 7.4). How easily, then, that Nero can receive his mandate for vice. The progeny of once great aristocratic households, now impoverished, give their name to Nero's desire to be on stage (*Ann.* 14.14.3): "Notable Roman equestrians too were driven by mighty gifts to promise their services to the arena, except that wages from one who can order carry with them the force of compulsion" (*Ann.* 14.14.4).[101] In the continual competition for recognition, the aristocracy willingly accepts servility as the path to power, status, and wealth (see, for example, *Ann.* 1.2.1; 14.15.5).

The irony is that over time the distinctions of rank and honor are undermined, producing a perverse equality among the different ranks of society in both their opposition to and affirmation of imperial rule.[102] If the Germans and Britons provide a diagnostic starting point for understanding what the aristocracy no longer was, then the mob serves as a dramatic image of what the aristocracy had become. Although the outlets of expression differ initially—the elites, as we will see, would have the courts as their circus—ultimately the aristocracy comes to inhabit even the spectacle of the theater. We catch a glimmer of the indiscriminant mixing that Tacitus associates with this form of equality with the mutinies. We get some sense of the blurring lines of rank and behavior in the prosecution of Gnaeus Piso when the senate joins with the frenzied people in "ferocious cries" (*infensas . . . voces*) and in expressing every "hostility and savagery" (*adversa et saeva*) against the defendant (*Ann.* 3.15.2). In the later Pisonian conspiracy against Nero, Tacitus emphasizes how "among people of different lineage, rank, age, and sex, rich and poor, everything was contained in silence" (*Ann.* 15.54.1).[103] In corruption, too, "Neither nobility nor age nor the holding of offices served as a hindrance to anyone's practicing the art of a Greek or Latin actor, right down to gestures and rhythms which were quite unmanly. Indeed illustrious ladies too gave grotesque performances" (*Ann.* 14.15.1–2; also 15.37). Every incentive existed for voluptuousness. Coins were distributed, "which the good were to spend from compulsion, the profligate from self-glorification" (*Ann.* 14.15.2). Among this competition of vices, few were left behind, including the emperor who appeared on stage before an audience now supplemented with centurions, tribunes, and the newest corps of Roman knights (*Ann.* 14.15.3–4): "And for days and nights they resounded with applause, calling the princeps's good looks and voice by divine designations: as if because of some excellence of theirs, they lived brilliant and honored lives" (*Ann.* 14.15.5).

The aristocracy under Nero had become no different from the slaves who, working on behalf of Tiberius, seek and bring the *patientias*, those made to endure unnatural lusts, either by gratuities, threats, or force (*Ann.* 6.1.2). The main difference is that Tiberius practices his depravity in the solitude of Capri, whereas Nero makes his depravity a public spectacle, treating the "whole City as his own house" (*Ann.* 15.37.1). Like the careful scrutinizing of words and facial expressions that figures into Tacitus's account of Tiberius's ascension to office, so one now fears to be missing from Nero's spectacles "since many people openly (and more in secret) were on hand to examine the names and faces, the eagerness and sourness, of the assembly" (*Ann.* 16.5.2). Tacitus's image of the theatricality of politics, described at the beginning of this section, now comes full circle: Nero becomes the leader of the theatrical claque, even encouraging brawls (*Ann.* 13.25), all to the raucous applause of the aristocracy. As the boundaries of fantasy and reality dissolve, Rome becomes enveloped in "a world of unreality," to use Woodman's words, a world in which individuals take their cues increasingly from the unknowable will of the emperor.[104]

THE INSTITUTIONALIZATION OF TERROR

In her discussion of the early principate, Levick observes, "The great issue of the late Republic, that of political supremacy in the state, had been fought and lost by the generation of Cicero and Cato. What remained to decide was how to stand in face of the new power: whether to defy, accept, or exploit it."[105] Despotism creates an environment, though, in which any calculation of these choices is made much more difficult. We have already seen how the gradual elimination of mediating functions makes political expression more vulnerable (since expression appears as personal rather than institutional) and political action more volatile (because of the immediacy of the interactions). When Montesquieu talks about the point at which the rising waters flooded the Roman political landscape, he is referring to an additional change in the political environment, the institutionalization of terror under Tiberius. Terror is formalized in procedures, sanctioned by state rewards, and carried out through state institutions. The effect of terror, and I think in this observation lies some of the insight of both Montesquieu and Tacitus, is not measured by a body count but by how it insinuates its way into, and ultimately corrodes, the forces of honor, liberty, and friendship, arguably the central animating principles of Roman political life.[106]

Terror had visited Rome before. The systematic prosecution of enemies had been made into a political tool by Sulla, and Augustus had followed this model—the extent is open to debate—in prosecuting political opponents.[107] Even the *lex maiestatis,* the law of majesty, once a republican concept used to prosecute public misdeeds, had been expanded by Augustus to include libels against leading men and women.[108] But Tiberius's broadening of the *lex maiestatis* to include intimations deemed hostile to the emperor proves to be the culmination for both Tacitus and Montesquieu of the forces of despotism. I say culmination because the form that the *maiestas* prosecutions take would not have been possible if viable institutions to mediate differences and grievances had existed, if alternate paths for political success had remained open (other than through the emperor's court), and if the majesty of the *res publica* had not become located in the body of the sovereign.[109]

The rise of the prosecutions occurs against the backdrop of an unmediated politics. They were kindled by Tiberius's insatiable suspicions.[110] And their sustenance points to how both institutions and norms become transformed into instruments of the emperor's will. Informing, as Tacitus writes, became a "form of life" (*Ann.* 1.74.1). *Maiestas* charges thrived, in part, because they gave easier access to evidence acquired from slaves under torture, evidence that could be used to prosecute other crimes, and because a defendant so charged did not have access to counsel.[111] The *delatores* had real earning power and opportunities for advancement as well, since informers acquired a portion of the estate if the accused were found guilty. Caepio Crispinus, for example, a pioneer in this new profession, showed the way from poverty to riches (*Ann.* 1.74.2).[112] And the prosecutions were supported by the material need to supplement the treasury.[113]

Tacitus portrays the rise of the prosecutions as an ailment or a contagious illness that was destined to eat away (*exedere*) the commonwealth (*Ann.* 2.27.1; 6.7.3; also 1.75.1; 1.73.1; 2.28.3; 4.52.4; 4.30.3; 4.66.1).[114] Drawing a startling comparison to the practice of medicine, and one that recalls his earlier description of the search for a healer in the final decades of the republic, Tacitus writes that "antagonisms, accusations, hatreds, and injustices were being fostered simply in order that the rottenness of the forum would bring money to advocates in the same way as the virulence of disease brought rewards for doctors" (*Ann.* 11.6.2). The physician becomes the purveyor of diseases, seeking not their cure but their spread. In part, such comparisons are common to other authors who identify the actions of the informers as a type of pollution that endangers the community.[115] Tacitus is speaking not just about pollution, though, but about the psychological malady of despotism. The persecutions, as they become institutionalized, contribute to the breakdown of the public cues that orient action.

The most telling point in the rise of the prosecutions (and the loss of traditional cues) occurs when the aristocracy joins together like a mob to bring down others. At that point, the aristocracy, already quick to humiliate itself, passes from degrading to dangerous (*infesta*) (*Ann.* 3.65–66). In describing how Mamercus Scaurus, an ex-consul, Junius Otho, a praetor, and Bruttedius Niger, an aedile, simultaneously seize (*simul corripiunt*) Gaius Silanus with the charge of treason, Tacitus points to the distortion, even inversion, of the traditional cues of aristocratic honor (*Ann.* 3.66.1).[116] Honor, the public recognition of status that is tied to family, position attained, and conduct, orients action by telling the individual nothing less than what is valued, what is virtuous, and what is to be obeyed.[117] Scaurus, in Tacitus's characterization, dishonors his illustrious ancestor, Marcus Scaurus. Junius Othos, elevated to the senate from his crude beginnings as a school teacher, defiles even these lowly origins through his shamelessness (*impudentibus*) and audacity (*ausis*) (*Ann.* 3.66.3). And Bruttedius's ambition, which sought rapid advancement through imperial ranks, "sent to the bottom (*pessum*) many good men" (*Ann.* 3.66.4).[118] Other accusers would join in: first a former quaestor, then his legate, and then the most fluent rhetoricians who press the case against Junius Othos.

The account may read like aristocratic wagons circling to fend off incursions of new men of influence into the camp. Rutledge argues that the *delatores* were actually acting according to traditional Roman motivations and, in fact, would have been "readily appreciated by their republican forebears."[119] In fact, as Rutledge observes, "In their larger social context, then, *delatores* are merely an instrument by which the moral fabric of Caesar's household is maintained, and Caesar's role as head of that *familia* is in essence an extension of the *patria potestas* underlying higher magisterial offices preexisting in the Republic."[120] The point is not that *delatores* are a "unique phenomenon" who act out of motives unknown in Rome before; it is that despotism functions by playing upon traditional motivations—the desire for honor, trust, and influence, for example, or the defense of the household—to ultimately undercut the stability of those markers of political behavior and to transfer the enforcement of those markers increasingly to the *princeps*.[121] In describing the *delatores* as exhibiting *audacia*, for example, Tacitus is employing a political term of disparagement that is applied in the late republic to individuals who display recklessness and unscrupulousness aimed at overthrowing the existing order (*Ann.* 4.1.3; 4.10.2; with 4.67.3).[122] In Tacitus, *audacia* can connote reckless courage or boldness (see, for example, *Ann.* 1.38.2). But the term is more ominously associated with sedition, applied, for example, to the stirrings of a slave war in Italy or the potential turbulence that threatens to overturn a community whenever the emperor or magistrates are absent (*Ann.* 4.27.2; 6.11.2). The sedition that Tacitus ascribes to the *delatores* appears not as the violent overthrow of the political body, but as an ailment that feeds on the vitals of the community, sapping it of the modes of differentiation, distinction, and collective expression that animate political life.[123] Terror's results are not measured by dead bodies, but by the paralysis of the spirit as individuals are isolated from the interactions between family, friends, and the political community.

Tacitus's account of Tiberius's reign (like his account of the reigns of Claudius, Nero, and, likely, Caligula) crescendos to outbreaks of terror that penetrate into even the most intimate of human realms.[124] No conversation (even those that never occurred) and no relationship (even the most intimate ones) were safe from the new "guardians" of the constitution (*Ann.* 4.30.2). Calpurnius Piso, for example, is charged with holding a "private conversation" against Tiberius (*Ann.* 4.21.2). A son prosecutes his father (*Ann.* 4.28). Domitius Afer accuses his mother, Claudia Pulchra (*Ann.* 4.52). Titius Sabinus, still in sorrow over the death of Germanicus, denounces in grief (to Latiaris) both Sejanus and Tiberius in what he believes to be the security of friendship, but was in fact a trap (*Ann.* 4.68.2). As Tacitus remarks more generally, "whether in the forum or at a dinner party, men were censured because each individual was frantic to forestall someone else in marking out a defendant" (*Ann.* 6.7.3).

Even women were not safe. Those who "could not be charged with taking over the state, were indicted for their tears" (*Ann.* 6.10.1). So Vitia, the mother of Fufius Germinus, is executed because she wept for the killing of her son (*Ann.* 6.10.1). The eyes of the friends and relatives of all those executed for complicity with Sejanus are checked for sorrow, as well (*Ann.* 6.19.3). Everyone thought to be connected is executed: "The wreckage stretched indefinitely—every sex, every age, illustrious, ignoble, scattered, or heaped" (*Ann.* 6.19.2).[125] Like the bloodlust that arises from the sight of gladiator fights, a sight that Tiberius avoided previously (*Ann.*

1.76.3–4), the executions now serve to whet his appetite (*Ann.* 6.19.2). There is no refuge: "encounters, dialogues, familiar and unfamiliar ears were avoided; even dumb and inanimate objects such as a roof and walls were treated with circumspection" (*Ann.* 4.69.3). Tacitus at one point characterizes his history as an account not of great deeds but of "savage orders, constant accusations, deceitful friendships, the ruin of innocents and always the same reasons for their extermination that I link together, confronted as I am by a satiety of similar material" (*Ann.* 4.33.3).

Tiberius's actions pale by modern standards of mass persecution. And, in fact, Tacitus's language likely exaggerates the actual number of persons executed by Tiberius.[126] But we should be careful not to miss Tacitus's point. Certainly, the persecutions are magnified because the targets are among the elite. But terror is difficult to measure because it saps the spirit by breaking down the categories by which people orient themselves: public and private, friend and enemy, virtue and vice, thought and expression.[127] If we do not see the mark of the lash on the bodies of the vast majority of the Romans, it is because despotism for Tacitus leaves its impression more on the mind. Tacitus's discussion of Libo's trial, for example, is less a court document and more an exploration of the profound disorientation and growing sense of isolation perpetrated by the prosecutions.[128] Tacitus's discussion becomes a veritable compendium of different types of public and private cues, all of them lost. Friendship: Libo is betrayed by his closest friend. Honor: Tiberius honors Libo with a praetorship and invitations to dinner even while the emperor secretly encourages the prosecution. Expression: Tiberius had buried his anger (*iram condiderat*), showed no strangeness (*alienatus*) in his expression, and no more of a disturbance (*commotior*) in his speech (*Ann.* 2.28.2).[129] Libo, thus, cannot read in Tiberius's expression a sense of the extent of danger, even appealing to the emperor who responds with unmoved expression (*immoto . . . vultu*) (*Ann.* 2.29.2). Law: laws provide no guide, either, since Tiberius invents "a new jurisprudence" in the course of the proceedings, ordering Libo's slaves to be sold to the treasury agent so that they could testify against him (*Ann.* 2.30.3).[130] Family: desperate, Libo wanders from house to house to seek support from his wife's relatives, but is refused. Libo, "exhausted by dread and illness" (*metus et aegritudine fessus*), is carried to the doors of the curia where he reaches out his hands in supplication to an impassive Tiberius (*Ann.* 2.29.2). Even while Libo prepares one last feast, soldiers surround his home, making themselves seen and heard as he sits at his table. Libo commits suicide, so tormented (*excruciatus*) was he by the very banquet that he desired as his last joy (*Ann.* 2.31.1). The sense of the sheer arbitrariness of the proceedings is reinforced when the trial continued "with the same assertiveness" until Tiberius could assert, in a moment of inconsequential magnanimity, that he would have spared Libo's life if he had not hastened to kill himself (*Ann.* 2.31.3; similarly, see 16.11.3).[131]

Like Libo, Othos is left "on his own (*solus*), and ignorant of advocacy, and in a state of dread (*metu*) (which cripples [*debilitat*] even practiced eloquence)" (*Ann.* 3.67.2). And King Archelaus, whom Tiberius seeks to punish for perceived slights while exiled earlier in Rhodes, is ultimately broken, not by the fictitious charges of treason, but through "tension" (*angore*) combined with the weariness of his age (*Ann.* 2.42.3). Tacitus describes the general psychological state as the terror progresses: everyone was "tense and panicked" (*anxia et pavens*) (*Ann.* 4.69.3). Later cases yield the same results. Tacitus comments how Petronius refuses to tolerate "the delay in his fear or hope" that normally accompanies the anticipation of the emperor's cruelty, as well as the desperate flattery that accompanies one's suicide (*Ann.* 16.19.1). There was a habitual sadness (*maestitia*) to the senate, but also a new terror (*pavor*) as they presided over the new round of prosecutions by Nero (*Ann.* 16.29.1). Even reporting the "servile passivity and so much blood wasted at home," as Tacitus comments on his own writing, "wear[ies] the spirit and numb[s] it with sorrowfulness" (*Ann.* 16.16.1).

Understood through its impact on the imagination, terror moves more by rumor than by the sword (*Ann.* 13.37.1). There is no basis for believing that one is ever safe when terror is now enforced by desire and formalized by law, announced from the palace (*Ann.* 6.24.1), reaches back in time to punish old grievances, extends beyond Rome, penetrates into private conversations between intimate friends, and reads thoughts. As the stable props by which one can orient oneself no longer exist, the individual mind is placed at the mercy of "vain imaginings," a form of insanity that expresses itself, as it had in Rome, variously as sadness, hilarity, rebellious violence, and melancholy (Cels. 3.18.3; 3.18.10).

What it means to "decide" to "accept" or even to "defy" imperial power (to recall Levick's terms) takes on a very different complexion under despotism since despotism affects one's ability to even orient oneself.[132] Despotism, Tacitus writes, dissolves the "dealings (*commercium*) which are the human lot," causing compassion to recede as cruelty advances (*Ann.* 6.19.3).[133] *Commercium* is associated with communication and fellowship that occurs between humans, a tie that is severed by the disorienting forces of terror. As Tacitus writes of Domitian's reign, the unleashing of the informers "deprived us even of the give and take of conversation" (*Agric.* 2.3). Prevented from normal outlets of expression, people stop acting from any collective impulse (see *Ann.* 4.12.1), except for punctuated moments of frenzy. More often people slip into a melancholic existence, neither accepting nor defying, but wasting away.[134] As Syme remarks, "It was the acute consciousness of personal insecurity and political impotence that depressed and perverted the morale of the aristocracy. There was no field left them now for action — or even for display."[135] Recounting Domitian's rule, Tacitus describes how the allure of listlessness (*inertiae dulcedo*) comes over (*subit*) us until "the languor we hate at first we learn to love" (*invisa primo desidia postremo amatur*) (*Agric.* 3.1). "Shackled" by silence, the soul is enfeebled (*debilitatur*) and broken down (*frangitur*) (*Dial.* 39.1–2).

Montesquieu, speaking as much from historical sense as the personal experience of a French court that extracted honor from the nobility as the price of privilege, similarly describes how the nobility succumbed to "a common affliction" (*une douleur commune*) (*C* 109), sinking into "dejection" (*abatement*) and "despair" (*désespoir*) (*C* 109). The people, like the eunuchs in Montesquieu's *Persian Letters,* became "conscious of nothing but their impotence" (*C* 133; *Persian* Essay 145). The Roman people, too, fell "ill" (*mal*), succumbing to "despair" (*désespoir*) and nearly a "frightful despondency" with the death of Germanicus because they had vested all their "fears and hopes" in this person (*C* 133). And the spirit of the community was "like a man who, laid low by disease (*maladie*), has no passions because he has not strength" (*S* 19.27).

DESPOTISM AND LIBERTY

The true measure of Rome's slide into despotism was the loss of liberty. As Montesquieu writes, by making speech and writing itself a crime, there was "no longer liberty" nor "even its shadow" (*S* 12.12; also *S* 12.13; *C* 129). Montesquieu himself provides several different, and not completely satisfactory, definitions of liberty that have in common their absence in despotism.[136] There is what might be called a constitutional liberty, which Montesquieu defines as the "right to do everything the laws permit" (*S* 11.3). Despotism undermines constitutional liberty since there are no longer laws that can be known, but only ever-changing wants that must be obeyed. There is also the liberty of citizens in relationship to each other, which Montesquieu defines as "that tranquility of spirit which comes from the opinion each one has of his security" which requires that "one citizen cannot fear another citizen" (*S* 11.6). In a despotic environment, everything from the "outpourings of the heart occasioned by the conversation of two friends" to political satire becomes suspect (*S* 12.13). As the bonds of trust that connect one person to another are broken, individuals become paralyzed by fear.

But there is a third sense of liberty, one that comes into view through our focus on the psychological portrait of despotism. The elevation of the mind — the ability to think, imagine, and judge — depends on the ability to "receive new impressions" (EC 146). Through the exercise of the will, since the will moves the spirit, an individual "creates himself" by knowing and feeling "the proper relation between the thing and himself" (EC 151). Despotism, though, has a stupefying effect as it debases and impoverishes the soul of ideas (see EC 148, 155). The despondency so characteristic of despotic regimes occurs because the mind is "no longer capable of lively movements" (EC 146).[137] The most serious loss of liberty is not the prohibition from speaking, but the loss of the will to speak — the paralysis of the spirit.[138]

When Montesquieu writes that the despotic community is not a union of citizens but "dead bodies buried one next to the other" (*C* 94), he is taking his cue from Tacitus, who points both to the lost lives and the lost souls that accompany despotism. Tacitus, too, recalls both the loss of constitutional liberty and the freedom of conversation. But the loss of liberty plays itself out most dramatically in the languor that comes over the political soul. The "energetic" perish and those who survive do so without ever "opening their lips" (*Agric.* 3.3). Across the political landscape of despotism, freedom flickers in the "free speaking" of Thrasea Paetus that momentarily "explode[s] the servitude of others" (*Ann.* 14.49.1) or in Lucius Vetus's "life lived next to freedom" (*Ann.* 16.11.1). Lucius Vetus's final act of freedom, before undertaking the suicide with his daughter and mother-in-law, is to refuse to name Nero as his majority heir. Tacitus's recounting of Octavia's brief life provides perhaps the most poignant image of the anxiety of existence under despotism as individuals are suspended between life and death: knowing they cannot survive, but not able to "rest in death" (*Ann.* 14.64.1).

THE HISTORIAN'S TASK

Montesquieu's attraction to Rome, like that of Machiavelli's, is unabashed. As Montesquieu proclaims, "One can never leave the Romans; thus it is that even today in their capital one leaves the new palaces to go in search of the ruins; thus it is that the eye that has rested on flower-strewn meadows likes to look at rocks and mountains" (*S* 11.13). Yet, Montesquieu's relationship to the Romans has always been difficult to reconcile with judgments about his intellectual contribution. Viewed as a social scientist, Montesquieu's seeming flights of fancy in recalling images of the Roman past stand uneasily with what is seen as his new, comparative methodology of social science.[139] As a historian, Montesquieu's analysis of the Romans appears flawed because, as scholars are quick to note, he neither compared nor examined the reliability of his sources.[140] As a political theorist, Montesquieu's discussion seems "hasty" and "episodic."[141] And as a proponent of particular forms of social life, Montesquieu's praise of Rome is diminished by his own critical stance toward Rome and by newer concerns, such as that of commerce, which cannot be found in this Roman past.[142] Even Levin, who provides one of the most extensive treatments of the classical roots of Montesquieu's thought, feels compelled to "disentangle" Montesquieu's ideas from the " 'chaotic mass of good things gone astray' " to identify a political doctrine.[143]

Those who have sought to locate the Roman contribution to Montesquieu's thought have largely focused on Livy. There is certainly support for Montesquieu's use of Livy. Montesquieu cites Livy extensively in his account of Roman development. And Montesquieu, too, seems to draw at points on the importance that Livy attributes to spectacles, though Montesquieu seems more to report than recreate these Livian moments (see *S* 11.15). Strikingly, Montesquieu criticizes Livy both for his rhetorical embellishments and his inability to enliven the past (*C* 55).[144] Furthermore, Livy can take Montesquieu only so far; namely, to the growth of the republic and premonitions of its decline. Livy cannot be found in Montesquieu's analysis of Rome's descent into despotism. Shackleton himself notes, after discussing Livy's influence, that Montesquieu must seek "non-European examples" for his description of despotism.[145]

And thus in interpreting Montesquieu's depiction of despotism, scholars almost universally look to accounts of the East, notably Persia, Turkey, and China.[146] Since the East was seen by Montesquieu as always, and perhaps naturally, subject to despotism, what is considered by many as the "basis" of his political theory and a warning to France appears, instead, as a "caricature" of the East, the least developed of his ideas, and essentially static.[147] The very monstrousness of despotism is often taken to point to its simplicity (see *C* 138, 140). Owing in no small part to some of Montesquieu's own characterizations, despotism appears as a stark, empty void: "uniform and simple," the "social equivalent of death," and "subpolitical."[148] Boesche expresses surprise that Montesquieu's notion of despotism, characterized "by fear, violence, isolation, and a general poverty supporting at best a subsistence living," also contains elements of "avarice, pleasure, urbanization, and at least enough production and commerce to distribute luxuries to some significant portion of the population."[149] And in describing the mechanisms by which despotism operates, Krause claims, "Fear not only arises automatically in despotism, but also has automatic effects."[150] There is "no need of education" because fear "is so well supported by instinct."[151]

These characterizations, though, follow from an essentially static model of despotism in which people have known only fear. Yet, in Montesquieu's relationship to Tacitus, what emerges is a subtler exploration of the sinew that connects and gives movement to the despotic political body. The tyrant may be able to change laws and institutions, but despotism, as a character of a community, requires a slower and more complex transformation in the habits and mores of a people. Despotism is not noisy; it is not sudden; it is not simple; and it is not always even uncomfortable. Despotism, instead, "gains its end" by "slowly grinding away" (*S* 14.13): an inexorability that over decades can deprive the nobility of their dignity and the people of their liberty.

If such a profound disorientation associated with despotism has so pervaded the soul of the community, then what is the role of the historian? Syme places Tacitus's vocation in the context of a senatorial tradition in which, mature in his years and exhausted from political battle, he retired to assert "a personal claim to glory and survival."[152] Tacitus's observations are impassioned: an attack on tyranny, a criticism of extremism, and a call to civic duty.[153] Mendell characterizes Tacitus's approach as "hardly that of a political theorist" but of a "good citizen shocked at the abuse of power."[154] Fornara connects Tacitus to the "bitter diagnostic style" of Sallust. Tacitus, as a senatorial historian in the age of empire, plays the role of "judge and jury" of the "tyrannous and base government[s]" under the emperors.[155] Marincola sees Tacitus as probing "beneath the surface" to "inquire into the truth behind the appearances of domestic policies at Rome."[156] Sinclair argues similarly that Tacitus's "procedure of 'looking beneath the surface' " is an attempt "to enlarge his reader's understanding of social reality by rending the veil of deception that surrounds so much of political life."[157] And in one recent reading of Tacitus, the disjunction between the real and ideal is seen as serving as an "ironic commentary" on the "position of the historian."[158] Alienation makes the historian's task possible by rendering all solutions, including the recollection of a republican past, incomplete, thus allowing a story to always be told.

I do not see Tacitus's task as avoiding "totality" in the name of irony. Writing in the dawn of despotism's retreat, Tacitus hardly seems to fear the looming terror of republican totality. Tacitus identifies, instead, the most extreme disorientation and melancholy caused by the altered world of despotism. Great men, when not seduced by greed, are afraid to speak or act. The political landscape of the despotic world lacks more than great deeds, though. If rhetoric is the way in which individuals construct themselves as citizens, as Connolly suggests in her discussion of Cicero, then the transformation of rhetoric in the imperial period alters the very nature of citizenship.[159] The "majority," as Tacitus recounts, "are taught by what happens to others" (*Ann.* 4.33.2), experiences that systematically denied memory. The altered political world of despotism is one in which few men are able to "distinguish the honorable from the baser" (*Ann.* 4.33.2) because there is no longer the public practice of judgment.

The weakness of despotism is that it must extinguish the memory of succeeding ages to effectively deny experience and expression. As Tacitus remarks of life under Domitian, "we should have lost memory itself as well as voice, had forgetfulness been as easy as silence" (*Agric.* 2.3). O'Gorman interprets this statement as suggesting that since "memory is silent," it "therefore has no perpetuation beyond the individual senators." Memory, because it cannot become history, "fails to be a vehicle for some future redemption of history."[160] But memory does leave its traces, which are difficult to completely expunge. Not that efforts to extinguish memory are not made. Augustus institutes public bonfires to burn offensive literature.[161] Both Augustus and Tiberius prosecute Cassius Severus, a man "hated and feared for his bitter tongue and incorrigible love of independence."[162] He is banished initially to Crete but when not silenced, he is stripped of his estate and sent to the rocks of Seriphus. And individuals can be legally removed from memory.[163] The difficulty of destroying all traces of memory is suggested, though, by the case of Cremutius Cordus, who is charged with publishing a history that praised Brutus and Cassius and, more damagingly, listed the authors of the proscriptions (*Ann.* 4.34–35). Memory, Cremutius declares to the senate, is enshrined in history (*Ann.* 4.35.2). Indeed, even with Cremutius's condemnation, self-starvation, and the burning of his books, copies of his account remain, "concealed and published" (*Ann.* 4.35.4). Veiled in the quiet of the despotism, genius punished grows in authority, eventually testifying against the malady of the age (*Ann.* 4.35.5).

The importance of memory for Tacitus, though, is not that it serves as a vehicle of redemption as much as an anchor of sanity. When Tacitus breaks the silence, he is puncturing the unreality of despotism that is fostered in fear, timidity, and isolation. The first duty of history, as Tacitus remarks, is to provide a record of this past "to prevent virtues from being silenced and so that crooked words and deeds should be attended by the dread of posterity and infamy" (*Ann.* 3.65.1; see also *Ann.* 4.33). In reversing the imperceptible way in which individuals suffer from the vain imaginings of a despotic realm, Tacitus's historiography is not simply diagnostic or evaluative, but curative.

If Tacitus's writings fly in the face of traditional modes of historiographic method, it may have a great deal to do with this task of restoring the lost sentiments of a political self. The treatment of insanity, as Celsus writes, requires that the mind of the patient be "slowly and imperceptibly" turned from vain imaginings to something more real (Cels. 3.18.11; see also 1.3.2). There are a variety of ways in which such changes may be effected, but all of them seem aimed at prompting the patient to recall whatever glimmers of sanity might remain. Fears must be allied and hope put forward (Cels. 3.18.10, 18); one's "interest" might be "awakened" by recalling activities that once excited the individual, such as having a patient read who likes literature (Cels. 3.18.11); patients should be "pressed to recite anything they can remember" (Cels. 3.18.11); and the spirit, in the case of melancholy, should be agitated (Cels. 3.18.22).

There can be "no beauty," as Tacitus remarks, "where the veins are prominent, or where one can count the bones: sound healthful blood must fill out the limbs, and riot over the muscles, concealing the sinews in turn under a ruddy complexion and a graceful exterior" (*Dial.* 21.8). But an altered world, as Tacitus notes in his *Dialogue on Oratory*, requires novel forms of eloquence (*Dial.* 19.2; 19.5). An audience no longer trained to hear argument and no longer used to public expression will be bored unless roused by a "striking and memorable utterance" (*Dial.* 20.4; also 28.2). In Tacitus's vivisection of the political body, he wants us to count the bones; he wants to peel away the skin to see the tortured soul. And this he does through the asymmetrical, often jarring syntax that highlights pretext, juxtaposes truth and falsehood, and emphasizes the discordant relationship between events.[164] The "obsession with variety," as Kraus and Woodman describe it—the changing of narrative modes, the unexpected sentence constructions, and the variation and misuse of technical words—does more than reflect the "essential truths" of the despotic world.[165] It agitates, prods, provokes, and awakens the community from its despotic slumber.[166] These moments might then be remembered and passed on to others (*Dial.* 20.4), reversing the course of despotic amnesia. As Montesquieu writes, in emulating the "sententious" style of Tacitus, to write well one must skip (*sauter*) the intermediate ideas just enough not to be boring but not so much as not to be understood (*Pensées* 802; see also *S* 11.20, 28.45).[167]

Montesquieu's works, like Tacitus's, become the artful response to the "dull rasp" of politics (*S* 14.13). Since servitude "begins with drowsiness," as Montesquieu writes, "a people who rest in no situation, who constantly pinch themselves to find the painful spots, could scarcely fall asleep" (*S* 14.13). To counter the debilitating effect of despotism, the political thinker extends the gaze from one's narrow preoccupations and introduces sensations, not just by portraying the infinite variety of experiences, but by exciting the soul by carrying it from one pleasure to another.[168]

If Montesquieu is engaged in a veiled (or not so veiled) critique of Louis XIV as despotic, then Montesquieu could find no better model than Tacitus, whose first essay, on Agricola, broke "the fifteen years of silence and humiliation" under Domitian.[169] It is the loss of communication that makes despotism so stark and so difficult to change precisely because people lose their political bearings. Tacitus's legacy in political thought does not lie in the construction, as Montesquieu would say of Malebranche, of "a magnificent palace in the air" that is "concealed from the eyes" and "lost in the clouds."[170] Tacitus, instead, makes visible an invisible reality: the mental map by which we navigate the political terrain. The problem of despotism, so Tacitus and Montesquieu seem to suggest, is that it isolates a person from the stable props by which one can confirm one's impressions and anticipate reactions. To explain this experience, both Tacitus and Montesquieu look to a medical language of insanity as much as any conventional political vocabulary to understand its virulence and its persistence. But Tacitus leaves us with a problem. He can perhaps awaken us. But where do we go from there? Since despotism extinguishes the integrity of public meaning, neither Cicero's call to care for the world nor Livy's attempt to reanimate felt meanings provides suitable solutions. In the final chapter, we turn to the question of how the political actor may find his or her bearings in a realm bereft of public meaning.

5

Seneca and Foucault

Restoring the Jurisdiction of the Political

No less for Seneca than for Tacitus, the politics of imperial Rome plays itself out in the hidden recesses of the human imagination. Seneca certainly experienced the vicissitudes of Roman political life: he was exiled by Claudius in 41 CE, recalled and appointed to a praetorship in 49 CE, acted as tutor and advisor to Nero, and was ultimately sentenced to death. "Even more than Tacitean history," Segal observes, "Senecan tragedy responds to this atmosphere of corruption by studying the soul's forced exploration of its innermost dark places."[1] Seneca's dramatic language parallels this shadowy existence: "The distortions and exaggerations of his language, the insistent grimness of his imagery, the deliberate vagueness of locale all create a realm that seems to float free of time and space," enveloping individuals in a "nightmarish atmosphere."[2]

Although scholars have often sought to separate Seneca's dramatic from his more sober (some even say "vapid") philosophic writings, I think we can read the *Epistles* as similarly inhabiting this interior realm.[3] The *Epistles* echo with images of madness: "shadowy terrors" (*tenebrae*) (*Ep.* 49.11), the "madness" (*demens*) and lassitude (*lassitudo*) that accompany our anticipation of the future (*Ep.* 74.33; see also *Ep.* 13.12), terrors (*metus*) and dangers (*pericula*) through which the soul must navigate (*Ep.* 74.21), the similarity between the "insanity (*insaniam*) of people in general" who suffer from false opinions and the insanity that is subject to medical treatment (*Ep.* 94.17), the comparison of life without philosophy to the life of a "madman" (*furiosi*) or "lunatic" (*phrenetici*) (*Ep.* 15.1), the Forum as dangerous to the mind that is recovering from its sickness (*Ep.* 28.6), the witty individuals who are seen "to laugh to excess and to rage to excess" (*acerrime ridere et acerrime rabere*) (*Ep.* 29.7), the disquiet (*inquieta*) that often parades as quiet (*quies*) (*Ep.* 56.8), the contagiousness of fear (*Ep.* 74.4), even the sense that the Stoic looks like a madman (*demens*) or lunatic (*alienatus*) (*Ep.* 85.24).

This language of madness speaks to Seneca's own exploration of the profound disorientation that accompanies the disintegration of public boundaries and the simultaneous insinuation of the political world into one's fantasies and fears. Yet, extracting a political argument from the *Epistles* has proven to be rather difficult for several reasons. First, the *Epistles*, with their mix of fact and fiction and with Seneca's seeming reluctance to refer to contemporaneous events, do not tell us a lot about imperial politics.[4] Attempts to infer events from passing allusions in Seneca's text turn out to be quite difficult. Second, Seneca is not a philosophic hero if we mean by that that he, like the figure of Socrates whose death he sought to emulate, was able to maintain the purity of his philosophic principles in his political life. Only with considerable caution, and even then without much success, can we make some assessment of the role that philosophy may have played in guiding his political actions under Claudius and then Nero. And that assessment seems to confirm Griffin's understated judgment of Seneca as never a man of "rigid principle."[5] Indeed,

Seneca's praise in *De Clementia* of Nero's innocence after the murder of Britannicus, Claudius's son, should tell us that Seneca was willing to cut some corners. From a comparison of his philosophic principles and political life, Seneca's *Epistles* come across to many commentators as uncritical, hypocritical, or self-justificatory.[6]

The third difficulty a political theorist faces is that the *Epistles*, like much of Roman imperial writing, seem to signal a retreat from the political world. Wolin, in his discussion of political thought in imperial Rome, concludes that "the 'moral' had overridden the 'political,' because the moral and the 'good' had come to be defined in relation to what transcended a determinate society existing in time and space" by finding refuge in a politicized nature: universal citizenship governed by natural law and justice.[7] Littlewood, speaking generally about Seneca's writings, sees Seneca's declamations of "disengagement and withdrawal from an irredeemably corrupt world" as characteristic of Seneca's "isolationist brand of Stoicism."[8] And Edwards describes Seneca's letters as "turned not towards the outside world of Roman political life but rather inwards."[9] By turning inward and "abandoning the world, the shared locus of human activity and human meaning," Seneca, as Littlewood concludes, "has abandoned any conceptual space for self-definition."[10]

Against the backdrop of these received interpretations, Michel Foucault's attempt to discern a political ethic in Seneca (specifically) and the Stoics (generally) can only be described as rather unexpected. Foucault's analysis in volume 3 of *The History of Sexuality* begins with the collapse of the ancient city-state, which, as he notes, has often been seen as "evidence of a general withdrawal from political life in a place where civic activities had constituted for citizens a true vocation" (*CS* 81).[11] Foucault suggests that "rather than imagining a reduction or cessation of political activities through the effects of a centralized imperialism, one should think in terms of the organization of a complex space," one that is "much vaster" and "much more discontinuous" than would have existed for the small city-states (*CS* 82). In this new space, and we saw this in the previous chapter, the "rules of the political game" change; the external signs of status correlate less and less with one's functions, activities, obligations, and power (*CS* 84). There is no longer an ethical relationship between "what one was, what one could be, and what one was expected to accomplish" (*CS* 84). Two responses emerge as an attempt to make sense of oneself as an "acting subject" (*CS* 85). One response is to cling to the visible signs of the Roman hierarchic society by emphasizing such status markers as physical bearing, clothing, gestures, and spending. A second response is to turn toward exercising increasing control over oneself as a response to the decreasing control that one has over external events and circumstances. The recourse to developing one's relationship to oneself would depend as little as possible on the maintenance of external signs of status or power. Although this turning to oneself would lead some philosophic circles to advise that one should withdraw from political activity, the emphasis on the return to oneself, Foucault argues, is less focused on drawing a line between "participation and abstention" and is "more concerned to define the principle of a relation to self that will make it possible to set the forms and conditions in which political action, participation in the offices of power, the exercise of a function, will be possible or not possible, acceptable or necessary" (*CS* 86).

Foucault's interpretation of Seneca has been greeted with something of a mixed reception: classicists seem as suspicious of Foucault as political theorists do of Seneca.[12] The true oddity of Foucault's use of Seneca is that Foucault would find himself so fond of a philosopher who sought to bring human practice into conformity with a universal, rational, and natural order.[13] Many commentators justifiably point out that Foucault perhaps overstates the subjective aspects of Stoicism, the range of possibilities of self-transformation available to the individual, and understates the objective aspects, the aim or end of that transformation in truth.[14] But lost in the intellectual shuffle is what I think is one of Foucault's important insights into Seneca, and what sheds some light on what was at least in part Foucault's affinity for the Stoic philosopher: the political role of thought.

Thought, as Foucault explains, "is not what inhabits a certain conduct and gives it its meaning; rather, it is what allows one to step back from this way of acting or reacting, to present it to oneself as an object of thought and to question it as to its meaning, its conditions, and its goals."[15] Through thought one does not simply analyze social ideas, historical forces, or ideologies; rather, one occupies a "vantage point" by which one can explore the "topography" of the self as it is shaped by the questions, practices, and goals employed by these political, social, and cultural forces.[16] Thought, to place this discussion in the trajectory of Foucault's scholarship, provides the way in which one becomes aware both of the ways in which forms of knowledge are constituted and defined and of the effects of that knowledge as it is organized and instrumentalized in relations of power. Thought, in other words, allows us to establish ourselves as an object of our own thinking and to see ourselves in our relationship to the sociocultural world of which we are a part.

An exploration of the political world begins for Foucault when we pose our political experience as a problem. This problematization, to use Foucault's term, can begin easily enough: what are the practices, beliefs, and thoughts by which society operates? What is the attainability of these expectations? How am I implicated in these expectations? What has been the effect of attempting to attain these expectations? I want to emphasize that for Foucault the material for problematizing one's relationship to the political world is, itself, the language and expectations of politics. Through thought one begins to give expression to, and thus give shape to, one's own experiences of political life. Or, as Foucault frames it, thought frees thought from what it silently thinks (*UP* 9).[17] That silent thinking is the social, cultural, and personal history that underlies and invisibly guides what we understand as our goals, hopes, capabilities, and possibilities. Thought, thus, can become political as it contributes to what Allen describes as "the power to modify the way individuals symbolize and interpret what they understand as their options or occasions for choice: liberties to be anticipated, repudiated, exercised, or denied."[18]

Foucault's language can get opaque, so let me lay out how I see Foucault's argument fitting into a Roman context. Foucault's suggestion that thought frees thought from what it silently thinks points to a central problem of despotism; namely, how thought loses its bearings by which it can orient itself. Despotism operates by eroding boundaries: legal and illegal, public and private, true and false, moral and immoral, innocent and guilty, and real and unreal. And in eroding these boundaries, despotism makes the self, in its relationship to the political world, increasingly unrecognizable and unknowable. Seneca's *Epistles*, from this perspective, serve as an activity of political thought. Through these letters, Seneca reflects on the experience of political life, seeking first to illuminate the contours of the despotic world by locating the self in this unbounded landscape and then to begin to restore the contours of the political self.

SUBJECTIVITY

Lest it appear that we are rapidly descending into anachronism, we should defend an assumption that underlies these claims: namely, that individuals are both aware of and capable of reflecting on themselves. For the Stoics, all living things are born with a primitive sort of self-awareness that activates an impulse toward self-preservation.[19] This attachment to oneself is what is referred to as *oikeiôsis*, a verbal noun that is translated into Latin in its verbal form as *conciliari* or the reflexive *sibi conciliari*.[20] Every living thing, Seneca writes, is attached to its own constitution (*constitutioni suae conciliari*) (*Ep.* 121.14; also 121.24: *conciliationem et caritatem sui*) and "has been entrusted to his own self" (*sibi . . . commissus est*) (*Ep.* 121.18). The claim is both descriptive and evaluative. Descriptively, we are provided with a faculty for avoiding what is dangerous to us (*Ep.* 121.20; also 121.23). Prescriptively, we are entrusted to act consistently, or in conformity (*homologia* = *concordia*), with what belongs to us and to lead a life "of vigilance and care" (*tutelae et diligentiae*) to avoid what is destructive to us (*Ep.* 121.20; also 121.23).

Even in its most primitive stage, the attachment to oneself creates a view of the world from the perspective of oneself. Seneca notes, "Since I gauge all my actions with reference to my own welfare, I am looking out for myself before all else" (*Ep.* 121.17). But as reasoning creatures, we also become conscious of ourselves as the "*bearer* of consciousness."[21] Such consciousness, as Engberg-Pedersen writes, "may be said to *create* a proper self (an I) that will constitute an unchangeable point of view from which everything *outside* that self will henceforth be seen."[22] As Seneca at one point enjoins Lucilius, employing this language of sight, you must act according to how you see yourself (*qualis tibi videaris*) rather than how others (*qualis aliis*) see you (*Ep.* 29.11; also 6.1).[23]

Through reflection, one comes to see oneself as belonging to a larger, rationally ordered system and to be concerned with acquiring knowledge about the value of objects in the world.[24] Such reflection, though, moves the Stoic both upwards in a process that Hadot describes as "rais[ing] oneself to universality."[25] And such reflection also moves the Stoic downward into "the lived experience of ourselves as concrete, living and perceiving subjects."[26] Speaking generally about Roman Stoicism, Reydams-Schils similarly notes that the individual is embedded ontologically and socially: "On the ontological level, this embeddedness indicates that the self is anchored both in a body and in a rational order that, Stoics would claim, structures all of reality as ultimately proceeding from an immanent divine principle. The social counterpart to this ontological aspect indicates that the self is intrinsically connected to others in a network of relationships that each has its specific claims and standards of behavior."[27] We "hate solitude," as Seneca writes, desire society, and, in fact, are expected to act politically (*Ep.* 9.17; *De Ot.* 3.2; also *Ep.* 6.4).

The Stoics claim that nothing in the external world can harm the moral virtue of the individual. But the individual does not become virtuous in isolation. In fact, in isolation the individual does not even become an agent capable of initiating action. Seneca writes of how "our powers can never inspire in us implicit faith in ourselves" (*Ep.* 13.1). Rather, we acquire knowledge of ourselves in our experience of the world. We will refuse to be under the "jurisdiction" (*arbitrium*) of that which is alien to us only when "many difficulties have confronted us on this side and on that, and have occasionally even come to close quarters with us" (*Ep.* 13.1). As Foucault writes, in language that captures some of the interactive nature of Stoic self-awareness, "By thought, I mean what establishes, in a variety of possible forms, the play of true and false, and which as a consequence constitutes the human being as a subject of learning; in other words, it is the basis for accepting or refusing rules, and constitutes human beings as social and juridical subjects; it is what establishes the relation with oneself and with others, and constitutes the human being as an ethical subject."[28]

Contained in both Seneca's and Foucault's claim is a notion of "jurisdiction": what are the extent and the limits of the power of that which is alien to me? Under the best of circumstances the external world seduces with its charms, inviting us to hand over any control of ourselves to the rule of license. But for Seneca, I will suggest, despotism is far more pernicious because its jurisdiction is boundless, subverting the operation of consciousness by undermining the ability of the mind to distinguish between the "boundaries" (*modi*) of truth and the boundlessness of the wordless and worldless imagination.

PROBLEMATIZING POLITICS

I have attempted to lay the groundwork, by way of Stoic psychology, for approaching Seneca's *Epistles* as a work of political thought. We can understand Seneca's turn inward as an exploration of the ways in which the political world comes to inhabit us. Political thinking, from this perspective, does not stand outside the world, but uses the political vocabulary of the time to reflect on the aspirations and experiences of political life — on what thought silently thinks. I want to now focus on three of these aspects of Roman political life that occupy Seneca's political thought: authority, recognition, and Fortune. Authority and recognition constitute the primary ways in which one locates oneself in the Roman political world. They ratify one's status, confer honor, grant power, and ensure remembrance. They, in short, are critical components of how one represents and differentiates oneself, both as an ethical and political subject. The question that Seneca addresses, though, is what happens when these markers become perverted by despotism. Where does one go? Who does one become? Seneca's *Epistles* become an exploration of how the individual gets caught in the discourses appropriated by despotism. One becomes unable to escape the language of authority and recognition that plays such an important part in defining one's worth as a person (*existimatio*), even as the terms are deprived of their meaning. Ultimately, a picture of the despotic world emerges in Seneca's analysis through a highly politicized reading of Fortune that empties the political world of difference, distinction, and value.

Authority without Jurisdiction

Rome's contribution to the Western political tradition, indeed to innovations in which the Romans themselves took great pride, was the identification of the individual as a political and juridical subject. As Mommsen writes, "The formal sovereignty of the people was expressed in the first instance in jurisdiction."[29] Politics and law defined individuals and bound individuals to each other and to the state. Law defined one's status: free or slave; type of freedom (either by birth or by grant of freedom from slavery); type of citizenship (Roman, Latin, or peregrines); independence of the citizen, and of those who were independent, whether they were under guardianship, under caretakership, or neither.[30] Law also defined a host of attendant rights and obligations: taxation, marriage, inheritance, ownership, commerce, political office, military service, and civil protections.[31] And law served as the formal (and often not so formal) expression of mutual duties (*officia*) that, as Nicolet writes, "preexisted all law and were contemporary to the foundation of the city itself."[32] Such duties encompassed political, military, social, and familial responsibilities. Enmeshed, as well, in this network of mutual obligations was the notion of authority (*auctoritas*), a distinctly Roman concept that, as we saw with Livy, was premised both on the founding of communities and on the subsequent reenactment and renovation of this foundation. Individuals, as the inheritors of this political past, were bound to the state just as they were obligated to their ancestors. With the rise of Augustus, that initiative (or reenactment) "would be carried out under Augustus' *auctoritas*," tying the significance and political meaningfulness of actions increasingly to the approval of the emperor.[33]

Seneca does not, and probably cannot, place himself outside these core assumptions of Roman political life.[34] The traces of the juridical self appear continually throughout the pages of Seneca's *Epistles*: of common law, statute, guardianship, judgment, imperial decree, imperial edicts, injury, jurisdiction, arbiter, authority, law, and duty.[35] Seneca, for example, affirms the underlying assumption of the Roman juridical self when he writes that duty is imposed by honor and encompasses the responsibilities of a good citizen, a good friend, and a good son as well as responsibilities to humanity, generally (*Ep.* 71.28; 93.4; 95.51).

The fulfillment of one's duties does not come without danger, though. In *On Leisure* (*De Otio*), Seneca provides a list of reasons why a person, though directed to engage in public affairs, might seek "safe retreat" from a corrupt state (*De Ot.* 3.4; also *De Tranq. An.* 5.5). And Seneca warns Lucilius of the increasing duties that he will inherit with his rise in political status (*Ep.* 19.5; also 19.8). But by the time of the *Epistles* the hope of safe retreat seems less and less an option. Seneca's life testifies to the difficulty of removing oneself from the physical reach of an increasingly corrupt and dangerous government. More than that, though, the *Epistles* explore the ways in which despotism perverts the legal and political categories by which we define ourselves, transforming the juridical self into a trap that binds the individual to unreality.[36]

Foucault notes that one change that occurs in Roman politics is that one becomes implicated in a complex interplay of power that, among other things, dissolves traditional hierarchy (see *CS* 92). Habinek and Shaw further confirm this dissolution of traditional hierarchy, pointing to the growing conflicts between birth and achievement, and between insider and outsider status, that inhere in Roman society at the time.[37] I do not want to understate the socioeconomic forces that underlie the transformation in status relations. Nor would I disagree with Habinek that Seneca's argument is conditioned, at least in part, by aristocratic and hierarchical sentiments that emphasize privilege and distinction (albeit based on criteria of achievement rather than birth). But Seneca is doing more than advocating for a new aristocracy. When he decries the change in status relations, he is pointing, not unlike Tacitus later, to the subversion of morals that underlies the political categories of governance so that there are neither reliable markers of authority nor limits to its jurisdiction (*Ep.* 95.29).

In the loss of boundaries lies madness. When Seneca exclaims, "We are mad, not only individually, but publicly" (*Non privatim solum, sed publice furimus*), he is employing a notion of madness that Cicero associates with having lost power (*exisse ex potestate*) over oneself because of fear, pain, lust, or wrath (*Ep.* 95.30; trans. modified; *Tusc.* 3.5.11). To have power over oneself requires a sense of limits: limits on what others can do to you, and limits on what you yourself can do. But the individual, as Seneca continues, no longer learns the proper limit (*modum novit*) of action because the experience of the political world teaches the opposite (*Ep.* 95.30). The political world has made itself master over us, but it is mastery that rests on criminality (*Ep.* 95.32). Individual crimes may still be punished, but official crimes at a much larger magnitude are celebrated: "We check manslaughter and isolated murders; but what of war and the much-vaunted crime of slaughtering whole peoples" (*Ep.* 95.30)? Cruelties (*saeva*), a term often associated with lawless tyranny, are now "practised in accordance with acts of senate and popular assembly, and the public is bidden to do what is forbidden to the individual" (*Ep.* 95.30).[38] Even Seneca's appeal for mercy suggests the change in the legal system. Where legal action is bound by procedure, the arbiter (in this case, the emperor) is "hampered by no bonds" (*De Ben.* 3.7.5).[39]

We might expect Seneca to associate this growing lawlessness with increasing concentration of power in a few hands and increasing powerlessness by the vast majority of people. He, instead, signals how deeply these perversions of power infiltrate all aspects of one's being. At its most general level, Rome's murderous lust undermines the traits of sympathy and sociability, the natural basis of a community sense (*sensus communis*) (see *Ep.* 5.4). As Seneca writes, "Man, an object of reverence in the eyes of man, is now slaughtered for jest and sport" (*Ep.* 95.33). But at a more specific level, such criminality becomes a mode of political action, practiced not by one but a thousand tyrants. The "temper" of the political times, Seneca writes, causes us to be "driven into wild rage by our luxurious lives, so that whatever does not answer to our whims arouses our anger" (*Ep.* 47.19). Like kings, we "insist" that we have "received an injury" (*iniuriam*), a legal term, so that we "may inflict them" (*Ep.* 47.20). The violence of the political times also rends the soul. "I shall be torn asunder (*distrahar*) or rather pulled to pieces" (*discerpar*) by the struggle between ambition, anger, and pleasure (*Ep.* 51.8), a tearing apart that Tacitus will later associate with the emergence of Tiberius.[40] Even if given great power (*magna potentia*), we, like Tiberius, would similarly make ungoverned (*inpotenter*) use of it (*Ep.* 42.3).

When such untempered violence comes to rule over the soul, then the political landscape, with its gradations of expectations, obligations, privileges, and power, dissolves into an undifferentiated rule of fear. Fear, as Seneca notes, places the individual under another's power (*aliena potentia*) (*CS* 92; *Ep.* 14.4). The problem is that the political sources of fear are not from one person but from many: "It is sometimes the people that we ought to fear; or sometimes a body of influential oligarchs in the Senate, if the method of governing the State is such that most of the business is done by that body; and sometimes individuals equipped with power by the people and against the people" (*Ep.* 14.7). The individual, as Foucault remarks, is "exposed on all sides" (*CS* 92). Slaves hold power over their masters (*Ep* 4.8; 47.5). Friends conspire against friends (*Ep.* 101.15). Children are sacrificed by their parents (*Ep.* 101.15). Political functionaries, as they thirst to become lords of many, become slaves of the desire for more (*Ep.* 9.22). And suggestive of the new equality, Cato, the last republican hero for Seneca, is condemned by both the mob and tyrant (*Ep.* 14.13).[41] "Everyone," Seneca writes, "possesses the power which inspires . . . fear" (*Ep.* 4.8).

Seneca does seem to suggest that with caution one can counter the hope, envy, hatred, fear, and contempt that motivate individuals to do evil (*Ep.* 105.1). Each motivation poses its own challenges for the person seeking to navigate through the political realm: hope can be avoided by "possessing nothing remarkable" (*Ep.* 105.3); envy can be escaped "if you do not force yourself upon the public view" (*Ep.* 105.3); fear can be tempered by a moderate disposition; contempt by "honourable occupations" and by influential friendships (*Ep.* 105.6); and hatred by not provoking others. But Seneca's qualifications seem more to unsettle. Hatred, for example, may be "uncalled for" and people can crave "even little things" (*Ep.* 105.3–4). Moreover, "flattery resembles friendship," even surpassing it for "wide-open and indulgent ears" (*Ep.* 45.7). Thus, the environment imposes an enormous price: an admonition by Seneca not to "trust the countenance of those you meet" (*Ep.* 103.2). One must, instead, "[keep] still—talking very little with others, and as much as may be with yourself" (*Ep.* 105.6).[42] We arrive where Tacitus does: at the breakdown of the bonds of human conversation.

To escape the madness of a political world without boundaries, the individual might seek stillness in some private existence. Seneca writes of his own "seclusion" that he sought out of "apprehension" (*timor*) and "weariness" (*lassitudo*) (*Ep.* 56.9). And he allows us to peer into the recesses of this despotic quiet where individuals, haunted by fear, "shrink into dark corners," burying their secrets deep in their heart and distrusting even themselves (*Ep.* 3.4). In fact, Seneca refers to this retreat as banishment (*Ep.* 55.5). In such seclusion one then enters a similarly boundless terrain of the imagination. The products of our imagination (for all but the sage) lack any limits or any standard by which to judge what is real because we are prone by habit to exaggerate (*augere*), imagine (*fingere*), and anticipate (*praecipere*) pain and sorrow (*Ep.* 13.5, 7). But perhaps most troubling is that such solitude produces, even in a better sort of person, a false quiet (*quies*) (*Ep.* 3.5), a quiet (as we saw) that Tacitus associates with despotism, as well. This quiet has a "pretence of soundness" (*simulata sanitate*) (*Ep.* 56.10), one that is actually "slackness and langor" (*dissolutio et languor*) (*Ep.* 3.5).[43] The individual who flees from human affairs ends up living like a "frightened and sluggish animal" in which even "sluggishness" (*inertia*) assumes "an air of authority (*auctoritatem*) with us" (*Ep.* 55.5). We find ourselves under the jurisdiction of our vain and limitless imaginings.

Perhaps the most telling image of this seclusion emerges in Seneca's recounting of Vatia, a wealthy praetorian and descendent of a politically active family. Vatia knew "how to hide" from the treachery of Tiberius's court (*Ep.* 55.4): "For whenever men were ruined by their friendship with Asinius Gallus," who died of starvation in a dungeon under Tiberius, "whenever others were ruined by their hatred of Sejanus, and later by their intimacy with him," people would say, "O Vatia, you alone know how to live" (*Ep.* 55.3). But, as Seneca observes, Vatia did not know how to live. Seneca remarks satirically on this living death: whenever he drove past Vatia's villa, where the dwelling places were closed off from even the glance of a passer-by, he would always say to himself, "Here lies Vatia" (*Vatia hic situs est*) (*Ep.* 55.4).[44] People think that one who withdraws from society is "free from care, self-sufficient, and lives for himself" (*Ep.* 55.4). The juridical subject, though, cannot just retreat from politics when there is no jurisdiction to put in its place: no authority to guide us, no duties that bind us to others, and no discourse to enliven us. In this absence of movement we succumb to the authority of *inertia* and reside with Vatia in his tomb.[45]

Recognition without Props

In contrast to those who "condemn all motion" (*Ep.* 3.5), Seneca calls for us to rouse ourselves to action (*ad rerum actus excitandi*) and emerge into view from "our sluggishness" (*inertia sui*) (*Ep.* 56.8). So deeply enmeshed is the importance of recognition in Greek and Roman society that even the Stoics (if we are to believe Cicero's account) were compelled, under the criticism of Carneades (a head of the skeptical or New Academy), to change their opinion that fame had no value other than as something useful and to declare that good fame (*bona fama*) was "preferred and desirable for its own sake"

(Cic. *Fin.* 3.17.57, trans. Rackham). A man of "good breeding and liberal education could desire to have the good opinion of his parents and relatives, and of good men in general, and that for its own sake and not for any practical advantage" (*Fin.* 3.17.57).

So, too, Seneca engages in a lengthy defense of *claritas* (renown), *fama* (fame), and *gloria* (glory), terms that overlap in their meaning. *Claritas*, Seneca argues as he employs a political vocabulary, does not need many votes (*multa suffragia*) but can be satisfied by the judgment (*iudicio*) of one good man (*Ep.* 102.11). In fact, *claritas* requires only the silent judgment, and not the actual words, of a good man (*Ep.* 102.14–15, 17). *Gloria*, which Seneca characterizes as "the shadow of virtue" that "will attend virtue even against her will" (*Ep.* 79.13), requires the judgments of the many (*Ep.* 102.17). However, the judgment of one good man "practically amounts" to being thought well by all good men since their judgment of what is true will be identical (*Ep.* 102.12). But even that shadow can lag behind, delayed by the envy and ignorance of one's contemporaries (*Ep.* 79.13). *Fama*, unlike *gloria*, requires the voices of many and, thus, has an even more tenuous existence (*Ep.* 102.17; also 102.13). *Fama*, for example, barely came to Socrates, Cato, Democritus, and Rutilius, almost resulting in the loss of our knowledge of their virtue, innocence, and worth (*Ep.* 79.14).

Seneca remarks in passing that there is no harm even if virtue is "lost to view" (*Ep.* 79.17). But he quickly qualifies the statement, suggesting that in the thousands of years and thousands of generations to come individual virtue will receive its reward of fame (*Ep.* 79.17). Underlying Seneca's qualification is his sense of the deeply human desire for recognition, not just as affirmation of greatness but also as confirmation of existence. He speaks of the pleasure of a letter that "brings us real traces (*vera . . . vestigia*), real evidences (*veras notas*), of an absent friend" (*Ep.* 40.1). "For that which is sweetest when we meet face to face is afforded by the impress of a friend's hand upon his letter, recognition" (*agnoscere*) (*Ep.* 40.1). Striking in Seneca's statement is the importance he places on recognition as something that is embodied. Images of friends "only refresh the memory and lighten our longing by a solace that is unreal" (*falso*) (*Ep.* 40.1). What is real, what reveals (*ostendit*) itself to us, is the physical traces of another's being (*Ep.* 40.1; also *Ep.* 31.1). Such visible traces of oneself are not limited to interactions among friends, but accompany one's political existence. Lucilius's ability and energy, for example, have thrust him into public view (*Ep.* 19.3–4): "You may sink yourself into the depths of obscurity (*in extrema mergaris*) and utterly hide yourself (*penitus recondaris*); yet your earlier acts will reveal you (*monstrabunt*). You cannot keep lurking in the dark; much of the old gleam will follow you wherever you fly" (*Ep.* 19.3–4; recall 3.6).

Despotism, though, alters the terms of recognition by requiring that individuals take on different guises—sometimes to be seen, sometimes not to be seen. The metaphor that Seneca uses, like the metaphor that Tacitus uses, is that of the theater. Seneca writes of how we must wear our different masks and play our different parts in life's drama. Edwards, for example, relates Seneca's "fascination with the slipperiness of the self, his urge to dramatize tensions within the self," to Neronian Rome and "Seneca's own place in the Neronian court." Rome under Nero, Edwards argues, required that one be able to assume different roles and dissimilate one's feelings, not unlike the stage-acting that had become so much a part of Nero's reign.[46] But the mask seems important not just as a way of hiding but of appearing. The challenge, as Seneca tells Lucilius, is to maintain a continuously recognizable character so that one is able to be praised (*laudari*) or at least to be identified by others (*adgnosci*) (*Ep.* 120.22; also 80.7). Yet, recognition can easily require "trickery," a sort of acting, because the people "will withhold their approval if they do not recognize you as one of themselves" (*Ep.* 29.11). As Seneca warns Lucilius, in continuing the theatrical image, "if I see you applauded by popular acclamation, if your entrance upon the scene is greeted by a roar of cheering and clapping—marks of distinction meet only for actors—if the whole state, even the women and children, sing your praises, how can I help pitying you" (*Ep.* 29.12)?

Seneca's warnings about the need to avoid such popular acclaim aside, there are few forces as powerful and irresistible as the people, in large part because of their ability to alter the terms of approbation and condemnation. Seneca admits, "There are things which, if done by the few, we should refuse to imitate; yet when the majority have begun to do them, we follow along—just as if anything were more honourable because it is more frequent! Furthermore, wrong views, when they have become prevalent, reach, in our eyes, the standard of righteousness" (*Ep.* 123.6). No doubt, our very sociability leads us to take our cues from others. When one person is "overwhelmed by disaster, the rest are overwhelmed by fear, and the possibility that they may suffer makes them as downcast as the actual sufferer" (*Ep.* 74.4). Similarly, we are easily seduced, like the siren songs, by the allure of others (*Ep.* 31.2). Not just the majority, but also those who immediately surround us can easily lead us to celebrate vice as virtue, rashness as bravery, moderation as sluggishness, and cowardice as prudence (*Ep.* 45.7). So powerful is the song in how it "reacts on the agent" that "even Socrates, Cato, and Laelius might have been shaken in their moral strength by a crowd that was unlike them" (*Ep.* 7.6–7).

Seneca calls us out of hiding so that we may be recognized. Yet our desire for recognition, our tendency to take our cues from others, implicates us, whether wittingly or unwittingly, in a world devoid of stable markers. "Put aside the opinion (*existimationem*) of the world," announces Seneca, since it is "always wavering" (*Ep.* 26.6). If Vatia's entombment speaks to the danger of burrowing out of sight, then the image of the political leader teetering on a sheer precipice points to the hazards of recognition. Elevated by opinion, "they are frightened (*exanimantur*) and in a flutter (*trepidant*) whenever they look down the abrupt steep of their greatness" (*Ep.* 94.73). In a play on words, Seneca remarks that what appears weighty (*graves*) in the eyes of others weighs more heavily (*gravior . . . incubat*) on those who ascend to these heights (*Ep.* 94.74). Heaviness appears in another passage in Seneca to describe how the heaviness of cargo can make a shifting ship more unstable (*Ep.* 28.3). Similarly, those who have weight are destined to "continually ebb and flow" and to be tossed "to and fro" by the shifting judgments of humankind (*Ep.* 95.57–58). On the seas we capsize; on a mountain we plummet, terrified at the height and exhausted from trying to keep our balance. The fate of recognition, like the fate of invisibility, as suggested by both *exanimare* and *incubare*, is exhaustion and death.[47]

The Politicization of Fortune

To be Roman is to base one's conduct on authority and one's success on recognition. Yet these categories get subverted so that we end up with authority without jurisdiction and recognition without stable props that can hold us up. Authority and recognition are but two instances, important ones, nonetheless, of how despotism functions by subverting any assignment of worth to things. The image of the political world under despotism as a liquid landscape in which everything can become something else is most fully played out in Seneca's highly politicized reading of Fortune.

The "precariousness" of Fortune, as Foucault describes it,

had long been a theme of reflection, meditation, and debate for both the Greeks and the Romans. The controversies surrounding the Stoic understanding of Chance (*casus*) and Fortune (*fortuna*) are known well enough (though hardly resolved). For Stoicism, generally, Chance and Fortune were "merely a matter of human ignorance: what seem to us like freak accidents are part of the overall order of nature."[48] The claim, as it related to the larger question of Fate, involved the Stoics in centuries of debate. Seneca seems at one point to evince some of the irresolution of the debate: "Whether the truth, Lucilius, lies in one or in all of these views, we must be philosophers; whether Fate binds us down by an inexorable law, or whether God as arbiter of the universe has arranged everything, or whether Chance drives and tosses human affairs without method, philosophy ought to be our defence. She will encourage us to obey God cheerfully, but Fortune defiantly; she will teach us to follow God and endure Chance" (*Ep.* 26.5). Seneca begs to sidestep the issue: "But it is not my purpose now to be led into a discussion as to what is within our own control (*quid sit iuris nostri*)—if foreknowledge is supreme, or if a chain of fated events drags us along in its clutches, or if the sudden and the unexpected play the tyrant (*dominantur*) over us" (*Ep.* 26.6).

Of interest to us here is Seneca's association of Fortune with *dominor*. *Dominor*, the verbal form of *dominus*, means to master or have dominion over something and carries an increasingly negative connotation as it moves from describing household rule and the rule of inanimate things to political rule (see Virg. *G.* 1.154). Cicero, for example, writes of how a king is transformed into a despot (*dominus*) when he turns to a mastery (*dominatum*) that is less just (Cic. *Rep.* 2.26.47–48).[49] For Seneca, the *dominus*, at home and in politics, is associated with "monstrous greed," cruelty toward his slaves (formerly citizens) (*Ep.* 47.2–4), and an unquenchable desire to extend one's rule over new territories and people (*Ep.* 113.30; 119.8).

So what does it mean to associate Fortune with the tyrant? Two answers come immediately to mind. First, like a tyrant, Fortune's movement seems arbitrary to those against whom it moves. It strikes, whether for good or bad, regardless of what one has done or what one deserves. Second, Fortune simply removes events from our control. It is our sovereign master. I want to suggest a third meaning. In associating Fortune with *iures nostri*, as we have seen Seneca do in *Epistle* 26, Seneca seems less interested in how Fortune treats us and more in how it transforms us. Fortune's jurisdiction comes to rule our character, transforming us in effect into slaves. However veiled, in Seneca's politicized rendering of Fortune, the political self, whether seeking or avoiding authority and recognition, is depicted as occupying an increasingly unknowable realm.

The precariousness of Fortune, as Foucault notes, has less to do with cycles of good and bad and more with the exposure of the political actor "on all sides to influence, intrigues, conspiracies, losses of favor" (*CS* 92). The hidden terrors of politics, as Seneca observes, arise not from "mere events" but from the hidden intrigues of our "fellow-man" (*Ep.* 91.7. 103.1; also 103.2). When not terrifying, politics borders on parody: candidates offering bribes, employing agents, "wearing down their hands with the kisses of those to whom they will refuse the least finger-touch after being elected"; others struggling for honors, triumph in war, permanent power, riches, and marriage (*Ep.* 118.3–4). As political activity is less and less premised on rank, responsibility, or position, it takes on the willy-nilly qualities of Fortune. Thus, Seneca gives political meaning to Fortune when he counsels Lucilius "to canvass (*petere*) for nothing, and to pass by all the elections (*comitia*) of Fortune" in order to achieve a free (*liberum*) outcome, a political category that requires paradoxically that one somehow absent oneself from politics (*Ep*. 118.3).

Fortune, in Seneca's *Epistles*, seems to keep appearing in overtly political occasions. Seneca has his reader imagine that Fortune is holding a festival and, like the emperor handing out the dole in the theater, is giving out honors, riches, and influence (*honores, divitias, gratiam*) (*Ep*. 74.7). Some of the gifts "have already been torn to pieces" by individuals trying to grab them; other gifts have been divided by "treacherous partnerships"; some gifts go to those not paying attention; and still other gifts have been knocked from the hands as the seeker grabs for other gifts (*Ep*. 74.7). In a sustained set of images, Seneca sets out the price that one pays for political favors (*Ep*. 74.7). Like the scramble for the coins at public games, so when we see Fortune's gifts we become impassioned and are torn apart as we "look back now in this direction and now in that," even more excited as we must grab for the few gifts that are awaited by all (*Ep*. 74.8). Worse than losing our gifts is getting them because the goods of Fortune "weigh heavily (*incubant gravia*) upon their owners, always pressing them down (*premunt*) and sometimes crushing them" (*Ep*. 76.30). Fortune can elevate us, but it is like we are perched perilously on a pedestal from which we tremble at the prospect of falling (*Ep*. 8.4). Or, as Seneca writes in another image, the gifts of Fortune are like "snares" that deceive us precisely because we think "we hold them in our grasp, but [they] hold us in theirs" (*Ep*. 8.3). Fortune transforms into chattel everything that falls under its *dominium*: "money, person, position," which are made "weak, shifting, prone to perish, and of uncertain tenure" (*Ep*. 66.23).

Fortune can find its way into our fears as easily as into our lusts. Seneca summons to our imagination the terror at the possibility of being tortured, a fate linked more to bad Fortune than good cause. The danger is that, like the spectacle of the games, so the spectacle of cruelty directed toward us haunts us. As Seneca notes, "of all the agencies which coerce and master (*subigunt et domant*) our minds, the most effective are those which can make a display" (*Ep.* 14.6). Strikingly, Seneca, in suggesting how to avoid giving offense (and thus how to minimize the risk of torture), seems only to magnify the potential sources of fear: the senate, the people and their allies, powerful individuals (read: the emperor) and their allies. The problem, as Seneca notes, is how one can limit Fortune's jurisdiction. "Fortune," as Seneca concludes his discussion of torture on a political note, "decides (*iudicat*) the issue, but I do not allow her to pass sentence (*sententiam*) upon myself" (*Ep.* 14.16). One can only avoid such a sentence by placing oneself "beyond the jurisdiction" (*extra ius dicionem*) of chance (*Ep.* 39.3).

What Fortune does (like despotism) is undermine any sense of the value of things. We saw this, for example, in Seneca's discussion of how criminality is given legal sanction. But Seneca broadens the picture: "Everything is slippery, treacherous, and more shifting than any weather (*Nihil non lubricum et fallax et omni tempestate mobilius*). The value of things is changed (*iactantur*) and everything changes into its opposite" (*in contrarium transeunt*) (*Ep.* 99.9). Like a bad-tempered master, Fortune moves with capricious glee (*Ep.* 4.4), attacking more violently those who shine most brilliantly (*Ep.* 91.4). The political tactics of Fortune also change. Fortune "does not always attack in one way, or even with her full strength; at one time she summons (*advocat*) our own hands against us; at another time, content with her own powers, she makes us of no agent (*auctore*) in devising perils for us. No time is exempt; in the midst of our very pleasures there spring up causes of suffering" (*Ep.* 91.5). And no one is immune. Fortune can always destroy what she had previously indulged (*Ep.* 4.7). To find examples, Seneca need look no further than Roman politics. Pompey's fate "was settled by a boy and a eunuch, that of Crassus by a cruel and insolent Parthian. Gaius Caesar ordered Lepidus to bare his neck for the axe of the tribune Dexter; and he himself offered his own throat to Chaerea" (*Ep.* 4.7). In this unpredictability, we are reminded of Seneca's earlier suggestion that everything is in turmoil (*Ep.* 91.7; also 99.9), but now Seneca gives us the political punchline. We cannot live under any authority that both destroyed Cato and made Vatinius (*Ep.* 98.4). To avoid being under the control of another, one must foreswear traditional modes of political involvement: canvass for nothing, pray to no man, ask no favors, and be at no one's service (*Ep.* 118.4).

ENVISIONING A POLITICAL SELF

Seneca locates the political actor in a treacherous political terrain with neither stable markers to orient oneself nor a place to hide. What makes the terrain so dangerous is that everything can mean its opposite: criminality is legal; *gravitas* is a weight that crushes rather than elevates us; and quiet is the stillness of death. Seneca's response to the political perils of imperial Rome is seen frequently as hinging on two moves: on creating sufficient exceptions so that one can withdraw from the political life of the local community and on redefining the political realm to encompass citizenship in the larger, universal community of humanity.[50] And, in fact, the notion of being a citizen of the world is seen frequently as Seneca's primary contribution to political thought.[51] Seneca does make both these claims, but I do not think even he believes they solve the problem because of how deeply, by his own analysis, despotism penetrates and disorients the individual, making withdrawal as troubling as involvement. One cannot escape oneself, as Seneca notes (*Ep.* 28.1–4). How can one limit the influence of the political world when the primary way of understanding oneself is political? How can one be alone with oneself when the experiences by which one even acquires a sense of oneself, or a trust in oneself, are disrupted (*Ep.* 104.26)? How can one orient oneself when isolated from others, from history, and from experience? How can one avoid simply getting lost in the boundlessness of one's own private fears and sorrows?

Foucault locates Seneca's response to the disorienting forces of Roman society in a turn toward a care of the self as a work of art in which the individual engages in a series of practices that transform the self. Foucault refers to the self as a work of art because the care of the self comes to be a part of the ancient concern with the art of living, or the techniques by which one establishes a relationship with the self so that one can know how to live.[52] The aspects of this art change from ancient Greece to Rome. For Socrates there is substantial emphasis on the role of dialogue in bringing the individual to reflect on oneself and to care for oneself as an ethical being. For the Stoics in the first two centuries CE in Rome, one sees instead a much greater emphasis on "looking and listening to the self."[53] One does not listen to an inner voice of conscience but brings together what has been done (one's actions) with what should be done (rules of conduct). The Stoic care of the self employs several practices that intensify this form of remembering: one memorizes what one has heard and converts that into rules of conduct; one engages in recollections, often in writing, of what one has done; and one imagines oneself in particular situations.[54] One adopts a visible mode of being and acting (an *ethos*) toward oneself and toward others by recognizing oneself and acting on oneself as a subject of both historical knowledge and systems of power that regulate the effects of that knowledge.[55] As Long notes, in identifying the role of self-fashioning in Stoic thought, "Our natures are such that we fashion our own selves, and correct self-fashioning requires the interrogative and reflective task."[56] The end of the "work of the self on the self" is a subject whose end is "to become capable of truth."[57] Truth in this context can be understood as the basis on which claims about oneself and about others are accepted and the basis on which these claims can be used to transform the self.[58] As Foucault writes, in language that we will return to in his discussion of frank speech, truth is "a force inherent to principles" that "has to be developed in discourse."[59]

The disagreement with Foucault comes with those who see his argument as slipping into a fundamental (and for some, a dangerous) error by making aesthetics itself and not living according to a universal, rational, and natural order as the end of self-fashioning.[60] Words like "nature" and "truth" end up as discourses for Foucault, a second order distancing from reality that Seneca would not make. Absent the goal of living in truth (or with the realization that living in truth is living in a constructed discourse of truth), self-fashioning for the sake of self-fashioning takes on a certain modern feel, a form of "dandyism," in Hadot's oft-quoted words.[61]

To be fair, whatever the "semantic slipperiness" of Foucault's use of aesthetics— whether he has in mind a modern aesthetic that is autonomous or an ancient aesthetic that is bound to a broader set of social, political, and ethical practices—Foucault is reasonably clear in his lectures on *The Hermeneutics of the Subject* that for Seneca the fashioning of oneself is meant to bring one into conformity with nature and truth.[62] That is, aesthetics is not autonomous. And Foucault takes care to distinguish an ancient and modern version of aesthetics by attributing the attitude of novelty (aesthetics as judged by its own criteria) specifically with modernity and not with the ancient care of the self.[63] But less clear is the point of alignment between Seneca's care of the self and Foucault's.

I want to locate this conjuncture in a less-noted aspect of Foucault's argument; namely in his suggestion that the care of the self involves a form of "looking" or a "conversion of the gaze."[64] The form of looking is not the self-styling of the dandy who asks, "How do I look?" Nor does the gaze peer out to a realm detached from this world to search for Truths we cannot see. Nor does the gaze look inward to a psychoanalytic deciphering of one's impulses to interpret the real meaning of one's desires. Rather, this conversion of the gaze has more to do with training one's sight so that we learn to see ourselves in our relationship to the world. As Foucault writes, we step back from ourselves so that we may "always have [ourselves] in sight" without losing "sight of any of the components that characterize the world in which we exist and, in particular, which characterize our own situation, in the very spot we occupy."[65]

We know from our discussion of Livy about the centrality of vision in the fashioning of ethical conduct. The imagination becomes the visual record by which we orient ourselves in the world.[66] But where Livy seeks to recall a set of felt meanings that have receded, though perhaps not entirely disappeared, Seneca has no such luxury. There is no recourse by which one can easily restore vision because of the complete subversion of the markers by which one orients oneself politically. As Seneca enjoins Lucilius, "Give your eyes time to unlearn what they have seen" (*sine dediscere oculos tuos*) (*Ep.* 69.2).[67] But the problem goes beyond unlearning. Contemplating the corruption of current affairs is like being "plunged into night" (*De Tranq. An.* 15.1). The concern is one of finding the materials by which the boundaries of real and unreal can be reconstructed and the individual brought back into view.

It is in the Roman context of visibility, of how I appear before others and how I appear before myself, that I want to recast Foucault's and Seneca's discussion of self-fashioning.

My suggestion is that the image of artistic making is less a solution than a strategy of power by which the individual is able to bring him or herself back into view.[68] Like the artist, the individual works with the cultural materials that are given. As Foucault notes, the "practices" by which a "subject constitutes itself" are "not something invented by the individual himself. They are models that he finds in his culture and are proposed, suggested, imposed upon him by his culture, his society, and his social group."[69] But those materials are rearranged. They can be rearranged because social systems are never completely closed but consist of discourses that potentially overlap, intersect, or conflict with other discourses. And, in fact, they have to be rearranged by the individual precisely because the cultural codes of behavior and authority have become so corrupted.[70] Thus, to respond to Thacker's question of why Foucault looks to aesthetics rather than "some reformulated version of ethics," the answer (at least in a Senecan context) is that the individual does not have the power to revise and put in place a different system of rules.[71] The effect of despotism, as we have seen, is to isolate individuals. The response to despotism must begin with this experience of isolation. The aesthetics of existence, thus, appears more as a starting point to the loss of ethical and political bearings and less as the mechanism by which these cultural codes are dismantled or a blueprint by which they are replaced.[72]

Seneca's artistic making begins with a Roman world that has made someone like Lucilius a "nobody" (*pusillum*) (*Ep.* 44.1) and with materials, however humble, by which to begin fashioning a someone (*Ep.* 85.40; also 31.11).[73] Playing upon a long discourse that associated noble birth with gold and silver, Seneca looks to a humbler raw material: clay. As Seneca reminds Lucilius, when men were closest to the gods in the Golden Age, they, too, were made from clay (*Ep.* 31.11). Seneca, thus, begins to fashion an alternate, philosophic genealogy, one that does not look to pedigrees (*stemma*) nor associates nobility with "a hall full of smoke-begrimed busts" (*fumosis imaginibus*) (*Ep.* 44.1, 5). Socrates, for example, was not an aristocrat. Cleanthes served as a laborer. And philosophy made Plato a nobleman (*Ep.* 44.3). A "noble mind is open to all men" and is the way in which "we may all gain distinction" (*nobiles*) (*Ep.* 44.2; trans. modified).[74] But the process of gaining distinction is hardly elevated: it (like the craft of ancient art) requires labor to shape the soul (*Ep.* 50.5).[75] As Seneca reminds Lucilius, in drawing a comparison to a building, some dispositions are "pliable and easy to manage, but others have to be laboriously wrought out by hand" and the materials exhausted in preparing the foundation (*Ep.* 52.6).

The individual, whose mind is distorted with error and confusion (*Ep.* 94.5), can no more begin shaping oneself than the novice artisan can begin sculpting clay. Both need patterns and practice.[76] Seneca, thus, arguing against Aristo, an early Stoic, points to precepts as a necessary beginning point. Like the treatment needed to restore eyesight, precepts help the mind to see (*videre*) by giving us guidance and practice in sorting the "jumbled mass" of matter into "proper classes" (*Ep.* 94.19, 21). One might be reminded of Cicero's suggestion that the senses can be trained, like an artist's, to see in the shadows and discern what others cannot see (*Acad.* 2.7.20). Paralleling the emergence of the individual from the shadowy netherworld of despotism, Seneca notes how teaching precepts functions much like the advice a physician gives to a recovering patient not to "expose your weak vision to a dangerous glare; begin with darkness, and then go into half-lights, and finally be more bold, accustoming yourself gradually to the bright light of the day" (*Ep.* 94.20). Precepts, furthermore, refresh memory (*memoriam renovant*) (*Ep.* 94.21, also 94.25) and add "new points of view" (*Ep.* 94.30), giving us additional resources for fashioning ourselves. Unlike for Plato where one leaves the world of shadows and enters the light of truth, for Seneca the world and one's place in that world acquires illumination and clarity. Patterns of conduct give the mind power "to make contact with the world."[77]

To find additional models for self-fashioning, one can also look to the "huge multitude" of maxims and quotations that are "scattered about in profusion" and need only "to be picked up" (*Ep.* 33.6). But there is a limit to the use of such passages. The artist cannot live in imitation of another.[78] Fearful of stunting the intellectual (and artistic) maturation of Lucilius, Seneca, in *Epistle* 33, eschews the further use of "extracts and quotations" or "mottos" (*Ep.* 33.3, 4). Seneca will continue to draw on the words of other philosophers; he will neither seek to encapsulate wisdom in a phrase nor attribute that wisdom to a particular source. That pedagogy seems to have a fairly explicit political reference. To have our words under "the leadership and commanding authority of one alone" (*unius ductu et auspiciis*) is to replicate despotism in one's thoughts (*Ep.* 33.4). But, as Seneca writes, in giving legal standing to the self, "We Stoics are not subjects of a despot (*rege*); each of us lays claim to his own freedom" (*Ep.* 33.4). The difference, the beginning of jurisdiction, lies in initiative: one must both initiate one's standing to act, and actually act. The individual must eventually "lean on himself" (*sibi . . . innitatur*) (*Ep.* 33.7), "take command" (*impera*) (as Seneca enjoins) (*Ep.* 33.7), and dare to create (*facere*) something for oneself and for posterity (*Ep.* 33.8). Only then, as Seneca combines an aesthetic with legal image, can one fashion one's own guardianship (*tutelae suae fiunt*) (*Ep.* 33.10).

Seneca's suggestion here is both conventional and unconventional, and speaks to distinctions that Foucault draws between domination, power, and freedom. Power is everywhere, operating through norms and social networks that are "borne by words, images, and the built environment."[79] And power is generative as it establishes relations that categorize, organize, and authorize forms (or discourses) of knowledge (e.g., medical knowledge, criminology, demography), modes of behavior and conduct (e.g., constraints on sexual desire, definitions of deviancy), types of institutions (e.g., prisons, hospitals, schools), regimes of truth (e.g., salvation, science), and valuations of worth (e.g., social hierarchy). Most significantly, power relations construct individuals as subjects. As Foucault writes, "This form of power applies itself to immediate everyday life which categorizes the individual, marks him by his own individuality, attaches him to his identity, imposes a law of truth on him which he must recognize and which others have to recognize in him."[80] Power is neither reducible to violence nor does is rest on consensus. Rather, power "is a total structure of actions brought to bear upon possible actions; it incites, it induces, it seduces, it makes easier or more difficult; in the extreme it constrains or forbids absolutely."[81] Foucault conceives of this power in the political language of "government": less the sovereign actions of a state on its subjects through laws and more the ways in which political, economic, and social powers guide the conduct of individuals and groups and mold the capacity of individuals and groups to govern themselves.[82] Government is "the way in which the conduct of individuals or of groups might be directed."[83]

Domination occurs when power relations become "frozen."[84] Domination constrains freedom because it prevents "any reversibility of movement."[85] But freedom, as an activity by which one establishes a relationship with oneself and others, is not in opposition to relations of power since power (as government over others and over oneself) "is exercised only over free subjects, and only insofar as they are free. By this we mean individual or collective subjects who are faced with a field of possibilities in which several ways of behaving, several reactions and diverse comportments may be realized."[86]

Interestingly, Foucault identifies the rise of "governmentality," which consists of the ways in which modern governments organize the conduct of vast populations through the "ritualization of the problem of personal conduct," with the sixteenth century Stoic revival.[87]

In his later works, Foucault continues to develop this Stoic relationship between government and freedom, exploring how freedom emerges as a turning of relations of authority onto oneself: a form of self-discipline by which one watches and learns to govern oneself. In a traditional Roman context, the individual would appoint a guardian (*custodem*) in order to have "someone whom you may look up to (*respicias*), someone whom you may regard as witnesses (*iudices*) of our thoughts" (*Ep.* 25.5; trans. modified).[88] But in an age in which authority is corrupted in crime, that guardian must be fashioned from history and memory. The past, thus, is not just a record of instruction; it is formed into a companion. Seneca, therefore, tells Lucilius, "guard (*custodi*) over yourself by means of the authority (*auctoritate*) of some man, whether your choice be the great Cato, or Scipio, or Laelius—or any man in whose presence even lost individuals (*perditi*) would check their bad impulses" (*Ep.* 25.6, trans. modified).[89] One might also look to philosophers who, because they are our ancestors, provide the measure for conduct that is worthy (*Ep.* 44.3). In reconceiving the relations of authority that inhere in despotism, Seneca is careful to note that these men of authority "are not our masters (*domini*), but our guides" (*duces*) (*Ep.* 23.11; also 33.4 and 80.1).

Seneca's point is not that an imagined companion is just like a real companion.[90] Rather, the fashioning of a companion serves, at least in part, to counter the isolating, enervating loneliness of despotism. The problem of loneliness for Seneca, as we saw in his warnings about secluding ourselves, is that we are hidden not only from the gaze of others, but also from our own view. In such invisibility lies lawlessness, which we can understand most basically as an inability to act according to a set of limits or boundaries. Seneca's letters, thus, seek to make us present to ourselves by way of an imagined other.[91] You are my "handiwork," Seneca declares to Lucilius (*Ep.* 34.2). The statement may refer as much to whatever effect Seneca has had on Lucilius's education as with how Seneca has created Lucilius as a partner in conversation. "I see you," Seneca writes in this moment of recognition, "and at this very moment I hear you" (*Ep.* 55.11). In this sensual appropriation by the imagination, time and distance are gathered together into the presentness of conversation with oneself as another. As a result, as Seneca writes, "I have begun to be a friend to myself" and thus can "never be alone" (*solus*) (*Ep.* 6.7). At the point at which "you have respect for yourself" (*tui reverentia*), and thus are ready to care for yourself, you can send away your guardian (*Ep.* 25.6).

But such presentness cannot occur only in the imagination because, as we have seen, one can easily be lost in its boundlessness. There must be tangibility, a way of leaving behind the contours of the self. For Seneca, this tangibility is comprised, at least in part, by writing (*Ep.* 84.5). Writing, as Foucault suggests, is an exercise of thought that "reactivates what it knows, calls to mind a principle, a rule, or an example, reflects on them, assimilates them, and in this manner prepares itself to face reality."[92] Like the application of paint, the materials themselves are hidden and what should be "[brought] to light" are what the individual has made of these materials (*Ep.* 84.7–8). Writing leaves behind the physical traces of oneself by which one can be recognized by others and by oneself. It gives body (*corpus*) to what we have read, heard, and practiced on ourselves.[93] As Foucault notes, writing "palliates the dangers of solitude; it offers what one has done or thought to a possible gaze; the fact of obliging oneself to write plays the role of a companion by giving rise to the fear of disapproval and to shame."[94]

Writing becomes "an agent of the transformation of truth into *êthos*" or what Foucault refers to also as the "subjectivation of truth."[95] The "subjectivation of truth" is the way in which the individual transforms truth into the practices that define one's character. From the "different and often conflicting normative structures and value systems," as Reydam-Schils notes, the Stoic individual must struggle to give some consistent and recognizable form to one's character.[96] To recall Livy's association of Roman monuments with *exempla*, we become the makers of ourselves as monuments, the outlines of the self (and what the self stands for) brought into relief so that we may live "in plain sight of all men" (*Ep.* 83.1).[97] Foucault's political writings, like Seneca's, are ways in which we can experience ourselves by asking questions about our limits and possibilities, who we are, and how we should act.[98]

The image of artistic making can take us only so far, but it takes us somewhere. It cannot tell us what form the art will take, but it does tell us something about how activity must be defined and organized by purpose. As Seneca writes, "The artist may have his colours all prepared, but he cannot produce a likeness unless he has already made up his mind what he wishes to paint" (*Ep.* 71.2; see also 65.5). Similarly, "no man can set in order the details unless he has already set before himself the chief purpose of his life" (*Ep.* 71.2). In pursuing this end, the artist also conveys how to learn how to be glad (*gaudere*), which, for Seneca, is the "foundation of a sound mind" (*Ep.* 23.3, 1; also 76.28). Being glad is contrasted with feeling hope, which might surprise us until we remember that it is precisely the human tendency to project oneself too far into the future that is the cause of so much anxiety (see, for example, *Ep.* 5.9). The artist teaches us that when one is "busy and absorbed in one's work, the very absorption affords great delight" (*Ep.* 9.7). Delight is not quite joy, but it is on the right track because delight, like joy, takes pleasure in the moment more than in anticipation of the future.

The image of artistic making also suggests how freedom emerges neither in opposition to networks of power nor in liberation from them, but in the initiative and ability to give shape to the materials of the cultural world and to define the boundaries of one's actions. One is not simply swallowed up in the march of time that, in Seneca's depiction, moves along, as though in night (*Ep.* 101.5). Nor does the artist simply "report to posterity the ills of others," as do the historical chroniclers (*Natl. Quest.* 3. pref.5). Artistic making, as a response to time, spatializes history by gathering together, and in turn giving shape to, the bits and pieces that comprise experience and memory.[99] Seneca's writing, in fact, might be seen as a way of painting through words, restoring and reshaping with vivid detail one's experience of the cultural landscape.[100]

In this re-imagining of the political landscape, Foucault is revising an Aristotelian philosophic tradition that identifies the political realm, with its habits, customs, traditions, and beliefs, as the site of our self-realization as political beings.[101] Foucault at one point addresses this Aristotelian position, taken up by Richard Rorty, who critiques Foucault for not "appeal[ing] to any 'we'—to any of those '*wes*' whose consensus, whose values, whose traditions constitute the framework for a thought and define the conditions in which it can be validated." Foucault responds that "the problem is, precisely, to decide if it is actually suitable to place oneself within a 'we' in order to assert the principles one recognizes and the values one accepts; or if it is not, rather, necessary to make the future formation of a "we' possible by elaborating the question."[102] But where Aristotle is perhaps more helpful in understanding the importance of a healthy political life, he is less instructive in answering to the problem of how one orients oneself, absent this realm. Foucault's project, and he is not far from Seneca at this point, takes on particular urgency against the backdrop of despotism in which the political realm disables, more than enables, individual self-realization. Neither Foucault nor Seneca leaves the individual floating freely in space, adrift in a vessel of empty autonomy (a critique interestingly made of both thinkers). For both Foucault and Seneca, one is engaged in an ongoing process of fixing "acquired elements" that are obtained from the practice, reflection, and modification of one's own cultural world.[103] Toward these reference points "it is always possible to turn back."[104] I am reminded of Václav Havel's discussion of how totalitarianism destroys the "basic instrument of human knowledge and self-knowledge" by attempting to deny the human ability to create stories.[105] In language that bears some similarity to Foucault's, Havel writes, "Every story presupposes a plurality of truths, of logics, of agents of decision, and of manners of behavior" that "resembles the logic of games, a logic of tension between what is known and not known, between rules and chance, between the inevitable and the unforeseeable."[106] Havel and Foucault, as I have explored more fully elsewhere, do not walk hand-in-hand.[107] But what they are talking about is the necessity of giving color and form to a self that is rendered invisible by despotism. The care of oneself does not, in my mind, create an ethic. But it may be a useful starting point for creating the condition for ethical thought by pointing to how one might establish the outlines, or jurisdiction, of the political self so that one can see oneself in relation to others.

GIVING LIFE TO FORM

Much of the scholarly discussion of Foucault's later work has focused on what Daraki refers to as Foucault's "journey to Greece."[108] Separate from appraisals of the accuracy of Foucault's reading of the ancient world, critics point to the ancient Greek model of the stylization of life as a barely sufficient response to the problems that Foucault had earlier diagnosed. Rochlitz, in commenting on Foucault's reliance on ancient Greece, remarks that there is something "laughable" about Foucault's proposing a new art of living, given his earlier concern with the genocidal dreams of bio-power.[109] Thacker attributes the failure of Foucault's aesthetic of power to be "more than simply a principle of absolute freedom or the rule of an empty autonomy" to his fascination with "the golden glow of Greek culture."[110] Smart, echoing a criticism frequently made of Foucault, argues that Foucault's notion of self-constitution, the process of elaborating the question of who I am, appears as a "relatively solitary or isolated process" that can occur "free of social, economic, or political structures."[111] Smart also attributes the stance to Foucault's "reflection on the moral world of ancient Greece."[112] And McNay, in looking at Foucault's work on the Greeks, suggests, "Without an interactional notion of the self— that is, without making the analytical links between one's own actions and the social context—the individual cannot distinguish between what constitutes a radical exploration of identity and what is simply an arbitrary stylization of life."[113]

My suggestion here is that attentiveness to Foucault's use of Seneca serves as something of a corrective to these characterizations of Foucault's project. Among other things, attention to Seneca invites a different interpretation of the challenge of the art of living, from how the individual fashions oneself in the context of a democratic *polis*, to how the individual orients oneself in the context of a world that is simultaneously expanding (with imperial conquest) and contracting (with the stultifying effects of despotism). The problem that Seneca faces is that neither outer nor inner limits of conquest are recognized or respected. The question that Foucault asks, by way of Seneca, is not whether a self can be constituted free of political, economic, and social structures, but whether it is possible to turn the experience of these structures into self-knowledge. "Rather than promoting a self-absorption," as Bernauer points out, "Foucault deprives the self of any illusion that it can become a sanctuary separated from the world."[114]

Foucault's turn to the Romans is instructive for another related reason. However much we may admire the Greeks for their creativity and dynamism, they are describing (often romanticizing) a form of political association that bears limited resemblance to the political structures and challenges of contemporary society. We do not live in Seneca's Rome. Nor do I find myself in agreement with either Jean-Luc Nancy and Philippe Lacoue-Labarthe or with Sheldon Wolin that modernity appears as a form totalitarianism.[115] But we find ourselves in an imperial society that is both expansive and isolating. It is expansive as it comes to dominate increasingly the political and economic landscape of the world.[116] And it is isolating because the duties of the imperial citizen become defined more and more by notions of unity and order, rules become organized more by capital markets for which there is little public recourse or accountability, and political discourse becomes constrained increasingly by secrecy and fear. On a purely anecdotal note, I cannot help but express some surprise that my undergraduate students associate democracy with, first-and-foremost, law abidingness. In such attitudes one expresses oneself as a juridical subject more than a political actor. The political problem of contemporary society is not whether the individual can flee the physical reach of a corrupt and violent state because, as both Foucault and Seneca suggest, the juridical self cannot flee what comprises it. The problem is how to assert a new jurisdiction of the self: of how to be political more than legal.

I find this question of how to assert a new jurisdiction of the self striking in contrast to the thrust of Foucault's earlier work. I understand Foucault as turning to this question of how to orient oneself when, in a 1978 roundtable, he asks, "Isn't the most general of political problems the problem of truth? How can one analyze the connection between ways of distinguishing true and false and ways of governing oneself and others?"[117] Foucault is inquiring, ultimately, about the task of political thought. Somewhat famously, Foucault points to what he calls the "Cartesian moment" when the ancient search for truth as a practice of the self was replaced with a more modern conception of truth that was "defined entirely in terms of knowledge."[118] As Foucault states in his lectures on *The Hermeneutics of the Subject*, the "modern age of the history of truth" begins "when knowledge itself and knowledge alone give access to the truth."[119] In juxtaposition to systems of knowledge, Foucault advances what he calls "political *spiritualité*."[120]

Odd words, indeed, coming from Foucault. Foucault once conceived of the soul as the "prison of the body" that is "born . . . out of methods of punishment, supervision and constraint."[121] The notion of "political spirituality" marks a fairly significant shift in Foucault's own thought (even as it may be linked to, and grow out of, some earlier aspects of his thought).[122] And scholars have drawn from the phrase quite different implications. Jambet sees the spiritual as the ability to invest the material domain (including humans as matter) with value.[123] Flynn interprets it generally as a "process of self-transformation."[124] Connolly characterizes it as pointing to an "ethical sensibility."[125] O'Leary understands it generally as a way for Foucault to connect "contemporary critique and the critical practices of the Socratic tradition in antiquity."[126] And Bernauer locates the "shift" in this concern with spirituality to Foucault's "study of Christian experience."[127] Foucault's final works appear as a form of "worldly mysticism" and "negative theology" that seeks to critique and transcend the "modern figure of finite man whose identity was put forward as capturing the essence of human being."[128] Foucault's form of "ecstatic thinking" for Bernauer is a practice of ethics precisely because it is a form of thinking that is free from any constraint, an "imaginative creativity" freed from the "scientifically knowable."[129]

I want to highlight a slightly different aspect of political spirituality. By way of his discussion of Seneca, Foucault emphasizes the dynamics of movement (more than, as in his earlier writings, the forces of imprisonment).[130] Foucault characterizes the principles of the care of the self, for example, as "restlessness and movement."[131] Perhaps most pertinent for our discussion here, political spirituality stands as a response to *stultitia*, a diagnosis of restlessness, listlessness, and directionlessness that Foucault takes from Seneca. The *stultus* is someone who "remembers nothing, who lets his life pass by, who does not try to restore unity to his life by recalling what is worth memorizing, and [who does not] direct his attention and will to a precise and well-determined end."[132] Reminiscent of the loss of any jurisdiction of the self, Foucault describes the *stultus* as "essentially someone who does not will, who does not will himself, who does not want the self, whose will is not directed towards the only object one can freely will, absolutely and always, which is oneself."[133] In the roundtable in which Foucault poses the notion of spirituality, he seems to refer back to "the will to discover a different way of governing oneself through a different way of dividing up true and false."[134]

But what are we to make of this conjuncture of political spirituality, the will, and truth, particularly since Foucault does not fully elaborate any of these ideas? I want to suggest that these three elements coalesce around Foucault's discussion of *parrhêsia*, a Greek notion of frank and truthful speech that plays itself out in the Roman idea of *libertas*.[135] Truthful speech is not simply a self-indulgent act of blurting out whatever comes to mind. Rather, truthful speech might be better understood as a response to a political realm that disorients by distancing how one speaks and acts from who one is or should be. Hypocrisy and flattery are only the opening salvos in a political system that relentlessly denies, and demands that one become complicit in that denial of, value or worth to the public language we use. The effect is a self that one "has never known at any moment of his life."[136] Truthful speech, as Foucault suggests, allows truth to appear by bringing together how one speaks and acts with whom one wants to be.[137] The beginning point of such speech is the conversion of the gaze toward oneself, a gaze associated with a conversion to truth. When Seneca directs the gaze toward truth, as Foucault writes, "It won't be a gaze directed towards the reality of essences, but one directed towards the truth of what we think. It is a matter of testing the truth of representations and of the opinions that accompany them."[138]

Truthful speech does not simply make the self into something to be viewed but also something to be lived. The difference between art and life, to return to Seneca, is that "a picture is a lifeless thing" (*Ep.* 84.8). What gives life to art is spirit: the ability to act. Truthful speech, though, does not follow from political spirituality but plays a critical role in the formation of that spirituality. Truthful speech develops and clarifies the principles of our beliefs and actions that serve as a "magnetic force" or a "point of attraction" that moves us to act.[139] Against the "dispersion and non-reflexivity of thought" associated with *stultitia* stands the reflexive self that "carries out the test of what one thinks, the test of oneself as the subject who actually thinks what he thinks and acts as he thinks."[140]

We can understand political spirituality as a will to truth about oneself that is enacted in public speech. Speech, as Seneca writes, must "harmonize with life" so that the "man has fulfilled his promise who is the same person both when you see him and when you hear him" (*Ep.* 75.4). But in Seneca's Rome rhetorical forms have become so corrupted that they seem more to ensnare than reveal. Thus, Seneca breaks from these rhetorical practices. As a response to the disjuncture between worth and acclaim, one should not speak with the audience in mind (as in rhetoric) but with the self in view. And as a break from the numbness of despotism one must feel what one says and be "wedded to it" (*Ep.* 75.3). To be able to have oneself in clear view, to be able to speak one's life, and to be able to articulate that life in a larger political terrain, is to have "perfect freedom" (*absoluta libertas*) (*Ep.* 75.18). The freedom of which Seneca speaks is the freedom that comes from being the "subject of my conduct": having power over oneself (*Ep.* 75.18).[141]

In this restoration of the jurisdiction of the self, the individual is no longer "prey to the winds of external representations": the habits, illusions, and desires that mix together in our minds from which we can neither flee nor embrace.[142] Foucault, like Seneca, is engaged in a political diagnosis of the numbing and disorienting effects of the political world. The recovery of the political self is the recovery of the animating spirit of political action that incites, elevates, and orients but is irreducible to power, class, or domination and undefinable through abstractions or systems of knowledge. In thought and speech one may begin again to form oneself politically.

Epilogue

Nunc demum redit animus. Tacitus sounds a note of hope: Now at last spirit returns (Tac. *Agric.* 3.1). Tacitus's hope speaks to a theme of this book. Even though the political thinkers that we have looked at have vastly different notions of spirit, what emerges by bringing together these modern and ancient thinkers is the role of political thought in giving life to political form — in activating our political world. More than questioning specific institutional forms, each of these thinkers is moved by a preliminary concern: a sense that the political markers by which communities form identities, establish boundaries, foster attachments, and organize purpose have been lost. In our contemporary world, as Barber notes, the "globalization of markets and of the consumer mentality has meant that global reasoning is dominated by private consumerist logic rather than public civic logic," a consuming impulse that, as we saw with Cicero and Arendt, pays little regard to the public worth of things.[1] We, like Cicero, can look around the republic, and, imagining it as a work of art that has fallen into decay through neglect, ask, "Is there anything worth saving?" What does it matter what happens to the things of this world, whether an object of art or a set of political institutions? There is, in part, a theological answer for Cicero: we are enjoined to care for the world. But there is a deeper, more secular response, born of Cicero's own sense of loss. Things matter because they give form to thought and aspiration. Ultimately, for Cicero and for Arendt, the political thinker restores a feel for the world, not by systematizing it or leaving it, but by illuminating it. The political thinker recognizes the life that gives form to our political world.

Like Livy and Machiavelli, we can survey a political landscape comprised of institutions, monuments, and buildings that appear as empty forms. What have been lost are felt meanings: the visceral connections that one not only has to the political world, but that one shares with others. Both Livy's and Machiavelli's works, I have sought to suggest, are ultimately works of political vision. They are engaged in an imaginative reconstruction of Roman life, to be sure, but the historical layering of their arguments is meant to replicate the ways in which felt meanings are publicly arrived at and shared. What emerges for Machiavelli from Livy's account is not necessarily harmony, but the animating, and often raucous, role of popular vision in the construction of the public meaning of liberty. The loss of publicly felt meanings, which I have associated with political blindness, underlies the corruption of the community.

There is a sober message that emerges. Political institutions (like judicial and legislative systems) and political concepts (like liberty) are not easily exported but are largely homegrown because their impetus, sustenance, and particular form depends so much on human passion—a collective sense of grievance, power, and opportunity—that arises from experience, action, and memory. These thinkers call into question, as well, the notion of politics as a "contract," recently extended in arguments about global civil society, that emphasizes "the role of human reason" against the "passions" in agreeing on particular "institutional outcomes."[2] To remove passion is to gut the institutions of the viscera that could give them life. There is perhaps a hopeful message: Citizens, moved finally by the corruption of ideals, might be able to reclaim democracy from the meaningless clichés, manufactured emotions, and ideological blinders that obscure vision.

These felt meanings become all the more significant against the backdrop of despotism, which, for Tacitus and Montesquieu, saps the community of its animating spirit. Tacitus's argument follows, to some extent, from Livy's. Livy's concern is with reanimating the felt meanings that one gives to the political world, meanings that had lost much of their salience in the wake of decades of political violence, in the undermining of political institutions and norms, and in the loss of civic attachments. For Tacitus, the political landscape of imperial Rome looks less like Augustus's "restored republic" (*res publica restituta*) and more like a *terra incognita*, a world no longer recognizable because of the absence of reliable markers by which one can orient oneself in the political terrain. For Montesquieu, Tacitus's political psychology takes us inside the individual, revealing how despotism plays itself out as a malady that depletes the animating spirit. One can hear in Barber's description of "Fear's Empire" the echoes of this Roman past. Fear "disempowers the powerful by provoking an anxiety that disables capacity" and "turns active citizens into fretful spectators."[3] The powerful feature of this fear that emerges from Tacitus and Montesquieu is that it can actually be comfortable: it can be an excuse not to ask questions of others or ourselves, it can serve as a salve to our consciences, and it (particularly when coupled with imperialism) can encourage our retreat to our private worlds where our silence can be bought through material prosperity.

Seneca's *Epistles* become a case study in how one becomes implicated in despotism, not only through his own complicity with Nero, but with how despotism insinuates its way into definitions of the political self. It is not unlike how we, as Foucault would argue, have come to define ourselves as bureaucratic subjects first, and only citizens in passing.[4] As we attempt to locate ourselves against both a domestic and global landscape rendered formless by rules that we had little role in making and decisions that we have little chance of knowing, we succumb, as Keane writes, to "inertness": a listlessness born of a sense of powerlessness and purposelessness.[5] Seneca is not an activist, but I think he asks an important question: what role can thought play in retrieving the materials by which we can recognize ourselves in the world? On what basis can we even constitute ourselves as a "we"? In a sense, we return to Arendt's own suggestion that the political thinker is like a pearl diver who retrieves gems—crystallized artifacts of human aspiration—from the depths of the past so that they may be used to inspire new generations to think again. More than a retreat from a threatening world, Seneca's *Epistles* and Foucault's project emerge as an attempt to define our possibilities in relation to the political world.

There are any number of reasons to condemn the Romans to continued theoretical obscurity, not the least of which, as Wolin has pointed out, is that they do not offer a particularly enticing vision of political life. The Romans do not engage in thought experiments. They do not provide us with blueprints for emancipation (from whatever). And they tell us very little that is persuasive today about systems or practices of government. Their contribution may lie in something quite different, namely, as a chronicle of the attempt to restore sensitivity and feeling to growing political numbness. In the readings that I have provided here, the legacy of Roman political thought extends beyond an inquiry into law and administration and beyond its traditional association with civic republicanism. Roman political thought is engaged most fundamentally in an exploration of what animates us as political beings. It is an inquiry into conditions of political resignation, cynicism, and despair. And it is an exploration of the possibilities of mutual recognition and collective action by way of the experiences of grief, indignation, anger, sorrow, compassion, trust, and joy. These thinkers recast our political vision from gazing at the perfection of an imagined world to seeking, through our return to the world, to recognize our attachments to and feelings for it again.

Notes

INTRODUCTION

1. Also Plutarch in his discussion of Cato the Elder (*Cato Mai.* 23); Cicero *Rep.* 6.11. On Cato the Elder, see Gruen 1992, 52–83.

2. Schiller 1993, 213.

3. Ibid.

4. See Nicgorski 1984, 1991; Saxonhouse 1975; Remer 1999; Seery 1999; Hammer 2002a; and Kalyvas 2007.

5. Hampsher-Monk 1990, 773–76.

6. Thiele 1997, xi.

7. Miller 1991, 450.

8. Ibid., 451.

9. Connolly 2007, 14.

10. Wolin 2004, 19.

11. Ibid.

12. Kaster 2005, 54.

13. See, for example, Vasaly's conclusion on Ciceronian oratory (1993, 256).

CHAPTER 1

This chapter was written with the assistance of Marina Lutova.

1. Gildersleeve 1890a, 44.

2. See, for example, Janet 1887; Woolsey 1893 (orig. 1877); Bluntschli 1885, 3, 7; Smith 1886, 5; and Willoughby 1907 (orig. 1896). For comments on the influence of these theories, see Merriam 1924, 15.

3. Bluntschli 1885, 5–6.

4. Ibid., 7, italics in orig. See also Carroll's Hegelian defense of classics (1908).

5. Ibid., 37.

6. Gildersleeve 1880, 1. *The Journal of Hellenic Studies* began publication in 1880, *Classical Review* in 1887, *Harvard Studies in Classical Philology* in 1890, *Classical Journal* in 1905, *Classical Quarterly* in 1907, and the *Journal of Roman Studies* in 1911.

7. See Benario 1989 and Stray 2003. Even now Kennedy argues that the primary goal of Latin study should be "an introduction to the nature of language, to concepts of grammar, to etymology, and to cultural concepts conveyed through words" and only secondarily should it aim to develop reading knowledge of texts (Kennedy 1987, 15).

8. See von Wilamowitz-Moellendorff 1982, 1; Lloyd-Jones 1982; Herzog 1983, 285; Halporn 1989, 308–10. On British classics in the nineteenth century, see Turner 1989. There were some efforts in England to incorporate more scientific approaches to historiography, including John Bagnall Bury's *History of the Later Roman Empire*.

9. Kelsey 1908, 374, 382. Also Gildersleeve 1884, 350. On Gildersleeve's contributions to the development of philology in the United States, see Kennedy 1980; Habinek 1998; Briggs 2002. Less influential was the comparative anthropological theorizing that informed British classicists (Phillips 1989, 643). Walter William Skeat and Henry Sweet were English philologists deemed as sufficiently scientific by Gildersleeve. On Gildersleeve's later (and more sympathetic) impressions of philology in England, see Gildersleeve 1917.

10. von Ranke 1973, 137. On the development of historiography generally, see Breisach 1994 and Novick 1988.

11. Momigliano 1994, 35.

12. Gildersleeve 1917, 399. For a discussion of how different twentieth century methodological approaches framed the study of ancient politics, see Hammer forthcoming.

13. Smith 1886, 6. Political philosophy appeared as a distinct subject as early as 1847 at Yale (Haddow 1939, 114). In the late nineteenth century, Columbia (with the appointment of Francis Lieber in 1857, and later with John Burgess, Munroe Smith, and William Dunning) and Johns Hopkins (with Herbert Adams and W.W. Willoughby) were the most important programs in establishing political science as a distinct discipline. For the early history of

political theory in the United States, see Haddow 1939 and Gunnell 1993. There was also important work in political science and political thought by Robert Blakey and Sir Francis Pollock in Britain (see Farr 2006, 232–34). The discipline, though, spread much more slowly in Britain in the first half of the twentieth century, with the UK Political Studies Association being formed in 1949 (see Goldsmith and Grant 2007). There was some growth in the academic study of jurisprudence in Britain, particularly in the late nineteenth century (see Duxbury 2004, 11). On the professionalization of the academy, see Wiebe 1967; Furner 1975; Haskell 1977; Ricci 1984.

14. Smith 1886, 5, 7, 2.

15. On the formation of the American Political Science Association, see Adcock 2003 and Gunnell 2006.

16. Bryce 1909, 3.

17. Ibid., 9–10.

18. Willoughby 1900, 78.

19. Ibid., 83.

20. Willoughby 1904, 108.

21. Dunning 1935 (orig. 1902), xix.

22. Ibid.

23. The proportion of books on the Romans devoted to law is stunning: Mommsen's works (reviewed in *Classical Review* and *American Journal of Philology*); Buckler's *The Origin and History of Contract in Roman Law Down to the End of the Republican Period* (reviewed in *Political Science Quarterly*); Zöller's *Römische Staats- und Rechtsaltertümer* (reviewed in *Classical Review*); Herzog's *Geschichte und System der Römischen Staatsverfassung* (reviewed in *Classical Review*); Liebenam's *Forschungen zur Verwaltungsgeschichte des Römischen Kaiserreichs* (reviewed in *Classical Review*); Libenam's *Zur Geschichte und Organisation des Römischen Vereinswesen* and Deloume's *Les Manieurs d'Argent à Rome* (reviewed in *Political Science Quarterly*); Arnold's *The Roman System of Provincial Administration* (reviewed in *Classical Journal* and *Classical Review*); Scrutton's *The Influence of the Roman Law on the Law of England* (reviewed in *Political Science Quarterly*); Taylor's *A Constitutional and Political History of Rome* (reviewed in *Classical Review*); Roby's *Roman Private Law* (reviewed in *Classical Review*); Clark's *History of Roman Private Law* (reviewed in the *American Political Science Review*); Bernard's *The First Year of Roman Law* (translated from French and reviewed in the *American Political Science Review*); Girard's *A Short History of Roman Law* (translated from French and

reviewed in the *American Political Science Review*); Leage's *Roman Private Law* (reviewed in the *American Political Science Review, Classical Journal,* and *Classical Philology*).

24. Willoughby 1907, 389 (orig. 1896). He cites Bluntschli, *Gesammelte kleine Schriften: Der Rechtsbegriff,* vol. 1.24. See also Dunning 1935 (orig. 1902), 106, 121.

25. Pollock 1935, 30–31 (orig.1890).

26. See Stray 2003, 34–35. On the debate about science education in England in the 1920s, see Mayer 1997.

27. Trowbridge Honey 1939, 37.

28. Ibid., 38.

29. Arnold 1920, 80.

30. Dewey 1989 (orig. 1944), 263.

31. Arnold 1920, 78.

32. For a discussion of the German educational system, see Burnet 1918.

33. Merriam 1921, 179; see also Merriam 1924, 43–44; Gettell 1923; and Sabine 1939.

34. On the establishment of the *Review of Politics,* see O'Malley 1948. Task of political education: Livingstone 1916; Hadzsits 1920; Morison 1939. For accounts of the Weimar years and its effects, see Brecht 1959 and Gunnell 1993, 146–74.

35. Herzog 1983, 287.

36. Mechanical state: Inge 1934 in Schofield 2003, 193; culture: Wagener 1938; Murray 1945, 3; restoration of values: Flickinger 1933; Murray 1943, 9; democratic populism: Inge 1934 in Schofield 2003, 193.

37. Granger 1919, 112, 111.

38. See Editorial 1917, 87.

39. Housman 1921, 73.

40. See Editorial 1917; West (ed.) 1917; Tavenner 1936.

41. Merriam 1921, 181.

42. Ibid., 174.

43. Catlin 1930, 12.

44. See Novick 1988, 145–50.

45. For example, Buckland 1921; Wenger 1925; Jolowicz 1932; and Monier 1935 and 1936.

46. Merriam 1931, 37 (orig. 1925); also Catlin 1930.

47. See Emmette Redford's reminiscence in Baer, Jewell, and Sigelman 1991, 56.

48. McIlwain 1968, 102 (orig. 1932).

49. Ibid., 121–22.

50. Carlyle and Carlyle 1950 (orig. 1936), 1:34.

51. Ibid., 1:3.

52. Ibid., 1:19.

53. Sabine 1939, 4.

54. Sabine and Smith 1976, 99 (orig. 1929).

55. Sabine 1946, 160.

56. Ibid., 161.

57. Ibid., 175.

58. See Haskell 1939; 1942; Marsh 1943 and later Abbott 1963.

59. Haskell 1942, iv.

60. See Rostovtzeff 1926; Frank 1927; 1933–40; Heinze 1930; Charlesworth 1937.

61. Broughton 1972, 251.

62. MacMullen 1988, 116. See also Gunnell 1986, 24.

63. Sabine 1939, 7–8.

64. Hammond 1951, 164–65. See also von Fritz 1954.

65. White 1946–47, 1. See also Agard 1953, 164–67. Bolgar explores the ideological shape that classical education took in its response to social, economic, and political changes over the centuries (1954).

66. See Calder 1994, xxxii–xxxiii.

67. Voegelin 1997, 1:131; 1971, 91 (orig. 1952).

68. See Hallowell and Porter 1997; Hallowell 1950, 16–19.

69. Strauss 1989a, 81. See also 1989b, especially 1–26, and the correspondence between Voegelin and Strauss in Emberley and Cooper 2004.

70. Holton 1963, 149; also Strauss 1958, 122–23 (historians not illuminate).

71. McDonald 1960, 135.

72. Examinations of ideology in Roman politics include contributions by Mazzarino 1951 and Béranger 1953.

73. Finley 1963, 19. On the gulf that opened between literary criticism and history, see Graff 1987, 183–94.

74. Starr 1960, 153.

75. Starr 1960, 151.

76. Starr 1963, 17, 3. Rostovtzeff compared the historian's task of discovering laws of development to that of the scientist (1930, 1:6). Not surprisingly, his work was singled out for approbation. See Starr

1960, 151, fn. 11. See also the comment in "News and Notes" in *Classical Review* that drew attention to a critique of Rostovtzeff by Meyer Reinhold. Although Rostovtzeff's work "constitutes a momentous contribution 'towards a scientific understanding of ancient Mediterranean civilization,' it is nevertheless strongly coloured by contemporary ideas and assumptions which have their origin in the society in which he was brought up" (1947, 1; also Reinhold 2002, 82–100).

77. Millar 1977, xii. See also Taylor 1949; Magie 1950; Broughton 1951 and 1952; 1972; Scullard 1951; Badian 1958. Later, see Badian 1967; Gruen 1974; Saller 1982; Paterson 1985; MacMullen 1988; Vishnia 1996; Lendon 1997; Mouritsen 2001; Kelly 2004.

78. Gruen 1974, 4.

79. Badian 1967, 5.

80. See Momigliano 1940.

81. Easton 1951, 36–37; 1971, 4 (orig. 1953). See also Whyte 1943, 695; Beard 1948, 214–15.

82. Braudel 1980, 10, 11. See Hexter 1972 and Iggers 1997, 51–64 for helpful discussions of the *Annales* school.

83. Ladurie 1979, 15; also Furet 1972.

84. Ebenstein 1960, 1 (orig. 1951).

85. Ibid., v.

86. Ibid., vi.

87. Ibid., 110, 121, 144. See also Elliot and McDonald 1950, 236.

88. Badian 1996, 189.

89. Ebenstein 1957, 87.

90. On these efforts to bring together the different methodological orientations of historiography and other social sciences, see the Social Science Research Council n.d. [1940s] and 1954.

91. Galston 1982, 492.

92. Galston 1993, 29.

93. See Brunt 1971b; Meier 1980; Raaflaub 1986a; 1986b; 1993; essays in Jehne 1995; Kienast 1999; Hölkeskamp 2004; also the Weberian approaches of Loewenstein 1973; Deininger 1985; Meier 1988; 1994; Hatscher 2000; Hölsher 2000; Ando 2000.

94. See Hahn 1975 and de Ste. Croix 1981. Ideology: Konstan 1983; Carandini 1988; Ando 2000 (using Althusser); Haynes 2003; Morstein-Marx 2004; Rose 2006.

95. See Pocock 1987, 335; 2006.

96. Pocock 1981, 50.

97. Pocock 1987, 336.

98. For a recent discussion of this republican tradition, see Nelson 2006.

99. I see Wolin's book as more influential in political theory, and constituting more of a break with past political theory, than does Saxonhouse 1993.

100. Wolin 2004, 4.

101. Ibid., 7. Jacobson articulated a similar view in which political theory should not succumb to either the false precision of scientism or the impatient virtue of moralism but should be a "search for political wisdom" that arises through a reflection on the activity of politics (1958, 117, 122).

102. Ibid., 19.

103. Ibid., 65.

104. Ibid.

105. Ibid.

106. Ibid., 70.

107. Ibid., 72.

108. Ibid.

109. Ibid., 75.

110. Ibid., 77.

111. Ibid., 81.

112. Ibid., 84.

113. Ibid., 85.

114. Habinek and Schiesaro 1997, xvii. Examples of different theoretical perspectives brought to classical scholarship include Konstan 1989; Peradotto 1989; M. Skinner 1989; 2000; the panel discussion by Branham, et al. 1997; the edited collection in Hallett and van Nortwick 1997; the edited collection in Wiseman 2002; Hammer 2006; Hammer forthcoming.

115. Significantly, see Habinek 1998.

116. Ricoeur 1981, 34. After writing this, I came across Konstan, who also employs Ricoeur in talking about the Old and the New Classical Humanities (1989).

117. Habinek 1998, 167–68.

118. See Ricoeur 1986. See also Hammer 2004; 2006. In this same vein, Connor expresses the concern that ancient history, as it has come to be influenced by the *Annales* school and the interest in broad themes of "space and time," has focused less (even devalued) public life (Connor 1989, 33). I find myself sympathetic to Galinsky's appeal for a hermeneutic approach that is sensitive to the "horizons of

expectations" between the ancient world and modern questions, concerns, and sensibilities (1992, 33). Segal also notes that "contemporary approaches can illuminate an ancient text, they can bring it into relationship with modern thought and ideas" (1992, 170).

CHAPTER 2

1. Passages in quotations are from Keyes' translation of *On the Republic*.

2. Wallace-Hadrill 1997, 14, 22; also Connolly 2007, 156 on how Cicero's rhetoric is a response to the "immanent fragility" of the republic.

3. The term is from Crawford 1978, 171–86.

4. Crawford 1978, 171–93.

5. *Rep.* 1.1.1; 1.4.7. See, for example, *Attic.* 4.2.2, referring to his oration *De Domo Sua*. On Cicero's association of pain with exile, see Narducci 1997.

6. See Schmidt 1978–79, 119–20; Glucker 1988, 66.

7. Douglas 1995, 208; also Colish 1990, 1:141. Clarke characterizes Cicero's philosophic writings, including the *Tusculans*, as motivated by an "unworldly spirit" (1956, 58; also 60).

8. Narducci 1997, 71. See also Plasberg 1926, 8–9; Alfonsi 1961, 182–85; Süss 1966, 68–69; Douglas 1995, 213, 214, 215 (from political concerns to introverted concerns).

9. Narducci 1997, 71.

10. Wood 1988, 58. Wood notes that for Cicero, "Philosophy's role is to inform politics, to set the course, to provide orientation and order" (1988, 57–8). Unfortunately, Wood does not explain how philosophy performs this function.

11. Douglas 1965, 148. See Smith 1995; Nederman 2000b, 249–53; and Remer 2004 for a more complimentary discussion of the relationship of Cicero's rhetoric to philosophic purpose.

12. Schofield 2002, 102.

13. Claassen writes of Cicero's exile: "For modern readers the puzzle in Cicero's presentation of self in these ingenuous letters [from his exile] lies in his apparent unawareness of a personal, private self separable from a civic self. Both are to him embodied in his material possessions, the support of his family, and the honours of which he has been stripped. In his appeals to friends his private and public *personae* are conflated" (1999, 110). See also Leach: "The

reason Cicero cannot separate the emotional gratification of friendship from its exercise in political interassociation is because politics, as the activity that absorbed all his thought and attention, was also that in which he placed his primary investment of emotion" (1993, 11). Nederman also emphasizes the patriotic attachments by Cicero to the country (2000c, 20).

14. I recognize that Cicero is creating a parallel to Crito not being convinced of the immortality of the soul in Plato's *Phaedo.* Schrenk argues that Cicero answers this uncertainty by introducing rhetoric to the argument; namely, by illustrating divine sanction for belief in the immortality of the soul (Schrenk 1994, 357–60). I agree that that is likely Cicero's purpose. I am not convinced, as I will argue, that Cicero convinces himself.

15. Quoted passages are from King's translation of the *Tusculans.*

16. MacKendrick 1989, 166.

17. See also *Attic.* 3.23.8 and Claassen 1999, 108, 161.

18. *Indolentia* is a word created by Cicero to correspond to the Stoic ideal of ἀναλγησία.

19. See *Tusc.* 2.4.11; 2.18.43; 3.1.1; 3.3.6; 3.34.84; 4.27.58; 4.38.83.

20. In translating *animi,* we should remember that as "mind" it refers to something less rational than the word connotes now, and as "soul" it refers to something less spiritual.

21. Arendt cites this as *Tusculan Disputations* 1, 13 in "The Crisis in Culture" (*BPF* 296, fn. 5). This incorrect citation is likely due to a printing error at the top of the page of her edition of the *Tusculan Disputations,* which incorrectly identified that page as "Disputations, I" rather than "Disputations, II."

22. On Cicero's use of the setting in *On the Republic* to parallel contemporaneous events, see *Q. Fr.* 3.5.2.; Leach 1993, 6. More generally, Paterson describes the violence of the 80s as the formative experience for "the last generation of the Republic" (1985, 27). See also Mitchell 1984, 32–34.

23. On Cicero's interpretation of natural law, see Watson 1971 and Tanner 1972.

24. See especially Cicero, *Rep.* 6.26.29.

25. See Long 1995. Specific mention is made by Cicero to Er in the beginning of Book 6 (*Rep.* 6.3.3).

26. On Scipio Aemilianus's relationship to philosophy, see Morford 2002, 16–17.

27. The suggestion has been taken still further; namely, that

Cicero's *On the Republic* was an anticipation of, and became the blueprint for, Augustus's founding of the principate. See Reitzenstein 1924 (Cicero as advocate of Augustus); Eduard Meyer 1922, 177–91 (Cicero as advocate of Pompey); and Richard Heinze 1924 (Cicero as advocate of aristocracy) for the origin of the debate. Radford goes so far as to describe Cicero as the "prophet of the Principate" (2002, 71; see also 66). Lind reviews the debate and concludes that there is no connection (1986, 94–5). Wirszubski (1950, 87; 1954, 9) and Galinsky (1996, 74) also reject the connection. Colish reviews and defends the view of the dream of Scipio as evoking "the apotheosis of Hercules the Stoic saint" (Colish 1990, 1:95).

28. Penwill writes that the promise of eternal rewards serves as "the ultimate in legitimating ideology" but also notes the ambivalence that accompanies Cicero's description of the disintegrating republic (1994, 74).

29. The meaning of *officium*, or a sense of duty, is fraught with interpretive difficulties. Cicero defines *officium* in his final philosophic work as actions concerned with the "end of the good" and actions that "consist of rules to which every part of our experience of life should conform" (*Offic.* 1.3.7; see Morford 2002, 90). The term undergoes some change in meaning when Cicero translates the Greek *kathekon* as *officium*. *Kathekon* had the philosophical meaning to Zeno as "an action in accordance with reason" and to Panaetius (also a Stoic) as "fitting or proper." Cicero, modeling *De Officiis* after Panaetius's *Peri tou Kathekontos*, gives the term the more Roman sense of "that which ought to be done," particularly toward others (see Morford 2002, 89).

30. See *Attic.* 12.28.2; 12.18.1; 12.15; *Tusc.* 3.31.76; 4.29.63; 5.2.5.

31. Unmanly: *Attic.* 12.38a.1; 12.40.2; also *Tusc.* 2.21.48; 2.24.58; syllogisms: *Tusc.* 2.18.42; 4.28.61; *Fin.* 4.5–7. Nederman points to two strands in Cicero's thought: rhetorical and Stoic (Nederman 2000b). My argument here suggests that Cicero recognized and worked through some of the implications of this ambivalence in his own thought. I think Mansfield overstates Cicero's own confidence in the *Tusculans* that "a man," as one who displays fortitude, "is in truth all that he ought to be" (1996, 33).

32. On ancient models of philosophy as therapy, see Nussbaum 1994; Erskine 1997; Sorabji 2000; Schofield 2002.

33. Also compare movements of the universe: *Rep.* 6.17.17–18.19 and *Tusc.* 5.24.69.

34. On the larger philosophic context for Cicero's love of humanity, see Wright 1995, 188–93. See also Cic. *Fin.* 3.67, 69.

35. See Graver 2002, 83. Although one should be free from passions, one may still have good emotions like "benevolence, mercy, sympathy, and the sober joys of friendship" (Colish 1990 1:42). Nussbaum sees Cicero as adopting the Stoic line that one should not have passions, or even "the approved variety of Stoic *erôs*" (2000, 188).

36. See Lendon on the relations of honor between "men and cities" (1997, 78–84).

37. On plans for the shrine, see also *Attic.* 12.18; 12.37a. Cicero provides an example of a burial monument built by Artemisia in *Tusc.* 3.31.75. Rawson writes that Cicero "wished to give Tullia the only immortality he was certain of, the immortality of glory, and to pay the highest honour he could to her transcendent qualities, to assert in all seriousness that they were transcendent" (1975, 227).

38. I disagree with Carter's assessment that Cicero viewed the struggle of civil war as though it were like a "game" (1972, 18). Certainly, at stake for Cicero were material interests. But I do not think that one can dismiss his genuine attachment to the republic, and the sense of loss that results from its dissolution.

39. See, for example, *Tusc.* 1.38.91; 3.1.2; *Amic.* 5.19; 14.50; 27.100; *Rep.* 1.1.1; 1.2.3; *Offic.* 2.5.17.

40. See Glucker 1988, 62.

41. Nicgorski notes that in Cicero's *Republic* "part of the very rationale or understanding of political life (*ratio rerum civilium*) is that political life *often* does not follow the way of reason (*rationis*)" (1991, 236). Connolly explores the tension that lies in Cicero's rhetoric (and republicanism generally) between reason and passion (2007, 158–97).

42. See Vassaly 1993; also Remer 1999, 41–42.

43. Morford 2002, 44.

44. Cicero, for example, requests that Lucceius write a eulogy to Cicero's consulship (*Fam.* 5.12). Cicero also expresses some consternation at Varro's failure to publish a work that he had promised to dedicate to Cicero (*Attic.* 13.12.3; 13.18).

45. See Mommsen *RG* 5:602–8 and Drumann 1919, 5:230–697. A survey of these views is made in Colish 1990 1:67–68.

46. As Hunt argues, in the *Tusculans* Cicero is taking up Antiochus's critique of two Stoic doctrines: (a) "the conception of the

ethical end as moral worth (*honestum*), absolute and removed from the world of the senses," and (b) "the doctrine that the pure state of virtue implies the complete excision of the emotions" (Hunt 1954, 6). On the Stoic denial of ethical significance to practical activity, see Hunt 1954, 160 and Cic. *Fin.* 3.58.

47. See also *Tusc.* 5.4.10: Pythagoras enriched public and private life of Magna Graecia with "the most excellent institutions and arts."

48. "City in speech" is the well-known term employed by Strauss to describe the Platonic republic (1964, 121). For a discussion of this relationship between Cicero and Plato, see Nicgorski 1991, 234–38. Connolly gives tangibility to Cicero's (and the Romans') notion of rhetoric in her book titled, *The State of Speech* (2007).

49. On Cicero's role in the creation of the word "*humanitas,*" see Lind 1994, 67–8. On *humanitas*, see also Hunt 1954; Clarke 1956, 135–45; Mitchell 1984, 37–38. On learning (*doctrina*), see Mitchell 1984, 35–37.

50. See *Pro Sestio* 98; *Fam* 1.9.21; *De Orat.* 1.1. On the scholarly debate about the meaning of this phrase, see Wirszubski 1954 and Nederman 2000c, 25 (*otium* as public tranquility and as leisure amidst a political career); Balsdon 1960 and Laidlaw 1968 (*otium* as contemplative life that Cicero must elevate when forced into retirement); Bringmann 1971 and Colish 1990, 1:77–78 (*otium* as evolving term as Cicero seeks to reconcile his actions with his own sense of duty).

51. Habinek also identifies the association of knowledge with discernment, seeing it as an aristocratic attempt to maintain "separation from the common people" based on taste rather than birth (1998, 129; also 126).

52. Davies 1971, 163.

53. On a discussion of these categories of beauty in Cicero, see Davies 1971.

54. McClure 1997, 71.

55. Critical: Jay 1978; R. Wolin 1986; Eagleton 1990. Sympathetic: Bennett 1996; Hammer 1997 (on taste); Curtis 1999.

56. Compare to *Rep.* 5.1.2: republic retains only the form but not the substance.

57. See also Habinek who points to *Tusc.* 1.1.2 as suggesting that "Rome is in danger of destroying its common wealth (*res publica*) through too much emphasis on private enrichment" (1994, 60).

58. See Mitchell 1984, 27–32.

59. *Cassell's Latin Dictionary* 617.

60. Cic. *Div.* 2.1.2; Schofield 2002, 102.

61. Macauley 1996, 117.

62. O'Sullivan 1975, 229. See also Adamson: "The main difficulty with an Arendtian dialectic conceived in this way is that it remains a disembodied ideal outside a romanticized, long-lost Athenian polis" (1978, 449).

63. Kateb 1983, 7.

64. Villa 1999, 132.

65. Springborg 1989, 15.

66. Examples of this reluctance include Bradshaw 1989, 46; Barnouw 1990, 26–27; Bowen–Moore 1989, 135–40; Canovan 1992, 147; Hansen 1993, 50; Gottsegen 1994, 98–99; McGowan 1998, 34, 65, 94; Markell 2006 (who talks about the Arendtian notion of beginning without ever making reference to the Romans). Some exceptions include McClure 1997; Seery 1999; Taminiaux 2000; and Hammer 2002a.

67. Brunkhorst 2000, 188.

68. See Villa 1996 and Curtis 1999 for two thoughtful attempts to link the idea of worldlessness back to Arendt's theoretical assumptions.

69. Villa 1996, 10, emphasis in original.

70. Ibid., 11, emphasis in original. See also Honig 1993.

71. Ibid. See also Kohn 2000.

72. Ibid., 247.

73. Arendt herself will use this language in talking about the role of fabrication. See, for example, *OR* 28.

74. On the abundance of images of fabrication, see Canovan 1994.

75. Canovan makes an important first step in noting the close relationship between Arendt's notion of politics and her understanding of culture (1994). Frampton looks at the relationship between political power and its "social and physical constitution" in architectural form (1979, 127).

76. It should be noted that both Arendt and Cicero are sympathetic to the idea of being citizens of the world. But that citizenship needs to be grounded in something more tangible. See Euben 2003, 126–32 for a critique of the Stoic idea of universal citizenship that I think is consistent with the arguments of both Cicero and Arendt.

77. See, for example, *RV* 10 ("limitless"), 21–22 (dissolves existing situation into "mood").

78. See, for example, *RV* 15 and Arendt 1978b.

79. Waldron 2000, 208.

80. Villa 1996, 158.

81. Curtis 1999, 121.

82. Ibid.

83. See my discussion of Arendt's use of a Roman conception of foundation in Hammer 2002a.

84. Lewis and Short; Cic. *Nat.* 2.60.151; 2.62.156; 2.63.157; Virg. *Ec.* 3.43.

85. Wolin 2004, 76.

86. Canovan 1992, 147.

87. Villa, for example, passes over Arendt's reference to the Romans at several critical stages, including in Arendt's image of the philosopher as spectator at the games (1996, 103–5) and Arendt's differentiation between a Greek and Roman incorporation of craft images into politics (1996, 246).

88. Wolin, in focusing exclusively on Arendt's Hellenism, criticizes Arendt for failing to give us "a politics without the divisive conflicts that have presented the main challenge to politicians" and that have led to the "broadening of citizenship" (1994, 293). Arendt does, however, recognize the generative role of conflict in the establishment and modification of Roman political life.

89. Brunkhorst, for example, sees Roman political freedom as fixed and defined within the walls of the city (2000, 180, 192).

90. Brunkhorst 2000, 183.

91. See, for example, Saller 1984; Wallace-Hadrill 1988; Edwards 1993, 150–60; Flower 1996. Frampton notes, "Again the Latin root of this verb—*aedificare*, from *aedes*, a 'building,' or, even more originally, a 'hearth,' and *ficare*, 'to make,' has latent within it the public connotation of the hearth as the aboriginal 'public' space of appearance" (1979, 103).

92. See, for example, Brunkhorst 2000, 178.

93. Canovan 1994, 184.

94. Wolin 1994, 300.

95. Cicero's emphasis on the transmission of culture, according to Habinek, is meant "as a tactic of social control and domination" by the literate class (1994, 65). I do not disagree that culture serves as a form of social control. I question the extent to which Cicero thought that cultural meanings and, in particular, the cultivation of taste, could and should remain the exclusive domain of one group.

96. Nederman 2000b, 253. See also Remer, who argues that Cic-

ero's emphasis on rhetoric in politics is attributable not just to an elitism but to a broader sense that "human beings are complex creatures—rational and emotional" (Remer 1999, 54). In particular, rhetoric is critical in animating political action (Remer 1999, 55).

97. Compare, for example, Arendt's discussion of Rahel Varnhagen, who remains lost in her interior world of feeling and introspection, to her discussion of Isak Dineson, whose sense of loss and despair is articulated through stories.

98. *OR* 207, citing Harrington, *The Commonwealth of Oceana* (1656) (Liberal Arts edition), 111.

99. Benjamin 1968, 241.

100. Arendt also writes that Rahel Varnhagen's great "error" was her attempt to "live life as if it were a work of art, to believe that by 'cultivation' one can make a work of art of one's own life" (*RV* xvi).

101. Montesquieu, "Discourse on Cicero." A new translation is provided by Fott 2002.

CHAPTER 3

1. Following Luce 1965 and Badian 1993, 17–19, the first publication of Book 1 appeared no later then 30 BCE, and the publication of the pentad around 27 BCE. We cannot tell if the preface was written with Book 1 or with the publication of the pentad. In any case, as Badian writes, "there was no enthusiastic welcome for the *nouus status rei publicae*" (1993, 19).

2. See Cic. *Tusc.* 3.17.36; 4.4.10–6.14; Woodman 1988, 133; Moles 1993, 133–34; Nussbaum 1994, 13–16, 48–77, 316–58.

3. See Moles 1993, 150–52; Woodman 1988, 133–34; *OLD*. All quotations from Livy are from the Foster translation unless otherwise noted.

4. Woodman 1988, 133–34. Further support in Livy at 3.20.8 and 22.8.5. See also Moles 1993, 151–53.

5. See Moles 1993, 146; also Livy 9.9.11.

6. On the reception of Livy's *History* by his contemporaneous audience, see Cichorius 1922, 261–63; Badian 1993, 14, 18. Wiseman suggests that histories, such as Livy's, were popular among a mass audience, not as written works, but as works read aloud (1987, 253–56).

7. Walsh 1966, 129. See also Kraus 1994a, 9–13.

8. Critical assessments of Livy's use of evidence are provided by Badian 1966 (on the early historians); Syme 1959, 28; Ogilvie 1965, 5–7; Rawson 1985, 219–20; and Raaflaub 1986, 16–22; 1993. More sympathetic assessments that place Livy in a broader rhetorical tradition are provided by Walbank 1960; Walsh 1961, chapts. 5–6; Walsh 1966; Burck 1964; Luce 1977; Fornara 1983, chapt. 3; Cornell 1986; Konstan 1986; Ungern-Sternberg 1986; Vasaly 1987, esp. 225; Wiseman 1987, 256–61 (ancient historiography, generally); Pauw 1991; Miles 1995; Jaeger 1997; Marincola 1997, 76–79; Kraus 1994b; Kraus and Woodman 1997; Feldherr 1998; Chaplin 2000.

9. Burck 1964, 195–233.

10. Walsh 1966, 129, 171. See also Walsh 1961, 168–72; Burck 1964, 195–233; Luce 1977, 231.

11. See, for example, Taylor 1918, 158–59; Syme 1939, 316–18, 464–65, modified to some extent in Syme 1959; Cochrane 1940, 98–99; Liebeschuetz 1967, 55; Strasburger 1983, 265–66; Joshel 1992, 114; Cizek 1992. Scholarship that has portrayed Livy as more critical of Augustus includes Walsh 1961; Mette 1961; Petersen 1961; Ogilvie 1965, 2–3; Gabba 1984, 79–80; Burck 1991 [distant]; Badian 1993; Miles 1995, 47–54. Luce sees Livy as able to "lift his eyes from the struggles of the immediate past" and, from the perspective of someone who is a provincial and who did not have a political career, could explain "Augustus' appeal and success" (1977, 298). Some recent scholars have allowed for the independence of Livy's work while noting its similarity to Augustus's project of building a new Rome (Levene 1993, 243–48; Kraus 1994a, 6–9; Galinsky 1996, 280–87; Feldherr 1998; Chaplin 2000, 192–96). For reviews of the scholarship, see Deininger 1985 and Badian 1993.

12. Hulliung 1983, 147. Even Coby, who takes seriously the influence of Livy on Machiavelli's thought, reduces Livy to one among "assorted others who write as apologists for Roman imperialism" (1999, 221).

13. Collingwood 1946, 44.

14. Wiedemann 2000, 523.

15. Moles 1993, 153.

16. Feldherr 1998, 8.

17. See Feldherr 1998, 34–37.

18. Feldherr 1997, 137.

19. Kraus and Woodman 1997, 55. See Jaeger 1997, 22.

20. Ibid., 55–56.

21. Matthes 2000, 47.

22. Chaplin 2000, 5.

23. Livy pref. 10. As Miles notes, etymologically, *monumentum* derives from the Indo-European root **men-*, "to think," and the causative suffix *-*yo*, suggesting "something that makes one think" (Miles 1995, 17). *Monumentum* is related, as well, to the Latin verb *monere*, "to remind." Historiography, like a monument, stands in some way as a visible reminder of past events that causes the reader to "to think" or "to behold" and "contemplate" (both senses are contained in *intueri*). A great deal of attention has been paid recently to Livy's notion of history as a monument. See Moles 1993; Miles 1995; Kraus and Woodman 1997; Jaeger 1997; Feldherr 1998; Chaplin 2000.

24. See Livy pref.10: "every kind of experience." Quoted passages from *The Discourses* are from the Mansfield and Tarcov translation unless otherwise noted.

25. I follow Parel in his definition of *virtù* as the disposition of individuals or groups to perform acts beneficial to the good of the state (1992, 86). The complexity of the term has been explored by numerous scholars, including Strauss 1958; Wood 1967; Pocock 1975; Skinner 1978, 176; Hulliung 1983; Newel 1987; Kahn 1994; Wolin 2004; Hörnqvist 2004.

26. Williams 1977, 132. See for example Peirce 1960, par. 5.283, 291, 294. Interestingly, Humphrey, in his Harvard lectures on consciousness, develops his entire talk around the sensation of seeing red (Humphrey 2006).

27. See Nietzsche, who argues that "consciousness is really only a net of communication" that arose as individuals, in order to express the need for help and protection, "needed to 'know' himself what distressed him, he needed to 'know' how he felt, he needed to 'know' what he thought" (1974, sect. 354).

28. This argument stands in contrast to Rahe's somewhat overstated claim that Livy's notion of the loss of liberty was "like most Roman notions, in its origins Greek" (2000, 284).

29. Mansfield, for example, argues that one lesson that Machiavelli takes from Livy is how the nobility can manipulate the people through "indirect rule" by getting the people to carry out punishments, but not actually letting them initiate or carry out policy (1996, 247–50; also 306–8). There is a growing scholarship that

seeks to argue against the view that Roman politics was largely divorced from the attitudes and opinions of the populace. The view of Rome as a largely closed oligarchy is articulated by Gelzer 1962 (= 1912); Münzer 1920; Syme 1939; Scullard 1973. Challenges to this approach (though not agreement) have been made by Meier 1980; Nicolet 1980; Millar 1984, 1986, 1998; Brunt 1966; 1971b: 74–111, 1982, 1988: 4–6, 23–56; Vanderbroeck 1987; North 1990a, 1990b; Badian 1996; Hölkeskamp 1994, 11–19, 75–81; Jehne (ed.) 1995; Bell 1997; Yakobson 1999; Lintott 1999; Morstein-Marx 2004; Williamson 2005; Connolly 2007, esp. 44. Even Mouritsen, who attempts to demonstrate that politics had little connection to popular interest, notes how leaders competed for popular support (2001).

30. The earliest appearances of the term define psychology as something that "treats of the soul" (*Blancard's Physiological Dictionary* [1693], from *OED*).

31. See Fleisher 1972; Parel 1991; 1992; Mansfield 1996; Fischer 1997; 2000; Nederman 2000a.

32. See Seneca *Ep.* 100.9; Rossbach 1882, 367, n. 3; Walsh 1958, 355; 1961, 4; Syme 1959, 51; Schindel 1983 (who takes a more critical look at the nature of this philosophy).

33. For the diffusion of medical knowledge in Rome, see Rawson 1985, 170–84.

34. Nussbaum 1994, 13–16. On the general diffusion of medical imagery in Latin literature, see Fantham 1972, 14–18. For the close relationship between philosophy and medicine, see Frede 1987a.

35. Walsh 1955; 1958; 1961, 46–81; also Ogilvie 1965, 48 (Livy's Stoicism as "polite"). Kajanto 1957, 53–63; Liebeschuetz 1967, 51–53; and Levene 1993, 30–33 provide criticisms of Walsh's argument.

36. Levene 1997, 130–31; also Rawson 1985, 289–91. On the influence of Aristotle on Cicero, see Frede 1989 (*On the Republic*); Classen 1989 (on the *Tusculans*) and Rawson 1985 (generally).

37. On the influence of Cicero on Livy, see Syme 1959, 51, 53; Walsh 1961, 42–43; Moles 1993, 146. On the influence of Posidonius on Livy, see Walsh 1958, 357; 1961, 49–50.

38. See, for example, Shaw 1985 on the ability of Stoicism to incorporate peripheral ideas.

39. See Graver 2002, 84 and Remer 2004.

40. On ancient debates about the qualities of *pneuma*, see Rawson 1985, 172–73 and Colish 1990 1.27–28. *Psuchê* may also carry a meaning that accords with *anima*, connoting the immortal part of

the soul. *Animus* (the mind) seems more appropriate to Livy's usage. So, too, Machiavelli emphasizes the role of spirit (*animo*) rather than the transcendent soul (*anima*) as performing "the functions of willing and intending" (Fischer 1997, 801; see also Parel 1991, 335; 1992, 88; Fleisher 1972, 118–25; Mansfield 1996, 40–45. Fischer 1997 also appears as Fischer 2000, 49–83).

41. On the difficulties of translation, see Sandbach 1971; von Staden 1978; Frede 1992; Nussbaum 1994, 327; Long 1996, 271.

42. Von Staden 1978, 97. See also Hahm 1978, 84–85.

43. Sandbach 1971; Frede 1987b, 152–57. See also Cic. *Acad.* 2.21.

44. Long 1996, 247. See Cic. *Acad.* 2.21.

45. Arist. *De An.* 431b7; Frede 1992, 289. See also von Staden who suggests that for the Stoics "all mental activity is hence at least to some degree dependent upon sensory experience" (1978, 109). Applied to Machiavelli, see Fischer 1997, 793.

46. Long 1996, 245.

47. Ibid., 247.

48. See Rist 1969, 86–91; von Staden 1978, 97; Inwood 1985, 164–65.

49. See also Cic. *Tusc.* 4.13.30; Graver 2002, 152, 154.

50. Graver 2002, 152.

51. Pico della Mirandola 1930, 51.

52. Ibid., 59.

53. Ibid.

54. Ibid.

55. Gal. *De Plac.* F. 164.53–54; see also F 165.26–28, 169.114–17; Cic. *Tusc.* 3.5.11; 3.1.2.

56. Much of our knowledge of Posidonius comes by way of Galen's *De Placitis*. For a careful discussion of both the limits and possibilities of interpretation, see Kidd 1971; 1988, vol. 2, pt. 1.

57. Jaeger 1999.

58. Pico della Mirandola 1930, 53; *D* 3.31.

59. Machiavelli, letter to Piero Soderini, Jan. 1512–(1513), No. 116 in Machiavelli 1965; see Parel 1992, 80 and Minogue 1972.

60. Gal. *De Plac.* F 162.8–9; see also Cic. *De Orat.* 2.186. For Cicero, the rhetorician (in this case, when in court), like the physician, must be able to recognize the malady as well as the disposition of the patient to provide proper treatment. This treatment includes exciting feelings that are in accord with the goals of the rhetorician. On

the relationship of the rhetorician to the historian, see *De Orat.* 2.51–70. On the influence of *De Orat.* on Livy, see Walsh 1961, 42–43.

61. Moles 1993, 154.

62. See Frede 1992, 289; Webb 1997, 117–21; Quint. *Inst.* 6.2.29–30; Cic. *Orat.* 2.357.

63. See Vasaly 1993, 26–39, esp. 29–30; Jaeger 1997, 22; Levene 1997, 139–47 (on an "internal audience").

64. Arnold 1911, 133.

65. Lloyd 1978, 243; also Rist 1969, 86–91

66. See Cic. *Tusc.* 2.27. 65; 2.23.55; Cic. *Acad.* 2.56.

67. See also Sen. *Ep.* 56.5.

68. Jaeger 1999.

69. On Roman population increases, see Brunt 1971a, 11–12.

70. See Cic. *Tusc.* 3.15.31.

71. See Cic. *Tusc.* 4.28.60.

72. See Arnold 1911, 68, 133; Cic. *Acad.* 1.41; 2.30.

73. See Vasaly who writes, "this constant reliance on the visual and the concrete was but the Roman gateway to the world of ideas" (1993, 257). On the power of words to effect *phantasia*, see Watson 1988, 215–19; Webb 1997; Quint. *Inst.* 6.2.29.

74. Wiseman surveys different interpretations of the Romulus and Remus myth (1995, 89–102). Bremmer 1987 places the myth in an Indo-European context. Gruen discusses the fixing of the Aeneas myth (1992, 6–51). Cornell 1975 discusses the relationship between the Romulus and Remus myth and the Aeneas myth.

75. Wiseman 1995, 13.

76. Strasburger 1968, 7–8, 38–43.

77. See, for example, Dougherty 1998 on murder legends in Greek colonization.

78. Cornell 1995, 60. See also Momigliano 1989, 58. An attempt to bring the Roman founding legends into line with Greek ideals can be seen in Dionysius of Halicarnassus, *Roman Antiquities*, 2.7–29. Cicero also portrays Romulus as a visionary founder more in keeping with Greek notions of founding (Cic. *Rep.* 2.2.4).

79. On the rape of the Sabines, see Hemker 1985; Miles 1995, 179–219.

80. See *D* 1.10: "And truly, if a prince seeks glory of the world, he ought to desire to possess a corrupt city—not to spoil it entirely as did Caesar but to reorder it as did Romulus."

81. Fischer understates the animating role of experience in shaping conceptions of justice when he claims that justice emerges only when a "strongman" makes laws and punishments (2000, 89). Sullivan ascribes the origin of justice to "calculation alone," understating the sentiments of love and hatred that underlie the conception of justice (1996, 92).

82. Machiavelli recognizes this in singling out for greatness those founders who are able to create a new order that lasts beyond their life (see *P* 6).

83. See Matthes 2000, 42. On Romulus's ability to direct the attention of the people, see Livy 1.9.6–7, 10.

84. Ogilvie 1965, 65.

85. When Machiavelli refers to Romulus as reordering the state (*D* 1.9), Coby interprets it as a "misnaming" (1999, 50). I think Machiavelli is following Livy here.

86. Penella notes that the association of *ferox* with Tullus underscores "the danger inherent in excessive devotion" to *vis* (force), which is associated with Romulus (1990, 211).

87. Liebeschuetz points to Livy's willingness to leave exposed the deliberate, human-made aspect of religion as the foundation for social order (1967, 48).

88. For a survey of scholarship on the Tarquins, see Cornell 1995, 215–26.

89. See Matthes 2000, 42–43.

90. Dunkle notes that for the Romans, "the opposite of *libido* was *lex*" (1967, 168). Machiavelli distinguishes between violence directed toward promoting the common good, such as was the case with Romulus, and violence intended to promote private interests (*D* 1.9).

91. I am reminded of Havel in his discussion of the foundation of totalitarianism (esp. 1991, 141–48).

92. See Ogilvie 1965, 217: "very different in intelligence from the mask which he had assumed."

93. The quotation is from Posidonius: Gal. *De Plac.* F 162.8–9. See Joshel 1992, 125. As Calhoon argues, Lucretia serves as a reminder of how much of Rome had sunk into self-indulgence and idleness, which breeds effeminacy (1997, 154). On differing interpretations of the Lucretia story over time, see Donaldson 1982.

94. Williams 1979, 164, italics in original.

95. For Lucretia as ritual scapegoat, see Klindienst Joplin 1990 and Calhoon 1997. The argument has been made that one sees the

unification of the roles of consular and father in the figure of Brutus, establishing a new relationship to the people that is both political and paternal (see Feldherr 1997, 153). One can read an interestingly parallel account of the Gdansk movement (Barker 2001).

96. See Joshel 1992, esp. 121–28 on women in Livy as catalysts for male action.

97. I disagree with Klindienst Joplin's claim, in talking about Machiavelli's recounting of the expulsion of the Tarquins, that "Memory of the female victim, raped and killed, is hard to sustain. Memory of the tyrant is not" (1990, 51). I also disagree with Jed who sees Brutus as the republican hero because he "subordinate[s] the emotions" of the people to "the cause of liberty" and employs the tale to help form habits of detachment (1989, 10). My suggestion is that the memories are tied together as felt meanings, and these felt meanings are integral to the Roman notion of liberty. Helpful discussions of the meaning of *libertas* in the republic are provided by Wirszubski 1950; Brunt 1988, 281–350; and Connolly 2007, 158–97. As Connolly writes, in rejecting attempts to define Roman liberty as either "positive" or "negative," "the binary at work in Roman *libertas* is not presence versus absence but master versus slave; the liberty prized by both patrician and plebs was the liberty of the free" (2007, 159).

98. Viroli 1998, 119.

99. See Viroli 1998, 120–21.

100. McCormick 2003, 634. See, for example, Skinner 1978, 157–58; Skinner 1990a, 134; Viroli 1998, 119. Colish, while exploring the range of meanings of liberty in Machiavelli, sees the importance of the Romans in Machiavelli as providing a "focus on liberty as the enjoyment of private legal rights" (1971, 349). Brunt, in contrast, suggests that Roman liberty was not simply a "cloak" for protection of material interests and rights (1988, 297).

101. McCormick 2003, 634–35.

102. See, for example, Pocock 1975, 186, 194; Skinner 1978, 181–82; Viroli 1990, 158–61; 1998, 126.

103. McCormick 2003, 617, 627. Distancing from Livy is also made by Rahe 2000, 298–301 (populism based on interest) and Sullivan 2000, 45–47 (importance of the people as soldier).

104. Viroli provides a useful discussion of the "passion for liberty" that lies at the heart of Machiavelli's thought (1998, 148–74).

105. Thus, I think Nicolet's claim that "from the individual's

point of view *libertas* was primarily a guarantee of equality under the law" is too limiting (1980, 320).

106. Walsh 1961, 69. On *concordia*, see, for example, Livy 5.7.10. On discord, see Momigliano 1942, 120. Fontana 2003 locates in Sallust the inspiration for Machiavelli's emphasis on public conflict as necessary for republican liberty.

107. This claim modifies Viroli's claim that Machiavelli "praises social conflict" as long as conflict does not violate "the rule of law and the common good" and as long as each component of the city stays in its "proper place" (Viroli 1998, 127, 125).

108. On publicness in Roman politics, see Millar 1984; 1986; 1998. Some examples of this publicness are striking. The *lex repetundarum* emphasizes "the necessity of the observance, under the eyes of the people, of the rules on the part of both the praetor and the *iudices* themselves" (Millar 1986, 8; also Sherwin-White 1982). Millar also notes that under the law of Bantia "not only must office-holders and senators swear within five days to obey the law, but they must do so in public, during daylight" (Millar 1986, 8).

109. Mansfield and Tarcov suggest that Livy, among other ancient authors, regards dictatorship "as an embarrassment to the Roman republic" and "play[s] it down" (1996, xxix). I see no evidence of this in Livy's account here.

110. Wiseman takes up the question of how, given the topography of Rome, the trial could be held out of sight. He sees it as a result of combining parts of different accounts for the purpose of sharpening the *exempla* rather than achieving historical truth (Wiseman 1987, 225–43).

111. The complexity of sorting out the historical evidence of the nature of the conflict between patricians and plebs in the early Roman Republic is discussed by Mitchell 1986; 1990; Raaflaub (ed.) 1986, especially Richard 1986; and Momigliano 1986.

112. On the tradition of the *decemviri*, see Ogilvie 1965, 451–89 and Wiseman 1979, 104–12. For a comparative analysis of the Twelve Tables in the context of broader legal and political developments, see Raaflaub 1986b and Eder 1986.

113. On the publicness of the *decemviri*, see 3.33.8; 3.33.10; 3.34.1. When the *decemviri* complete the ten tablets, they make them public so that the proposed laws might be debated and modified before being finally confirmed (3.34.2; *D* 1.40). A consensus emerges that the *decemviri* should be reappointed to give time for two more tablets

to be added. Machiavelli adds that Appius started a "rumor" that the laws could be perfected if the *decemviri* are appointed for another year so that they can draw up two more tablets (*D* 1.40). There is no textual support in Livy for that interpretation.

114. Livy is reconciling two traditions, one of Appius's achievements in establishing the first ten tables, the other of Appius's tyranny associated with the final two tablets. See Vasaly 1987, 212–16; Ogilvie 1965, 461–62, 503–6. On the historicity of the latter tradition, see von Ungern-Sternberg 1986. Ogilvie sees Livy's treatment of Appius's character as "a good example of the Roman—Stoic—preconception that a man's character cannot change and that he is at twenty what he will be at fifty and that what he is at fifty he must have been at twenty" (1965, 463). I am reluctant, however, to describe Livy as a Stoic.

115. Livy employs what Vasaly refers to as the "stock" traits of the "tyrannical personality" (1987, 218). See also Dunkle 1967 and 1971 on how tyrants are characterized.

116. For the connection of Verginia to Roman (especially plebeian) liberty, see Syme 1939, 155, 306, 469; Wirszubski 1960, 103–6; Vasaly 1987, 220–21.

117. Scholars generally, and rightly, emphasize the religious aspects of the Camillus legend. See Ogilvie 1965, 626; Miles 1971; Dumézil 1980; Feldherr 1998, 79–81. The Camillus legend is generally seen, as Ogilvie aptly states, as "one of the most daring fabrications in Roman history" (1965, 289). On the development of the legend, see Luce 1971, 289–97.

118. See Kraus 1994, 279.

119. See Balsdon 1979, 65; Ogilvie 1965, 727–29.

120. Traditional view of Gauls: 5.33.11; 5.48.3; 5.37.4–5, 8. Rashness of Romans: 5.36.1; 5.37.3; 5.37.7; 5.38.1; 5.38.5; 5.38.7–8. Temperance of Gauls: 5.38.3–4; 5.39.1; 5.41.4. Luce notes that Livy's account differs from those in Diodorus and Plutarch by emphasizing the guilt of all elements of Roman society, not just the Fabii (1971, 277).

121. Ogilvie 1965, 727.

122. Ogilvie 1965, 727. See Williams 1955, 229. Ogilvie corrects the manuscript to *concipere* from *consipere.*

123. Luce notes the contrast between the considerable time Livy spends on the trial of the siege and the brevity by which he addresses the culmination of the siege (1971, 281–82).

124. On avarice as a theme of Book 5, see Miles 1986.

125. Viroli 1998, 150.

126. See, for example, Hölkeskamp 2004, 138–68, on the role of visual monuments in the cultural memory (*kulturellen Gedächtnis*) of the Roman Republic.

127. Pitkin 1984, 151.

128. See Greene 1986; Mousley 1995; Najemy 1993, 8; 1995.

129. Rubinstein 1982, 153–55, 181–84. Rubinstein does recognize the importance of Roman history in providing a republican genealogy for Italy. But, as Rubinstein notes, it was "only in the fourteenth century that Italian historiography became a major source of our knowledge of contemporary political ideas, and in the meantime, the rediscovery and absorption of Aristotle's *Politics* had transformed Italian political thought" (1982, 155). Arguments for the ongoing importance of the Romans in Italian political thought are provided by Pocock 1975; Skinner 1981, 1990a, 1990b; Blythe 2000; Hörnqvist 2004.

130. Garver 1987, 8.

131. Ibid., 134–35.

132. Hulliung 1983, 139.

133. Ibid.

134. Ibid., 151.

135. See Strauss 1958; also Mansfield 1979; 1996; Mansfield and Tarcov 1996, xix; Sullivan 1996; 2004; MacFarland 1999; Rahe 2000, esp. 305–8. Sullivan claims, for example, that Machiavelli's "changes in Livy's account" suggest "a measure of disrespect toward his ancient master" (1996, 137). Mansfield and Tarcov write, "when examined, ancient virtue [for Machiavelli] turns out to show little respect for things ancient" (1996, xix).

136. Strauss 1958, 122.

137. Ibid., 123.

138. Ibid., 86.

139. See Gilbert 1965, 197; Gilbert 1977, 133; Bondanella 1973, 22; Hulliung 1983, 154–55.

140. Cassirer 1955, 155.

141. Ibid., 156.

142. Parel 1972, 7. See also Olschki where he compares Machiavelli's "science of motion" to Galileo's (1945, 26).

143. Parel 1972, 9.

144. Wolin 2004, 193; also Butterfield 1960, 28–33 and de Grazia 1989, 197.

145. Gilbert 1977, 132.

146. Ibid., 124.

147. Ibid., 131–2; also Gilbert 1965, 168 and Walker 1950, 1–2, 65–74, 82–84, 92–99.

148. Gilbert 1965, 169. At the very least, the creation of examples would seem to diminish the credibility of Machiavelli's intellectual achievement as a scientist.

149. Coby 1999, 210.

150. Ibid.

151. Ibid., 213–14. Coby's conclusion that ultimately Machiavelli's project lies in the elevation of spiritedness seems consistent with the role of history as the cultivation of felt meanings which directs this spirit (1999, 283).

152. For a review of this new rhetorical approach to Machiavellian studies, see Hörnqvist 2004, 1–37. Viroli sees Machiavelli as articulating a Roman practice of "deliberative rhetoric" (1998, 4). Bondanella places Machiavelli's work, in part, in a classical rhetorical tradition that emphasizes the persuasive role of history (1973, 21–22). *The Prince* and *The Discourses* are "theoretical treatises which argue abstract ideas by examining the actions and personalities of great men" (Bondanella 1973, 52). Machiavelli's "historical illustrations function rhetorically as a means of persuading his audience that his theories actually have the status of rhetorical fact" (Bondanella 1973, 59).

153. Mansfield 1996, 61. I think this characterization of rhetoric as fraud does not fully capture the moral character of rhetoric as envisioned by the ancient authors, including Aristotle and Cicero (see for example Remer 2004).

154. Kahn 1994, 8.

155. Ibid., 26, 56; also 32.

156. Ibid., 45.

157. Hörnqvist 2004, 35; also 11.

158. Ibid., 34.

159. Matthes 2000, 75.

160. Ibid., 76.

161. Ibid., 75–76.

162. Ibid., 76.

163. Viroli recognizes the "rhetorical power of history" to "move" and "incite" the reader (1998, 97; also 99–100). Viroli places this

argument in the context of a classical rhetorical tradition. I am attempting to draw out the psychological assumptions that underlie this claim.

164. Minogue 1972, 157.

165. Traditionally this vision is seen as the desire for a self-contained republican community (see for example Baron 1955, 438; Skinner 1978; Viroli 1992, 154–77). Others emphasize the more imperial aspects of this vision (see Strauss 1958, 89; Hulliung 1983, 26–7, 96; Sullivan 2000; Hörnqvist 2000; 2004).

166. As Coby writes, "Moderation is thus the consequence of involvement in affairs" (1999, 35).

167. Pocock 1975, 180, 184; also Pocock 1972; Skinner 1978.

168. Ibid., 192.

169. Ibid.

170. *D* 1.47; Fischer 2000, 131.

171. Fischer 1997, 804–5.

172. Fischer 2000, 131; also Mansfield 1996, 94; Sullivan 2000, 46; 2004, 54–55. As Sullivan writes, "the wisdom of the people" seems "to be founded in the very gullibility that made them so vulnerable to the deceptions of the great" (2004, 55).

173. Fischer 1997, 822, 820.

174. Ibid., 820.

175. Fischer 2000, 68–69.

176. Nederman 2000a, 361.

177. Fischer 2000, 132. See also *D* 1.57: multitude creates a chief for itself; *D* 1.58: hold rank equally and honorably. On a related note, the example that Fischer cites of Nicias's failed effort to dissuade the people from launching an assault on Sicily points more to tendencies of a people to engage in "daring enterprises" (*D* 1.53).

178. Hulliung 1983, 147–48; Sullivan 2004, 58, 68.

179. Linderski identifies this Samnite oath as a corrupt religious form (1993, 61).

180. Sullivan argues that "the Roman commander inspired his own troops by actually making light of the importance of religion" (1996, 110). Not quite. Papirius, in both Machiavelli's and Livy's account, points to a corrupt form of religious ritual that seeks only to inspire terror rather than religion that is an ongoing and integrated aspect of a community's education, training, and experience.

181. Hörnqvist 2004, 191.

182. Along these same lines, Wood associates *virtù* with a successful army in which there is authority but also vigor and initiative displayed by all the soldiers (1967, 171–72).

CHAPTER 4

1. Martin 1981, 104.

2. Ibid., 142. So Benario sees Tacitus as affirming the necessity of the principate, "provided the emperor was good" (1972, 19). The focus on the personality of the emperor can be seen, for example, in debates about the nature of Tiberius. Tiberius as dissembling hypocrite: Marsh 1931, 14; Pippidi 1944, 37; Walker 1952, 238–39; Alexander 1954, 356–57; Syme 1958, 422–23; Martin 1981, 113; Gill 1983, 486; Sinclair 1995, 82; Griffin 1995, 36; Boesche 1996, 87–109. More complex portraits of Tiberius: Tarver 1902, 294–319; Rogers 1943; Syme 1958, 426–29; Levick 1976, 75–8; Woodman 1998, 69; Seager 2005.

3. Martin 1981, 143. As Tacitus writes in his obituary of Tiberius, "he erupted into crimes and degradations alike when at last, with his shame and dread removed, he had only himself to rely on" (*Ann.* 6.51.3). Quoted passages from *The Annals* are from Woodman, unless otherwise noted.

4. See Goodyear 1972, 92.

5. *Decemviral* power actually lasted into the third year, though legal power only lasted two years (see Goodyear 1972, 92).

6. The military tribunes actually lasted from 444–367 BCE, "oscillating with consulship or dictatorship down to 406, thereafter almost unbroken" (Goodyear 1972, 93).

7. O'Gorman describes the variety of words Tacitus uses for power in this opening section (2000, 8).

8. On the cruelty of Sulla, see Tac. *Hist.* 2.38.

9. Eder 1990, 74. Raaflaub and Samons, too, ask this question (1990, 450–54).

10. Schellhase 1976, 114–16.

11. Ibid., 133–34.

12. Tuck 1999, 101.

13. For discussions of the difference between Aristotle's and Montesquieu's account, see Koebner 1951, 291, 299; Kassem 1960, 107; Pangle 1973, 70; Richter 1973, 1; 1995, 333–37; Schaub 1995,

23; Krause 2001, 233. For Aristotle, the *despotês* was the head of the household who exercised absolute rule over what, for Aristotle, were slaves by nature (see *Pol.* 1253b–1255b; 1278b–1279a). Politically, the despot was a tyrant who ruled over free men as if they were slaves. *Dominus* is the common Latin word for the master of a slave.

14. Wirszurbski 1950, 160.

15. On the association of psychology with character, see Miller 1964, 293; Häussler 1965; Martin 1981, 215; Mellor 1993, 70–71. Alexander concludes that the frequent characterization of Tacitus's historical approach as psychological probably "arose in relation to his interest in persons and their characters" but has little relationship to what we might describe as "psychological" today (Alexander 1952, 327; also Alexander 1954, 352–57). See also Henry and Walker who wonder how Tacitus ever acquired the reputation as an "acute psychologist" since his description of individual motivation and behavior is "entirely lacking in subtlety and penetration" (1963, 106).

16. Luce 1986, 156.

17. Ibid., 151.

18. I am probably closer to Betensky's position that Tacitus is searching "for psychological rather than historical truth" (Betensky 1978, 420). As von Fritz writes, there is "a problem not only of the psychology of Tiberius and of other individual emperors but also of the political psychology of the institution of the Principate itself that is to a large extent independent of the personal psychological equation both of the emperors and of Tacitus" (1957, 79). Cousin notes the instances of Tacitus's use of words that reflect the psychological response to the insecurity and unrest of the time: *pertimescere* 2, *pavescere* 8, *tristitia* 14, *timor* 16, *maestitia* 17, *maestus* 31, *pavere* 32, *pavidus* 33, *anxius* 33, *tristis* 39, *trepidus* 39, *timere* 44, *metuere* 57, *terror* 75, *pavor* 81, *metus* 402 (Cousin 1969, 121). See also Williams 1990, 154–56. Political psychology points to the role of collective perceptions, emotions, moods, preferences, motivations, and calculations as the impetus for political action. See McGraw 2003, 395–96.

19. Compare to Cels. pro. 15: *inflammatio talem motum efficit, qualis in febre est.* For Tacitus's conception of the state as a biological organism, see Havas 1991. Similarly, Berlin sees Montesquieu's model as "biological, not chemical" because Montesquieu is exploring the " 'inner' forces," rather than the "mechanical causes," by which a social organism functions (1997, 140).

20. On the use of *tabes*, see, for example, *Ann.* 1.53.2; 11.6.2;

12.50.2; 12.66.1 and Cels. 3.22.1. On the practice of ancient psychology, see Roccatagliata 1986.

21. For a discussion of the different forms of sensualist psychology in the French Enlightenment, or what O'Neal refers to as "sensationism," see O'Neal 1996.

22. Scholars have sought to resolve what is seen as a tension in Montesquieu's analysis between the development of a state as the product of individual choices and development that is determined by inexorable processes. Carrithers claims that Montesquieu provides "contrasting historical explanations" that take on a "distinctively determinist orientation" in his discussion of Rome (1986, 69, 77). Wolin sees Montesquieu as emphasizing the "undesigned, unpremeditated qualities" of society (1989, 107). Collingwood argues that Montesquieu views society as an organism governed by natural and ineluctable laws (1946, 79). Manent suggests that Montesquieu initially indicates the diversity of different societies and then "abolishes this diversity or deprives it of its meaning by drawing out the general laws under which all particular cases fall and which thereby regulate the functioning of human societies" (1998, 57). Shackleton seeks to reconcile "organic determinism and individual freedom" by suggesting that as the state develops, moral causes (which are in the realm of freedom of the will) take precedence over physical causes. The role of the legislator is to harmonize the laws of the state with "organic law" (Shackleton 1988c, 37). Keohane characterizes the collective spirit as a form of "political culture" that is inculcated through "socialization" (Keohane 1972, 388).

23. Levin emphasizes the influence of Lucretius's *De Rerum Natura* for Montesquieu's account of primitive society (1936, 45–7). Montesquieu's discussion of the Germanic tribes reveals a primitive form of community that is neither as determined by natural factors as those who emphasize Montesquieu's use of climate theory would suggest (see *S* 14.3), nor as romantic as those who see in this form of community the operation of untainted virtue that points, as one political theorist suggests, "the way forward to 'the liberty of the citizen'" (Mosher 2001, 171). Environment creates only the most general conditions of human character, and even those conditions are highly variable. As Montesquieu notes, climate alone "contributes in an infinite number of ways to the formation of the human mind" (EC 143). Tacitus's most thorough discussion of the role of climate on the character of a people appears in *Germania*.

24. In describing these effects of climate on a people's character, Montesquieu is influenced most significantly by Arbuthnot, whose theory of climate has an ancient lineage. For the influence on Arbuthnot, see Levin 1936, 28; Shackleton 1988c, 24. For Montesquieu's notes on Hippocrates, see *Spicilège* 379, 392, 398.

25. Montesquieu is making a pointed contrast between contract theorists who identified the origins of society in a hypothetical agreement and a more anthropological, historical account that saw societies (and the reasons they were formed) as shaped by the concrete particulars of the physical conditions, customs, and mores of a people. The Germanic tribes left the state of nature, as Montesquieu notes, when they established laws that formalized political relations (*S* 30.19). The tribes in this state of nature, though, were already a long-standing, functioning community. Pangle construes Montesquieu as agreeing with Hobbes "that the state of nature is a state of war" (Pangle 1973, 33). See Richter 1977, 62–63 for a discussion of Montesquieu's explicit opposition to Hobbes. Waddicor sees in Montesquieu the continuation of the ideas that societies originate through a contract that guarantees natural rights to liberty and property (1970, 86–99).

26. On the role of discussions of primitive times in ancient society, see Jens 1956, 349–52; Syme 1958, 125–26; Edelstein 1967; Wallace-Hadrill 1982, 19–36; Heilmann 1989. On *Germania* as mirror of Rome, see Syme 1958, 48, 126; Dudley 1968, 221; Dorey 1969; Mellor 1993, 14–16, 62; O'Gorman 1993; Rives 1999; Benario 1999; Haynes 2003, 13.

27. Woodman and Martin 1996, 236, 239 and Langslow 2000, 199.

28. Also, "Plain vices could be treated by plain cures (*remedia simplicia*)" because bodies were still strong and unspoiled by luxury (Sen. *Ep.* 95.14).

29. On Tacitus's purpose in writing the *Germania,* see Timpe 1989 (arguing against the work as either simply a moral treatise or political tract); Rives 1999; Benario 1999.

30. Seneca similarly describes how too rich a soil will load down the branches and prevent the fruit from maturing, just as "uncontrolled prosperity" will weigh down and prevent the full development of the soul (Sen. *Ep.* 39.4). See also Sallust *Jug.* 1.1–4, 4.7–8. On the use of language used to describe plants in this passage, see Woodman and Martin 1996, 242.

31. Interpretations of the passage are controversial. Tacitus may

be saying that there are three developmental trajectories that follow the appearance of ambition and violence: despotism, lawful government, or kingship that leads ultimately to lawful government (see Martin, in Woodman and Martin 1996, 242–43). Others see despotism as a more universal aspect of development from which despotism may become permanent, or may evolve into either kingships or democracies (see Woodman in Woodman and Martin, 1996, 243). In the case of early Rome, the developmental trajectory described by Tacitus seems to be kingship, despotism, and then law. Griffin suggests that the ambiguity of the formula may be the result of a compromise between "traditional Roman history and a formula that put the development of law subsequent to a period of monarchy" (1976, 200). There is a second controversy about whether Tacitus sees Romulus as a lawgiver or despot (see Woodman and Martin 1996, 245–6). Resolving the ambiguity is probably impossible and for my argument here unnecessary.

32. *Pravus* also said of Sempronius Gracchus (*Ann.* 1.53.3); of the Parthian view of Vonones (*Ann.* 2.2.4); of Piso's confession (*Ann.* 3.16.4); of the depravity of Roman wives (*Ann.* 3.34.3); of the depravity of the nobility and the sickness of the age (*Ann.* 3.65.1); of Junius Rusticus (*Ann.* 5.4.1); and of Agrippina's charge against Nero's preceptors (*Ann.* 12.41.3).

33. Medical use of *turbor*, see Langslow 2000, 297.

34. On *corrigere* in medicine, see Woodman and Martin 1996, 255. On *gravis* in medicine, see Celsus pro. 39; 1.3.1.

35. See Gruen 1974, 224–35; Habicht 1990, 58–9; Morstein-Marx 2004, 3–4.

36. Tacitus also notes that the increased speed of the judicial proceedings served to bridle eloquence (*Dial.* 38.2).

37. Compare to Tacitus's statement that for the Germans "good habits" had more force than "good laws elsewhere" (*Germ.* 19.5; also *Ann.* 3.26.1).

38. On *gliscere*, see Goodyear 1972, 96–7. *Gliscere* appears 19 times in the *Annals*, replacing the more commonly used *crescere*. See also *S* 5.14 where Montesquieu talks about the end of despotism as "tranquillity," not as "peace" but as "silence."

39. Eder 1990, 103. See also Lacey 1996, 210 and Nicolet 1984.

40. Nicolet 1984.

41. Galinsky 1996, 8.

42. See Goodyear 1972, 104.

43. On Augustus's consolidation of power, see Cotton and Yakobson 2002.

44. On proscriptions, see Syme 1939, 187–201.

45. *Adulatio* in Livy: 9.28.4. The extent and nature of censorship under Augustus are assessed by Raaflaub and Samons 1990, 436–47. Galinsky provides a rather sympathetic account of the flourishing of art, literature, and expression under Augustus (1996, 225–87, 370). Tacitus provides an account of the prosecution of Cremutius Cordus by clients of Sejanus for publishing annals praising M. Brutus (*Ann.* 4.33).

46. See also *Ann.* 3.26.2: "equality was cast aside." On Tacitus's use of *aequalitas* in a political context, see Goodyear 1972, 118.

47. So, too, Augustus would appropriate the private religious cults to make himself *pater patriae* (Lacey 1996, 5, 13, 169–89). On the model of emperor as father, see Stevenson 1992.

48. Woodman and Martin 1996, 260.

49. See, for example, *Ann.* 1.3.2; 1.4.2; 1.10.1. On the use of *dominus* by Tacitus to describe imperial rule, see Benario 1964 and Fontana 1993.

50. See Lana 1989 for Tacitus's distinctive use of *introspicere.*

51. Thus, I think that Dunkle makes Tacitus's portrait of Tiberius too stereotypical (Dunkle 1971, 17–18).

52. I think Brunt is quite right to note, "Fear can hardly account for servility before Tiberius' last years. The explanation may lie partly in the equivocal position of the 'first man in the state'. All real power was in his hands, and yet he professed to be an accountable minister. How could men be sure when he was seeking advice for form's sake, or sincerely wished for counsel and was prepared to act in accordance with the general wish" (Brunt 1984, 444)? See also Rudich, who writes that "the intellectual and psychological landscape of that period was fraught with mental anguish, confused and discordant attitudes, and inconsistent behavior encapsulated in each individual's quest for self-adjustment, when the realities of life stood in painful conflict with heartfelt beliefs" (1993, xxii).

53. Eder 1990, 83–4. On continuities of Augustus's reign with the earlier republican system, see Raaflaub 1987, 41–45 and Galinsky 1996.

54. See *S* 5.14; 5.16.

55. Rudich 1993, xvii.

56. Syme 1939, 336; Millar 1966 (on the evolving role of the

emperor's power of *imperium proconsulare*); 1973, 63 (on changes in 27 BCE); Campbell 1984, 32; Eder 1990, 106–7; Badian 1986, 81–83; Galinksy 1996, 70–71, 365, 377; Bleicken 1998, 326; Kienast 1999, 99–109.

57. Syme 1939, 337. Also Bleicken 1998, 352–53; Kienast 1999, 104–9. Tacitus describes the tribunician power as the title for the highest power in the Roman world (*summi fastigii vocabulum* [*Ann.* 3.56.2]). Even Eder, who attempts to understand the principate as at least being seen at the time as consistent with republican traditions, admits that Augustus holding *tribunicia potestas* was "without precedent" and "greatly contradicted the practices of the traditional *res publica*" since tribunician power had always been vested in plebeians (Eder 1990, 109). Reference to the emperor's use of the veto is made in *Ann.* 1.13.4; 1.73; 3.70.3; 4.30.1; 5.2; 15.74.3; 13.43.5; 14.45.2; 14.48.2; 16.11.3.

58. Jones 1960, 52–54; 1960c, 86–98. As Jones writes, "Here the emperor seems to have taken the place of the people as the ultimate arbiter of life and death. *Provocatio ad populum* has become *appellatio ad Caesarem*, and the emperor, instead of the people, decides whether to uphold the magistrate's sentence or not" (1960, 94).

59. On Tacitus's selection of material to highlight the insignificance of the senate, see Ginsburg 1981, 87–95. On Tiberius's continual intrusions into senate affairs, see Ginsburg 1981, 124–26, fn. 27–34. On limitations of senatorial self-representation, see Eck 1984. Confirming evidence of the irrelevance of senatorial careers: the difficulty of finding candidates for quaestorships, tribuneships, and aedileships (Levick 1985, 60). Tiberius laments the difficulty of finding suitable people to fill governorships (*Ann.* 6.27.3).

60. See Talbert 1984, 221–289; Rudich 1993, xx–xxi.

61. See Brunt 1984, 423–44; Talbert 1984, 362–64; Wallace-Hadrill 1990, 146–47; Rowe 2002, 41–42, 60–66. As Wiseman observes, "In one sense, the history of the Julio-Claudians is the history of the slow extinction of this tradition [of the competition for individual glory]. The extinction was inevitable, since ultimately an ethos of personal aggrandisement could not co-exist with devotion to the *princeps;* the surprising thing is how long it took to come about" (1985, 8–9).

62. See Rowe 2002, 54–57. Thrasea warns Arulenus Rusticus, to exercise the veto would be "an empty initiative, of no advantage to the defendant and ruinous to the intervener" (*Ann.* 16.26.5). And

Julius Agricola realizes, in holding the tribunate, that "to be passive was to be wise" (*Agric.* 6.3).

63. Yavetz 1969, 96.

64. Rowe 2002, 96. See also Veyne 1990, 383–86.

65. Transfer of elections from the people to the senate: *Ann.* 1.15.1; 1.81. Tiberius's refusal of the senate's request to nominate additional candidates for the praetorship: *Ann.* 1.14.4. Augustus restored popular elections in 27 BCE, though he continued to exercise influence in the choice of candidates by personally canvassing for a candidate (an act of *suffragatio*) or writing in support of a candidate (an act of *commendatio*). The emperors could officially only recommend candidates; neither the senate nor the assembly of the people was officially required to ratify these choices. The emperor's influence rested on his *auctoritas* (see Jones 1960a; Levick 1967, 216–19; Brunt 1984, 429–32). With the change in elections, the ambitious no longer relied on elections for rank but relied more on the emperor's favor. One result is the change in household architecture. The *atrium*, which had housed the *imagines* (ancestor masks), provided a form of advertising to the public of one's own status. As elections receded in importance, and "power came to be exercised by friends and advisers of the emperor who never held traditional senatorial office," the *atrium* receded in importance and was replaced by peristyles and gardens (Flower 1996, 69–70, 193; also 256).

66. Syme 1939, 355; Brunt 1983.

67. Brunt 1983, 51. Brunt suggests that there is little to suggest a rivalry between the equestrian and senatorial orders and some evidence to point to shared perceptions of imperial rule (1983, 65–66).

68. See Syme 1939, 352–53; Campbell 1984, 158–62; Rowe 2002, 172. See, for example, *Ann.* 1.2.1 and 1.28.4.

69. See Campbell 1984, 19–32.

70. Campbell 1984, 122–33; Talbert 1984, 363–64. Acclamations as *imperator* ("holder of supreme power" [Talbert 1984, 363, n.18]) could be awarded to senators, but only by personal concession of the emperor. The last award to a senator occurred in 22 CE as a concession by Tiberius to Junius Blaesus, the uncle of Sejanus (see *Ann.* 3.74.4; Campbell 1984, 127–8).

71. See Campbell 1984, 109–20; Keppie 1996. As Campbell writes, "In general the Praetorians remained quiescent and loyal to the

reigning emperor whether he was a conscientious ruler or a rogue, and, with the exception of the civil wars in 68–9 and the events of 193, they had little direct impact on imperial politics" (1984, 120).

72. Ideology of *corpus imperii*: Goodyear 1972, 180; Häussler 1965, 273–57; Béranger 1953, 218–37. See also Pliny *Ep.* 3.20.12: everything depends on will of one man, and Sen. *Clem.* 1.5.1: the emperor is the "soul of the state and the state your body." On the visual language that now focused on the image of the emperor, see Zanker 1988.

73. Fontana 1993, 30. See also *S* 5.14; 8.2; 8.7.

74. Augustus, for example, codifies the customary procedures of the senate in the *lex Julia de senatu habendo* in 9 BCE. See Talbert 1984, 222–24.

75. Ross 1973, 226–27. Ross is following Shotter 1968. For the tradition of Germanicus as hero (or exemplary leader), see Walker 1952, 9, 118–19; Mendell 1970, 30; Daitz 1960, 37; Koestermann 1963, 39; Syme 1958, 418; Dudley 1968, 100; Mellor 1993, 75–76; Williams 1997. More ambiguous treatments of Germanicus's heroism are offered by Goodyear 1972, 239–41; Williams 1990, 141–45; Pelling 1993.

76. Woodman 2006, 324.

77. Ibid., 325.

78. Rowe 2002, 163.

79. Ibid., 162.

80. Ibid., 172.

81. On politics as performance, see Hammer 1998, 2002b. As Potter writes, "The exercise of authority in the ancient world was highly theatrical, and for the performance of power to succeed, it was necessary for the audience to be drawn into the act, to be made to feel a part of the action" (1996, 131); also Bartsch 1994 and Beacham 1999, 35–43.

82. See *Ann.* 1.7.1 (Tiberius mixes tears with joy, regrets with adulation); 1.16.3 (Percennius stirring crowd); 1.18.2 (mixing of legions); 1.54.2 (Augustus mixes in the pleasures of the crowd); 1.64.1 (mingling of cries in battle); 3.22.2 (Tiberius confuses symptoms of anger and mercy); 3.67.4 (Silanus, desperate under criminal attack, mingles reproaches with petitions); 4.51.2 (confusion of battle because of inability to distinguish friend from foe). *Miscere* forms the root, as well, for *promiscuus*, an indiscriminate mixing.

83. See Woodman 2006, 315.

84. On the *adlocutio,* see Campbell 1984, 72–76.

85. Similarly, Ash notes that in Tacitus's recounting of civil wars in the *Histories,* "soldiers on all sides gradually develop a mistrust of their immediate commanding officers" (1999, 168).

86. On forms of mass unrest in the principate, see Yavetz 1969, chapts. 2, 5; Bollinger 1969, 50–71; Gilbert 1976, 71–79; Nippel 1995, 85–90; Kienast 1999, 201–3.

87. For the importance of the theater as the primary forum of political expression, see Veyne 1990; 398–403; Nippel 1995, 87; Potter 1996, 144; Beacham 1999, 160–61.

88. I disagree with Bartsch that Tacitus presents a view of the emperor as controlling and manipulating the crowds, without the crowd being able to exert control (1994, 24–26). On the need for even absolute rulers to respond to and anticipate forms of collective expression, see Levick 1967, 230 and Rowe 2002.

89. Campbell 1984, 18.

90. See Shotter 1968, 195–96.

91. For Tacitus, public discourse was "the index of social health" (Walker 1952, 151). See also Ranun 1980, 550–51.

92. Tiberius, too, is able to "overturn and exchange the signs of anger and clemency" (*Ann.* 3.22.2). On the growing variance between "gesture" and "feeling," see Betensky 1978. Rudich points to how the need to dissimulate, a growing feature of Roman political life captured in the term *dissimulatio,* "operated on the conscious level but also, if it became habitual, on the subconscious. It was a condition of mental entropy, capable of perpetuating itself or of becoming self-destructive through a nervous breakdown or even a split of personality" (1993, xxii).

93. Syme 1958, 365.

94. See Dupont 1997, 49.

95. Saxonhouse 1975, 56. See also Syme 1939, 483; Henderson 1990, 192; Fontana 1993; Rudich 1993, xxx–xxxii ("rhetoricized mentality"); Edwards 1994, 92–93; Boesche 1996, 88–95. Goldberg 1999 and Connolly 2007, 237–61 provide cautionary notes to interpretations of oratory's decline in the imperial era. Both note, however, that oratory is redefined to accommodate to imperial power.

96. See, for example, *Ann.* 3.31.2–4 (senate engages in trivial quarrel); 3.35.1 (Tiberius's abmonition for senate's failure to act); 13.26.1 (debate governed by fear); 14.45 (ineffectual protest); 14.64.3 (senate's willingness to approve crime). On a comparison of

speeches in Livy to their inferior counterparts by Tacitean senators, see Ginsburg 1993. Also Marshall 1975, 15–16. In comparing the accounts of Tacitus and Dio for the year 16, Ginsburg notes that Tacitus rather tends to include "a number of debates in the senate which were largely inconsequential (2.33–38) than to record, as Dio does, the administrative actions taken by that body (57.16.1–2)" (Ginsburg 1981, 82). In addition, in contrast to Livy, who forms a narrative around the "repetitive and recurrent nature of government at Rome," particularly the annual term of its magistrates, for Tacitus the election of magistrates "was no longer significant" (Ginsburg 1981, 86). On the infrequency of senatorial disagreement with the emperors, see Talbert 1984, 172–4.

97. See Levick 1985, 62. The options open to individual forms of protest were fairly limited and appeared more as opting out of things, a largely passive and ineffective form of protest (see *Ann.* 14.12.2; 16.21).

98. Examples of *equites* who saw more power in the emperor's service rather than in a senatorial career include Maecenas and C. Sallustius Crispus (*Ann.* 3.30). Mela "abstained from seeking office, having the inverted ambition that as a Roman equestrian he might match consulars in powerfulness. At the same time he believed that a shorter way to acquiring money was through the procuratorships for administering the princeps's business" (*Ann.* 16.17.3). See Mommsen, *Ges. Schr.* 4.311; Syme 1939, 385; Talbert 1984, 77–80; Levick 1985, 63.

99. High rank, for example, was a cause for attack by Nero. See *Ann.* 13.1; 15.35; 16.7. So was virtue (*Ann.* 16.21.1; 16.23.1).

100. See also *Hist.* 1.4; Yavetz 1969, 115, 124; Sullivan 1985, 40–41; Beacham 1999, 200–1.

101. On the nearly unavoidable moral complicity in despotism, see Liebeschuetz 1966, 33–34.

102. See *S* 3.8; 8.2. This perverse equality occurs even as the social order continues to be enforced in theatrical seating (see Zanker 1988, 149–52; Edwards 1993, 110–13; Edmondson 1996, 84–95).

103. On the Pisonian conspiracy, see Rudich 1993, 87–112.

104. Woodman 1993, 127. See also MacDonald 1965, 177 (Domus Aurea as disorienting); Betensky 1978, 420 (everything "staged"); Edwards 1994, 92–93 (inversion of real and unreal); Beacham 1999, 228 (the city as a "stage set"); Haynes 2003, 23–24, 31; Bartsch 1994, 47. Also Sen. *Natl. Quaes.* 1.16–17 (illusion).

105. Levick 1985, 64.

106. See Tac. *Hist.* 1.15: "*Fidem, libertatem, amicitiam, praecipua humani animi bona.*"

107. On the use of proscriptions as a form of "legal murder," see Syme 1939, 187–201 (quote from 187). For a review of the evidence of opposition to Augustus, see Raaflaub 1987 and Raaflaub and Samons 1990. On opposition to Nero, see Rudich 1993. For a broader discussion of the extent of opposition, and the responses of the emperors, see the contributions to *Opposition et résistances à l'empire d'Auguste à Trajan.*

108. Bauman 1974, 14–15, 25–51; Levick 1985, 56; Raaflaub and Samons 1990, 444. On the inconsistency of the use of this term, and the types of crimes associated with the term, by literary sources, including Tacitus, see Bauman 1974, 1–24.

109. See, for example, Raaflaub 1987, 41–45.

110. Tacitus traces the source of the *maiestas* prosecutions back to Tiberius's own troubled soul, which had been excited by satires of his life and character (*Ann.* 1.72.4). On *asperavere* in medicine, see Cels. 4.5.6; Langslow 2000, 175, 305.

111. Bauman 1974, 55–59, 93.

112. On advancement, see Rutledge 2001, 20–53. On the continued rewards for informers, see *Hist.* 1.2 and Rudich 1993. Rutledge argues, by way of prosopography, that advancement is likely exaggerated. Rutledge's table that indicates "Office held in wake of prosecution" fails to distinguish between those about whom we have knowledge from those about whom we know little or nothing (2001, 25–6). Absence of evidence is not evidence of absence. Nonetheless, it is as much the hope, as any realization, of rewards that is important as a motivation.

113. Necessity of prosecutions for treasury: Levick 1985, 56–7.

114. *Exedere* in medical terminology, see Langslow 2000, 197.

115. Rutledge 2001, 14.

116. On *corripiunt* in medical terminology, see Woodman and Martin 1996, 459, 260. The inversion of the moral order in which individuals are honored for their vices becomes the standard of society under subsequent emperors. See *Ann.* 14.3; 14.13; 14.15; 14.59; 14.62; 14.64; 15.50. See also Walker 1952, 78–81.

117. See Lendon 1997 for a discussion of the operation of honor in imperial Rome.

118. On *pessum* in medical vocabulary, see Cels. 5.21.

119. Rutledge 2001, 53. On the role of *delatores* in republican Rome, see Rutledge 2001, 37–39, 44–46. Rutledge argues that *delatores* were not just instruments of tyranny but were driven by a number of forces that were "deeply embedded in Roman society" (2001, 4).

120. Rutledge 2001, 65.

121. Ibid., 52.

122. See Wirszubski 1961, 14; Wood 1986, 37–39; Kaster 2005, 55.

123. Related, Keitel sees Tacitus using images of civil war to describe the mutinies and the actions of the nobles and the *delatores* (1984, 317–25).

124. On the continued and pernicious role of the informers in subsequent reigns, see *Ann.* 11.5.1 (Claudius); *Ann.* 14.48; 16.7–35 (Nero); *Hist.* 1.2 (Nero); *Agric.* 2.3 (Domitian). As Levick writes, "The Emperor might be induced to renounce *maiestas*, for example; so with Gaius, Claudius, and (tacitly) Nero. What that meant is not clear. Not the repeal of the Lex, which was never re-enacted; nor did the Senate suspend the statute; the state could not do without it" (1985, 57).

125. For a discussion of this passage as invoking an image of the captured city, see Keitel 1984, 307.

126. The actual number of prosecutions under Tiberius appears to be much lower than suggested by Tacitus. Suetonius places the number of prosecutions in 33 CE, described by Tacitus as *immensa strages*, at no more than twenty individuals (Suet. *Tib.* 61; *Ann.* 6.19.2). In total, as calculated by Walker, eighteen individuals were executed for treason during Tiberius's rule (1952, 84–5, 263–70). There is, however, a substantial increase in suicides after 31 CE (Walker 1952, 84). Rutledge argues that the *delatores* played only a "limited part in curtailing the freedoms of others" in the early principate (2001, 4).

127. See Barthes' evocative discussion of death in Tacitus's *Annals* (1982).

128. In other ancient versions, Libo is portrayed as a plotter who is suspected of seeking to overthrow Tiberius. See Valleius 2.130; Suet. *Tib.* 25; Sen *Ep.* 70.10; also Marsh 1926, 294–96. See Rogers 1952, 285 on Tacitus's accounts of treason trials. The discovery of the *Tabula Siarensis* and the *Senatus Consultum de Cn. Pisone Patre*, both of which deal with affairs surrounding the death of Germanicus and the trial of Piso, suggest that Tacitus (at least in the case

of Piso) is generally accurate in his account. See Eck, Caballos, and Fernández 1996, 289–98; Woodman and Martin 1996, 114–18; Flower 1996, 246–54; 1999, 110–15; Griffin 1997, 258–61; Talbert 1999, 95–96. For a survey of the controversy surrounding Tacitus's use of the *acta senatus,* specifically, and his accuracy, generally, see Talbert 1984, 326–34. Häussler (1965) more generally makes an argument for Tacitus's objectivity and detachment as a historican.

129. On *condere* in medical terminology, see Cels. 3.25.3. O'Gorman suggests that Tiberius "is estranged not from Libo but from his own expressions of inner thought" because his intention to bring Libo to trial does not appear in his face (2000, 84).

130. Dio suggests that selling a master's slaves to the treasury so that they could testify against their master was practiced, in fact, by Augustus (Dio 55.5).

131. See also *Ann.* 15.35.3 when Nero declares in his "usual speech" that he would have granted clemency to Torquatus Silanus, who committed suicide when his condemnation appeared imminent.

132. Levick 1985, 64. Henderson, for example, writes, "It will not be the mere performance—the 'score'—of Tiberian or Neronian Treason Trials that we are to consider, it is the (anti-)logic in its re-oriented functioning around the *persona* of the Emperor that we are to trace from its inception. In the new Order, there is *no* 'Trial'; it is a matter of the tyrant's (however benign) perception of how threatened he feels, of how the sum adds up in confirming his grasp of power ('Should it be generosity, liquidation or menace *this time?*'): power as power over meaning, *Wor(l)d-Power.* The misnomer *maiestas* de-stabilizes Roman discourse. Systematically. Into pieces" (1990, 177).

133. Tacitus seems to connect Claudius's suppression of any symptoms of human emotion with forgetfulness (*Ann.* 11.38.3).

134. See Jens 1956 who traces Tacitus's growing sense of the impossibility of individuals under imperial rule not slipping into listlessness.

135. Syme 1939, 504.

136. For discussions of Montesquieu's notion of liberty, see Richter 1977, 95–7; Shklar 1987, 86–92; Carrithers 2001, 291–334.

137. "Despotic authority is inanimate" because "it lacks the *animus* of politics—both the animating spirit of reason that sparks deliberation and the courageous opposition, even animosity, that sustains it" (Krause 2001, 241).

138. On fear as a "physiological reaction" that paralyzes the body, see Shklar 1987, 84.

139. See Comte 1974, 442–43; Durkheim 1960, 21, 51; Merry 1970. For a thoughtful comparison of the methodological concerns of Durkheim and Montesquieu, see Jones 1994. Berlin provides a sympathetic assessment of Montesquieu as a social scientist when he writes that one of Montesquieu's "great merits lies in the very fact that although he claims to be founding a new science in the spirit of Descartes, his practice is better than his professions, and he is, in fact, doing nothing of the kind, because he realizes that the material will not allow of it" (1997, 137–38).

140. Shackleton 1961, 158; Richter 1977, 52–3.

141. Sabine 1946, 551, 556.

142. Critical stance: Shklar 1987, esp. 49–66, 1990; Rahe 2001; Larrère 2001; commerce: Larrère 2001, 354–55.

143. Levin 1936, 1, quoting E.P. Dargan, *The Aesthetic Doctrine of Montesquieu*, Diss. Johns Hopkins: Baltimore, 1907, p. 198.

144. Criticism of Livy: *Pensées*, Barckhausen classification 881, MS 1475, in Montesquieu 1964; *C* 55; History as monument: *Pensées*, Bkn. 611, MS 1260, in Montesquieu 1964. Romans as providing "spectacle of things human" (*C* 15).

145. Shackleton 1988b, 130.

146. See Levin 1936, 112–3; Aron 1968, 1:25; Richter 1977, 71–2; Young 1978; Shackleton 1988b, 130; Cohler 1988, 73–5; Hundert and Nelles 1989; Boesche 1990. Montesquieu, like Tacitus, recognizes differences between Roman and Eastern forms of despotism (see Tac. *Hist.* 1.16; 4.17).

147. Naturally subject to despotism: Richter 1973, 1; 1995, 340; Hulliung 1976, 38–9; Shklar 1987, 95–6; Shackleton 1988a, 239; basis: Dodds 1929, 149; also Schaub 1995, 19; Richter 1995, 347; warning to France and more generally about encroaching monarchical power: Levin 1936, 112; Koebner 1951, 302; Richter 1995, 334–37; Shackleton 1961, 15–17, 226–28, 271–72; 1988a, 239; Shklar 1987, 2–5, 85; Young 1978, 404–5; Venturi 1963, 134–36; Mosher 2001, 168–70; caricature: Young 1978, 401, 403; undeveloped: Dodds 1929, 169–70; Waddicor 1970, 29, 105; Durkheim 1960, 31. Corrections are made by Hundert and Nelles 1989; Schaub 1995; and Krause 2001.

148. Shackleton 1961, 271 (uniform); Shklar 1987, 85 (death); Aron 1968, 21 (subpolitical).

149. Boesche 1990, 742. See also Veyne 1990, 405–6, who sees Montesquieu's notion of despotism as not being able to account for the popularity of someone like Nero.

150. Krause 2001, 238.

151. Ibid. See also Shklar 1987, 83–84.

152. Syme 1970, 2.

153. Ibid., 2–3, 13.

154. Mendell 1970, 68.

155. Fornara 1983, 76, 118–19. See also O'Gorman, who sees Tacitus as engaged in part of a larger struggle between senatorial and imperial history over historical memory. O'Gorman emphasizes, in particular, the attempt by Tacitus to undermine dynastic attempts to "naturalise hereditary power" (2000, 106).

156. Marincola 1997, 95. Also, Haynes: "However, looking down into the abyss, as Tacitus does, means understanding that there is no Truth, no historical necessity, outside of the symbolic" (2003, 13; also 20–21).

157. Sinclair 1995, 63.

158. O'Gorman 2000, 182.

159. Connolly 2007.

160. O'Gorman 2000, 177.

161. Syme 1939, 486.

162. Ibid.; *Ann.* 1.72.3; 4.21.3. See Bauman 1974, 48–49.

163. *Ann.* 2.32 (Libo Drusus); 3.17–18 (Piso); 3.76 (Brutus and Cassius); 11.38 (Messalina). On the practice of *damnatio memoriae,* see Flower 2006.

164. On Tacitus's style see Boissier 1906, 22–23; Walker 1952, 57–66; Klingner 1955, 193; Syme 1958, 1:199; Martin 1981, 214–35; Goodyear 1981, 185–87; Henderson 1990, 193–94; Sinclair 1995; Kraus and Woodman 1997, 110–11; O'Gorman 2000, 4–10. Syme characterizes Tacitus's *Annals* as "much more condensed, austere, and enigmatic" than the *History*, making it "Sallust rather than Livy" (1958, 1:340).

165. Kraus and Woodman 1997, 110–11.

166. Walker writes, "*In the style*, there is a conscious artistry, a development of all the potentialities of words to startle, impress, fascinate and move the listener" (1952, 53). Henderson describes the *Annals* as a "discursive clash between language and desire, meaning and power, challenging any civic mentality to suffer, probe and resist the draining away of Rome from itself that unwinds from first to last" (1990, 194).

167. Richter writes, "A second emphasis of philosophical history, if a negative one, consisted in the rejection of fact, detail, or erudition for its own sake. Montesquieu's style in this book reflects its author's preoccupations: its sparse, stripped-down maxims are historical generalizations at a high level of abstraction" (1977, 56). On the emulation of Tacitus's use of *sententiae* in the eighteenth century, see Sinclair 1995, 3.

168. See "Essay sur le gout." *OC* (1964), 846. See also 848 for Montesquieu's praise of Suetonius for being able to elicit different feelings through surprise.

169. Syme 1970, 2; see *Agric.* 3.2.

170. *Pensées* 673. On influence of Malebranche, see Shackleton 1961, 24–6; Riley 1986, 143–80.

CHAPTER 5

1. Segal 1986, 12. See also Herington 1966, 430: "What does seem relevant is the clear fact that Seneca himself lived through and witnessed, in his own person or in the persons of those near him, almost every evil and horror that is the theme of his writings, prose, or verse" (1966, 430).

2. Segal 1986, 6.

3. Dingel, for example, attempts to separate Seneca's philosophic from his tragic writings (1974, 94–100). Henry and Walker characterize Seneca's philosophic writings as "vapid" (1963, 108–9). In contrast, Inwood describes Seneca's work as "a rare example of first-order Latin philosophy" (1995, 75). Too suggests that Seneca "privileges psychological space at the expense of literal, physical space," but does not suggest how politics inhabits this interior realm (1994, 220). And von Albrecht explores the idea of change or transformation (*Verwandlung*) as it relates to both the style and theme of the tragedies and *Epistles* (2004).

4. On the *Epistles* as fictional, see von Albrecht 1989, 114, n. 25; Bourgery 1911; Leeman 1951; Maurach 1970, 21; Griffin 1976, p. 349–55, 416–19; Griffin 1988, 136; Too 1994; Nussbaum 1994, 337; Edwards 1999. Those seeing historicity (and growing personal relationship with Lucilius) of the *Epistles*: Albertini 1923, 136–46; Grimal 1978, 155–64; 315–27; Müller 1980, 139–42; Wilson 2001.

5. Griffin 1976, 135. See also Sandbach 1975, 161–62. For a de-

fense of Seneca's own sincerity in the practice of his ethics as proclaimed in the *Epistles*, see Andrews 1930.

6. Uncritical: Veyne 1987, 45; 2003, 13, 227–30; Brown 1987, 248–51; unphilosophical: Strozier 2002, 162 ("not particularly analytic"); hypocritical: Coleman 1974, 286, n.2; Sandbach 1975, 162; Too 1994; aristocratic: Habinek 1992 = 1998; self-justificatory: Sullivan 1985, 144.

7. Wolin 2004, 85. *The Cambridge Companion to the Stoics* (2003), for example, contains no chapter on politics. On Seneca as focused on individual morality, see I. Hadot 1969, 80–84; Griffin 1976, 210; Coleman 1974, 289 ("novel form of moral essay"); Reydams-Schils 2005, 85.

8. Littlewood 2004, 16. See also Momigliano 1969 (orig. 1950), 253, 255 ("His best, most profound, words were about private virtues and intimate feelings."); Ferguson 1958, 137; I. Hadot 1969, 80–1; Griffin 1976, 8 (surveying scholarship); Cooper and Procopé 1995, xxv–xxvi ("apolitical" and "an inward looking moralist"); Strozier 2002, 164 (interiority as protection from world), 169; Fitch and McElduff 2002, 20.

9. Edwards 1997, 24.

10. Littlewood 2004, 44.

11. See also Foucault 2005a, 12–13.

12. Classicists sympathetic to Foucault have generally focused on explorations of the social and historical construction of sexuality and gender. See Winkler 1990; Halperin 1990; Halperin, Winkler, and Zeitlin (eds.) 1990; Konstan 1994; Halperin, 1995, 73–76; Hallet and Skinner (eds.) 1997; Larmour, Miller, and Platter (eds.) 1998; Nussbaum and Sihvola (eds.) 2002; Rabinowitz and Auanger (eds.) 2002. Other classical readings: Jambet 1992; Davidson 1994; Platter 1995 (on Catallus and Propertius); Edwards 1997; 1999; O'Leary 2002; Strozier 2002. Critical: Daraki 1986; Hadot 1989; Thornton 1991; Nussbaum 1994, 5–6, 353–54; Cohen and Saller 1994; Detel 1998; Foxhall 1998; Richlin 1991; 1998; Miller 1998; Porter 2005. Often, scholars seem to sidestep (when not dismissing) Foucault's discussion of the ancient Roman texts. Poster relates the question of the self-constitution of the subject more to Sartre than to anything Roman (Poster 1993, 65). He further suggests that readers might well find the turn to the ancients in this later work as "an exercise of paraphraxis, a string of banal summaries of well-known texts, a succession of unimaginative readings of the classics by some-

one who is hardly versed in the field" (Poster 1986, 206). Jay chooses to dismiss this ethical turn in Foucault's work, even while critiquing him for not addressing the issue of values (Jay 1986, 194–5). Dreyfus and Rabinow suggest that only when Foucault "goes back and reconstructs in detail the Stoic understanding of the relation between ethics and politics does it become clear that the Stoics faced a problem similar to Kant's," namely the normalization of life through the rule of reason (1983a, 260). Thacker suggests that "the main problem with Foucault's [aesthetic] map is that it is a Greek one" (1993, 19). A collection of essays entitled *The Later Foucault* manages to avoid any reference to the Romans (ed. Moss 1998). Despite a focus on the notion of the subject, Fraser's 1989 publication of her essays on Foucault mentions the Stoics only once, and that is at the beginning of "hermeneutical subjectification" (1989, 48). Richlin notes this "disappearance of Rome," which she attributes as much to Foucault as to his interpreters (1991, 168).

13. On Foucault's personal fondness for Seneca's letters, in particular, see Veyne's elegant reminiscence (1993, 1). There is some controversy about whether nature, for Seneca, defines the ends of human action or provides the capacity for thought and action so that one, in employing that capacity, lives in accordance with nature. For the former view, see Long and Sedley 1987, 1:352, 374 and Inwood 1985, 156, 199, 210. For the latter view, see Engberg-Pedersen, who argues that "there is no suggestion in the theory that nature (whether external or internal in Long's terms) has the role of an external criterion of goodness as setting up goals for human beings and conferring value on the world" (1990b, 40). Instead, "it is *because* human beings (and animals too) see certain things as valuable that these things are valuable" (1990b, 40, italics in orig.; also 46).

14. See, for example, Hadot 1992, 229–30; O'Leary 2002, 85. Both Davidson (1990, 1994) and Flynn (2005a) attempt to bridge some of the differences between Hadot and Foucault.

15. Foucault 1997c, 117.

16. Foucault *UP*, 11; Dean 1996, 214.

17. Deleuze, on Foucault, writes, "The unthought is therefore not external to thought but lies at its very heart, as that impossibility of thinking which doubles or hollows out the outside" (1988, 97). He later writes, "I do not encounter myself on the outside, I find the other in me" (1988, 98). See also Deleuze 1988, 116.

18. Allen 1993, 157.

19. Blundell points out that *oikeiôsis* does not direct us toward self-preservation in "any crude sense, but towards the proper maintenance of one's constitution in its natural condition" (1990, 221).

20. *Oikeiôsis* is translated variously as "Zueignung" (Pohlenz 1947, 1:57); "a perception and grasp of what is akin" (Rist 1969, 44, following Plutarch); "well-disposed" (Pembroke 1971, 116); "endearment" (Rist 1978, 263); "a process of taking something to oneself, or accepting or appropriating it or making it one's own" (White 1979, 145); "attachment" (Engberg-Pedersen 1990b, 80–82); a "mental process by which a human being will, if things go rightly, arrive at the true grasp of the good" (Engberg-Pedersen 1990a, 119); "affinity" (Erskine 1990, 115–16); "appropriation" or "affective relationships" (Long 1996, 172); "a natural impulse to *identify with* other humans" (Schofield 2000, 449); "appropriation" (Reydams-Schils 2005, 55).

21. Engberg-Pedersen 1990b, 70. Also 1990a, 120. Compare to Foucault, who seeks to trace the "desiring man" who comes to recognize himself as the subject of desire (*UP* 5). That recognition of the self is not epistemological (i.e., the soul is not a source of knowledge to be deciphered) but is ontological (i.e., as a recognition of its own being) (*UP* 89).

22. Engberg-Pedersen 1990b, 70.

23. On the connection of *oikeiôsis* to seeing, including seeing oneself, see Pembroke 1971, 118–19; Engberg-Pedersen 1990b, 42–46, 95.

24. See White 1979, 176–77 and Engberg-Pedersen 1990b, 95, 101.

25. Hadot 1992, 229.

26. Ibid., 230.

27. Reydams-Schils 2005, 17. See also Long 1996, 283 and Horowitz 1998, 26–31.

28. Foucault, Preface to *The History of Sexuality*, vol. 2, not published with English translation. From Foucault 1984, 334.

29. Mommsen 1996, 82.

30. See Crook 1967, 36.

31. On Roman law and society, see Crook 1967 and Johnston 1999. Mommsen emphasizes the importance of jurisdiction: "With regard to a specific sphere of competence: all spheres of competence in the Republic were clearly defined. All magistrates, even

subordinate ones, were autonomous within their own spheres of competence; they could, and indeed were obliged to, refrain from complying with orders from senior magistrates if these contravened the law" (1996, 85).

32. Nicolet 1993, 23.

33. Galinsky 1996, 13.

34. Habinek, for example, sees Seneca's writings as maintaining the "fixity and stratification of the Roman social system" (1998, 137). Griffin, more sympathetically, contends that Seneca sought to raise "to the level of theory the concepts and standards of Roman society" (2000, 534).

35. Law: Sen. *Ep.* 3.3 (applied to friendship), 18.1 (license is law), 36.6 (fortune has no jurisdiction), 39.3 (fortune has no jurisdiction), 47.14 (slaves allowed to pronounce judgment), 48.3 (rights of humanity), 57.3 (and fortune), 65.22 (soul brings quarrels to tribunal), 107.6 (apply law to self), 113.30 (push limits of empire), 123.16 (death); statute: see Inwood 2004 and Sen. *Ep.* 63.2, 86.2, 106.2; guardianship: *Ep.* 25.6; judgment: see Düll 1976, 375–77 and Inwood 2004; decree: *Ep.* 18.11; edicts by a praetor: 48.10; 117.30; injury: *Ep.* 47.20; jurisdiction: *Ep.* 118.11; Düll 1976, 371–74; duty: *Ep.* 3.2; 19.5; 19.8; 20.2; 22.3; 22.7; 45.2; 71.28; 74.20; 77.19; 78.20; 86.10; 90.5; 93.4; 94.5; 94.33; 94.37; 95.41 (human relations generally); 99.6; 103.3; 99.19; 101.1; 101.3; 102.6; 114.23; 120.2; 120.11; 122.2; 122.3; arbiter: *De Ben.* 3.7.5; authority: *Ep.* 11.9; 25.6; 29.3; 30.7; 55.5; 71.7; 94.27; 115.3.

36. See Foucault 1997c, 114. As Hindess writes, speaking generally about Foucault's project, "The *political* problem here is to help us to escape from the traps of our history" (Hindess 1998, 55). My argument diverges substantially from Too's claim that "Power and domination are the programme of Senecan pedagogy" (1994, 212).

37. See Shaw 1985, 25–26 and Habinek 1998, 137–38.

38. Lawless tyranny: Ovid *M.* 6.581; Livy 34.32. Compare to Foucault's discussion of the contemporary mechanisms of power that fashion our souls to reflect how "entire populations are mobilized for the purpose of wholesale slaughter in the name of life necessity: massacres have become vital" (1990 1:137).

39. For Seneca's attempt to place clemency in the context of social roles and duties, see Griffin 2000, 538–43.

40. See Tacitus: Tiberius and mother tear state apart (*Ann.* 1.4.5).

41. On Seneca's view of Cato, see Griffin 1968.

42. On the Senecan idea of stillness, see Too 1994, 220–21.

43. The alternative of retreat to the country is explored, as well, in Senecan drama. See *Thy.* 401–3, 455, 468; *HF* 159–85; and Fitch and McElduff 2002, 37–38.

44. See, as well, the discussion by Motto and Clark 1993, 115–24 and Henderson 2004, 73–77.

45. See also Sen. *De Tranq. An.* 2.11: "For it is the nature of the human mind to be active and prone to movement."

46. Edwards 1997, 35.

47. On associations of *incubare* with death in Seneca, see 1986, 53–54.

48. Frede 2003, 183–84. On determinism in Stoic philosophy generally, see also Bobzien 1998. In Seneca, see *Ep.* 101.5: "Time does indeed roll along by fixed law, but as in darkness; and what is it to me whether Nature's course is sure, when my own is unsure?"

49. See also Cic. *Rep.* 1.33.50; 2.19.34.

50. See, for example, Momigliano 1969, 249; Macintyre 1984, 169; Nussbaum 1994, 341–44; Griffin 2000, 555–58. For the different allowances to abstain from participation, see Sen. *De Otio* 3.2–3; 7.1–4. For Seneca, even cosmopolitanism is not at expense of local attachments. See Reydams-Schils 2005, 48–9; Sen. *Cons. Helv*; *Ep.* 78.2; 98.15–16; 104.2–5.

51. See, for example, Euben's critique of Nussbaum (Euben 2003, 126–29).

52. Foucault 2005a, 447–48.

53. Foucault 1997f, 236.

54. Ibid., 238.

55. Foucault 1997a, 286.

56. Long 1996, 281. As Seneca writes, "all art is but imitation of nature" (*Ep.* 65.3).

57. Foucault 2005a, 16.

58. Foucault 1997e, 178–79.

59. Ibid., 194.

60. For general discussions and defenses of Foucault's aesthetics, see Connolly 1993; Bennett 1996; Bevir 1999; O'Leary 2002, 121–38. For more critical appraisals of Foucault's aesthetics, see R. Wolin 1986; Hadot 1989; Taylor 1989, 489–90; Eagleton 1990; Thornton 1991; Thacker 1993; Detel 1998; Porter 2005.

61. Hadot 1992, 230. See also Thacker 1993.

62. Thacker 1993, 14; also Porter 2005, 121, 128–29. See, for example, Foucault 2005a, 271–85.

63. Foucault 1997g, 310. That Foucault is appealing to a classical rather than a modern notion of aesthetics (as work rather than genius), see O'Leary 2002, 128–29. See also Davidson 1994, 76–77. On the role of the classical artist, see Smith 2002, 71.

64. Foucault 2005a, 10, 217.

65. Ibid., 217, 282; see also Foucault 1988a, 49.

66. On the role of the imagined gaze of others in defining one's sense of worth, see Kaster 2005, 35–65. Connolly argues that for Cicero "communication involves the whole self, body and mind, for both speaker and audience" (2007, 136).

67. See Foucault 1997b, 97.

68. Contra Bell who argues that "the idea of aesthetics of existence in Foucault's later work is not a solution to the analyses of power of which he had previously written" (1996, 86).

69. Foucault, 1997a, 291; also 1998a, 50–51. For the world as an archive, see Deleuze 1988, 128 and Flynn 2005a, 30–32. Littlewood 2004, 44 suggests that the Stoic self does not have materials for its own self–construction.

70. See Foucault 1988a, 49.

71. Thacker 1993, 15.

72. See, for example, Fraser's critique of Foucault as failing to provide "any conception of what is to replace [modernity]" (1989, 33). Boyne notes that Foucault's aesthetics of existence is a "mechanism without a principle" (1990, 149).

73. Foucault 1997b, 99–100. On a related note, see Cruikshank, who employs Foucault to explore how "the question of governance becomes a question of self-governance in the discourse of self-esteem" (1996, 232).

74. Seneca, furthermore, rejects the view that "only young minds are moulded" and that an older man, thus, "cannot be re-shaped" (*Ep.* 25.2).

75. As Veyne notes, "*Style* does not mean distinction here; the word is to be taken in the sense of the Greeks, for whom an artist was first of all an artisan and a work of art was first of all a work" (1993, 7).

76. For Seneca, there are general moral principles (*decreta*) and specific moral rules (*praecepta*). For a discussion of the relationship between general moral rules and determinate moral precepts in

Seneca, see Mitsis 1993. I agree with Mitsis that for Seneca, precepts do not need to be immune to exceptions but are useful in helping individuals acquire awareness of the moral demands in different situations (Mitsis 1993, 294–98).

77. Mitsis 1993, 304.

78. See Foucault 2005a, 424.

79. Brown 2006, 66.

80. Foucault 1983b, 212.

81. Ibid., 220.

82. Foucault 1991a, 87; see Dean 1996 on Foucault's discussion of government and authority.

83. Foucault 1983b, 221.

84. Foucault 1997a, 283.

85. Ibid.

86. Foucault 1983b, 221.

87. Foucault 1991a, 87.

88. Mayer describes Seneca's exemplary figure as "a sort of guardian angel" (1991, 167).

89. See also *Ep.* 11.10; 24.3–6; 42.7–8; 104.21; 104.27.

90. The creation of companionship is an aspect of Seneca's thought that has been frequently noticed. See, for example, Edwards 1997, 30. References in Seneca include *Ep.* 6.7; 24.17; 25.4–5; 26.7; 27.1; 28.10; 35.2; 78.21.

91. On the self in dialogue with the self in a Greek context, see Gill 1996.

92. Foucault 1997d, 209.

93. See *Ep.* 40.1; 83.1; 84; Foucault 1997d; 2005a, 359.

94. Foucault 1997d, 207.

95. See Foucault 1997d, 209; 1997f, 238.

96. Reydams-Schils 2005, 17.

97. O'Leary defends Foucault's aestheticism by pointing to writing (rather than plastic arts) as a model of artistic fashioning. O'Leary makes this defense, though, by way of Nietzsche (O'Leary 2002, 134–38).

98. See Dean 1996.

99. Time had become a moral, rather than simply a physics, problem for the Stoics. See Goldschmidt 1953, 55–73; Rist 1969, 273–88; Motto and Clark 1993, 54–64. On the spatialization of history, see Foucault 1997f, 238 and Brown 1998, 45.

100. Herington 1966, 443. Edwards 1999 emphasizes Seneca's

display of pain and suffering. Henderson emphasizes the "spatialized environment" created in the *Epistles* (2004, 2). Motto and Clark point to Seneca's extensive use of Virgil (1993, 125–32).

101. See, for example, Bennett 1996, 661.

102. Foucault 1997c, 114.

103. Foucault 1997d, 212.

104. Ibid. Also *Ep.* 52.1–2.

105. Havel 1991, 330.

106. Ibid., 332.

107. See Hammer 1995 (= 1999).

108. Daraki 1986, 87.

109. Rochlitz 1992, 251, 257. See Foucault 1990, 1:137.

110. Thacker 1993, 18–19.

111. Smart 1998, 20, 22; also 25. See also McNay 1992, 157, 164–65. Foucault argues against a "necessary link" between ethics and sociopolitical structures, not the absence of a relationship (Foucault 1983a, 236; see also 1997a, 291).

112. Smart 1998, 21; also 22. Han sees Foucault as oscillating "in a contradictory manner" between the self as a "free actor in the practices through which he transforms himself" and as a self "inserted into a set of relations of power and practices" (2002, 172).

113. McNay 1992, 165.

114. Bernauer 1990, 181; see also Rajchman 1985, 97–125.

115. See Dolan 2005; Wolin 2004, 590–94.

116. For a sense of the extent of the United States' imperial reach, see Johnson 2004.

117. Foucault 1991b, 82.

118. Foucault 2005a, 14; 1997a, 294.

119. Ibid., 17. Although for a very different purpose, Charles Taylor, in critiquing the assimilation of political theory into a natural science model of validity and truth, points similarly to "a powerful current in our culture [that] resists strongly the idea of political theory as transforming its object" (Taylor 1985, 102). Taylor's concern is ultimately with how one validates social theory. But the concern points to the idea of theory as "knowledge" that is separate from, and does not implicate, the individual.

120. Foucault, 1991b, 82.

121. Foucault 1979, 29–30.

122. This continuity is developed by Carrette 2000.

123. Jambet 1992, 240–43.

124. Flynn 2005b, 614.

125. Connolly 1993, 378.

126. O'Leary 2002, 152.

127. Bernauer 1990, 159.

128. Ibid., 178; also 1987.

129. Ibid., 178, 182–83.

130. As Dean writes, "For, while the earlier writings may have given the impression of a kind of denial of interiority of the subject, there is now an explicit theorisation of this 'inside' " (Dean 1994, 201).

131. Foucault 2005a, 8. Foucault is similarly, and I think erroneously, drawn to the "political dynamic" of the Iranian Revolution. See Foucault 1988b, 212–13; 2005b, 207.

132. Foucault 2005a, 131; see Sen. *De Tranq. An.* 1.1–14; *Ep.* 52.

133. Ibid., 133.

134. Foucault 1991b, 82.

135. On *parrhêsia* in Foucault, see Foucault 2001; Flynn 1988.

136. Foucault 2005a, 129.

137. See Foucault 1997e, 195.

138. Foucault 2005a, 459.

139. Foucault 1997e, 194.

140. Foucault 2005a, 465, 460.

141. Ibid., 406–7.

142. Ibid., 131.

EPILOGUE

1. Barber 2003, 166.

2. Kaldor 2003, 45.

3. Barber 2003, 26. See also Wood 2004 on the ways in which tyranny and comfort join each other in what he sees as the emergence of a contemporary form of tyranny in the United States. See also the edited collection by Koivukoski and Tabachnick 2005 on ancient lessons about tyranny, though the essays (except for Boesche's) focus overwhelmingly on Greek philosophy.

4. Bureaucratization and despotism, in this sense, are so potent not because of raw power but because they are able to graft themselves onto the notion of citizenship. See Foucault 1988c.

5. Keane 2003, 112.

Bibliography

Abbott, Frank. 1963. *Roman Politics*. New York: Cooper Square Publishers.

Adcock, Robert. 2003. "The Emergence of Political Science as a Discipline: History and the Study of Politics in America, 1875–1910." *History of Political Thought* 24:481–508.

Agard, Walter. 1953. "Classical Scholarship." In *American Scholarship in the Twentieth Century*. Edited by Merle Curti. Cambridge: Harvard University Press, 146–67.

Albertini, Eugéne. 1923. *La Composition dans les ouvrages philosophiques de Sénèque*. Paris: E. de Boccard.

Alexander, William. 1952. "The 'Psychology' of Tacitus." *Classical Journal* 47:326–28.

——. 1954. *The Tacitean 'non liquet' on Seneca*. Berkeley: University of California Press.

Allen, Barry. 1993. *Truth in Philosophy*. Cambridge: Harvard University Press.

Ando, Clifford. 2000. *Imperial Ideology and Provincial Loyalty in the Roman Empire*. Berkeley: University of California Press.

Andrews, Alfred. 1930. "Did Seneca Practice the Ethics of His Epistles?" *Classical Journal* 25: 611–25.

Arendt, Hannah. 1958a. *The Human Condition*. Chicago: University of Chicago Press (cited as *HC*).

——. 1958b. *The Origins of Totalitarianism*. 2nd edition. Cleveland: Meridian Books (cited as *OT*).

——. 1965. *On Revolution*. New York: Penguin (cited as *OR*).

———. 1968a. *Between Past and Future*. Enlarged Edition. New York: Penguin (cited as *BPF*).

———. 1968b. *Men in Dark Times*. New York: Harvest (cited as *MDT*).

———. 1974. *Rahel Varnhagen: The Life of a Jewish Woman*. Revised Edition. Translated by Richard and Clara Winston. New York: Harcourt Brace Jovanovich (cited as *RV*).

———. 1978a. *The Life of the Mind*. New York: Harvest (cited as *LM*).

———. 1978b. "Martin Heidegger at Eighty." In *Heidegger and Modern Philosophy: Critical Essays*. Edited by Michael Murray. New Haven: Yale University Press.

———. 1982. *Lectures on Kant's Political Philosophy*. Edited by Ronald Beiner. Chicago: University of Chicago Press (cited as *LK*).

———. 1993. *Was ist Politik?: Fragmente aus dem Nachlaß*. Edited by Ursula Ludz. München: Piper (cited as *WP*).

Arnold, Edward. 1911. *Roman Stoicism*. Cambridge: Cambridge University Press.

Aron, Raymond. 1968. *Main Currents in Sociological Thought*. Vol. 1. Translated by Richard Howard and Helen Weaver. New York: Anchor Books.

Ash, Rhiannon. 1999. *Ordering Anarchy: Armies and Leaders in Tacitus'* Histories. Ann Arbor: University of Michigan Press.

Badian, Ernst. 1958. *Foreign Clientelae (264–70 B.C.)*. Oxford: Clarendon.

———. 1966. "The Early Historians." In *Latin Historians*. Edited by T. A. Dorey. New York: Basic Books, 1–38.

———. 1967. *Roman Imperialism in the Late Republic*. Pretoria: Communications of the University of South Africa.

———. 1986. "The Young Betti and the Practice of History." In *Costituzione romana e crisi della repubblica: Atti del convegno su Emilio Betti*. Edited by Giuliano Crifò. Napoli: Edizioni Scientifiche Italiane.

———. 1993. "Livy and Augustus." In *Livius: Aspekte seines Werkes*. Edited by Wolfgang Schuller. Konstanz: Universitätsverlag Konstanz, 9–38.

———. 1996. "*Tribuni Plebis* and *Res Publica*." In *Imperium Sine Fine: T. Robert S. Broughton and the Roman Republic*. Edited by Jerzy Linkerski. Stuttgart: Franz Steiner Verlag, 187–213.

Baer, Michael, Malcolm Jewell, and Lee Sigelman, Eds. 1991. *Political Science in America: Oral Histories of a Discipline*. Lexington: University Press of Kentucky.

Ball, Terence. 1995. *Reappraising Political Theory: Revisionist Studies in the History of Political Thought*. Oxford: Clarendon Press.

Balsdon, J.P.V.D. 1960. "*AUCTORITAS, DIGNITAS, OTIUM*." *Classical Quarterly* n.s. 10: 43–50.

———. 1979. *Romans and Aliens*. London: Duckworth.

Barber, Benjamin. 2003. *Fear's Empire: War, Terrorism, and Democracy*. New York: W.W. Norton.

Barker, Colin. 2001. "Fear, Laughter, and Collective Power: The Making of Solidarity at the Lenin Shipyard in Gdansk, Poland, August 1989." *Passionate Politics: Emotions and Social Movements*. Edited by Jeff Goodwin, James Jasper, and Francesca Polletta. Chicago: University of Chicago Press, 175–94.

Barnouw, Dagmar. 1990. *Visible Spaces: Hannah Arendt and the German–Jewish Experience*. Baltimore: Johns Hopkins University Press.

Baron, Hans. 1966. *The Crisis of the Early Italian Renaissance: Civic Humanism and Republican Liberty in an Age of Classicism and Tyranny*. Princeton: Princeton University Press.

Barthes, Roland. 1982. "Tacitus and the Funerary Baroque." In *A Barthes Reader*. Edited by Susan Sontag. New York: Hill and Wang, 162–66.

Bartsch, Shadi. 1994. *Actors in the Audience: Theatricality and Doublespeak from Nero to Hadrian*. Cambridge: Harvard University Press.

Bauman, Richard. 1974. *Impietas in Principem*. München: C.H. Beck.

Beacham, Richard. 1999. *Spectacle Entertainments of Early Imperial Rome*. New Haven: Yale University.

Beard, Charles. 1948. "Neglected Aspects of Political Science." *American Political Science Review* 42:211–22.

Bell, Andrew. 1997. "Cicero and the Spectacle of Power." *Journal of Roman Studies* 87:1–22.

Bell, Vikki. 1996. "The Promise of Liberalism and the Performance of Freedom." In *Foucault and Political Reason: Liberalism, Neo-Liberalism and Rationalities of Government*. Edited by Andrew Barry, Thomas Osborne, and Nikolas Rose. Chicago: University of Chicago Press, 81–97.

Benario, Herbert. 1964. "Tacitus and the Principate." *Classical Journal* 60:97–106.

———. 1972. "*Imperium* and *Capaces Imperii* in Tacitus." *American Journal of Philology* 93:14–26.

———. 1989. *The Classical Association of the Middle West and South: A*

History of the First Eighty Years. Greenville: Classical Association of the Middle West and South.

——. 1999. *Tacitus, Germany, Germania.* Warminster: Aris & Phillips.

Benjamin, Walter. 1968. *Illuminations.* Edited by Hannah Arendt. New York,: Schocken.

Bennett, Jane. 1996. " 'How is it, Then, That We Still Remain Barbarians?' Foucault, Schiller, and the Aestheticization of Ethics." *Political Theory* 24:653–72.

Béranger, Jean. 1953. *Recherches sur l'aspect idéologique du principat.* Basel: Verlag Friedrich Reinhardt AG.

Berlin, Isaiah. 1997. "Montesquieu." In *Against the Current: Essays in the History of Ideas.* Edited by Henry Hardy. Princeton: Princeton University Press, 130–61.

Bernauer, James. 1987. "Michel Foucault's Ecstatic Thinking." In *The Final Foucault.* Edited by Bernauer and David Rasmussen. Cambridge: MIT Press, 45–82.

——. 1990. *Michel Foucault's Force of Flight: Toward an Ethics for Thought.* New Jersey: Humanities Press.

Betensky, Aya. 1978. "Neronian Style, Tacitean Content: The Use of Ambiguous Confrontations in the *Annals.*" *Latomus* 37:419–35.

Bevir, Mark. 1999. "Foucault and Critique: Deploying Agency against Autonomy." *Political Theory* 27:65–84.

Bleicken, Jochen. 1998. *Augustus: Eine Biographie.* Berlin: Alexander Fest Verlag.

Blundell, Mary Whitlock. 1990. "Parental Nature and Stoic Οἰχείωσις." *Ancient Philosophy* 10:221–42.

Bluntschli, J. K. 1885. *The Theory of the State.* Oxford: Clarendon Press.

Blythe, James. 2000. " 'Civic humanism' and Medieval Political Thought." In *Renaissance Civic Humanism: Reappraisals and Reflections.* Edited by James Hankins. Cambridge: Cambridge University Press, 30–74.

Bobzien, Susanne. 1998. *Determinism and Freedom in Stoic Philosophy.* Oxford: Clarendon.

Boesche, Roger. 1990. "Fearing Monarchs and Merchants: Montesquieu's Two Theories of Despotism." *Western Political Quarterly* 43:741–61.

——. 1996. *Theories of Tyranny from Plato to Arendt.* University Park: Penn State Press.

Boissier, Gaston. 1906. *Tacitus and Other Roman Studies.* Translated by W.G. Hutchison. New York: G.P. Putnam's Sons.

Bolgar, R. R. 1954. *The Classical Heritage and its Beneficiaries*. Cambridge: Cambridge University Press.

Bollinger, Traugott. 1969. *Theatralis licentia: Die Publikumsdemonstration an den öffentlichen Spielen im Rom des früheren Kaiserzeit und ihre Bedeutung im politischen Leben*. Winterthur: Verglag Hans Schellenberg.

Bondanella, Peter. 1973. *Machiavelli and the Art of Renaissance History*. Detroit: Wayne State University Press.

Bourgery, A. 1911. "Les lettres a Lucilius: sont-elles de vraies lettres?" *Revue de philologie* 35:40–55.

Bowen-Moore, Patricia. 1989. *Hannah Arendt's Philosophy of Natality*. New York: St. Martin's Press.

Boyne, Roy. 1990. *Foucault and Derrida: The Other Side of Reason*. London: Unwin Hyman.

Bradshaw, Leah. 1989. *Acting and Thinking: The Political Thought of Hannah Arendt*. Toronto: University of Toronto Press.

Branham, R. Bracht, Glenn Most, Ralph Hexter, Sissa Giulia, Daniel Selden, Page duBois, and W. R. Johnson. 1997. "Panel Discussion: Classics and Comparative Literature: Agenda for the 90s." *Classical Philology* 92:153–88.

Braudel, Fernand. 1980. *On History*. Translated by Sarah Matthews. Chicago: University of Chicago Press.

Brecht, Arnold. 1947. "Political Theory: Beyond Relativism in Political Theory." *American Political Science Review* 41:470–88.

———. 1959. *Political Theory: The Foundations of Twentieth Century Political Thought*. Princeton: Princeton University Press.

Breisach, Ernst. 1994. *Historiography: Ancient, Medieval and Modern*. 2nd ed. Chicago: University of Chicago Press.

Bremmer, J. N. 1987. "Romulus, Remus and the Foundation of Rome." In *Roman Myth and Mythology*. Edited by J. N. Bremmer and N.M Horsfall. London: Institute of Classical Studies, 25–48.

Broughton, T. Robert S. 1951 and 1952. *The Magistrates of the Roman Republic*. 2 vols. New York: American Philological Association.

———. 1972. "Senate and Senators of the Roman Republic: The Prosopographical Approach." *Aufstieg und Niedergang der römischen Welt*. 1.1. Edited by Hildegard Temporini. Berlin: Walter de Gruyter, 250–65.

Brown, Peter. 1987. "Late Antiquity." In *A History of Private Life:* I. *From Pagan Rome to Byzantium*. Edited by Paul Veyne. Translated by Arthur Goldhammer. Cambridge: Belknap, 235–312.

Brown, Wendy. 1998. "Genealogical Politics." In *The Later Foucault:*

Politics and Philosophy. Edited by Jeremy Moss. London: Sage, 33–49.

——. 2006. "Power after Foucault." In *The Oxford Handbook of Political Theory*. Edited by John Dryzek, Bonnie Honig, and Anne Phillips. Oxford: Oxford University Press, 65–84.

Brunkhorst, Hauke. 2000. "Equality and Elitism in Arendt." In *The Cambridge Companion to Hannah Arendt*. Edited by Dana Villa. Cambridge: Cambridge University Press, 178–98.

Brunt, P.A. 1966. "The Roman Mob." *Past and Present* 35:3–27.

——. 1971a. *Italian Manpower: 225 B.C.–A.D. 14*. Oxford: Clarendon Press.

——. 1971b. *Social Conflicts in the Roman Republic*. New York: W. W. Norton and Company.

——. 1982. "*Nobilitas* and *Novitas*." *Journal of Roman Studies* 72:1–17.

——. 1983. "Princeps and Equites." *Journal of Roman Studies* 73:42–75.

——. 1984. "The Role of the Senate in the Augustan Regime." *Classical Quarterly* 34:423–44.

——. 1988. *The Fall of the Roman Republic: And Related Essays*. Oxford: Clarendon Press.

Buckland, W. W. 1921. *A Text-Book of Roman Law from Augustus to Justinian*. Cambridge: Cambridge University Press.

Burnet, John. 1918. *Higher Education and the War.* London: Macmillan.

Burck, Erich. 1964. *Die Erzählungskunst des T. Livius*. Berlin: Weidmannsche.

——. 1991. "Livius und Augustus." *Illinois Classical Studies* 16:269–81.

Butterfield, Herbert. 1960. *The Statecraft of Machiavelli*. London: Collier Books.

Bryce, James. 1909. "The Relations of Political Science to History and to Practice." *American Political Science Review* 3:1–20.

Calder, William III. 1994. "Classical Scholarship in the United States: An Introductory Essay." In *Biographical Dictionary of North American Classicists*. Edited by Ward Briggs, Jr. Westport: Greenwood Press, xix–xxxix.

Calhoon, Cristina. 1997. "Lucretia, Savior and Scapegoat: The Dynamics of Sacrifice in Livy 1.57–59." *Helios* 24:151–69.

Campbell, J. B. 1984. *The Emperor and the Roman Empire, 31 BC–AD 235*. Oxford: Clarendon Press.

Canovan, Margaret. 1992. *Hannah Arendt: A Reinterpretation of Her Political Thought.* Cambridge: Cambridge University Press.

———. 1994. "Politics as Culture: Hannah Arendt and the Public Realm." In *Hannah Arendt: Critical Essays.* Edited by Lewis Hinchman and Sandra Hinchman. Albany: SUNY Press, 179–210.

Carandini, Andrea. 1988. *Schiavi in Italia: Gli strumenti pensanti dei Romani fra tarda Repubblica e medio impero.* Roma: La Nuova Italia Scientifica.

Carlyle, Robert Warrand and Alexander James Carlyle. 1950 (orig. 1936). *A History of Mediaeval Political Theory in the West.* Edinburgh: William Blackwood and Sons.

Carrette, Jeremy. 2000. *Foucault and Religion: Spiritual Corporality and Political Spirituality.* London: Routledge.

Carrithers, David. 1986. "Montesquieu's Philosophy of History." *Journal of the History of Ideas* 47:61–80.

———. 2001. "Montesquieu and the Liberal Philosophy of Jurisprudence." In *Montesquieu's Science of Politics: Essays on* The Spirit of Laws. Edited by Carrithers, Michael Mosher, and Paul Rahe. Lanham: Rowman and Littlefield, 291–334.

Carter, J. M. 1972. "Cicero: Politics and Philosophy." In *Cicero and Virgil: Studies in Honour of Harold Hunt.* Edited by John Martyn. Amsterdam: Adolf M. Hakkert, 15–36.

Cassirer, Ernst. 1955. *The Myth of the State.* Garden City, NY: Doubleday.

Catlin, George. 1930. *A Study of the Principles of Politics: Being an Essay Towards Political Rationalization.* New York: Macmillan.

Celsus. 1971. *On Medicine.* Translated by W.G. Spencer. Cambridge: Harvard University Press.

Chaplin, Jane. 2000. *Livy's Exemplary History.* Oxford: Oxford University Press.

Charlesworth, M. P. 1937. *The Virtues of a Roman Emperor: Propaganda and the Creation of Belief.* London: Milford.

Cicero, Marcus Tullius. 1913. *On Duties.* Translated by Walter Miller. Cambridge: Harvard University Press.

———. 1914. *On Ends.* Translated by H. Rackham. Cambridge: Harvard University Press.

———. 1952. *Orator.* Translated by H.M. Hubbell. Cambridge: Harvard University Press.

———. 1996. *Laelius on Friendship.* Translated by William Armistead Falconer. Cambridge: Harvard University Press.

——. 1996. *On the Orator*. Translated by E. W. Sutton. Cambridge: Harvard University Press.

——. 1996. *Tusculan Disputations*. Translated by J. E. King. Cambridge: Harvard University Press.

——. 2000. *Academics*. Translated by H. Rackham. Cambridge: Harvard University Press.

——. 2000. *On the Laws*. Translated by Clinton Walker Keyes. Cambridge: Harvard University Press.

——. 2000. *On the Republic*. Translated by Clinton Walker Keyes. Cambridge: Harvard University Press.

——. 2001. *Letters to Friends*. Translated by D.R. Shackleton Bailey. Cambridge: Harvard University Press.

Cichorius, Conrad. 1922. *Römische Studien*. Leipzig: Teubner.

Cizek, Eugen. 1992. "A propos de la poétique de l'histoire chez Tite-Live." *Latomus* 51:354–64.

Claasen, Jo-Marie. 1999. *Displaced Persons: The Literature of Exile from Cicero to Boethius*. Madison: University of Wisconsin Press.

Clarke, M.L. 1956. *The Roman Mind: Studies in the History of Thought from Cicero to Marcus Aurelius*. Cambridge: Harvard University Press.

Classen, C. Joachim. 1989. "Die Peripatetiker in Cicero's *Tuskulanen*." In *Cicero's Knowledge of the Peripatos*. Edited by William Fortenbaugh and Peter Steinmetz. New Brunswick: Transaction, 186–200.

Coby, J. Patrick. 1999. *Machiavelli's Romans: Liberty and Greatness in* The Discourses on Livy. Lanham: Lexington Books.

Cochrane, Charles. 1940. *Christianity and Classical Culture: A Study of Thought and Action from Augustus to Augustine*. Oxford: Clarendon.

Cohen, David and Richard Saller. 1994. "Foucault on Sexuality in Greco-Roman Antiquity." In *Foucault and the Writing of History*. Edited by Jan Goldstein. Oxford: Blackwell, 35–59.

Cohler, Anne. 1988. *Montesquieu's Comparative Politics and the Spirit of American Constitutionalism*. Lawrence: University Press of Kansas.

Coleman, Robert. 1974. "The Artful Moralist: A Study of Seneca's Epistolary Style." *Classical Quarterly* 24:276–89.

Colish, Marcia. 1971. "The Idea of Liberty in Machiavelli." *Journal of the History of Ideas* 32:323–50.

——. 1990. *The Stoic Tradition from Antiquity to the Early Middle Ages*. 2nd ed. 2 vols. Leiden: E. J. Brill.

Collingwood, R. G. 1946. *The Idea of History*. Oxford: Clarendon Press.

Comte, Auguste. 1974. *The Positive Philosophy*. Translated by C. Blanchard. New York: AMS Press.

Condren, Conal. 1985. *The Status and Appraisal of Classical Texts: An Essay on Political Theory, Its Inheritance, and the History of Ideas*. Princeton: Princeton University Press.

Connolly, Joy. 2007. *The State of Speech: Rhetoric and Political Thought in Ancient Rome*. Princeton: Princeton University Press.

Connolly, William. 1993. "Beyond Good and Evil: The Ethical Sensibility of Michel Foucault." *Political Theory* 21:365–89.

Connor, W. R. 1989. "The New Classical Humanities and the Old." In *Classics: A Discipline and Profession in Crisis?* Edited by Phyllis Culham and Lowell Edmunds. New York: University Press of America, 25–38.

Cooper, John and J. F. Procopé. 1995. *Seneca, Moral and Political Essays*. Cambridge: Cambridge University Press.

Cornell, T. J. 1975. "Aeneas and the Twins: The Development of the Roman Foundation Legend." *Proceedings of the Cambridge Philological Society* 21:1–32.

———. 1986. "The Value of the Literary Tradition Concerning Archaic Rome." In *Social Struggles in Archaic Rome: New Perspectives on the Conflict of the Orders*. Edited by Kurt Raaflaub. Berkeley: University of California Press, 52–76.

———. 1995. *The Beginnings of Rome: Italy and Rome from the Bronze Age to the Punic Wars (c. 1000–264 BC)*. London: Routledge.

Cotton, Hannah and Alexander Yakobson. 2002. "*Arcanum Imperii*: The Powers of Augustus." In *Philosophy and Power in the Graeco-Roman World: Essays in Honour of Miriam Griffin*. Edited by Gillian Clark and Tessa Rajak. Oxford: Oxford University Press, 193–209.

Cousin, Jean. 1969. "Rhetorik und Psychologie bei Tacitus im Hinblick auf seine ΑΕΙΝΩΣΙΣ." In *Tacitus*. Edited by Viktor Pöschl. *Wege der Forschung* 97. Darmstadt: Wissenschaftliche Buchgesellschaft.

Crawford, Michael. 1978. *The Roman Republic*. Cambridge: Harvard University Press.

Crook, John. 1967. *Law and Life of Rome*. Ithaca: Cornell University Press.

Cruikshank, Barbara. 1996. "Revolution Within: Self-Government and Self-Esteem." In *Foucault and Political Reason: Liberalism, Neo-Liberalism and Rationalities of Government*. Edited by Andrew Barry,

Thomas Osborne, and Nikolas Rose. Chicago: University of Chicago Press, 231–51.

Curtis, Kimberley. 1999. *Our Sense of the Real: Aesthetic Experience and Arendtian Politics*. Ithaca: Cornell University Press.

Daitz, Stephen. 1960. "Tacitus' Technique of Character Portrayal." *American Journal of Philology* 81:30–52.

Daraki, Maria. 1986. "Michel Foucault's Journey to Greece." *Telos* 67:87–110.

Davidson, Arnold. 1990. "Spiritual Exercises and Ancient Philosophy: An Introduction to Pierre Hadot." *Critical Inquiry* 16:475–82.

———. 1994. "Ethics as Ascetics: Foucault, the History of Ethics, and Ancient Thought." In *Foucault and the Writing of History*. Edited by Jan Goldstein. Oxford: Blackwell, 63–80.

Davies, J.C. 1971. "Was Cicero Aware of Natural Beauty?" *Greece and Rome,* 2nd series, 18:152–65.

Dean, Mitchell. 1994. *Critical and Effective Histories: Foucault's Methods and Historical Sociology*. London: Routledge.

———. 1996. "Foucault, Government and the Enfolding of Authority." In *Foucault and Political Reason: Liberalism, Neo-Liberalism and Rationalities of Government*. Edited by Andrew Barry, Thomas Osborne, and Nikolas Rose. Chicago: University of Chicago Press, 209–29.

de Grazia, Sebastian. 1989. *Machiavelli in Hell*. Princeton: Princeton University Press.

de Ste. Croix, G. E. M. 1981. *The Class Struggle in the Ancient Greek World from the Archaic Age to the Arab Conquests*. Ithaca: Cornell University Press.

Deininger, Jürgen. 1985. "Livius und der Prinzipat." *Klio* 67:265–72.

Deleuze, Gilles. 1988. *Foucault*. Translated by Seán Hand. Minneapolis: University of Minnesota Press.

Detel, Wolfgang. 1998. *Foucault and Classical Antiquity: Power, Ethics and Knowledge*. Translated by David Wigg-Wolf. Cambridge: Cambridge University Press.

Dewey, John. 1989 (orig. 1944). "Challenge to Liberal Thought." In *The Later Works, 1925–1953*. Vol. 15. Edited by Jo Ann Boydston. Carbondale: Southern Illinois University Press, 261–75.

Dingel, Joachim. 1974. *Seneca und die Dichtung*. Heidelberg: Carl Winter Universitätsverlag.

Dodds, Muriel. 1929. *Les récits de voyages: sources de l'Esprit des lois de Montesquieu*. Paris: Librairie Ancienne Honoré Champion.

Dolan, Frederick. 2005. "The Paradoxical Liberty of Bio-power: Hannah Arendt and Michel Foucault on Modern Politics." *Philosophy and Social Criticism* 31:369–80.

Donaldson, Ian. 1982. *The Rapes of Lucretia: A Myth and its Transformations*. Oxford: Clarendon Press.

Donlan, Walter. n.d. "A Brief History of the Classical Association of the Atlantic States and *The Classical World*: 1907–1980." Website of the Classical Association of the Atlantic States.

Dorey, T. A. 1969. " '*Agricola*' and '*Germania*.' " In *Tacitus*. Edited by Dorey. London: Routledge, 1–18.

Dougherty, Carol. 1998. "It's Murder to Found a Colony." In *Cultural Poetics in Archaic Greece: Cult, Performance, Politics*. Edited by Carol Dougherty and Leslie Kurke. New York: Oxford University Press, 178–98.

Douglas, A. E. 1965. "Cicero the Philosopher." In *Cicero*. Edited by T.A. Dorey. London: Routledge and Kegan Paul, 135–70.

———. 1995. "Form and Content in the *Tusculan Disputations*." In *Cicero the Philosopher: Twelve Papers*. Edited by J. G. F. Powell. Oxford: Clarendon Press, 197–218.

Dreyfus, Hubert and Paul Rabinow. 1983. *Michel Foucault: Beyond Structuralism and Hermeneutics*. 2nd ed. Chicago: University of Chicago Press.

Drumann, W. 1919. *Geschichte Roms*. Leipzig: Verlag von Gebrüder Borntraeger.

duBois, Page. 1998. "The Subject in Antiquity after Foucault." In *Rethinking Sexuality: Foucault and Classical Antiquity*. Edited by David Larmour, Paul Miller, and Charles Platter. Princeton: Princeton University Press, 85–103.

Dudley, Donald. 1968. *The World of Tacitus*. London: Secker and Warburg.

Düll, Rudolf. 1976. "Seneca iurisconsultus." *Aufstieg und Niedergang der römischen Welt*. 2.15. Edited by Hildegard Temporini and Wolfgang Haase. Berlin: Walter de Gruyter, 364–80.

Dumézil, Georges. 1980. *Camillus: A Study of Indo-European Religion as Roman History*. Edited by Udo Strutynski. Translated by Annette Aronowicz and Josette Bryson. Berkeley: University of California Press.

Dunkle, J. Roger. 1967. "The Greek Tyrant and Roman Political Invective of the Late Republic." *Transactions of the American Philological Association* 98:151–71.

——. 1971. "The Rhetorical Tyrant in Roman Historiography: Sallust, Livy and Tacitus." *Classical World* 65:12–20.

Dunn, John. 1996. *The History of Political Theory and Other Essays*. Cambridge: Cambridge University Press.

Dunning, William. 1935 (orig. 1902). *A History of Political Theories: Ancient and Mediaeval*. New York: Macmillan.

Dupont, Florence. 1997. "*Recitatio* and the Reorganization of the Space of Public Discourse." In *The Roman Cultural Revolution*. Edited by Thomas Habinek and Alessandro Schiesaro. Cambridge: Cambridge University Press, 44–59.

Durkheim, Emile. 1960. *Montesquieu and Rousseau: Forerunners of Sociology*. Translated by Ralph Manheim. Ann Arbor: University of Michigan Press.

Duxbury, Neil. 2004. *Frederick Pollock and the English Juristic Tradition*. Oxford: Oxford University Press.

Eagleton, Terry. 1990. *The Ideology of the Aesthetic*. Oxford: Basil Blackwell.

Easton, David. 1951. "The Decline of Modern Political Theory." *Journal of Politics* 13:36–58.

——. 1971 (orig. 1953). *The Political System: An Inquiry into the State of Political Science*. New York: Alfred A. Knopf.

Ebenstein, William. 1957. *Political Thought in Perspective*. New York: McGraw-Hill.

——. 1960 (orig. 1951). *Great Political Thinkers: Plato to the Present*. New York: Holt, Rinehart and Winston.

Eck, Werner. 1984. "Senatorial Self-Representation: Developments in the Augustan Period." In *Caesar Augustus: Seven Aspects*. Edited by Fergus Millar and Erich Segal. Oxford: Clarendon Press, 129–67.

Eck, Werner, Antonio Caballos, and Fernando Fernández. 1996. *Das senatus consultum de Cn. Pisone patre*. München: C.H. Beck'sche Verlagsbuchhandlung.

Edelstein, Ludwig. 1967. *The Idea of Progress in Classical Antiquity*. Baltimore: Johns Hopkins University Press.

Eder, Walter. 1986. "The Political Significance of the Codification of Law in Archaic Societies: An Unconventional Hypothesis." In *Social Struggles in Archaic Rome: New Perspective on the Conflict of the Orders*. Edited by Kurt Raaflaub. Berkeley: University of California Press, 262–300.

——. 1990. "Augustus and the Power of Tradition: The Augustan Principate as Binding Link between Republic and Empire." In

Between Republic and Empire: Interpretations of Augustus and His Principate. Edited by Kurt Raaflaub and Mark Toher. Berkeley: University of California Press, 71–122.

Editorial. 1917. "The Classical Conference at Princeton." *Classical Journal* 13:81–87.

Edmondson, J. C. 1996. "Dynamic Arenas: Gladiatorial Presentations in the City of Rome and the Construction of Roman Society during the Early Empire." In *Roman Theater and Society: E. Togo Salmon Papers I*. Edited by William Slater. Ann Arbor: University of Michigan Press, 669–712.

Edmunds, Lowell. 1989. "Introduction." In *Classics: A Discipline and Profession in Crisis?* Edited by Phyllis Culham and Lowell Edmunds. New York: University Press of America, ix–xxxviii.

Edwards, Catharine. 1993. *The Politics of Immorality in Ancient Rome*. Cambridge: Cambridge University Press

——. 1994. "Beware of Imitations: Theatre and the Subversion of Imperial Identity." In *Reflections of Nero: Culture, History & Representation*. Edited by Jas Elsner and Jamie Masters. Chapel Hill: University of North Carolina Press, 83–97.

——. 1997. "Self-Scrutiny and Self-Transformation in Seneca's Letters." *Greece and Rome* 44:23–38.

——. 1999. "The Suffering Body: Philosophy and Pain in Seneca's *Letters*." In *Constructions of the Classical Body*. Edited by James Porter. Ann Arbor: University of Michigan Press, 252–68.

Elliot, William and Neil McDonald. 1950. *Western Political Heritage*. New York: Prentice-Hall.

Ellis, Ellen. 1927. "Political Science at the Crossroads." *American Political Science Review* 21:773–91.

Emberly, Peter and Barry Cooper, Eds. 2004. *Faith and Political Philosophy: The Correspondence Between Leo Strauss and Eric Voegelin, 1934–1964*. Columbia: University of Missouri Press.

Engberg-Pedersen, Troels. 1990a. "Stoic Philosophy and the Concept of the Person." In *The Person and the Human Mind: Issues in Ancient and Modern Philosophy*. Edited by Christopher Gill. Oxford: Clarendon Press, 109–35.

——. 1990b. *The Stoic Theory of Oikeiosis: Moral Development and Social Interaction in Early Stoic Philosophy*. Aarhus: Aarhus University Press.

Erskine, Andrew. 1990. *The Hellenistic Stoa: Political Thought and Action*. Ithaca: Cornell University Press.

———. 1997. "Cicero and the Expression of Grief." In *The Passions in Roman Thought and Literature*. Edited by Susanna Morton Braund and Christopher Gill. Cambridge: Cambridge University Press, 36–47.

Euben, J. Peter. 2003. *Platonic Noise*. Princeton: Princeton University Press.

Fantham, Elaine. 1972. *Comparative Studies in Republican Latin Imagery*. Toronto: University of Toronto Press.

Farr, James. 2006. "The History of Political Thought as Disciplinary Genre." In *The Oxford Handbook of Political Theory*. Edited by John Dryzek, Bonnie Honig, and Anne Phillips. Oxford: Oxford University Press, 225–42.

Feldherr, Andrew. 1997. "Livy's Revolution: Civic Identity and the Creation of the *res publica*." In *The Roman Cultural Revolution*. Edited by Thomas Habinek and Alessandro Schiesaro. Cambridge: Cambridge University Press, 136–57.

———. 1998. *Spectacle and Society in Livy's* History. Berkeley: University of California Press.

Ferguson, John. 1958. *Moral Values in the Ancient World*. London: Methuen.

Finley, M. I. 1963. "Generalizations in Ancient History." In *Generalization in the Writing of History*. Edited by Louis Gottschalk. Chicago: University of Chicago Press, 19–35.

Fischer, Markus. 1997. "Machiavelli's Political Psychology." *Review of Politics* 59:789–829.

———. 2000. *Well-Ordered License: On the Unity of Machiavelli's Thought*. Lanham: Lexington.

Fitch, John and Siobhan McElduff. 2002. "Construction of the Self in Senecan Drama." *Mnemosyne* 55:18–40.

Fleisher, Martin. 1972. "A Passion for Politics: The Vital Core of the World of Machiavelli." In *Machiavelli and the Nature of Political Thought*. Edited by Martin Fleisher. New York: Atheneum, 114–47.

Flickinger, Roy. 1933. "Our Message in a Time of Depression." *Classical Journal* 28:561–73.

Flower, Harriet. 1996. *Ancestor Masks and Aristocratic Power in Roman Culture*. Oxford: Clarendon Press.

———. 1999. "Piso in Chicago: A Commentary on the APA/AIA Joint Seminar on the *Senatus Consultum de Cn. Pisone Patre*." *American Journal of Philology* 120:99–115.

——. 2004. "Spectacle and Political Culture in the Roman Republic." In *The Cambridge Companion to the Roman Republic*. Edited by Harriet Flower. Cambridge: Cambridge University Press, 322–43.

——. 2006. *The Art of Forgetting: Disgrace and Oblivion in Roman Political Culture*. Chapel Hill: University of North Carolina Press.

Flynn, Thomas. 1988. "Foucault as Parrhesiast: His Last Course at the Collège de France (1984)." In *The Final Foucault*. Edited by James Bernauer and David Rasmussen. Cambridge: MIT Press, 102–18.

——. 2005a. "Foucault's Mapping of History." In *The Cambridge Companion to Foucault*. 2nd ed. Edited by Gary Cutting. Cambridge: Cambridge University Press, 29–48.

——. 2005b. "Philosophy as a Way of Life: Foucault and Hadot." *Philosophy and Social Criticism* 31:609–22.

Fontana, Benedetto. 2003. "Sallust and the Politics of Machiavelli." *History of Political Thought* 24:86–108.

Fornara, Charles. 1983. *The Nature of History in Ancient Greece and Rome*. Berkeley: University of California Press.

Foucault, Michel. 1979. *Discipline and Punish: The Birth of the Prison*. Translated by Alan Sheridan. New York: Vintage.

——. 1983a. "On the Genealogy of Ethics: An Overview of Work in Progress." In *Michel Foucault: Beyond Structuralism and Hermeneutics*. 2nd ed. Edited by Hubert Dreyfus and Paul Rabinow. Chicago: University of Chicago Press, 229–52.

——. 1983b. "The Subject and Power." In *Michel Foucault: Beyond Structuralism and Hermeneutics*. 2nd ed. Edited by Hubert Dreyfus and Paul Rabinow. Chicago: University of Chicago Press, 208–26.

——. 1984. *Foucault Reader*. Edited by Paul Rabinow. New York: Pantheon.

——. 1988a. "An Aesthetics of Existence." In *Politics, Philosophy, Culture*. Edited by Lawrence Kritzman. New York: Routledge, 47–53.

——. 1988b. "Iran: The Spirit of a World Without a Spirit." In *Politics, Philosophy, Culture*. Edited by Lawrence Kritzman. New York: Routledge, 211–24.

——. 1988c. "Politics and Reason." In *Politics, Philosophy, Culture*. Edited by Lawrence Kritzman. New York: Routledge, 57–85.

——. 1990. *The History of Sexuality*. Vol. 1. *An Introduction*. Translated by Robert Hurley. New York: Vintage.

———. 1990. *The History of Sexuality*. Vol. 2. *The Use of Pleasure*. Translated by Robert Hurley. New York: Vintage (cited as *UP*).

———. 1990. *The History of Sexuality*. Vol. 3. *The Care of the Self*. Translated by Robert Hurley. New York: Vintage (cited as *CS*).

———. 1991a. "Governmentality." *The Foucault Effect: Studies in Governmentality*. Edited by Graham Burchell, Colin Gordon, and Peter Miller. Chicago: University of Chicago Press, 87–104.

———. 1991b. "Questions of Method." *The Foucault Effect: Studies in Governmentality*. Edited by Graham Burchell, Colin Gordon, and Peter Miller. Chicago: University of Chicago Press, 73–86.

———. 1997a. "The Ethics of the Concern for Self as a Practice of Freedom." In *Ethics: Subjectivity and Truth*. Vol. 1. Edited by Paul Rabinow. New York: Free Press, 281–301.

———. 1997b. "The Hermeneutics of the Subject." In *Ethics: Subjectivity and Truth*. Vol. 1. Edited by Paul Rabinow. New York: Free Press, 93–106.

———. 1997c. "Polemics, Politics, and Problematizations." In *Ethics: Subjectivity and Truth*. Vol. 1. Edited by Paul Rabinow. New York: Free Press, 111–19.

———. 1997d. "Self Writing." In *Ethics: Subjectivity and Truth*. Vol. 1. Edited by Paul Rabinow. New York: Free Press, 207–22.

———. 1997e. "Subjectivity and Truth." In *The Politics of Truth*. Edited by Sylvère Lotringer. Los Angeles: Semiotext(e).

———. 1997f. "Technologies of the Self." In *Ethics: Subjectivity and Truth*. Vol. 1. Edited by Paul Rabinow. New York: Free Press, 223–52.

———. 1997g. "What is Enlightenment?" In *Ethics: Subjectivity and Truth*. Vol. 1. Edited by Paul Rabinow. New York: Free Press, 303–19.

———. 2001. *Fearless Speech*. Edited by Joseph Pearson. Los Angeles: Semiotext(e).

———. 2005a. *The Hermeneutics of the Subject: Lectures at the Collège de France 1981–1982*. Edited by Frédéric Gros. Translated by Graham Burchell. New York: Palgrave.

———. 2005b. "What are the Iranians Dreaming About?" In *Foucault and the Iranian Revolution: Gender and the Seductions of Islamism*. Edited by Janet Afary and Kevin Anderson. Chicago: University of Chicago Press, 203–9.

Foxhall, Lin. 1998. "Pandora Unbound: A Feminist Critique of Foucault's *History of Sexuality*." In *Rethinking Sexuality: Foucault and Classical Antiquity*. Edited by David Larmour, Paul Miller, and Charles Platter. Princeton: Princeton University Press, 122–37.

Frampton, Kenneth. 1979. "The Status of Man and the Status of His Objects: A Reading of *The Human Condition*." In *Hannah Arendt: The Recovery of the Public World*. Edited by Melvyn Hill. New York: St. Martin's Press, 101–30.

Frank, Tenney. 1927. *An Economic History of Rome*. 2nd ed. Baltimore: Johns Hopkins University Press.

———. 1933–40. *An Economic Survey of Ancient Rome*. 6 vols. Baltimore: Johns Hopkins University Press.

———. 1941. "Our Changing Program." *American Journal of Philology* 62: 257–60.

Frede, Dorothea. "Constitution and Citizenship: Peripatetic Influence on Cicero's Political Conceptions in the *De re publica*." In *Cicero's Knowledge of the Peripatos*. Edited by William Fortenbaugh and Peter Steinmetz. New Brunswick: Transaction, 77–100.

———. 1992. "The Cognitive Role of *Phantasia* in Aristotle." In *Essays on Aristotle's* De Anima. Edited by Martha Nussbaum and Amélie Oksonberg Rorty. Oxford: Clarendon Press, 279–95.

———. 2003. "Stoic Determinism." In *The Cambridge Companion to the Stoics*. Edited by Brad Inwood. Cambridge: Cambridge University Press, 179–205.

Frede, Michael. 1987a. "Philosophy and Medicine in Antiquity." *Essays in Ancient Philosophy*. Minneapolis: University of Minnesota Press, 225–42.

———. 1987b. "Stoics and Skeptics on Clear and Distinct Impressions." *Essays in Ancient Philosophy*. Minneapolis: University of Minnesota Press, 151–76.

Furner, Mary. 1975. *Advocacy and Objectivity: A Crisis in the Professionalization of American Social Science, 1865–1905*. Lexington: University of Kentucky Press.

Gabba, Emilio. 1984. "The Historians and Augustus." In *Caesar Augustus: Seven Aspects*. Edited by Fergus Millar and Erich Segal. Oxford: Clarendon Press, 61–88.

Galen. 1972, 1988, 1999. *De Placitis Hippocratis et Platonis*. In Kidd and Edelstein, *Posidonius*.

Galinsky, Karl, Ed. 1992. "Introduction: The Current State of the Interpretation of Roman Poetry and the Contemporary Critical Scene." In *The Interpretation of Roman Poetry: Empiricism or Hermeneutics?* Frankfurt am Main: Peter Lang, 1–40.

——. 1996. *Augustan Culture: An Interpretive Introduction*. Princeton: Princeton University Press.

Galston, William. 1993. "Political Theory in the 1980s: Perplexity Amidst Diversity." In *Political Science: The State of the Discipline II*. Edited by Ada Finifter. Washington, D.C.: American Political Science Association, 27–53.

Garver, Eugene. 1987. *Machiavelli and the History of Prudence*. Madison: University of Wisconsin Press.

Gelzer, Matthias. 1962. "Die Nobilität der römischen Republik." *Kleine Schriften* 1. Wiesbaden: Franz Steiner Verlag, 17–135.

Gilbert, Alan. 1965. *Machiavelli: The Chief Works and Others*. 3 vols. Durham: Duke University Press.

——. 1994. " 'Internal Restlessness': Individuality and Community in Montesquieu." *Political Theory* 22:45–70.

Gilbert, Felix. 1965. *Machiavelli and Guicciardini: Politics and History in Sixteenth Century Florence*. Princeton: Princeton University Press.

——. 1977 (orig. 1953). "The Composition and Structure of Machiavelli's *Discorsi*." *History: Choice and Commitment*. Cambridge: Belknap Press, 115–33.

Gilbert, Rolf. 1976. *Die Beziehungen zwischen Princeps und stadtrömischen Plebs im frühen Principat*. Bochum: Studienverlag Dr. N. Brockmeyer.

Gildersleeve, Basil. 1880. "Editorial Note." *American Journal of Philology* 1:1–3.

——. 1884. "Friedrich Ritschl." *American Journal of Philology* 5:339–53.

——. 1890a. "Classics and Colleges." *Essays and Studies: Educational and Literary*. Baltimore: N. Murray, 43–84.

——. 1890b. "Limits of Culture." *Essays and Studies: Educational and Literary*. Baltimore: N. Murray, 3–40.

——. 1917. "An Oxford Scholar." *American Journal of Philology* 38:392–410.

Gill, Christopher. 1983. "The Question of Character-Development: Plutarch and Tacitus." *Classical Quarterly* 33:469–87.

——. 1985. "Ancient Psychotherapy." *Journal of the History of Ideas*. 46:307–25.

——. 1987. "Two Monologues of Self-Division: Euripides, *Medea* 1021–80 and Seneca, *Medea* 893–977." In *Homo Viator: Classical Essays for John Bramble*. Edited by Michael Whitby, Philip Hardie, and Mary Whitby. Bristol: Bristol Classical Press, 25–37.

——. 1996. *Personality in Greek Epic, Tragedy, and Philosophy: The Self in Dialogue*. Oxford: Clarendon Press.

——. 2000. "Stoic Writers of the Imperial Era." In *The Cambridge History of Greek and Roman Political Thought*. Edited by Christopher Rowe and Malcolm Schofield. Cambridge: Cambridge University Press, 597–615.

Ginsburg, Judith. 1981. *Tradition and Theme in the* Annals *of Tacitus*. Salem: The Ayer Company.

——. 1993. "*In Maiores Certamina:* Past and Present in the *Annals*." In *Tacitus and the Tacitean Tradition*. Edited by T. J. Luce and A. J. Woodman. Princeton: Princeton University Press.

Glucker, John. 1988. "Cicero's Philosophical Affiliations." In *The Question of "Eclecticism": Studies in Later Greek Philosophy*. Edited by John Dillon and A. A. Long. Berkeley: University of California Press, 34–69.

Goldberg, Sander. 1999. "Appreciating Aper: The Defence of Modernity in Tacitus' *Dialogus de oratoribus*." *Classical Quarterly* 19: 224–37.

Goldschmidt, Victor. 1953. *Le système Stoïcien et l'idée de temps*. Paris: Librairie Philosphique J. Vrin.

Goodwin, Jeff, James Jasper, and Francesca Polletta, Eds. 2001. "Introduction: Why Emotions Matter." In *Passionate Politics: Emotions and Social Movements*. Chicago: University of Chicago Press, 1–24.

Goodyear, F. R. D. 1968. "Development of Language and Style in the *Annals* of Tacitus." *Journal of Roman Studies* 58:22–31.

——. 1972. *The Annals of Tacitus, Books 1–6*. Vol. 1. Cambridge: Cambridge University Press.

——. 1981. *The Annals of Tacitus, Books 1–6*. Vol. 2. Cambridge: Cambridge University Press.

Gottsegen, Michael. 1994. *The Political Thought of Hannah Arendt*. Albany: State University of New York Press.

Graff, Gerald. 1987. *Professing Literature: An Institutional History*. Chicago: University of Chicago Press.

Granger, Frank. 1919. "Review: Natural Science and the Classical System in Education." *Classical Review* 33:110–13.

Graver, Margaret. 2002. *Cicero on the Emotions:* Tusculan Disputations *3 and 4*. Chicago: University of Chicago Press.

Greene, Thomas. 1986. "The End of Discourse in Machiavelli's *Prince*." In *Literary Theory/Renaissance Texts*. Edited by Patricia Parker and David Quint. Baltimore: Johns Hopkins University Press, 63–77.

Griffin, Miriam. 1968. "Seneca on Cato's Politics: *Epistle* 14, 12–13." *Classical Quarterly* 18:373–75.

———. 1976. *Seneca: A Philosopher in Politics*. Oxford: Clarendon.

———. 1988. "Philosophy for Statesmen: Cicero and Seneca." In *Antikes Denken-Moderne Schule: Beiträge zu den antiken Grundlagen unseres Denkens*. Edited by H. W. Schmidt and P. Wülfing. Heidelberg: Carl Winter Universitätsverlag, 133–50.

———. 1995. "Tacitus, Tiberius and the Principate." In *Leaders and Masses in the Roman World: Studies in Honor of Zvi Yavetz*. Edited by I. Malkin and Z. W. Rubinsohn. Leiden: E. J. Brill, 33–57.

———. 1997. "The Senate's Story." *Journal of Roman Studies* 87:249–63.

———. 2000. "Seneca and Pliny." In *The Cambridge History of Greek and Roman Political Thought*. Edited by Christopher Rowe and Malcolm Schofield. Cambridge: Cambridge University Press, 532–58.

Grimal, Pierre. 1978. *Seneca: Macht und Ohnmacht des Geistes*. Darmstadt: Wissenschaftliche Buchgesellschaft.

Gruen, Erich. 1974. *The Last Generation of the Roman Republic*. Berkeley: University of California Press.

———. 1992. *Culture and National Identity in Republican Rome*. Ithaca: Cornell University Press.

Gunnell, John. 1983. "Political Theory: The Evolution of a Sub-Field." In *Political Science: The Discipline and Its Scope and Theory*. Edited by Ada Finifter. Washington, D.C.: American Political Science Association, 3–45.

———. 1986. *Between Philosophy and Politics: The Alienation of Political Theory*. Amherst: University of Massachusetts Press.

———. 1993. *The Descent of Political Theory: The Genealogy of an American Vocation*. Chicago: University of Chicago Press.

———. 2006. "The Founding of the American Political Science Association: Discipline, Profession, Political Theory, and Politics." *American Political Science Review* 100:479–86.

Habicht, Christian. 1990. *Cicero the Politician*. Baltimore: Johns Hopkins University Press.

Habinek, Thomas. 1992. "An Aristocracy of Virtue: Seneca on the Beginnings of Wisdom." In *Beginnings in the Classical Literature*. Edited by Francis Dunn and Thomas Cole. *Yale Classical Studies* 24. Cambridge: Cambridge University Press, 187–203.

———. 1994. "Ideology for an Empire in the Prefaces to Cicero's Dialogues." *Ramus* 23:55–67.

———. 1997. "The Invention of Sexuality in the World-City of Rome." In *The Roman Cultural Revolution*. Edited by Habinek and Alessandro Schiesaro. Cambridge: Cambridge University Press, 23–43.

———. 1998. *The Politics of Latin Literature: Writings, Identity, and Empire in Ancient Rome*. Princeton: Princeton University Press.

Habinek, Thomas and Alessandro Schiesaro. 1997. "Introduction." In *The Roman Cultural Revolution*. Edited by Habinek and Alessandro Schiesaro. Cambridge: Cambridge University Press, xv–xxi.

Haddow, Anna. 1939. *Political Science in American Colleges and Universities, 1636–1900*. New York: D. Appleton-Century Co.

Hadot, Ilsetraut. 1969. *Seneca und die griechisch-römische Tradition der Seelenleitung*. Berlin: Walter de Gruyter.

Hadot, Pierre. 1992. "Reflections on the Notion of 'The Cultivation of the Self.'" In *Michel Foucault, Philosopher*. Edited by François Ewald. Translated by Timothy Armstrong. New York: Routledge, 225–31 (= Hadot 1995).

———. 1995. *Philosophy as a Way of Life: Spiritual Exercises from Socrates to Foucault*. Edited by Arnold Davidson. Translated by Michael Chase. Oxford: Blackwell.

Hadzsits, George Depue. 1920. "The Classics in a Democracy." *Classical Journal* 15:226–34.

Hahm, David. 1978. "Early Hellenistic Theories of Vision and the Perception of Color." In *Studies in Perception: Interrelations in the History of Philosophy and Science*. Edited by Peter Machamer and Robert Turnbull. Columbus: Ohio State University Press, 60–95.

Hahn, István. 1975. "Der Klassenkampf der *plebs urbana* in den letzten Jahrzehnten der römischen Republik." *Die Rolle der Volksmassen in der Geschichte der vorkapitalistischen Gesellschaftsformation*. Edited by Joachim Herrmann and Irmgard Sellnow. Berlin: Akademie Verlag, 121–46.

Hallett, Judith and Marilyn Skinner, Eds. 1997. *Roman Sexualities*. Princeton: Princeton University Press.

Hallett, Judith and Thomas van Nortwick. 1997. *Compromising Traditions: The Personal Voice in Classical Scholarship*. London: Routledge.

Hallowell, John. 1960 (orig. 1950). *Main Currents in Modern Political Thought*. New York: Holt, Rinehart and Winston.

Hallowell, John and Jene Porter. 1997. *Political Philosophy: The Search for Humanity and Order*. Scarborough, Ontario: Prentice Hall.

Halperin, David. 1990. *One Hundred Years of Homosexuality and Other Essays on Greek Love*. London: Routledge.

——. 1995. *Saint Foucault: Towards a Gay Hagiography*. New York: Oxford University Press.

Halperin, David, John Winkler, and Froma Zeitlin, Eds. 1990. *Before Sexuality: The Construction of Erotic Experience in the Ancient Greek World*. Princeton: Princeton University Press.

Halporn, James. 1989. "Foreign Scholars and American Classical Education." In *Classics: A Discipline and Profession in Crisis?* Edited by Phyllis Culham and Lowell Edmunds. New York: University Press of America, 305–15.

Hammer, Dean. 1995. "Václav Havel's Construction of a Democratic Discourse: Politics in a Postmodern Age." *Philosophy Today* 39:119–30. Reprinted in *Critical Essays on Václav Havel*. Edited by Marketa Goetz-Stankiewicz and Phyllis Carey. New York: G. K. Hall & Co., 1999.

——. 1997. "Incommensurable Phrases and Narrative Discourse: Lyotard and Arendt on the Possibility of Politics." *Philosophy Today* 41:475–90.

——. 1998. "The Politics of the *Iliad*." *The Classical Journal* 94:1–30.

——. 2002a. "Hannah Arendt and Roman Political Thought: The Practice of Theory." *Political Theory* 30:124–49. Reprinted in *Hannah Arendt: Critical Assessments of Leading Philosophers*. Edited by Garrath Williams. London: Routledge, 2006.

——. 2002b. *The* Iliad *as Politics: The Performance of Political Thought*. Norman: University of Oklahoma Press.

——. 2004. "Ideology, the Symposium, and Archaic Greek Politics." *American Journal of Philology* 125:479–512.

——. 2006. "Bourdieu, Ideology, and the Ancient World." *American Journal of Semiotics* 22:85–106.

——. forthcoming. "What is in the Ancient World Politics?" In *The Blackwell Companion to Greek and Roman Political Thought*. Edited by Ryan Balot. Oxford: Blackwell.

Hammond, Mason. 1951. *City-State and World State in Greek and Roman Political Theory until Augustus*. Cambridge: Harvard University Press.

Hampsher-Monk, Iain. 1990. "Ten Year Report on Article Submissions to *History of Political Thought*." *History of Political Thought*. Supplement to Vol. 11: 773–94.

Han, Béatrice. 2002. *Foucault's Critical Project: Between the Transcenden-*

tal and the Historical. Translated by Edward Pile. Stanford: Stanford University Press.

Handley, Carol. 2003. "Things that Matter." In *The Classical Association: The First Century 1903–2003.* Edited by Christopher Stray. Oxford: Oxford University Press, 209–25.

Hansen, Phillip. 1993. *Hannah Arendt: Politics, History and Citizenship.* Stanford: Stanford University Press.

Haskell, H. J. 1939. *The New Deal in Old Rome: How Government in the Ancient World Tried to Deal with Modern Problems.* New York: Alfred A. Knopf.

———. 1942. *This Was Cicero: Modern Politics in a Roman Toga.* New York: Alfred A. Knopf.

Haskell, Thomas. 1977. *The Emergence of Professional Social Science.* Urbana: University of Illinois Press.

Hatscher, Christoph. 2000. *Charisma und Res Publica: Max Webers Herrschaftssoziologie und die römische Republik.* Stuttgart: Franz Steiner Verlag.

Häussler, Reinhard. 1965. *Tacitus und das historische Bewusstsein.* Heidelberg: Carl Winter Universitätsverlag.

Havas, László. 1991. "Éléments du biologisme dans la conception historique de Tacite." *Aufstieg und Niedergang der römischen Welt.* 33.4. Edited by Wolfgang Haase and Hildegard Temporini, Part 2: *Principat.* Berlin: Walter de Gruyter, 2949–86.

Havel, Václav. 1991. *Open Letters: Selected Writings 1965–1990.* Edited by Paul Wilson. New York: Alfred A. Knopf.

Haynes, Holly. 2003. *The History of Make-Believe: Tacitus on Imperial Rome.* Berkeley: University of California Press.

Heilmann, Willibald. 1989. " 'Goldene Zeit' und geschichtliche Zeit im Dialogus de oratoribus. Zur Geschichtsauffasung des Tacitus." *Gymnasium* 96:385–405.

Heinze, Richard. 1924. "Ciceros 'Staat' als politische Tendenzschrift." *Hermes* 59: 73–94.

———. 1930. *Die Augusteische Kultur.* Leipzig: B. G. Teubner.

Hemker, Julie. 1985. "Rape and the Founding of Rome." *Helios* n.s. 12:41–47.

Henderson, John. 1990. "Tacitus/ The World in Pieces." In *The Imperial Muse: Flavian Epicist to Claudian.* Edited by A. J. Boyle. Bendigo: Aureal Publications, 167–210.

———. 2004. *Morals and Villas in Seneca's* Letters: *Places to Dwell.* Cambridge: Cambridge University Press.

Henry, Denis and Bessie Walker. 1963. "Tacitus and Seneca." *Greece and Rome* 2nd series, 10:98–110.

Herington, C. J. 1966. "Senecan Tragedy." *Arion* 5:422–71.

Hexter, J. H. 1972. "Fernand Braudel and the *Monde Braudellien*..." *Journal of Modern History* 44:480–539.

Hindess, Barry. 1998. "Politics and Liberation." In *The Later Foucault: Politics and Philosophy*. Edited by Jeremy Moss. London: Sage, 50–63.

Hölkeskamp, Karl-Joachim. 2004. *Senatus Populusque Romanus: Die politische Kultur der Republik-Dimensionen und Deutungen*. Stuttgart: Franz Steiner Verlag.

Hölscher, Tonio. 2000. "Augustus und die Macht der Archäologie." In *La révolution romaine après Ronald Syme: Bilans et perspectives*. Edited by Adalberto Giovannini. Genève: Fondation Hardt, 237–73.

Holton, James. 1963. "Marcus Tullius Cicero." In *History of Political Philosophy*. Edited by Leo Strauss and Joseph Cropsey. Chicago: Rand McNally and Co., 130–50.

Honig, Bonnie. 1993. *Political Theory and the Displacement of Politics*. Ithaca: Cornell University Press.

Hörnqvist, Mikael. 2000. "The Two Myths of Civic Humanism." In *Renaissance Civic Humanism: Reappraisals and Reflections*. Edited by James Hankins. Cambridge: Cambridge University Press, 105–42.

———. 2004. *Machiavelli and Empire*. Cambridge: Cambridge University Press.

Horowitz, Maryanne Cline. 1998. *Seeds of Virtue and Knowledge*. Princeton: Princeton University Press.

Housman, A. E. 1921. "The Application of Thought to Textual Criticism." *Proceedings of the Classical Association* 18:67–84.

Howes, J. R. 1972. "Cicero's Moral Philosophy in the *De Finibus*." In *Cicero and Virgil: Studies in Honour of Harold Hunt*. Edited by John Martyn. Amsterdam: Adolf M. Hakkert, 37–59.

Hulliung, Mark. 1976. *Montesquieu and the Old Regime*. Berkeley: University of California Press.

———. 1983. *Citizen Machiavelli*. Princeton: Princeton University Press.

Humphrey, Nicholas. 2006. *Seeing Red: A Study in Consciousness*. Cambridge: Belknap Press.

Hundert, E. J. and Paul Nelles. 1989. "Liberty and Theatrical Space in Montesquieu's Political Theory: The Poetics of Public Life in *The Persian Letters*." *Political Theory* 17:223–46.

Hunt, H. A. K. 1954. *The Humanism of Cicero*. Melbourne: Melbourne University Press.

Iggers, Georg. 1997. *Historiography in the Twentieth Century: From Scientific Objectivity to the Postmodern Challenge*. Hanover: Wesleyan University Press.

Inwood, Brad. 1985. *Ethics and Human Action in Early Stoicism*. Oxford: Clarendon Press.

———. 1993. "Seneca and Psychological Dualism." In *Passions and Perceptions: Studies in Hellenistic Philosophy of Mind, Proceedings of the Fifth Symposium Hellenisticum*. Edited by Jacques Brunschwig and Martha Nussbaum. Cambridge: Cambridge University Press, 150–83.

———. 1995. "Seneca in His Philosophical Milieu." *Harvard Studies in Classical Philology* 97:63–76.

———. 2004. "Moral Judgment in Seneca." In *Stoicism: Traditions and Transformations*. Edited by Steven Strange and Jack Zupko. Cambridge: Cambridge University Press, 76–94.

Jaeger, Mary. 1997. *Livy's Written Rome*. Ann Arbor: University of Michigan Press.

———. 1999. "Guiding Metaphor and Narrative Point of View in Livy's *AB VRBE CONDITA*." In *The Limits of Historiography: Genre and Narrative in Ancient Historical Texts*. Edited by Christina Kraus. Leiden: Brill, 169–95.

Jambet, Christian. 1992. "The Constitution of the Subject and Spiritual Practice: Observations on *L'Histoire de la sexualité*." In *Michel Foucault, Philosopher*. Translated by Timothy Armstrong. New York: Routledge, 233–47.

Janet, Paul. 1872. *Histoire de la science politique dans ses rapports avec la morale*. 2nd ed. Paris: Librairie philosophique de Ladrange.

Jay, Martin. 1978. "Hannah Arendt: Opposing Views." *Partisan Review* 45:348–68.

———. 1986. "In the Empire of the Gaze: Foucault and the Denigration of Vision in Twentieth-century French Thought." In *Foucault: A Critical Reader*. Edited by David Couzens Hoy. Oxford: Basil Blackwell, 175–204.

Jed, Stephanie. 1989. *Chaste Thinking: The Rape of Lucretia and the Birth of Humanism*. Bloomington: Indiana University Press.

Jehne, Martin, Ed. 1995. *Demokratie in Rom?: Die Rolle des Volkes in der Politik der römischen Republik*. Stuttgart: Franz Steiner Verlag.

Jens, Walter. 1956. "Libertas bei Tacitus." *Hermes* 84:331–52.

Johnson, Chalmers. 2004. *The Sorrows of Empire: Militarism, Secrecy, and the End of the Republic.* New York: Metropolitan Books.

Johnston, David. 1999. *Roman Law in Context.* Cambridge: Cambridge University Press.

Jolowicz, H. F. 1932. *Historical Introduction to the Study of Roman Law.* Cambridge: Cambridge University Press.

Jones, A. H. M. 1960a. "The Elections under Augustus." *Studies in Roman Government and Law.* Oxford: Basil Blackwell, 29–50.

———. 1960b. "I Appeal unto Caesar." *Studies in Roman Government and Law.* Oxford: Basil Blackwell, 51–65.

———. 1960c. "Imperial and Senatorial Jurisdiction in the Early Principate." *Studies in Roman Government and Law.* Oxford: Basil Blackwell, 69–98.

Jones, Robert. 1994. "Ambivalent Cartesians: Durkheim, Montesquieu, and Method." *American Journal of Sociology* 100:1–39.

Joshel, Sandra. 1992. "The Body Female and the Body Politic: Livy's Lucretia and Verginia." In *Pornography and Representation in Greece and Rome.* Edited by Amy Richlin. New York: Oxford University Press, 112–30.

Kahn, Victoria. 1994. *Machiavellian Rhetoric: From the Counter-Reformation to Milton.* Princeton: Princeton University Press.

Kajanto, Iiro. 1957. *God and Fate in Livy.* Turku: Turun Yliopiston Kustantama.

Kaldor, Mary. 2003. *Global Civil Society: An Answer to War.* Cambridge: Polity.

Kalyvas, Andreas. 2007. "The Tyranny of Dictatorship: When the Greek Tyrant Met the Roman Dictator." *Political Theory* 35:412–42.

Kaser, Max. 1955. *Das römische Privatrecht.* Munich: C. H. Beck.

Kassem, Badreddine. 1960. *Décadence et absolutisme dans l'oeuvre de Montesquieu.* Geneva: Librairie E. Droz.

Kaster, Robert. 1997. "Fruitful Disputes: Controversy and Its Consequences in the (More or Less Recent) History of Classical Studies." *Transactions of the American Philological Association* 127:345–47.

———. 2005. *Emotion, Restraint, and Community in Ancient Rome.* Oxford: Oxford University Press.

Kateb, George. 1977. "Freedom and Worldliness in the Thought of Hannah Arendt." *Political Theory* 5:141–81.

———. 1983. *Hannah Arendt: Politics, Conscience, Evil.* Totowa, N.J.: Rowman & Allanheld.

Keane, John. 2003. *Global Civil Society?* Cambridge: Cambridge University Press.

Keitel, Elizabeth. 1984. "Principate and Civil War in the *Annals* of Tacitus." *American Journal of Philology* 105:306–25.

Kelly, Christopher. 2004. *Ruling the Later Roman Empire.* Cambridge: Harvard University Press.

Kelsey, Francis. 1908. "Is there a Science of Classical Philology?" *Classical Philology* 3:369–85.

Kennedy, George. 1987. "The History of Latin Education." *Helios* 14:7–16.

Keohane, Nannerl. 1972. "Virtuous Republics and Glorious Monarchies: Two Models in Montesquieu's Political Thought." *Political Studies* 20:383–96.

Keppie, L. 1996. "The Praetorian Guard Before Sejanus." *Athenaeum* 84:101–24.

Kidd, I. G. 1971. "Posidonius on Emotions." *Problems in Stoicism.* Edited by A. A. Long. London: Athlone Press, 200–15.

Kidd, I. G. and L. Edelstein (on volume 1), Eds. 1972, 1988, 1999. *Posidonius.* 4 vols. Cambridge: Cambridge University Press.

Kienast, Dietmar. 1999. *Augustus: Prinzeps und Monarch.* 3rd ed. Darmstadt: Wissenschaftliche Buchgesellschalt.

Klindienst Joplin, Patricia. 1990. "Ritual Work on Human Flesh: Livy's Lucretia and the Rape of the Body Politic." *Helios* 17:51–70.

Klingner, Friedrich. 1955. "Beobachtungen über Sprache und Stil des Tacitus am Anfang des 13. Annalenbuches." *Hermes* 83:187–200.

Klosko, George. 1993. *History of Political Theory: An Introduction.* Vol. 1. Fort Worth, TX: Harcourt Brace.

Koebner, R. 1951. "Despot and Despotism: Vicissitudes of a Political Term." *Journal of the Warburg and Courtauld Institutes* 14:275–302.

Koestermann, Erich. 1963. *Cornelius Tacitus, Annalen Band 1, Buch 1–3.* Heidelberg: Carl Winter Universitätsverlag.

Kohn, Jerome. 2000. "Freedom: The Priority of the Political." In *The Cambridge Companion to Hannah Arendt.* Edited by Dana Villa. Cambridge: Cambridge University Press, 113–29.

Koivukoski, Toivo and David Tabachnick, Eds. 2005. *Confronting Tyranny: Ancient Lessons for Global Politics.* Lanham: Rowman and Littlefield.

Konstan, David. 1983. *Roman Comedy.* Ithaca: Cornell University Press.

———. 1986. "Narrative and Ideology in Livy: Book 1." *Classical Antiquity* 5:198–216.

———. 1989. "What is New in the New Approaches to Classical Literature?" In *Classics: A Discipline and Profession in Crisis?* Edited by Phyllis Culham and Lowell Edmunds. New York: University Press of America, 45–49.

———. 1994. *Sexual Symmetry: Love in the Ancient Novel and Related Genres*. Princeton: Princeton University Press.

Kraus, Christina. 1994a. *Livy.* Ab urbe condita. *Book VI.* Cambridge: Cambridge University Press.

———. 1994b. " 'No Second Troy': Topoi and Refoundation in Livy, Book V." *Transactions of the American Philological Association* 124:267–89.

Kraus, Christina, and A. J. Woodman. 1997. *Latin Historians.* Oxford: Oxford University Press.

Krause, Sharon. 2001. "Despotism in *The Spirit of Laws.*" In *Montesquieu's Science of Politics: Essays on* The Spirit of Laws. Edited by David Carrithers, Michael Mosher, and Paul Rahe. Lanham: Rowman and Littlefield, 232–271.

———. 2002. "The Uncertain Inevitability of Decline in Montesquieu." *Political Theory* 30:702–27.

Lacey, W. K. 1996. *Augustus and the Principate: The Evolution of the System.* Leeds: Francis Cairns.

Ladurie, Emmanuel Le Roy. 1979. *The Territory of the Historian.* Translated by Ben and Siân Reynolds. Chicago: University of Chicago Press.

Laidlaw, W. A. 1968. "*Otium.*" *Greece and Rome* 2nd series, 15:42–52.

Lana, Italo. 1989. "Introspicere in Tacito." *Orpheus* 10:26–57.

Langslow, D. R. 2000. *Medical Latin in the Roman Empire.* Oxford: Oxford University Press.

Larmour, David, Paul Miller, and Charles Platter, Eds. 1998. *Rethinking Sexuality: Foucault and Classical Antiquity*. Princeton: Princeton University Press.

Larrère, Catherine. 2001. "Montesquieu on Economics and Commerce." In *Montesquieu's Science of Politics: Essays on* The Spirit of Laws. Edited by David Carrithers, Michael Mosher, and Paul Rahe. Lanham: Rowman and Littlefield, 335–73.

Latimer, John. 1970. "Pedagogy, Progress, and the Profession." *Transactions of the American Philological Association* 101: 253–62.

Leach, Eleanor. 1993. "Absence and Desire in Cicero's *De Amicitia.*" *Classical World* 89:3–20.

Leeman, A. D. 1951. "The Epistolary Form of Sen. *Ep.* 102." *Mnemosyne* 4, ser. 4:175–81.

Lendon, J. E. 1997. *Empire of Honour: The Art of Government in the Roman World.* Oxford: Clarendon Press.

———. 2002. "Historical Thought in Ancient Rome." In *A Companion to Western Historical Thought.* Edited by Lloyd Kramer and Sarah Maza. Oxford: Blackwell, 60–77.

Levene, D. S. 1993. *Religion in Livy.* Leiden: E. J. Brill.

———. 1997. "Pity, Fear and the Historical Audience: Tacitus on the Fall of Vitellius." In *The Passions in Roman Thought and Literature.* Edited by Susanna Morton Braund and Christopher Gill. Cambridge: Cambridge University Press, 128–49.

Levick, Barbara. 1967. "Imperial Control of the Elections under the Early Principate: Commendatio, Suffragatio, and 'Nominatio.' " *Historia* 16:207–30.

———. 1976. *Tiberius the Politician.* London: Thames and Hudson.

———. 1985. "The Politics of the Early Principate." In *Roman Political Life: 90 B.C.–A.D. 69.* Edited by T. P. Wiseman. Exeter: University of Exeter, 45–68.

Levin, Lawrence Meyer. 1936. *The Political Doctrine of Montesquieu's* Espirit des Lois*: Its Classical Background.* New York: Columbia University.

Liebeschuetz, W. 1966. "The Theme of Liberty in the *Agricola* of Tacitus." *Classical Quarterly* 16:126–39.

———. 1967. "The Religious Position of Livy's History." *Journal of Roman Studies* 57: 45–55.

Lind, J. R. 1986. "The Idea of the Republic and the Foundations of Roman Political Liberty." In *Studies in Latin Literature and Roman History* 4. Edited by Carl Deroux. Bruxelles: Revue D' Etudes Latines, 44–108.

Linderski, Jerzy. 1993. "Roman Religion in the Livy." In *Livius: Aspekte seines Werkes.* Edited by Wolfgang Schuller. Konstanz: Universitätsverlag Konstanz, 53–70.

Lintott, Andrew. 1999. *The Constitution of the Roman Republic.* Oxford: Clarendon Press.

Littlewood, C. A. J. 2004. *Self-Representation and Illusion in Senecan Tragedy.* Oxford: Oxford University Press.

Livingstone, Richard. 1916. *A Defence of Classical Education*. London: Macmillan.

Livy. 1998. *History of Rome*. Translated by B. O. Foster. Cambridge: Harvard University Press.

Lloyd, A. C. 1978. "Emotion and Decision in Stoic Psychology." In *The Stoics*. Edited by John Rist. Berkeley: University of California Press, 233–46.

Loyd-Jones, Hugh, Ed. 1982. "Introduction." In *History of Classical Scholarship*. Translated by Alan Harris. Baltimore: Johns Hopkins University Press, v–xxxii.

Loewenstein, Karl. 1973. *The Government of Rome*. The Hague: Martinus Nijhoff.

Long, A. A. 1995. "Cicero's Plato and Aristotle." In *Cicero the Philosopher: Twelve Papers*. Edited by J. G. F. Powell. Oxford: Clarendon Press, 37–61.

———. 1996. "Soul and Body in Stoicism." In *Stoic Studies*. Berkeley: University of California Press, 224–49.

Long, A. A. and D. N. Sedley. 1987. *The Hellenistic Philosophers*. 2 vols. Cambridge: Cambridge University Press.

Longrigg, James. 1963. "Philosophy and Medicine." *Harvard Studies in Classical Philology* 67:147–75.

Luce, T. J. 1965. "The Dating of Livy's First Decade." *Transactions of the American Philological Association* 96:209–40.

———. 1971. "Design and the Structure in Livy: 5.32–55." *Transactions of the American Philological Association* 102:265–302.

———. 1977. *Livy: The Composition of his History*. Princeton: Princeton University Press.

———. 1986. Tacitus' Conception of Historical Change: The Problem of Discovering the Historian's Opinions." In *Past Perspectives: Studies in Greek and Roman Historical Writing*. Edited by I. S. Moxon, J. D. Smart, and A. J. Woodman. Cambridge: Cambridge University Press, 143–57.

Macauley, David. 1996. "Hannah Arendt and the Politics of Place: From Earth Alienation to *Oikos*." In *Minding Nature: The Philosophers of Ecology*. Edited by Macauley. New York: Guilford Press, 102–33.

MacFarland, Joseph. 1999. "Machiavelli's Imagination of Excellent Men: An Appraisal of the Lives of Cosimo de Medici and Castruccio Castracani." *American Political Science Review* 93:133–46.

Machiavelli, Niccolò. 1950. *The Prince and the Discourses*. Translated by

Luigi Ricci (for *The Prince*) and Christian Detmold (for *Discourses*). New York: Modern Library (cited as *P*).

———. 1965. "Familiar Letters." In *Machiavelli: The Chief Works and Others*. Translated by Allan Gilbert. Durham: Duke University Press.

———. 1996. *Discourses on Livy*. Translated by Harvey Mansfield and Nathan Tarcov. Chicago: University of Chicago Press (cited as *D*).

MacIntyre, Alasdair. 1984. *After Virtue*. 2nd edition. Notre Dame: University of Notre Dame Press.

MacKendrick, Paul. 1989. *The Philosophical Books of Cicero*. New York: St. Martin's Press.

MacMullen, Ramsay. 1988. *Corruption and the Decline of Rome*. New Haven: Yale University Press.

Magie, David. 1950. *Roman Rule in the Asia Minor to the End of the Third Century after Christ*. 2 vols. Princeton: Princeton University Press.

Manent, Pierre. 1998. *The City of Man*. Translated by Marc LePain. Princeton: Princeton University Press.

Mansfield, Harvey. 1979. *Machiavelli's New Modes and Orders: A Study of the Discourses on Livy*. Ithaca: Cornell University Press.

———. 1996. *Machiavelli's Virtue*. Chicago: University of Chicago Press.

Mansfield, Harvey and Nathan Tarcov. 1996. "Introduction" to *Discourses on Livy*. Chicago: University of Chicago Press, xvii–xliv.

Marcus, George. 2002. *The Sentimental Citizen: Emotion in Democratic Politics*. University Park: Penn State University Press.

Marincola, John. 1997. *Authority and Tradition in Ancient Historiography*. Cambridge: Cambridge University Press.

Markell, Patchen. 2006. "The Rule of the People: Arendt, *Archê*, and Democracy." *American Political Science Review* 100:1–14.

Marsh, Frank. 1926. "Tacitus and Aristocratic Tradition." *Classical Philology* 21:289–310.

———. 1931. *The Reign of Tiberius*. London: Oxford University Press.

———. 1943. *Modern Problems in the Ancient World*. Austin: University of Texas Press.

Marshall, A. J. 1975. "Tacitus and the Governor's Lady: A Note on *Annals* III.33–34." *Greece and Rome* 22:11–18.

Martin, Ronald. 1981. *Tacitus*. Berkeley: University of California Press.

Matthes, Melissa. 2000. *The Rape of Lucretia and the Founding of Republics*. University Park: Penn State University Press.

Maurach, Gregor. 1970. *Der Bau von Senecas Epistulae morales*. Heidelberg: Carl Winter Universitätsverlag.

Mayer, Anna-Katherina. 1997. "Moralizing Science: The Use of Science's Past in National Education in the 1920s." *British Journal for the History of Science* 30:51–70.

Mayer, R. G. 1991. "Roman Historical Exempla in Seneca." In *Sénèque et la prose latine: neuf exposés suivis de discussions*. Edited by Pierre Grimal. Vandoeuvres-Genève: Fondation Hardt, 141–76.

Mazzarino, Santo. 1951. *Aspetti Sociali del Quarto Secolo*. Rome: L'Erma di Bretschneider.

McClure, Kirstie. 1997. "The Odor of Judgment: Exemplarity, Propriety, and Politics in the Company of Hannah Arendt." In *Hannah Arendt and the Meaning of Politics*. Edited by Craig Calhoun and John McGowan. Minneapolis: University of Minnesota Press, 53–84.

McCormick, John. 2001. "Machiavellian Democracy: Controlling Elites with Ferocious Populism." *American Political Science Review* 95:297–313.

———. 2003. "Machiavelli against Republicanism: On the Cambridge School's 'Guicciardinian Moments.'" *Political Theory* 31: 615–43.

McDonald, A. H. 1960. "Fifty Years of Republican History." *Journal of Roman Studies* 50:135–48.

McDonald, Neil and James Rosenau. 1968. "Political Theory as Academic Field and Intellectual Activity." In *Political Science: Advance of the Discipline*. Edited by Marian Irish. Englewood Cliffs, NJ: Prentice-Hall, 21–54.

McGowan, John. 1998. *Hannah Arendt: An Introduction*. Minneapolis: University of Minnesota Press.

McGraw, Kathleen. 2003. "Political Impressions: Formation and Management." In *Oxford Handbook of Political Psychology*. Edited by David Sears, Leonie Huddy, and Robert Jervis. New York: Oxford University Press, 394–432.

McIlwain, Charles. 1947 (orig. 1940). *Constitutionalism: Ancient & Modern*. Ithaca: Cornell University Press.

———. 1968 (orig. 1932). *The Growth of Political Thought in the West: From the Greeks to the End of the Middle Ages*. New York: Cooper Square Publishers.

McNay, Lois. 1992. *Foucault and Feminism*. Boston: Northeastern University Press.

Meier, Christian. 1980. *Res Publica Amissa: Eine Studie zu Verfassung und Geschichte der späten römischen Republik.* 2nd ed. Wiesbaden: Franz Steiner Verlag GMBH.

———. 1988. "Max Weber und die Antike." In *Max Weber: Ein Symposion.* Edited by Christian Gneuss and Jürgen Kocka. München: Deutscher Taschenbuch Verlag, 11–24.

———, Ed. 1994. "Bemerkungen zum Problem der 'Verbrüderung' in Athen und Rom." In *Die Okzidentale Stadt nach Max Weber: Zum Problem der Zugehörigkeit in Antike und Mittelatter.* München: R. Oldenbourg Verlag, 18–33.

Mellor, Ronald. 1993. *Tacitus.* New York: Routledge.

Mendell, Clarence. 1970. *Tacitus: The Man and His Work.* Hamden: Archon Books.

Merriam, Charles. 1921. "The Present State of the Study of Politics." *American Political Science Review* 15:173–85.

———. 1924. "Recent Tendencies in Political Thought." In *A History of Political Theories: Recent Times.* Edited by Merriam and Harry Barnes. New York: Macmillan, 1–45.

———. 1931 (orig. 1925). *New Aspects of Politics.* 2nd ed. Chicago: University of Chicago Press.

Merry, Henry J. 1970. *Montesquieu's System of Natural Government.* West Lafayette: Purdue University Studies.

Mette, Hans Joachim. 1961. "Livius und Augustus." *Gymnasium* 68:269–85.

Meyer, Eduard. 1922. *Caesars Monarchie und das Principat des Pompeius.* Stuttgart: J.G. Cotta'sche Buchhandlung Nachfolger.

Miles, Gary. 1986. "The Cycle of Roman History in Livy's First Pentad." *American Journal of Philology* 107:1–33.

———. 1995. *Livy: Reconstructing Early Rome.* Ithaca: Cornell University Press.

Millar, Fergus. 1966. "The Emperor, the Senate, and the Provinces." *Journal of Roman Studies* 56, parts 1 & 2:156–66.

———. 1973. "Triumvirate and Principate." *Journal of Roman Studies* 63:50–67.

———. 1977. *The Emperor in the Roman World (31 B.C.–A.D. 337).* London: Duckworth.

———. 1984. "The Political Character of the Classical Roman Republic, 200–151 B.C." *Journal of Roman Studies* 74:1–19.

———. 1986. "Politics, Persuasion, and the People Before the Social War (150–90 B.C.)." *Journal of Roman Studies* 76:1–11.

———. 1998. *The Crowd in Rome in the Late Republic.* Ann Arbor: University of Michigan Press.

———. 2002. *The Roman Republic in Political Thought.* Hanover: University Press of New England for Brandeis University Press.

Miller, David, Ed. 1991. *The Blackwell Encyclopaedia of Political Thought.* Cambridge: Basil Blackwell.

Miller, N. P. 1964. "Dramatic Speech in Tacitus." *American Journal of Philology* 85:279–96.

———. 1977. "Tacitus' Narrative Technique." *Greece and Rome* 24:13–22.

Miller, Paul. 1998. "Catullan Consciousness, the 'Care of the Self,' and the Force of the Negative in History." In *Rethinking Sexuality: Foucault and Classical Antiquity.* Edited by David Larmour, Paul Miller, and Charles Platter. Princeton: Princeton University Press, 171–203.

Minogue, K. R. 1972. "Theatricality and Politics: Machiavelli's Concept of Fantasia." In *The Morality of Politics.* Edited by Bhikhu Parekh and R. N. Berki. London: George Allen and Unwin, 148–62.

Mitchell, Richard. 1986. "The Definition of *patres* and *plebs*: An End to the Struggle of the Orders." In *Social Struggle in Archaic Rome: New Perspectives on the Conflict of the Orders.* Edited by Kurt Raaflaub. Berkeley: University of California Press, 130–74.

———. 1990. *Patricians and Plebeians: The Origin of the Roman State.* Ithaca: Cornell University Press.

Mitchell, T. N. 1984. "Cicero on the Moral Crisis of the Late Republic." *Hermathena* 136:21–410.

Mitsis, Phillip. 1993. "Seneca on Reason, Rules, and Moral Development." In *Passions and Perceptions: Studies in Hellenistic Philosophy of Mind, Proceedings of the Fifth Symposium Hellenisticum.* Edited by Jacques Brunschwig and Martha Nussbaum. Cambridge: Cambridge University Press, 285–312.

Moles, John. 1993. "Livy's Preface." *Proceedings of the Cambridge Philological Society* 39:141–68.

Momigliano, Arnaldo. 1940. "Review: *The Roman Revolution.*" *Journal of Roman Studies* 30:75–80.

———. 1942. "Camillus and Concord." *Classical Quarterly* 36:111–20.

———. 1969. "Seneca between Political and Contemplative Life." *Quarto contributo alla storia degli studi classici e del mondo antico.* Rome: Edizioni di Storia e Letteratura, 239–56.

——. 1986. "The Rise of the *plebs* in the Archaic Age of Rome." In *Social Struggles in Archaic Rome: New Perspectives on the Conflict of the Orders*. Edited by Kurt Raaflaub. Berkeley: University of California Press, 175–97.

——. 1989. "The Origins of Rome." *Cambridge Ancient History* 2nd ed., vol. 7, pt. 2. Edited by F. W. Walbank, A. E. Astin, M. W. Frederiksen, and R. M. Ogilvie. Cambridge: Cambridge University Press, 52–112.

——. 1994. *Studies on Modern Scholarship*. Edited by G. W. Bowersock and T. J. Cornell. Berkeley: University of California Press.

Mommsen, Theodor. 1869. *Römische Geschichte*. Berlin: Weidmannsche Buchhandlung (abbreviated as *RG*).

——. 1996. *A History of Rome under the Emperors*. Edited by Barbara and Alexander Demandt. Translated by Clare Krojzl. London: Routledge.

Monier, Raymond. 1935 and 1936. *Manuel élémentaire de Droit Romain*. 2 vols. Paris: Les éditions Domat-Montchrestien.

Montesquieu. 1964a. *Oeuvres Complètes*. Edited by Daniel Oster. Paris: Aux Éditions du Seuil (abbreviated as *OC*).

——. 1964b. "De la politique." *Oeuvres Complètes*. Edited by Daniel Oster. Paris: Aux Éditions du Seuil, 172–75.

——. 1964c. "Essay sur le gout." *Oeuvres Complètes*. Edited by Daniel Oster. Paris: Aux Éditions du Seuil, 845–52.

——. 1964d. "Spicilège." *Oeuvres Complètes*. Edited by Daniel Oster. Paris: Aux Éditions du Seuil, 379–435.

——. 1965. *Considerations on the Causes of the Greatness of the Romans and Their Decline*. Translated by David Lowenthal. Ithaca: Cornell University Press (abbreviated as *C*).

——. 1976. "An Essay on the Causes that may Affect Men's Minds and Characters." Translated by Melvin Richter. *Political Theory* 4:139–62 (abbreviated as EC).

——. 1997. *The Spirit of the Laws*. Edited and translated by Anne Cohler, Basia Miller, and Harold Stone. New York: Cambridge University Press (abbreviated as *S*).

——. 2002. "Discourse on Cicero." Translated by David Fott. *Political Theory*, 30:733–37.

Morison, Samuel Eliot. 1939. *The Ancient Classics in a Modern Democracy*. London: Oxford University Press.

Morford, Mark. 2002. *The Roman Philosophers: From the Time of Cato the Censor to the Death of Marcus Aurelius*. London: Routledge.

Morstein-Marx, Robert. 2004. *Mass Oratory and Political Power in the Late Roman Republic*. Cambridge: Cambridge University Press.

Mosher, Michael. 2001. "Monarchy's Paradox: Honor in the Face of Sovereign Power." *Montesquieu's Science of Politics: Essays on* The Spirit of Laws. Edited by David Carrithers, Michael Mosher, and Paul Rahe. Lanham: Rowman and Littlefield, 159–229.

Most, Glenn. 1992. "Professionalizing Politics, Politicizing the Profession." *Transactions of the American Philological Association* 122: 381–84.

Motto, Anna Lydia and John Clark. 1993. *Essays on Seneca*. New York: Peter Lang.

Mouritsen, Henrik. 2001. Plebs *and Politics in the Late Roman Republic*. Cambridge: Cambridge University Press.

Mousley, Andrew. 1995. "*The Prince* and Textual Politics." In *Niccolò Machiavelli's* The Prince*: New Interdisciplinary Essays*. Edited by Martin Coyle. Manchester: Manchester University Press, 151–73.

Müller, Wolfgang. 1980. "Der Brief als Spiegel der Seele." *Antike und Abendland* 26:138–57.

Münzer, Friedrich. 1920. *Römische Adelsparteien und Adelsfamilien*. Stuttgart: J. B. Metzlersche Verlagsbuchhandlung.

Murray, Gilbert. 1945. "The Future of Greek Studies." *Journal of Hellenic Studies* 65:1–9.

Myers, Richard. 1989-90. "Christianity and Politics in Montesquieu's *Greatness and Decline of the Romans*." *Interpretation* 17:223–38.

Najemy, John. 1993. *Between Friends: Discourses of Power and Desire in the Machiavelli-Vettori Letters of 1513–1515*. Princeton: Princeton University Press.

———. 1995. "Language and *The Prince*" In *Niccolò Machiavelli's* The Prince: *New Interdisciplinary Essays*. Edited by Martin Coyle. Manchester: Manchester University Press, 89–114.

Narducci, Emanuele. 1997. "Perceptions of Exile in Cicero: The Philosophical Interpretation of a Real Experience." *American Journal of Philology* 118:55–73.

Nederman, Cary. 2000a. "Machiavelli and Moral Character: Principality, Republic and the Psychology of *Virtù*." *History of Political Thought* 21:349–64.

———. 2000b. "Rhetoric, Reason, and Republic: Republicanisms—Ancient, Medieval, and Modern." In *Renaissance Civic Humanism: Reappraisals and Reflections*. Edited by James Hankins. Cambridge: Cambridge University Press, 247–69.

———. 2000c. "War, Peace, and Republican Virtue: Patriotism and the Neglected Legacy of Cicero." In *Instilling Ethics*. Edited by Norma Thompson. Lanham: Rowman and Littlefield, 17–29.

Nelson, Eric. 2006. "Republican Visions." In *The Oxford Handbook of Political Theory*. Edited by John Dryzek, Bonnie Honig, and Anne Phillips. Oxford: Oxford University Press, 193–210.

Newell, W. R. 1987. "How Original is Machiavelli? A Consideration of Skinner's Interpretation of Virtue and Fortune." *Political Theory* 15:612–34.

Nicgorski, Walter. 1984. "Cicero's Paradoxes and His Idea of Utility." *Political Theory* 12:557–78.

———. 1991. "Cicero's Focus: From the Best Regime to the Model Statesman." *Political Theory* 19:230–51.

Nicolet, Claude. 1980. *The World of the Citizen in Republican Rome*. Translated by P.S. Falla. Berkeley: University of California Press.

———. 1984. "Augustus, Government, and the Propertied Classes." In *Caesar Augustus: Seven Aspects*. Edited by Fergus Millar and Erich Segal. Oxford: Clarendon Press, 89–128.

———. 1993. "The Citizen: The Political Man." In *The Romans*. Edited by Andrea Giardina. Translated by Lydia Cochrane. Chicago: University of Chicago Press, 16–54.

Nietzsche, Friedrich. 1974. *The Gay Science*. Translated by Walter Kaufmann. New York: Vintage.

Nippel, Wilfried. 1995. *Public Order in Ancient Rome*. Cambridge: Cambridge University Press.

North, J. A. 1990a. "Democratic Politics in Republican Rome." *Past and Present* 126:3–21.

———. 1990b. "Politics and Aristocracy in the Roman Republic." *Classical Philology* 85:277–87.

Novick, Peter. 1988. *The Noble Dream: The "Objectivity Question" and the American Historical Profession*. Cambridge: Cambridge University Press.

Nussbaum, Martha. 1994. *The Therapy of Desire: Theory and Practice in Hellenistic Ethics*. Princeton: Princeton University Press.

———. 2000. "Duties of Justice, Duties of Material Aid: Cicero's Problematic Legacy." *Journal of Political Philosophy* 2:176–206.

Nussbaum, Martha and Juha Sihvola, Eds. 2002. *The Sleep of Reason: Erotic Experience and Sexual Ethics in Ancient Greece and Rome*. Chicago: University of Chicago Press.

Oake, Roger. 1955. "Montesquieu's Analysis of Roman History." *Journal of the History of Ideas* 16:44–59.

Ogilvie, R. M. 1965. *A Commentary on Livy: Books 1–5.* Oxford: Clarendon Press.

O'Gorman, Ellen. 1993. "No Place like Rome: Identity and Difference in the *Germania* of Tacitus." *Ramus* 22:135–54.

———. 2000. *Irony and Misreading in the* Annals *of Tacitus.* Cambridge: Cambridge University Press.

O'Leary, Timothy. 2002. *Foucault: The Art of Ethics.* London: Continuum.

Olschki, Leonardo. 1945. *Machiavelli the Scientist.* Berkeley: University of California Press.

O'Malley, Frank. 1948. "Editorial: The Image of Man: Ten Years of *The Review of Politics.*" *Review of Politics* 10:395–98.

O'Neal, John. 1996. *The Authority of Experience: Sensationist Theory in the French Enlightenment.* University Park: Pennsylvania State University Press.

O'Sullivan, Noel. 1975. "Hannah Arendt: Hellenic Nostalgia and Industrial Society." In *Contemporary Political Philosophers.* Edited by Anthony de Crespigny and Kenneth Minogue. New York: Dodd, Mead & Co., 228–51.

Pangle, Thomas. 1973. *Montesquieu's Philosophy of Liberalism: A Commentary on* The Spirit of the Laws. Chicago: University of Chicago Press.

Parel, Anthony. 1972. "Introduction: Machiavelli's Method and His Interpreters." In *The Political Calculus: Essays on Machiavelli's Philosophy.* Edited by Parel. Toronto: University of Toronto Press, 3–27.

———. 1991. "The Question of Machiavelli's Modernity." *Review of Politics* 53:320–39.

———. 1992. *The Machiavellian Cosmos.* New Haven: Yale University Press.

Paterson, Jeremy. 1985. "Politics in the Late Republic." In *Roman Political Life: 90 BC–AD 69.* Edited by T. P. Wiseman. Exeter: University of Exeter, 21–43.

Pauw, Dirk. 1991. "The Dramatic Elements in Livy's History." *Acta Classica* 34:33–49.

Peirce, Charles. 1960. "Some Consequences of Four Incapacities." *Collected Papers of Charles Andrew Peirce.* Vol. 5. Edited by Charles Hartshorne and Paul Weiss. Cambridge: Belknap, 156–89.

Pelling, Christopher. 1993. "Tacitus and Germanicus." In *Tacitus and the Tacitean Tradition.* Edited by T. J. Luce and A. J. Woodman. Princeton: Princeton University Press, 59–85.

Pembroke, S. G. 1971. "Oikeiôsis." In *Problems in Stoicism*. Edited by A. A. Long. London: Athlone Press, 114–49.

Penella, Robert. 1990. "*Vires/Robur/Opes* and *Ferocia* in Livy's Account of Romulus and Tullus Hostilius." *Classical Quarterly* 40:207–13.

Penwill, J. L. 1994. "Image, Ideology, and Action in Cicero and Lucretius." *Ramus* 23:68–91.

Peradotto, John. 1989. "Texts and Unrefracted Facts: Philology, Hermeneutics and Semiotics." In *Classics: A Discipline and Profession in Crisis?* Edited by Phyllis Culham and Lowell Edmunds. New York: University Press of America, 179–98.

Petersen, Hans. 1961. "Livy and Augustus." *Transactions of the American Philological Association* 92:440–52.

Phillips, Robert, III. 1989. "Classical Scholarship against Its History." *American Journal of Philology* 110:636–57.

Pico della Mirandola, Gianfrancesco. 1930. *On the Imagination*. Translated by Harry Caplan. New Haven: Yale University Press.

Pippidi, D. M. 1944. *Autur de Tibère*. Bucaresti: Institutal di Istorie universala "N. Iorga."

Pitkin, Hanna. 1984. *Fortune Is a Woman: Gender and Politics in the Thought of Niccolò Machiavelli*. Berkeley: University of California Press.

Plasberg, Otto. 1926. *Cicero in seinen Werken und Briefen*. Leipzig: Dieterich'sche Verlagsbuchshandlung.

Platter, Charles. 1995. "*Officium* in Catullus and Propertius: A Foucauldian Reading." *Classical Philology* 90:211–24.

Pocock, J. G. A. 1972. "Custom and Grace, Form and Matter: An Approach to Machiavelli's Concept of Innovation." *Machiavelli and the Nature of Political Thought*. Edited by Martin Fleisher. New York: Atheneum, 153–74.

———. 1975. *The Machiavellian Moment: Florentine Political Thought and the Atlantic Republic Tradition*. Princeton: Princeton University Press.

———. 1981. "The *Machiavellian Moment* Revisited: A Study in History and Ideology." *Journal of Modern History* 53:49–72.

———. 1987. "Between Gog and Magog: The Republican Thesis and the *Ideologia Americana*." *Journal of the History of Ideas* 48:325–46.

———. 2006. "Theory in History: Problems of Context and Narrative." In *The Oxford Handbook of Political Theory*. Edited by John Dryzek, Bonnie Honig, and Anne Phillips. Oxford: Oxford University Press, 163–74.

Pohlenz, Max. 1947. *Die Stoa: Geschichte einer geistigen Bewegung*. 2 vols. Göttingen: Vandenhoeck und Ruprecht.

Pollock, Sir Frederick. 1935 (orig. 1890). *An Introduction to the History of the Science of Politics*. London: Macmillan.

Porter, James. 2005. "Foucault's Ascetic Ancients." *Phoenix* 59:121–32.

Posidonius. 1972, 1988, 1999. Edited by I. G. Kidd and L. Edelstein (on vol. 1). 4 vols. Cambridge: Cambridge University Press.

Poster, Mark. 1986. "Foucault and the Tyranny of Greece." In *Foucault: A Critical Reader*. Edited by David Couzens Hoy. Oxford: Basil Blackwell, 205–20.

——. 1993. "Foucault and the Problem of Self-Constitution." In *Foucault and the Critique of Institutions*. Edited by John Caputo and Mark Yount. University Park: Penn State University Press, 63–80.

Potter, David. 1996. "Performance, Power and Justice in the High Empire." In *Roman Theater and Society: E. Togo Salmon Paper I*. Edited by William Slater. Ann Arbor: University of Michigan Press, 129–59.

——. 1999. "Political Theory in the *Senatus Consultum Pisonianum*." *American Journal of Philology* 120:65–88.

Powell, J. G. F. 1995. "Introduction: Cicero's Philosophical Works and their Background." In *Cicero the Philosopher: Twelve Papers*. Edited by J. G. F. Powell. Oxford: Clarendon Press, 1–35.

Raaflaub, Kurt. 1986a. "The Conflict of the Orders in Archaic Rome: A Comprehensive and Comparative Approach." In *Social Struggles in Archaic Rome: New Perspective on the Conflict of the Orders*. Edited by Raaflaub. Berkeley: University of California Press, 1–57.

——. 1986b. "From Protection and Defense to Offense and Participation: Stages in the Conflict of the Orders." In *Social Struggles in Archaic Rome: New Perspective on the Conflict of the Orders*. Edited by Kurt Raaflaub. Berkeley: University of California Press, 198–243.

——. 1987. "Grundzüge, Ziele und Ideen der Opposition gegen die Kaiser IM 1.JH.N. CHR: Versuch einer Standortbestimmung." In *Opposition et resistances a l'Empire d'Auguste a Trajan*. Edited by Giovanni Adalberto and Denis van Berchem. Vandoeuvres-Genève: Fondation Hardt, 1–63.

——. 1993. "Politics and Society in Fifth-Century Rome." In *Bilancio Critico su Roma arcaica fra monarchia e repubblica, in memoria di Ferdinando Castagnoli*. Edited by M. A. Levi. Rome: Accademia Nazionale dei Lincei, 129–57.

Raaflaub, Kurt and L. J. Samons II. 1990. "Opposition to Augustus." In *Between Republic and Empire: Interpretations of Augustus and His Principate*. Edited by Kurt Raaflaub and Mark Toher. Berkeley: University of California Press, 417–54.

Rabel, Robert. 1981. "Diseases of Soul in Stoic Psychology." *Greek, Roman, and Byzantine Studies* 22:385–93.

Rabinowitz, Nancy Sorkin and Lisa Auanger, Eds. 2002. *Among Women: From the Homosocial to the Homoerotic in the Ancient World*. Austin: University of Texas Press.

Radford, Robert. 2002. *Cicero: A Study in the Origins of Republican Philosophy*. Amsterdam: Rodopi.

Rahe, Paul. 2000. "Situating Machiavelli." In *Renaissance Civic Humanism: Reappraisals and Reflections*. Edited by James Hankins. Cambridge: Cambridge University Press, 270–308.

——. 2001. "Forms of Government: Structure, Principle, Object, and Aim." *Montesquieu's Science of Politics: Essays on* The Spirit of Laws. Edited by David Carrithers, Michael Mosher, and Paul Rahe. Lanham: Rowman and Littlefield, 69–108.

Rajchman, John. 1985. *Michel Foucault: The Freedom of Philosophy*. New York: Columbia University Press.

Ranum, Orest. 1980. "D'Alembert, Tacitus, and the Political Sociology of Despotism." *Transactions of the Fifth International Congress of the Enlightenment*. Vol 2: *Studies on Voltaire and the Eighteenth Century* 191. Oxford: Voltaire Foundation, 547–58.

Rawson, Elizabeth. 1972. "Cicero the Historian and Cicero the Antiquarian." *Journal of Roman Studies* 62:33–45.

——. 1975. *Cicero: A Portrait*. Ithaca: Cornell University Press.

——. 1985. *Intellectual Life in the Late Roman Republic*. Baltimore: Johns Hopkins University Press.

Reinhold, Meyer. 2002. *Studies in Classical History and Society*. Oxford: Oxford University Press.

Reitzenstein, R. 1924. "Zu Cicero de re publica." *Hermes* 59:356–62.

Remer, Gary. 1999. "Political Oratory and Conversation: Cicero versus Deliberative Democracy." *Political Theory* 27:39–64.

——. 2004. "Cicero and the Ethics of Deliberative Rhetoric." In *Talking Democracy: Historical Perspectives on Rhetoric and Democracy*. Edited by Benedetto Fontana, Cary Nederman, and Gary Remer. University Park: Penn State University Press, 135–61.

Reydams-Schils, Gretchen. 2005. *The Roman Stoics: Self, Responsibility, and Affection*. Chicago: University of Chicago Press.

Ricci, David. 1984. *The Tragedy of Political Science: Politics, Scholarship, and Democracy.* New Haven: Yale University Press.

Richard, J. C. 1986. "Patricians and Plebeians: The Origin of a Social Dichotomy." In *Social Struggles in Archaic Rome: New Perspectives on the Conflict of the Orders.* Edited by Kurt Raaflaub. Berkeley: University of California Press, 105–29.

Richlin, Amy. 1991. "Zeus and Metis: Foucault, Feminism, Classics." *Helios* 18:160–80.

———. 1998. "Foucault's *History of Sexuality:* A Useful Theory for Women?" In *Rethinking Sexuality: Foucault and Classical Antiquity.* Edited by David Larmour, Paul Miller, and Charles Platter. Princeton: Princeton University Press, 138–70.

Richter, Melvin. 1973. "Despotism." In *Dictionary of the History of Ideas.* Vol. 2 of 4. Edited by Philip Wiener. New York: Charles Scribner's Sons, 1–18.

———. 1976. "An Introduction to Montesquieu's 'An Essay on the Causes That May Affect Men's Minds and Characters.'" *Political Theory* 4:132–37.

———. 1977. *The Political Theory of Montesquieu.* Cambridge: Cambridge University Press.

———. 1995. "Montesquieu's Comparative Analysis of Europe and Asia: Intended and Unintended Consequences." In *L'Europe de Montesquieu.* Edited by Alberto Postigliola and Maria Grazia Bottaro Palumbo. Oxford: Voltaire Foundation, 329–48.

Ricoeur, Paul. 1981. *Hermeneutics and the Human Sciences.* Edited and translated by John Thompson. Cambridge: Cambridge University Press.

———. 1986. *Lectures on Ideology and Utopia.* Edited by George Taylor. New York: Columbia University Press.

Riley, Patrick. 1986. *The General Will Before Rousseau: The Transformation of the Divine into the Civic.* Princeton: Princeton University Press.

Rist, John. 1969. *Stoic Philosophy.* Cambridge: Cambridge University Press.

———. 1978. "The Stoic Concept of Detachment." In *The Stoics.* Edited by John Rist. Berkeley: University of California Press, 259–72.

Robin, Corey. 2000. "Reflections on Fear: Montesquieu in Retrieval." *American Political Science Review* 94:347–60.

Roccatagliata, Giuseppe. 1986. *A History of Ancient Psychiatry.* New York: Greenwood Press.

Rochlitz, Rainer. 1992. "The Aesthetics of Existence: Post-conventional Morality and the Theory of Power in Michel Foucault." In *Michel Foucault, Philosopher*. Translated by Timothy Armstrong. New York: Routledge, 248–59.

Rogers, Robert. 1943. *Studies in the Reign of Tiberius: Some Imperial Virtues of Tiberius and Drusus Julius Caesar.* Westport: Greenwood Press.

———. 1952. "A Tacitean Pattern in Narrating Treason-Trials." *Transactions of the American Philological Association* 83:279–311.

Rose, Peter. 2006. "Divorcing Ideology from Marxism and Marxism from Ideology: Some Problems." *Arethusa* 39:101–36.

Ross, Jr., D. O. 1973. "The Tacitean Germanicus." *Yale Classical Studies* 23:209–27.

Rossbach, Otto. 1882. "De Senecae Dialogis." *Hermes* 17:365–76.

Rostovtzeff, Michael. 1930. *A History of the Ancient World.* 2nd ed. 2 vols. Translated by J. D. Duff. Oxford: Clarendon.

Rowe, Greg. 2002. *Princes and Political Cultures: The New Tiberian Senatorial Decrees.* Ann Arbor: University of Michigan Press.

Rubinstein, Nicolai. 1982. "Political Theories in the Renaissance." In *The Renaissance: Essays in Interpretation.* Edited by André Chastel. London: Methuen, 153–200.

Rudich, Vasily. 1993. *Political Dissidence under Nero: The Price of Dissimulation.* London: Routledge.

Russo, Elena. 1999. "Monstrous Virtue: Montesquieu's *Considérations sur les Romains.*" *The Roman Review* 90:333–51.

Sabia, Daniel. 2001. "Machiavelli's Soderini and the Problem of Necessity." *Social Science Journal* 38:53–67.

Sabine, George. 1939. "What is a Political Theory?" *Journal of Politics* 1:1–16.

———. 1946 (orig. 1937). *A History of Political Theory.* New York: Henry Holt and Co.

Sabine, George, and Stanley Smith. 1976 (orig. 1929). "Introduction." *On the Commonwealth.* Indianapolis: Bobbs-Merrill Co., 1–102.

Saller, Richard. 1982. *Personal Patronage under the Early Empire.* Cambridge: Cambridge University Press.

———. 1984. "*Familia, Domus*, and the Roman Conception of the Family." *Phoenix* 38:336–55.

Sandbach, F. H. 1971. "Phantasia Katalêptikê." In *Problems in Stoicism.* Edited by A. A. Long. London: Athlone Press, 9–21.

———. 1975. *The Stoics*. New York: W.W. Norton and Company.

Sartori, Giovanni. 1973. "What is 'Politics.' " *Political Theory* 1:5–26.

Saxonhouse, Arlene. 1975. "Tacitus' *Dialogue on Oratory*: Political Activity under a Tyrant." *Political Theory* 3:53–68.

———. 1993. "Texts and Canons: The Status of the 'Great Books' in Political Theory." In *Political Science: The State of the Discipline II*. Edited by Ada Finifter. Washington, D.C.: American Political Science Association, 3–26.

Schaub, Diana. 1995. *Erotic Liberalism: Women and Revolution in Montesquieu's* Persian Letters. Lanham: Rowman and Littlefield.

Schellhase, Kenneth. 1976. *Tacitus in Renaissance Political Thought*. Chicago: University of Chicago Press.

Schiller, Friedrich. 1993. "On Naïve and Sentimental Poetry." Translated by Daniel Dahlstrom. In *Essays*. Edited by Walter Hinderer and Dahlstrom. New York: Continuum.

Schindel, Ulrich. 1983. "Livius philosophus?" In *Livius: Werk und Rezeption. Festschrift für Erich Burck zum 80. Geburtstag*. Edited by Eckard Lefèvre and Eckart Olshausen. München: C. H. Beck, 411–19.

Schmidt, P. L. 1978–79. "Cicero's Place in Roman Philosophy: A Study of His Prefaces." *Classical Journal* 74:115–27.

Schofield, Malcolm. 1995. "Cicero's Definition of *Res Publica*." In *Cicero the Philosopher: Twelve Papers*. Edited by J. G. F. Powell. Oxford: Clarendon Press, 63–83.

———. 2000. "Epicurean and Stoic Political Thought." In *The Cambridge History of Greek and Roman Political Thought*. Edited by Christopher Rowe and Malcolm Schofield. Cambridge: Cambridge University Press, 435–56.

———. 2002. "Academic Therapy: Philo of Larissa and Cicero's Project in the *Tusculans*." In *Philosophy and Power in the Graeco-Roman World: Essays in Honour of Miriam Griffin*. Edited by Gillian Clark and Tessa Rajak. Oxford: Oxford University Press, 91–109.

Schrenk, Lawrence. 1994. "Cicero on Rhetoric and Philosophy: *Tusculan Disputations*." *Ancient Philosophy* 14:355–60.

Scullard, H. H. 1951. *Roman Politics, 220–150 B.C.* Oxford: Clarendon.

Seager, Robin. 2005. *Tiberius*. 2nd ed. Oxford: Blackwell.

Seery, John. 1999. "Castles in the Air: An Essay on Political Foundations." *Political Theory* 27:460–90

Segal, Charles. 1986. *Language and Desire in Seneca's* Phaedra. Princeton: Princeton University Press.

———. 1992. "Discussion." In *The Interpretation of Roman Poetry: Empiricism or Hermeneutics?* Edited by Karl Valinsky. Frankfurt am Main: Peter Lang, 170–75.

Seneca. 1932. "On Tranquillity of Mind." In *Moral Essays*. Translated by John Basore. Cambridge: Harvard University Press.

———. 1935. "On Benefits." In *Moral Essays*. Translated by John Basore. Cambridge: Harvard University Press.

———. 1971. *Natural Questions*. Translated by Thomas Corcoran. Cambridge: Harvard University Press.

———. 1996. *Epistles*. Translated by Richard Gummere. Cambridge: Harvard University Press.

Serres, Michel. 1991. *Rome: The Book of Foundations*. Translated by Felicia McCarren. Stanford: Stanford University Press.

Shackleton, Robert. 1961. *Montesquieu: A Critical Biography*. Oxford: Oxford University Press.

———. 1988a. "Asia as Seen by the French Enlightenment." In *Essays on Montesquieu and on the Enlightenment*. Edited by David Gilson and Martin Smith. Oxford: Voltaire Foundation, 231–41.

———. 1988b. "Montesquieu and Machiavelli: A Reappraisal." In *Essays on Montesquieu and on the Enlightenment*. Edited by David Gilson and Martin Smith. Oxford: Voltaire Foundation, 117–31.

———. 1988c. "Montesquieu in 1948." In *Essays on Montesquieu and on the Enlightenment*. Edited by David Gilson and Martin Smith. Oxford: Voltaire Foundation, 17–40.

———. 1989. "Les mots 'despote' et 'despotisme'." In *Essays on Montesquieu and on the Enlightenment*. Edited by David Gilson and Martin Smith. Oxford: Voltaire Foundation, 481–86.

Shapiro, Gary. 2003. *Archaeologies of Vision: Foucault and Nietzsche on Seeing and Saying*. Chicago: University of Chicago.

Shaw, Brent. 1985. "The Divine Economy: Stoicism as Ideology." *Latomus* 44:16–54.

Sherwin-White, A. N. 1982. "The *lex repetundarum* and the Political Ideas of Gaius Gracchus." *Journal of Roman Studies* 72:18–31.

Shklar, Judith. 1987. *Montesquieu*. Oxford: Oxford University Press.

———. 1990. "Montesquieu and the New Republicanism." In *Machiavelli and Republicanism*. Edited by Gisela Bock, Quentin Skinner, and Maurizio Viroli. Cambridge: Cambridge University Press, 265–79.

Shorey, Paul. 1919. "Fifty Years of Classical Studies in America." *Transactions of the American Philological Association* 50:33–61.

Shotter, D. C. A. 1968. "Tacitus, Tiberius and Germanicus." *Historia* 17:194–214.

Sinclair, Patrick. 1995. *Tacitus the Sententious Historian: A Sociology of Rhetoric in* Annales *1–6*. University Park: Penn State University Press.

Skinner, Marilyn. 1989. "Expecting the Barbarians: Feminism, Nostalgia, and the 'Epistemic Shift' in Classical Studies." In *Classics: A Discipline and Profession in Crisis?* Edited by Phyllis Culham and Lowell Edmunds. New York: University Press of America, 199–210.

———. 2000. "Valedictory." *Transactions of the American Philological Association* 130:459–60.

Skinner, Quentin. 1978. *The Foundations of Modern Political Thought*. Vol. 1. *The Renaissance*. Cambridge: Cambridge University Press.

———. 1981. *Machiavelli*. New York: Hill and Wang.

———. 1990a. "Machiavelli's *Discorsi* and the Pre-Humanist Origins of Republican Ideas." In *Machiavelli and Republicanism*. Edited by Gisela Bock, Quentin Skinner, and Maurizio Viroli. Cambridge: Cambridge University Press, 121–41.

———. 1990b. "The Republican Ideal of Political Liberty." In *Machiavelli and Republicanism*. Edited by Gisela Bock, Quentin Skinner, and Maurizio Viroli. Cambridge: Cambridge University Press, 293–309.

Small, Jocelyn. 1976. "The Death of Lucretia." *American Journal of Archaeology* 80:349–60.

Smart, Barry. 1998. "Foucault, Levinas and the Subject of Responsibility." In *The Later Foucault: Politics and Philosophy*. Edited by Jeremy Moss. London: Sage, 18–32.

Smith, Munroe. 1886. "Introduction: The Domain of Political Science." *Political Science Quarterly* 1:1–8.

Smith, Philippa. 1995. "A Self-Indulgent Misuse of Leisure and Writing? How Not to Write Philosophy: Did Cicero Get it Right?" In *Cicero the Philosopher: Twelve Papers*. Edited by J. G. F. Powell. Oxford: Clarendon Press, 301–23.

Smith, R. R. R. 2002. "The Use of Images: Visual History and Ancient History." In *Classics in Progress: Essays on Ancient Greece and Rome*. Oxford: Oxford University Press, 59–102.

Social Science Research Council. n.d. *Theory and Practice in Historical Study: A Report of the Committee on Historiography*. New York: Social Science Research Council.

———. 1954. *The Social Sciences in Historical Study.* New York: Social Science Research Council.

Sorabji, Richard. 2000. *Emotion and Peace of Mind: From Stoic Agitation to Christian Temptation.* Oxford: Oxford University Press.

Springborg, Patricia. 1989. "Hannah Arendt and the Classical Republican Tradition." In *Hannah Arendt: Thinking, Judging, Freedom.* Edited by Gisela Kaplan and Clive Kessler. Sydney: Allen & Unwin, 9–17.

Stadter, P. A. 1972. "The Structure of Livy's History." *Historia* 21:287–307.

Starr, Chester. 1960. "The History of the Roman Empire 1911–1960." *Journal of Roman Studies* 50:149–60.

———. "Reflections upon the Problem of Generalization." In *Generalization in the Writing of History.* Edited by Louis Gottschalk. Chicago: University of Chicago Press, 3–18.

Strasburger, Hermann. 1968. *Zur Sage von der Gründung Roms.* Heidelberg: Carl Winter.

———. 1983. "Livius über Caesar: Unvollständige Überlegungen." In *Livius: Werk und Rezeption. Festchrift für Erich Burck zum 80. Geburtstag.* Edited by Eckard Lefèvre and Eckart Olshausen. München: C. H. Beck, 265–91.

Strauss, Leo. 1958. *Thoughts on Machiavelli.* Glencoe: Free Press.

———. 1959. *What is Political Philosophy? and Other Studies.* Glencoe: Free Press.

———. 1989a. *An Introduction to Political Philosophy.* Edited by Hilail Gildin. Detroit: Wayne State University Press.

———. 1989b. *The Rebirth of Classical Political Rationalism: An Introduction to the Thought of Leo Strauss.* Edited by Thomas Pangle. Chicago: University of Chicago Press.

Stray, Christopher. 2003. *The Classical Association: The First Century 1903–2003.* Oxford: Oxford University Press.

Strong, Tracy. 1983. "Nihilism and Political Theory." In *What Should Political Theory Be Now?* Edited by John Nelson. Albany: State University of New York Press, 243–63.

———. 1990. *The Idea of Political Theory: Reflections on the Self in Political Time and Space.* Notre Dame: University of Notre Dame Press.

Strozier, Robert. 2002. *Foucault, Subjectivity, and Identity: Historical Constructions of Subject and Self.* Detroit: Wayne State University Press.

Sullivan, J. P. 1985. *Literature and Politics in the Age of Nero.* Ithaca: Cornell University Press.

Sullivan, Vicki. 1996. *Machiavelli's Three Romes: Religion, Human Liberty, and Politics Reformed*. DeKalb: Northern Illinois University Press.

———. 2000. "In Defense of the City: Machiavelli's Bludgeoning of the Classical and Christian Traditions." In *Instilling Ethics*. Edited by Norma Thompson. Lanham: Rowman and Littlefield, 39–59.

———. 2004. *Machiavelli, Hobbes, and the Formation of a Liberal Republicanism in England*. Cambridge: Cambridge University Press.

Süss, Wilhelm. 1966. *Cicero: Eine Einführung in seine philosophischen Schriften (mit Ausschluß der staatsphilosophischen Werke)*. Weisbaden: Franz Steiner Verlag.

Syme, Ronald. 1939. *The Roman Revolution*. Oxford: Oxford University Press.

———. 1958. *Tacitus*. 2 vols. Oxford: Clarendon Press.

———. 1959. "Livy and Augustus." *Harvard Studies in Classical Philology* 64:27–87.

———. 1970. *Ten Studies in Tacitus*. Oxford: Clarendon Press.

Tacitus. 1970. *Agricola. Germania. Dialogus*. Translated by M. Hutton and W. Peterson. Revised by R. M. Ogilvie, E. H. Warmington, and M. Winterbottom. Cambridge: Harvard University Press.

———. 1994. *Annales*. Edited by Henrich Heubner. Stuttgart: B. J. Teubner.

———. 1996. *The Histories*. Translated by C. H. Moore. Cambridge: Harvard University Press.

———. 2004. *The Annals*. Translated by A.J. Woodman. Indianapolis: Hackett.

Talbert, Richard. 1984. *The Senate of Imperial Rome*. Princeton: Princeton University Press.

———. 1999. "Tacitus and the *Senatus Consultum de Cn. Pisone Patre*." *American Journal of Philology* 120:89–97.

Taminiaux, Jacques. 2000. "Athens and Rome." In *The Cambridge Companion to Hannah Arendt*. Edited by Dana Villa. Cambridge: Cambridge University Press, 165–77.

Tanner, R.G. 1972. "Cicero on Conscience and Morality." In *Cicero and Virgil: Studies in Honour of Harold Hunt*. Edited by John Martyn. Amsterdam: Adolf M. Hakkert, 87–112.

Tavenner, Eugene. 1936. "An Invitation to All Lovers of Literature." *Classical Journal* 32:1–3.

Tarver, J. C. 1902. *Tiberius the Tyrant*. Westminster: Archibald Constable and Co., Ltd.

Taylor, Charles. 1985. "Social Theory as Practice." *Philosophy and the Human Sciences: Philosophical Papers* 2. Cambridge: Cambridge University Press, 91–115.

——. 1989. *Sources of the Self: The Making of the Modern Identity*. Cambridge: Harvard University Press.

Taylor, Lily Ross. 1918. "Livy and the Name Augustus." *Classical Review* 32:158–61.

——. 1949. *Party Politics in the Age of Caesar.* Berkeley: University of California Press.

Thacker, Andrew. 1993. "Foucault's Aesthetics of Existence." *Radical Philosophy* 63:13–21.

Thiele, Leslie. 1997. *Thinking Politics: Perspectives in Ancient, Modern, and Postmodern Political Theory*. Chatham, N.J: Chatham House.

Thompson, William. 1958. "Relevant or Irrelevant.? Classics in the Curriculum Today." *Greece and Rome* 2nd series. 5:196–99.

Thornton, Bruce. 1991. "Idolon Theatri: Foucault and the Classicists." *Classical and Modern Literature* 12:81–100.

Timpe, Dieter. 1989. "Die Absicht der Germania des Tacitus." In *Beiträge zum Verständnis der Germania des Tacitus.* Vol. I: *Bericht über die Kolloquien der Kommission für die Altertumskunde Nord- und Mitteleuropas in Jahr 1986.* Edited by Herbert Jankuhn and Dieter Timpe. Göttingen: Vandenhoeck and Rubrecht, 106–27.

Too, Yun Lee. 1994. "Educating Nero: A Reading of Seneca's *Moral Epistles*." In *Reflections of Nero: Culture, History, and Representation.* Edited by Jas Elsner and Jamie Masters. Chapel Hill: University of North Carolina Press, 211–24.

Trowbridge Honey, Mary. 1939. "The Classics in America." *Greece and Rome* 9:36–42.

Tuck, Richard. 1999. *The Rights of War and Peace: Political Thought and the International Order from Grotius to Kant.* Oxford: Oxford University Press.

Turner, Frank. 1989. "Why the Greeks and not the Romans in Victorian Britain?" In *Rediscovering Hellenism: The Hellenic Inheritance and the English Imagination.* Edited by G. W. Clarke. New York: Cambridge University Press, 61 –81.

Vanderbroeck, Paul. 1987. *Popular Leadership and Collective Behavior in the Late Roman Republic (ca. 80–50 B.C.)*. Amsterdam: J. C. Gieben.

Vasaly, Ann. 1987. "Personality and Power: Livy's Depiction of the Appii Claudii in the First Pentad." *Transactions of the American Philological Association* 117:203–26.

———. 1993. *Representations: Images of the World in Ciceronian Oratory.* Berkeley: University of California Press.

Venturi, Franco. 1963. "Oriental Despotism." *Journal of the History of Ideas* 24:133–42.

Veyne, Paul. 1987. "The Roman Empire." *A History of Private Life.* I. *From Pagan Rome to Byzantium.* Edited by Paul Veyne. Translated by Arthur Goldhammer. Cambridge: Belknap Press, 5–234.

———. 1990. *Bread and Circuses: Historical Sociology and Political Pluralism.* Edited by Oswyn Murray. Translated by Brian Pearce. New York: Penguin.

———. 1993. "The Final Foucault and His Ethics." *Critical Inquiry* 20:1–9.

Villa, Dana R. 1992. "Beyond Good and Evil: Arendt, Nietzsche, and the Aestheticization of Political Action." *Political Theory* 20:274–308.

———. 1996. *Arendt and Heidegger: The Fate of the Political.* Princeton: Princeton University Press.

———. 1997. "Hannah Arendt: Modernity, Alienation, and Critique." In *Hannah Arendt and the Meaning of Politics.* Edited by Craig Calhoun and John McGowan. Minneapolis: University of Minnesota Press, 179–206.

———. 1999. *Politics, Philosophy, Terror: Essays on the Thought of Hannah Arendt.* Princeton: Princeton University Press.

Viroli, Maurizio. 1990. "Machiavelli and the Republican Idea of Politics." In *Machiavelli and Republicanism.* Edited by Gisela Bock, Quentin Skinner, and Maurizio Viroli. Cambridge: Cambridge University Press, 143–71.

———. 1992. *From Politics to Reason of State: The Acquisition and Transformation of the Language of Politics 1250–1600.* Cambridge: Cambridge University Press.

———. 1998. *Machiavelli.* Oxford: Oxford University Press.

Vishnia, Rachel. 1996. *State, Society, and Popular Leaders in Mid-Republican Rome, 241–167 B.C.* London: Routledge.

Voegelin, Eric. 1971 (orig. 1952). *The New Science of Politics: An Introduction.* Chicago: University of Chicago Press.

———. 1975. *From Enlightenment to Revolution.* Edited by John Hallowell. Durham: Duke University Press.

———. 1997. *History of Political Ideas.* Vol. 1. *Hellenism, Rome, and Early Christianity.* In *The Collected Works of Eric Voegelin.* Vol. 19. Edited by Athanasios Moulakis. Columbia: University of Missouri Press.

von Albrecht, Michael. 1989. *Masters of Roman Prose from Cato to Apuleius: Interpretative Studies*. Translated by Neil Adkin. Leeds: Francis Cairns.

———. 2004. *Wort und Wandlung: Senecas Lebenskunst*. Leiden: Brill.

von Fritz, Kurt. 1954. *The Theory of the Mixed Constitution in Antiquity: A Critical Analysis of Polybius' Political Ideas*. New York: Columbia University Press.

———. 1957. "Tacitus, Agricola, Domitian, and the Problem of the Principate." *Classical Philology* 52:73–97.

von Ranke, Leopold. 1973. *The Theory and Practice of History*. Edited by Georg Iggers and Konrad von Moltke. Indianapolis: Bobbs-Merrill.

von Staden, Heinrich. 1978. "The Stoic Theory of Perception and its 'Platonic' Critics." In *Studies in Perception: Interrelations in the History of Philosophy and Science*. Edited by Peter Machamer and Robert Turnbull. Columbus: Ohio State University Press, 96–136.

von Ungern-Sternberg, Jürgen. 1986. "The Formation of the 'Annalistic Tradition': The Example of the Decemvirate." In *Social Struggles in Archaic Rome: New Perspectives on the Conflict of the Orders*. Edited by Kurt Raaflaub. Berkeley: University of California Press, 77–104.

von Wilamowitz-Moellendorff, Ulrich. 1982. *History of Classical Scholarship*. Translated by Alan Harris. Baltimore: Johns Hopkins University Press.

Waddicor, Mark. 1970. *Montesquieu and the Philosophy of Natural Law*. The Hague: Mantinus Nijhoff.

Wagener, A. Pelzer. 1938. "Progress and Problems of the Committee on the Present Status of Classical Education." *Classical Journal* 34:1–8.

Walbank, F. W. A. 1960. "History and Tragedy." *Historia* 9:216–34.

Walcot, Peter. 1981. "*Greece and Rome*, the First Half-Century." *Greece and Rome* 2nd series. 28:1–9.

Waldron, Jeremy. 2000. "Arendt's Constitutional Politics." In *The Cambridge Companion to Hannah Arendt*. Edited by Dana Villa. Cambridge: Cambridge University Press, 201–19.

Walker, Andrew. 1993. "*Enargeia* and the Spectator in Greek Historiography." *Transactions of the American Philological Association* 123:353–77.

Walker, Bessie. 1952. *The* Annals *of Tacitus: A Study in the Writing of History*. Manchester: University of Manchester Press.

Wallace-Hadrill, Andrew. 1982. "The Golden Age and Sin in Augustan Ideology." *Past and Present* 95:19–36.

———. 1988. "The Social Structure of the Roman House." *Papers of the British School at Rome* 56:43–97.

———. 1990. "Roman Arches and Greek Honours: The Language of Power at Rome." *Proceedings of the Cambridge Philological Society.* 36:143–81.

———. 1997. "*Mutatio morum*: The Idea of a Cultural Revolution." In *The Roman Cultural Revolution.* Edited by Thomas Habinek and Alessandro Schiesaro. Cambridge: Cambridge University Press, 3–22.

Walsh, P. G. 1955. "Livy's Preface and the Distortion of History." *American Journal of Philology* 76:369–83.

———. 1958. "Livy and Stoicism." *American Journal of Philology* 79:355–75.

———. 1961. *Livy: His Historical Aims and Methods.* Cambridge: Cambridge University Press.

———. 1966. "Livy." In *Latin Historians.* Edited by T. A. Dorey. New York: Basic Books, 115–42.

Watson, Gerard. 1971. "The Natural Law and Stoicism." In *Problems in Stoicism.* Edited by A. A. Long. London: Athlone Press, 216–38.

———. 1988. "Discovering the Imagination: Platonists and Stoics on *phantasia.*" In *The Question of "Eclecticism": Studies in Later Greek Philosophy.* Edited by John Dillon and A. A. Long. Berkeley: University of California Press, 208–33.

Webb, Ruth. 1997. "Imagination and the Arousal of the Emotions in Greco-Roman Rhetoric." In *The Passions in Roman Thought and Literature.* Edited by Susanna Morton Braund and Christopher Gill. Cambridge: Cambridge University Press, 112–27.

Wenger, Leopold. 1925. *Institutionen des römischen Zivilprozessrechts.* München: Verlag der Hochschulbuchhandlung Max Hueber.

White, Mary. 1946–47. "A Point of View." *Phoenix* 1:1.

White, Nicholas. 1979. "The Basis of Stoic Ethics." *Harvard Studies in Classical Philology* 83:143–78.

White, Stephen. 1995. "Cicero and the Therapists." In *Cicero the Philosopher: Twelve Papers.* Edited by J. G. F. Powell. Oxford: Clarendon, 219–46.

Whitfield, J. H. 1971. "Machiavelli's Use of Livy." In *Livy.* Edited by T. A. Dorey. London: Routledge and Kegan Paul, 73–96.

———. 1976. "Livy>Tacitus." In *Classical Influences on European Culture, AD 1500–1700.* Edited by R. R. Bolgar. Cambridge: Cambridge University Press, 281–93.

Whyte, William Foote. 1943. "A Challenge to Political Scientists." *American Political Science Review* 37:692–97.

Wiebe, Robert. 1967. *The Search for Order: 1877–1920.* New York: Hill and Wang.

Wiedemann, Thomas. 2000. "Reflections of Roman Political Thought in Latin Historical Writing." In *The Cambridge History of Greek and Roman Political Thought.* Edited by Christopher Rowe and Malcolm Schofield. Cambridge: Cambridge University Press, 517–31.

Williams, Bronwyn. 1990. "Reading Tacitus' Tiberian Annals." In *The Imperial Muse: Flavian Epicist to Claudian.* Edited by A. J. Boyle. Bendigo, Australia: Aureal Publications, 140–66.

Williams, Gordon. 1955. "Review of *Tite-Live, Histoire Romaine.*" *Journal of Roman Studies* 45:227–29.

Williams, Mary Frances. 1997. "Four Mutinies: Tacitus *Annals* 1.16–30; 1.31–49 and Ammianus Marcellinus *Res Gestae* 20.4.9–20.5.7; 24.3.1–8." *Phoenix* 51:44–74.

Williams, Raymond. 1977. *Marxism and Literature.* Oxford: Oxford University Press.

———. 1979. *Politics and Letters: Interviews with* New Left Review. London: NLB.

Williamson, Callie. 2005. *The Laws of the Roman People: Public Law in the Expansion and Decline of the Roman Republic.* Ann Arbor: University of Michigan Press.

Willoughby, W. F. 1933. "A Program for Research in Political Science." *American Political Science Review* 27:1–23.

Willoughby, W. W. 1900. "The Value of Political Philosophy." *Political Science Quarterly* 15:75–95.

———. 1904. "The American Political Science Association." *Political Science Quarterly* 19:107–11.

———. 1907 (orig. 1896). *An Examination of the Nature of the State: A Study in Political Philosophy.* New York: Macmillan.

Wilson, Marcus. 2001. "Seneca's *Epistles* Reclassified." In *Texts, Ideas, and the Classics: Scholarship, Theory, and Classical Literature.* Edited by S. J. Harrison. Oxford: Oxford University Press, 164–87.

Winkler, John. 1990. *The Constraints of Desire: The Anthropology of Sex and Gender in Ancient Greece.* London: Routledge.

Wirszubski, Chaim. 1950. *Libertas as a Political Idea at Rome During the Late Republic and Early Principate.* Cambridge: Cambridge University Press.

———. 1954. "Cicero's *CVM DIGNITATE OTIVM*: A Reconsideration." *Journal of Roman Studies* 44:1–13.

———. 1961. "*AVDACES*: A Study in Political Phraseology." *Journal of Roman Studies* 51:12–22.

Wiseman, T. P. 1979. *Clio's Cosmetics: Three Studies in Greco-Roman Literature.* Totowa, N.J.: Rowman and Littlefield.

———. 1985. "Competition and Co-operation." In *Roman Political Life: 90 B.C.–A.D. 69.* Edited by Wiseman. Exeter: University of Exeter, 3–19.

———. 1986. "Monuments and the Roman Annalists." In *Past Perspectives: Studies in Greek and Roman Historical Writing.* Edited by I.S. Moxon, J.D. Smart and A.J. Woodman. Cambridge: Cambridge University Press, 87–100.

———. 1987. *Roman Studies: Literary and Historical.* Liverpool: Francis Cairns.

———. 1994. "The Origins of Roman Historiography." *Historiography and Imagination: Eight Essays on Roman Culture.* Exeter: University of Exeter Press, 1–22.

———. 1995. *Remus: A Roman Myth.* Cambridge: Cambridge University Press.

———. 2002. "Roman History and the Ideological Vacuum." In *Classics in Progress: Eight Essays on Ancient Greece and Rome.* Edited by Wiseman. Oxford: Oxford University Press, 285–310.

Wittgenstein, Ludwig. 1953. *Philosophical Investigations.* Translated by G. E. M. Anscombe. New York: Macmillan.

Wolin, Richard. 1986. "Foucault's Aesthetic Decisionism." *Telos* 67:71–81.

Wolin, Sheldon. 1989. *The Presence of the Past: Essays on the State and the Constitution.* Baltimore: Johns Hopkins University Press.

———. 1994. "Hannah Arendt: Democracy and the Political." In *Hannah Arendt: Critical Essays.* Edited by Lewis Hinchman and Sandra Hinchman. Albany: SUNY Press, 289–306.

———. 2004. *Politics and Vision.* Expanded Edition. Princeton: Princeton University Press.

Wood, Neal. 1967. "Machiavelli's Concept of *Virtù* Reconsidered." *Political Studies* 15:159–72.

———. 1986. "*Populares* and *Circumcelliones:* The Vocabulary of 'Fallen

Man' in Cicero and St. Augustine." *History of Political Thought* 7:33–51.

———. 1988. *Cicero's Social and Political Thought*. Berkeley: University of California Press.

———. 2004. *Tyranny in America: Capitalism and National Decay*. London: Verso.

Woodman, A. J. 1988. *Rhetoric in Classical Historiography: Four Studies*. London: Croom Helm.

———. 1993. "Amateur Dramatics at the Court of Nero: *Annals* 15.48.74." In *Tacitus and the Tacitean Tradition*. Edited by T. J. Luce and Woodman. Princeton: Princeton University Press, 104–28.

———. 1998. *Tacitus Reviewed*. Oxford: Clarendon.

———. 2006. "Mutiny and Madness: Tacitus, *Annals* 1.16–49." *Arethusa* 39:303–29.

Woodman, A. J. and R. H. Martin. 1996. *The* Annals *of Tacitus. Book 3*. New York: Cambridge University Press.

Woolsey, Theodore. 1893 (orig. 1877). *Political Science or the State Theoretically and Practically Considered*. 2 Vols. New York: Charles Scribner's Sons.

Wright, M. R. 1995. "Cicero on Self-Love and Love of Humanity in *De Finibus* 3." In *Cicero the Philosopher*. Edited by J. G. F. Powell. Oxford: Clarendon.

Yakobson, Alexander. 1999. *Elections and Electioneering in Rome: A Study in the Political System of the Late Republic*. Stuttgart: Franz Steiner Verlag.

Yavetz, Zvi. 1969. *Plebs and Princeps*. Oxford: Clarendon Press.

Young, David. 1978. "Montesquieu's View of Despotism and His Use of Travel Literature." *Review of Politics* 40:392–405.

Zanker, Paul. 1988. *The Power of Images in the Age of Augustus*. Translated by Alan Shapiro. Ann Arbor: University of Michigan Press.

Index of Classical Sources Cited

Aristotle

De An.
431b7 247n45

Pol.
1253b–1255b 257n13
1278b–1279a 257n13

Celsus

De Med.
pro. 4 137
pro. 5 140
pro. 14 137
pro. 15 257n19
pro. 23 137
pro. 39 260n34
1.3.1 260n34
1.3.2 158, 177
3.18.2 157
3.18.3 169
3.18.5 143
3.18.10 169, 177
3.18.11 177
3.18.18 177
3.18.22 177
3.22.1 137, 258n20
3.25.3 269n129
3.27.1A 144
5.21 267n118

Cicero

Acad.
1.41 248n72
2.7.20 89, 209
2.10.30 90
2.21 247n43–44
2.30 92, 248n72
2.56 248n66
3.23.8 237n17

Amic.
5.19 52, 239n39
6.22 52
7.23 50
9.32 51
12.15 238n30
12.18.1 52, 238n30
12.28.2 238n30
13.47 49
13.48 49
14.50 239n39
27.100 239n39
27.102 51

Attic.
1.8.2 53
3.14 40
4.2.2 236n5
9.10.2 39
12.13.1 46

12.14.3 47, 52
12.15 47
12.16 52
12.18 239n33
12.18.1 47
12.28.2 47
12.36.1 50
12.37a 239n34
12.38a.1 238n31
12.40.2 238n31
12.43 51
13.12.3 239n44
13.18 239n44

De Orat.
1.1 240n50
2.9.36 53
2.51–70 248n60
2.186 247n60
2.357 248n62
3.50.195 57
3.51.197 57

Div.
2.1.2 241n60
2.2.4 60

Fam.
1.9.21 240n50
2.12.2 46
5.12 239n44

Fin.
3.17.57 196
3.58 240n46
3.67 239n34
3.69 239n34
4.5–7 238n31

Leg.
2.1.3 53
2.2.4 53

Nat.
1.4.9 47
2.60.151 242n84
2.62.156 242n84
2.63.157 242n84

Offic.
1.3.7 238n29
2.5.17 44, 239n39
3.10.41 93

Orator
120 52

Pro Sestio
98 240n50

Q. Fr.
3.5.1–2 45, 237n22

Rep.
1.1.1 43, 45, 236n5, 239n39
1.1.1–2 69
1.2.2 45
1.2.3 43, 44, 239n39
1.3.4 45
1.4.7 46, 236n7
1.7.12 44, 69
1.33.50 277n49
2.1.2 71
2.2.4 93, 248n78
2.19.34 277n49
2.26.47–48 200
5.1.2 38, 46, 76, 240n56
6.3.3 237n25
6.12.12 43
6.13.13 43
6.14.15 43
6.17.17–18.19 238n23
6.18.18–19 65
6.19.20 44, 45
6.21.23 45
6.24.26 45, 48
6.26.28 48
6.26.29 45, 51, 59, 65, 76, 237n24

Tusc.
1.1.2 240n57
1.3.5 54
1.3.6 54, 73
1.11.24 40
1.13.30 50

1.14.31 50, 55
1.14.32 48
1.14.33 50
1.15.32 50
1.19.14 47
1.20.45 47, 54
1.20.47 55
1.25.62 54, 56
1.26.64 55
1.28.68 54, 55
1.28.69 54
1.31.76 47
1.34.84 40
1.37.90 51
1.38.91 239n39
2.4.11 237n19
2.4.13 42
2.5.13 55
2.18.42 238n31
2.18.43 237n19
2.21.48 238n31
2.23.55 248n66
2.23.56 89
2.24.58 238n31
2.27.65 248n66
3.1.1 55, 237n19
3.1.2 89, 239n39, 247n55
3.2.3 59
3.2.4 59, 91
3.3.6 41, 47, 237n19
3.5.11 91, 191, 247n55
3.6.12 41, 49
3.6.13 49
3.10.23 87
3.15.31 248n70
3.17.36–18.43 41, 48, 243n2
3.22.54 91
3.23.55 51
3.23.56 52
3.24.58 52
3.29.72 51
3.31.75 239n37
3.31.76 238n30
3.34.84 237n19
4.1.1 56
4.1.2 55
4.2.3 58
4.4.10–6.14 243n2
4.10.23 87
4.10.23–11.27 88
4.13.30 247n49
4.13.31 55, 58
4.23.51 48, 59
4.27.58 237n19
4.28.60 51, 248n71
4.28.61 238n31
4.29.63 238n30
4.35.74 47
4.38.83 47, 237n19
5.1.1 40
5.1.3 40, 49, 50
5.2.5 56, 238n30
5.3.9 59
5.4.10 48, 240n47
5.22.63 52
5.23.66 56
5.24.69 238n33
5.25.70 48
5.25.71 48
5.25.72 48, 59
5.36.105 56
5.37.108 48
5.39.114 61, 77
5.41.121 40

Dio Cassius

55.5 269n130

Dionysius of Halicarnassus

Roman Antiquities

2.7–29 248n78

Galen

De Plac.

F. 162.4–8 89

F. 162.8–9 247n60, 249n93
F. 163.8 89
F. 164.41–50 88
F. 164.48–50 88
F. 164.53–54 247n55
F. 165.26–28 247n55
F. 169.114–17 247n55

Horace

Epode
7 93

Livy

pref. 1 245n24
pref. 4 79
pref. 5 78
pref. 6 92
pref. 7 92
pref. 9 79, 90
pref. 10 79, 90, 92, 245n23–24
pref. 12 79
1.2.9 103
1.4.5 276n40
1.4.9 93
1.6.3 93
1.7.2 93
1.7.11 69
1.8.1 94
1.8.2 93
1.8.3 95
1.8.5 93
1.8.6 93
1.9.6–7 249n83
1.9.10 249n83
1.9.14 95
1.10.1 95
1.10.2 96
1.10.3–4 95
1.10.5–6 95
1.11.2 95
1.11.4 95
1.11.6 96
1.12.3 96
1.12.4 96
1.12.7 96
1.13.2 96
1.13.4 96
1.13.6 96
1.14.3 97
1.14.9 111
1.15.6 96, 97
1.18.4 97
1.18.6 97
1.19.1 97
1.19.2 97
1.19.4–5 97
1.21.1–2 97
1.23.11 100
1.32.2 97
1.47.6–7 99
1.49.4 99, 111
1.49.5 99
1.51.1 99, 111
1.51.9 100
1.52.4 100
1.52.6 99
1.54.10 100
1.56.7 100
1.56.8 100
1.58.2 100
1.58.4 101
1.58.5 100, 101
1.59.3 101
1.59.4 101
1.59.8 101
1.59.9 101
1.59.11 101
2.1.1 102
2.1.2 94
2.1.3–6 103
2.1.4 110
2.1.5 94
2.1.7 103
2.1.8 103
2.1.9 110
2.2.7 103

2.7.7 104
2.7.11 104
2.9.7 104
2.29.9 110
2.30.2 110
2.52.2 110
2.52.3 110
3.20.8 243n4
3.31.8 110
3.33.8 251n113
3.33.10 251n113
3.34.1 251n113
3.34.2 251n113
3.34.8 110
3.36.1 111
3.36.4 111
3.36.5 111
3.36.6 111
3.36.7–9 112
3.36.8 111, 112
3.37.3 111
3.37.8 111, 112
3.38.1 112
3.38.2 112
3.38.8 112
3.38.10 112
3.38.11 112
3.39.3 112
3.39.4 112
3.41.4 112
3.44.4 113
3.44.8 113
3.44.9 113
3.45.4 113
3.45.8 113
3.46.1 113
3.46.2 113
3.47.4 114
3.48.9 114
3.49.1 114
3.49.5 114
3.49.6 114
3.50.2–3 114
3.50.7 114
3.50.10 114
3.50.13 114
3.65.11 105
4.13.3 106
4.15.6 144
5.2.2 118
5.2.6–8 118
5.6.2 118
5.6.8 118
5.7.10 251n106
5.33.11 116, 252n120
5.36.1 252n120
5.37.3 252n120
5.37.4–5 116, 252n120
5.37.7 252n120
5.37.8 116
5.38.1 252n120
5.38.3–4 252n120
5.38.5 252n120
5.38.7–8 252n120
5.39.1 252n120
5.41.4 252n120
5.42.3 116
5.42.4 117
5.42.8 117
5.44.2 117
5.44.6 117
5.46.5 117
5.46.6 117
5.48.3 116, 252n120
5.49.3 117
5.49.7 118
5.51.3 119
5.51.4 119
5.52.2–3 119
5.52.7 119
5.52.8 119
5.52.12 119
5.53.1 119
5.53.5 119
5.53.7 119
5.53.9 119

5.54.3 119
5.55.1 119
6.1.2 116
6.7.5 128
6.7.6 130
6.15.5 108
6.15.13 108
6.18.14 108
6.19.7 108
6.20.10 108
6.20.11 108
7.2.2 92
9.9.11 243n5
9.17.3 130
9.28.4 261n45
22.8.5 243n4
34.32 276n38

Lucan

1.95 93

Ovid

M.
6.438–570 276n38

Plutarch

Cato Mai.
23 229n1

Quintilian

Inst.
6.2.29–30 248n62

Sallust

Jug.
1.1–4 259n30
4.7–8 259n30
41.5 39, 91
41.9 91

Seneca

Clem.
1.5.1 264n72

De Ben.
3.7.5 192, 276n35

De Ot.
3.2 187
3.2–3.3 277n50
3.4 190
7.1–4 277n50

De Tranq. An.
1.1–14 281n132
2.11 277n45
5.5 190
15.1 207

Ep.
3.2 276n35
3.3 276n35
3.4 194
3.5 194, 195
3.6 197
3.20 264n72
4.4 203
4.7 203, 204
4.8 193
5.4 192
5.9 215
6.1 186
6.4 187
6.7 213, 279n90
7.6–7 198
8.3 202
8.4 202
9.7 215
9.17 187
9.22 193
11.9 276n35
11.10 279n89
13.1 187
13.5 194
13.7 194
13.12 181
14.4 193
14.6 203
14.7 193
14.13 193

15.1 181
18.1 276n35
18.11 276n35
19.3–4 197
19.5 190, 276n35
19.8 190, 276n35
20.2 276n35
22.3 276n35
22.7 276n35
23.1 214
23.3 214
23.11 212
24.3–6 279n89
24.17 279n90
25.2 278n74
25.4–5 279n90
25.5 212
25.6 212, 213, 276n35
26.5 200
26.6 199, 200
26.7 279n90
27.1 279n90
28.1–4 204
28.3 199
28.6 181
28.10 279n90
29.3 276n35
29.7 181
29.11 186, 198
29.12 198
30.7 276n35
31.1 197
31.2 198
31.11 208
33.3 210
33.4 210, 212
33.6 210
33.7 210
33.8 210
33.10 210
34.2 213
35.2 279n90
36.6 276n35
39.3 203, 276n35
39.4 259n30
40.1 197, 279n93
42.3 193
42.7–8 279n89
44.1 208, 209
44.2 209
44.3 212
44.5 209
45.2 276n35
45.7 194, 198
47.2–4 200
47.5 193
47.14 276n35
47.19 192
47.20 192, 276n35
48.3 276n35
48.10 276n35
49.11 180
50.5 209
51.8 192
52 281n132
52.1–2 280n104
52.6 209
55.3 195
55.4 195
55.5 194, 276n35
55.11 213
56.5 248n67
56.8 181, 195
56.9 194
56.10 194
57.3 276n35
63.2 276n35
65.5 214
65.22 276n35
66.23 202
70.10 268n128
71.2 214
71.7 276n35
71.28 190, 276n35
74.4 181, 198
74.7 202

74.8 202
74.20 276n35
74.21 181
74.33 181
75.3 222
75.4 222
75.18 222
76.28 214
76.30 202
77.19 276n35
78.2 277n50
78.20 276n35
78.21 279n90
79.13 196
79.14 196
79.17 196
80.1 212
80.7 197
83.1 214, 279n93
84 279n93
84.5 213
84.7–8 213, 221
85.24 181
85.40 208
86.2 276n35
86.10 276n35
90.5 276n35
91.4 203
91.5 203
91.7 201, 204
93.4 190, 276n35
94.5 209, 276n35
94.17 181
94.19 209
94.20 209
94.21 209
94.25 209
94.27 276n35
94.30 209
94.33 276n35
94.37 276n35
94.73 199
94.74 199
95.14 140, 259n28
95.15 140
95.29 191
95.30 191, 192
95.32 192
95.33 192
95.41 276n35
95.51 190
95.57–58 199
98.4 204
98.15–16 277n50
99.6 276n35
99.9 203, 204
99.19 276n35
100.9 246n32
101.1 276n35
101.3 276n35
101.5 215, 277n48
101.15 193
102.6 276n35
102.11 196
102.12 196
102.13 196
102.14–15 196
102.17 196
103.1 201
103.2 194, 201
103.3 276n35
104.2–5 277n50
104.21 279n89
104.26 205
104.27 279n89
105.1 193
105.3 193, 194
105.4 194
105.6 193, 194
106.2 276n35
107.6 276n35
113.30 201, 276n35
114.23 276n35
115.3 276n35
117.30 276n35
118.3–4 201, 202, 204

118.11 276n35
119.8 201
120.2 276n35
120.11 276n35
120.22 197
121.14 186
121.17 186
121.18 186
121.20 186
121.23 186
121.24 186
122.2 276n35
122.3 276n35
123.6 198
123.16 276n35
HF
159–85 277n43
Natl. Quest.
1.16–17 266n104
3.pref.5 215
Thys.
401–3 277n43
455 277n43
468 277n43

Seutonius

Tib.
25 268n128
61 268n126

Tacitus

Agric.
2.3 169, 176, 268n124
3.1 170, 223
3.2 272n169
3.3 172
11.4 142
21.2 141, 142
Ann.
1.1.1 133
1.1.2 143, 144
1.2.1 137, 144, 160, 263n68
1.2.2 143
1.3.2 261n49
1.3.7 144
1.4.1 144
1.4.2 145, 158, 261n49
1.7.1 145, 157, 264n82
1.7.3 146
1.8.5–6 156
1.9.4–5 143
1.10.1 145, 261n49
1.11.2 157
1.11.3 157
1.12.3 149
1.13.4 262n57
1.14.4 263n65
1.15.1 263n65
1.16.3 152, 264n82
1.18.2 153, 155, 264n82
1.19.2 153
1.19.5 153
1.21.3 153
1.22.1 153
1.23.1 154
1.24.1 154
1.24.3 154
1.25.2 154, 158
1.26.1 154
1.26.3 154
1.28.4 263n68
1.28.6 155
1.31.1 155, 156
1.31.3 155
1.32.1 155
1.34.3 155
1.35.3 156
1.37.1 155
1.38.2 165
1.46.1 155
1.46.3 155
1.52.1 156
1.53.2 257n20
1.53.3 260n32
1.54.2 264n82
1.64.1 264n82

1.72.3 271n162
1.72.4 267n110
1.73 262n57
1.73.1 163
1.74.1 163
1.74.2 163
1.74.5 146
1.75.1 163
1.76.3–4 166
1.77.1 156
1.78.2 155
2.2.4 260n32
2.27.1 163
2.28.2 167
2.28.3 163
2.29.2 168
2.30.3 168
2.31.1 168
2.31.3 168
2.32 271n163
2.33 160
2.38.1 146
2.42.3 168
2.87.1 156, 157
3.11.2 158
3.15.2 160
3.16.4 260n32
3.17–18 271n163
3.19.2 158
3.22.2 264n82, 265n92
3.23.1 156
3.25.2 140
3.26.1 260n37
3.26.2 141, 142, 261n46
3.27.1 142
3.27.2 142
3.27.3 142
3.28.1 142, 143
3.28.3 144
3.29 157
3.31.2–4 265n96
3.34.3 260n32
3.35.1 146, 265n96
3.35.2 146
3.36.1 156
3.52–54 146
3.56.2 262n57
3.60.1 147
3.65–66 164
3.65.1 177
3.65.2 157
3.65.3 146
3.66.1 164, 260n32
3.66.3 164
3.66.4 165
3.67.2 168
3.67.4 264n82
3.69.2–6 146
3.70.3 262n57
3.76 271n163
4.1.3 159, 165
4.6 146
4.6.1 146
4.6.2 146
4.7.1 146
4.10.2 165
4.11.2 158
4.12.1 169
4.14.3 156, 157
4.17.1 158
4.21.2 166
4.21.3 271n162
4.27.2 165
4.28 166
4.30.1 262n57
4.30.2 166
4.30.3 163
4.32.2 135, 137, 145
4.33 177
4.33.2 175
4.33.3 167
4.34–35 176
4.35.2 176
4.35.4 176
4.35.5 176
4.51.2 264n82

4.52 166
4.52.4 163
4.66.1 163
4.67.3 165
4.68.2 166
4.69.3 167, 168
5.2 262n57
5.4.1 260n32
5.4.2 156
6.1.2 161
6.7.3 163, 166
6.8.2 159
6.8.4 159
6.10.1 166
6.11.2 165
6.13.1 156
6.19.2 166, 167, 268n126
6.19.3 166, 169
6.24.1 169
6.27.3 262n59
11.5.1 268n124
11.6.2 164, 257n20
11.11.2 157
11.13.1 156
11.38 271n163
11.38.3 269n133
12.7.1 157
12.41.3 260n32
12.50.2 258n20
12.66.1 258n20
13.1 266n99
13.25 161
13.26.1 158, 265n96
13.37.1 169
13.43.5 262n57
14.3 267n116
14.12.2 266n97
14.13 267n116
14.14 158
14.14.2 159
14.14.3 160
14.14.4 160
14.15 267n116
14.15.1–2 161
14.15.3–4 161
14.15.5 160, 161
14.45 265n96
14.45.2 262n57
14.48 268n124
14.48.2 262n57
14.49.1 172
14.50.1 158
14.59 267n116
14.60.1 158
14.61 157
14.62 267n116
14.64 267n116
14.64.1 172
14.64.3 265n96
15.35 266n99, 269n131
15.37 161
15.50 267n116
15.54.1 161
15.74.3 262n57
16.5.2 161
16.7 266n99
16.7–35 268n124
16.11.1 172
16.11.3 168, 262n57
16.16.1 169
16.19.1 168
16.21 266n97
16.21.1 266n99
16.23.1 266n99
16.26.5 262n62
16.29.1 169
Dial.
19.2 177
19.5 177
20.4 178
21.8 177
28.2 177
38.2 260n36
39.1–2 170
Germ.
6.6 141

7.1 141
7.3–4 141
12.2 141
13.3–4 141
19 141
19.1 141
19.5 260n37
21.1 141
22.4 141
Hist.
1.2 267n112, 268n124
1.4 266n100
1.5 158
1.15 267n106
1.16 270n146
1.72 156
1.85 158
4.17 270n146

Valleius
2.130 268n128

Virgil
Aen.
1.276–77 69
6.851 3
Ec.
3.43 242n84
6.7 69
G.
1.154 200

General Index

Achilles, 72
Ancus, 97
Animi medicina (art of healing the soul), 41, 46–54
Annales school, 30
Antiochus, 239n46
Antony, Mark, 78, 133
Arendt: and beauty, 56–61; and Cicero, 41–42, 61–68; and citizenship, 241n76; and common sense, 57–58; and culture, 9, 53–54, 68, 75; elitism of, 62, 72–73; and fabrication, 62–64, 66, 69–77; and founding, 69–71; Greek influence on, 61–63; and judgment, 57–58, 68–69, 72–73; and law, 69–72; and medicine, 41; philosophy as cultivation, 54–61; Rahel Varnhagen, 67, 243n97, 243n100; role of philosophy for, 54–61, 74–77; Roman influence on, 12, 41–42, 61–77; and "Scipio's Dream," 64–66; and spectacle, 53, 57, 73; and totalitarianism, 6, 66; and worldlessness, 61–68
Aristo, 209
Aristotle: and despotism, 134, 145, 256–57n13; and emotions, 85–86; and lawmaking, 69–70; in Livy, 85–86; and *phronesis*, 10, 12, 83, 124; and reason, 12; and self-realization, 215–16
Art: and culture, 53, 55–61, 215; as model of political theory, 60–61, 63–64, 66, 69–70, 73–74, 76–77, 89, 98, 205–16; Plato's conception of, 76, 98; Roman Republic compared to, 8–9, 38, 46, 53, 55–61, 69–70, 73–74; and the self, 205–16
Atticus, 40, 46, 52–53
Augustus: *auctoritas* of, 80, 190; and Cicero, 237n27; persecution under, 162–63, 176, 261n45; power of, 147–49; restored republic under, 144, 225; rise of, 78; Tacitus's view of, 143–45

Barbatus, Marcus Horatius, 112
Benjamin, Walter, 74–76
Bentley, Arthur, 26
Bruni, Leonardo, 133
Brutus, 101–103, 110, 113–14

Caesar, Julius, 42, 78
Caligula, 166
Cambridge School, 33–34, 102–103, 123, 125–26

Camillus, 50–51, 107, 115–20, 128–30, 157; legend of, 252n117
Carneades, 195
Catlin, George, 22
Cato the Elder, 3, 193, 196, 198, 204, 212
Celsus, 136–37, 140, 143–44, 169, 177
Cicero: and Augustus, 237n27; and beauty, 56–61; and care, 42, 45, 59–61; and citizenship, 241n76; and common sense, 57–58; and culture, 8–9, 53–61, 242n95; death of Tullia, 39, 46–47, 50, 52, 67; and disease (*see* Cicero, and medicine); and duty, 43, 46, 238n29; and ethics, 60–61; and Epicureanism, 41; exile of, 39–40, 42, 46, 236n13; and founding, 69, 71, 93; and grief, 38–41, 46–52; and *humanitas,* 56; and judgment, 57–58, 72–73; and leisure, 56, 250n50; and medicine, 40–42, 46–54, 87–89, 92, 247n60; and monuments, 52–53; and nature, 51, 54–58; and oratory (*see* Cicero, and rhetoric); and passion, 48–49, 239n35; philosophy as cultivation, 54–61; philosophy as therapy, 40, 46–54; and Plato, 44–46; political psychology of, 46–54, 87–88, 91; as political theorist, 46–61, 223–24; *The Republic,* 8–9, 40, 42–46; and rhetoric, 53, 236n2, 236n11, 240n48, 242n96, 247–48n60; role of philosophy in, 46–61, 236n10; role of sight in, 57, 61, 73, 90–92, 209, 248n73; Roman Republic, 38–39, 58–59, 78; "Scipio's Dream" in, 8–9, 40, 42–48, 59; and sickness (*see* Cicero, and medicine); and spectacle, 48, 57–61, 73; and Stoicism, 40, 45–52, 239n35, 239n46; and Tullia (*see* Cicero, death of Tullia); *Tusculan Disputations,* 8–9, 39–42, 46–61, 73; views by scholars of, 24, 35, 39–40; and virtue, 51
Civic republicanism, 34, 102, 125–26
Classics: *Altertumswissenschaft,* 15; contributions of, 15–16, 20–22, 26–28; cultural approaches in, 36–37; and democracy, 19–22, 26–28; and ethics, 20–21; historiography in, 15–16, 28–30; and idealism, 13–15; origins as a discipline, 13–16, 230n8–9; philology in, 15; prosopography, 25–26; and science, 21–22; social power approaches, 25–26; and theory, 28–30
Claudius, 156–57, 166, 180
Claudius, Appius (grandfather), 110–15, 133
Claudius, Appius (grandson), 118
Claudius, Marcus, 113
Cordus, Cremutius, 176
Crantor, 48–49
Crassus, Marcus Licinius, in the First Triumvirate, 42
Cultura animi (care of the soul), 42, 54–61, 76

Dahl, Robert, 26
Decemvirate. *See Decemviri*
Decemviri, 104–106, 109–15, 133; traditions of, 252n114
Delatores, 163–70
Despotism: in Aristotle, 134, 145, 256–57n13; in Foucault, 185,

216, 218; modern, 11–12; in Montesquieu, 10–11, 133–36, 150–51, 159, 162, 170–74; in Tacitus, 11, 185, 189–204, 210, 212–13, 216. *See also* Arendt, and totalitarianism; Livy, and tyranny; Machiavelli, and tyranny; Tyranny
Dewey, John, 19
Dineson, Isak, 76–77
Domitian, 132, 135, 169–70, 176, 178
Dream of Scipio. *See* "Scipio's Dream"
Drusus Caesar (son of Tiberius), 153–55
Dunning, William, 17–18

Easton, David, 30

First Triumvirate, 42
Fortune: in Cicero, 45; in Livy, 117; in Machiavelli, 130; in Seneca, 199–204
Foucault: aesthetics, 206–208, 217; and art, 206–16, 221–22; care of the self, 11, 183–85, 205–16; and Christianity, 220; and Descartes, 219; and despotism, 185, 216, 218; and domination, 211–12; and ethics, 187–88, 205–207, 214, 216, 220; and fortune, 199–201; and freedom, 211–12, 215, 222; governmentality, 211–12, 220–21; Greek influence on, 217; and jurisdiction, 188–95, 216, 220; and liberty, 212, 215; and medicine, 137; *parrhêsia*, 221–22; political spirituality, 219–22; power, 183–84, 191, 193, 210–11; problematization, 184–85; and rhetoric (*see* Foucault, and speech); role of sight, 207–16, 221–22; role of thought in, 184–85, 217–22; Roman influence on, 182–84, 217–22, 274n13; scholarly views of, 183–84, 217, 219–20, 273–74n12; self-fashioning, 207–16; and speech, 221–22

Gallus, Asinius, 149, 195
Gauls, 115–19
Gelzer, Matthias, 25
Germanicus Caesar (adopted son of Tiberius), 151, 156, 166, 170
Gildersleeve, Basil, 13, 15, 18–19
Globalization, 12, 64, 218–19, 223–26
Gracchus, Tiberius, 42–43
Guicciardini, Francesco, 133

Hallowell, John, 28
Havel, Václav, 216
Hegel, 7, 14, 41
Heidegger, Martin, 68
Hektor, 72
Hippocrates, 86
Homer, 60–61, 63
Homo faber. See Arendt, and fabrication
Honor: corruption of, 143, 146, 150, 159–60, 162, 164–65, 170, 175, 183, 198, 201–202; desire for, 50; imperial, 148; role of, 150, 162, 164–65, 183, 188
Humors, 86–92, 105–106. *See also* Medicine

Icilius, 113
Imperialism, 12, 182–83, 218, 225

Lepidus, M. Aemilius, in Second Triumvirate, 78, 133, 142

Lex de ambitu, 143
Lex maiestatis, 163
Lex Pompeia de vi, 142–43
Liberty: in Foucault, 212, 215; in Livy, 10, 84, 98–106, 117; in Machiavelli, 10, 84, 102–106, 250n100; in Montesquieu, 149, 170–72; in Rome, 71–72, 221–22, 242n89, 250n97, 250n100, 250n105; in Seneca, 215, 221–22; in Tacitus, 142, 171–72
Libo Drusus (M. Scribonius Libo Drusus), 167–68
Livy, 7; and Aristotle, 85–86; and Augustus, 79–80, 244n11; and authority, 94–99; and civic virtue, 92; and climate, 116; and corruption, 90–91, 100, 104–16; and *exempla*, 80–82, 214; felt meanings in, 9–10, 82–83, 90, 94–98, 104, 109, 112–15, 118–20, 207, 224–25; and founding, 92–98, 118–20; and the humors, 86–92; and liberty, 10, 84, 98–106, 117; medicine in, 78–79, 91–93, 108–109; and monuments, 9–10, 80, 214, 245n23; and the New Academy, 86; and Plato, 86; political psychology of, 9–10, 79–92, 108–109, 116–20, 246–47n40; as political theorist, 79–84, 89–92, 116, 118, 125, 223–24; rhetoric in, 115–16, 118–20; role of historiography, 101–102, 114, 116, 118, 120–25; role of sight in, 80–84, 89–92, 94–95, 100–102, 104–120, 214; and sickness (*see* Livy, medicine in); and the skeptical Academy, 86; and spectacle, 9–10, 78–81, 86–92, 94–98, 100–103, 108–109, 112–14, 116–20; and the Stoics, 85; and the Tarquins, 98–102, 111; and tyranny, 100–102, 110–15; views by scholars of, 79–81, 120–22
Lucretia, 100–104, 119

Machiavelli: and Camillus, 128–30; and character (*see* Machiavelli, and political character); and Christianity, 10, 124; civic republicanism of, 125–26; corruption in, 10, 84, 104–15, 125; and the decemvirate (*see* Machiavelli, and the *decemviri*); and the *decemviri*, 110–15; and dictators, 106–107; and disease (*see* Machiavelli, medicine in); felt meanings, 82–83, 94, 104, 109, 115, 131, 127–29, 224; and founding, 93–94, 97–98; and the humors, 86–92, 105–106; and judgment, 124–25, 127; and justice, 94, 249n81; and kingship, 99, 124; liberty in, 10, 84, 102–106, 250n100; and Lucretia, 101–102, 250n97; medicine in, 86–92, 105–106, 108–109; and monuments, 81–82, 98; and necessity, 128–30; political character, 107, 125–31, 246–47n40; political psychology of, 10, 82–92, 108–109, 124–25, 127–31; as political theorist, 120–25, 130–31, 224; and rhetoric, 123–25; role of historiography, 120–25, 130–31; role of sight in, 81–84, 89–90, 94–98, 103, 104–15, 123–25, 130; Roman influence, 81–82, 102–103, 120–25; and sickness (*see* Machiavelli, medicine in); scholarly views of, 120–28; and spectacle, 81–84, 88–90,

94–98, 103–15, 123–25, 129–31; and Tacitus, 133–38; and tyranny, 106, 110; *virtù*, 81, 106–107, 123, 245n25
Maelius, Spurius, 106–107
Manlius, Spurius, 107–109
Marxian approaches, 7, 33
McIlwain, Charles, 23
Medicine: analogy to politics, 40–42, 46–54, 78–79, 85–92, 100–102, 105–106, 108–109, 116, 136–46, 157–62, 163–66, 175–79, 191–95, 209, 220, 246n34; ancient, 85–92, 136–38, 140, 143–44, 177–79; in Arendt, 41; in Cicero, 40–42, 46–54, 87–89, 92, 247n60; in Foucault, 137; and Hippocrates, 86; humors in, 86–92, 105–106; and madness, 110, 145–46, 150–55, 157, 168–70, 176–81, 191–95, 246n33, 247n60; relationship to sight, 86–92; in Seneca, 140, 180–81, 189–204, 220–22
Merriam, Charles, 17, 22, 27
Michels, Robert, 26
Mirandola, Pico della, 88–89
Mommsen, Theodor, 16, 18, 23, 54, 189, 275n31
Montaigne, 134
Montesquieu and Aristotle, 134, 256–57n13; and the Britons, 139–46; and Cicero, 77; climate theory in, 258n23–24; collective spirit (*see* Montesquieu, spirit of the community); contract theory, 259n25; despotism, 10–11, 133–36, 150–51, 159, 162, 170–74; and determinism in, 258n22; and Eastern despotisms, 173–74; and the Germans, 139–46; and Hobbes, 259n25; and liberty, 149, 170–72; and Livy, 173; and madness, 171–72; political psychology of, 135–40, 143, 171–72; as political theorist, 178–79, 225; and primitive societies, 139–47, 258n23; Roman influence on, 133–35, 172–74; and spectacle, 173; and the spirit of the community, 134, 137–40, 258n22; view by scholars of, 172–74
Mosco, Gaetano, 26
Mos maiorum, 5
Münzer, Friedrich, 25

Nero, 157, 159–61, 166, 169, 172, 181–82, 197
New Criticism, 28–29
New Historicism, 36
Niger, Bruttedius, 164
Numa, 97
Numitor, 96

Octavia (wife of Nero), 172
Octavian. *See* Augustus
Oratory. *See* Rhetoric
Othos, Junius, 164–65, 168

Panaetius, 238n29
Pareto, Vilfredo, 26
Piso, Calpurnius, 166
Piso, Gnaeus, 146–47
Plato: corruption in, 84; *eidos*, 73, 76; and founding, 93, 97–98; and lawmaking, 69–70; Myth of Er, 44–45; and the New Academy, 86; philosopher-king in, 10, 46, 83, 130; and reason, 12, 131; in Seneca, 209–10; vision of, 6, 56
Plebs. *See* Power, of the people
Pocock, J.G.A. *See* Cambridge School

Political psychology: of Cicero, 46–54, 87–88, 91; of Livy, 9–10, 79–92, 116–20, 246–47n40; of Machiavelli, 10, 82–92, 124–25, 127–31; of Montesquieu, 135–40, 143, 171–72; of Seneca, 180–81, 186–88, 212–15; of the Stoics, 186–88; of Tacitus, 135–46, 164, 176–79, 257n15, 257n18
Political theory: and behavioralism, 30, 34; and Cambridge School, 33–34; in Cicero, 46–61, 223–24; and classics, 13–14; contributions of, 16–18, 20–22, 26–28; cultural approaches to, 36–37; and democracy, 19–22, 26–28; and ethics, 20–21, 27–28; group power approaches in, 26; and history, 16–17, 30; and idealism, 13–15; as intellectual history, 3–34; in Livy, 79–84, 89–92, 116, 118, 125, 223–24; in Machiavelli, 120–25, 130–31, 224; in Montesquieu, 178–79, 225; normative, 33; origin as a discipline, 13–14, 16–18, 230n13; as political vision, 34–35; and science, 16–18; 21–22, 30–31; in Seneca, 185, 188, 226; as social history, 17–18; 33; in Tacitus, 176–79, 225
Pollock, Sir Frederick, 18
Polybius, 31, 35, 85, 105
Pompey, 42, 133, 142–43, 204
Posidonius, 88–89
Power: of the army, 148, 156; of the consuls, 103; of the decemvirate (*see* Power, of the *decemviri*); of the *decemviri*, 110–14; of the equestrian order (*see* Power, of the knights); of the kings, 96–99; of the knights, 148, 161; of Lucretia, 100–101; over oneself, 183, 191, 193, 201, 210–12, 220–22; of patronage, 147–48; of the people, 84, 103–104, 108–110, 112–13, 133, 148, 155, 245n29, 251n108; of the plebs (*see* Power, of the people); of the praetorian guard, 149, 156; in the principate, 132–36, 143–44, 147–51, 154, 182–83, 188–95, 201–202, 261n52, 263n65, 264n72, 266n98; in the republic, 103, 132–33; of the senate, 109–110, 112, 133, 142, 144, 146–48, 154–55, 157–62, 262n59, 263n65, 265–66n96; and terror, 162–70; of the tribunes, 108, 110, 112–13, 114, 118, 142, 148, 161, 262n57
Propaganda, 20, 25–27
Prosopography, 25

Rawls, John, 7, 33
Remus, 93
Rhetoric: in Cicero, 53, 236n2, 236n11, 240n48, 242n96, 247–48n60; in Foucault, 221–22; in Livy, 115–16, 118–20; in Machiavelli, 123–25; role of, 175; in Rome, 222, 265n95; in Seneca, 194, 221–22; in Tacitus, 157–58, 175–79, 221–22
Roman political thought: and Christianity, 10, 24, 27–28; compared to Greek political thought, 3–4, 6–7, 11–13, 28, 31–32, 35, 44–45, 56, 61–62, 67–74, 76, 93–94, 97–98, 120–22, 131, 134, 209–10, 215–16, 218, 226–27; as constitutionalism, 3, 14, 16, 18–19, 22–25, 56;

as cultivation, 74–77; as fabrication, 74–77; and law, 70–72; as nostalgic, 6, 37; vision provided by, 6–10, 12, 31–32, 35, 60–61, 73–77, 118–20, 125, 172–79
Rome: armies in, 148, 151–56; authority in (*see* Rome, institutions); civil war in, 38–39, 78–79, 143, 155–57; corruption of, 60, 104–15, 159–60; the *decemviri* in, 104–106, 109–15; despotism in (*see* Despotism); and duty, 43–46, 48, 50–54, 189–90, 238n29; and fame, 195–99; founding, 69–71, 92–98, 118–20; institutions of, 96–97, 102–107, 135–36, 143, 147–51, 154, 158–59, 168, 188–91, 251n108, 262n57, 262n59, 263n65; and laws (*see* Rome, institutions of); lawyers in, 23–24; liberty in, 71–72, 151, 221–22, 242n89, 250n97, 250n100, 250n105; *maiestas* prosecutions, 162–70; mutinies, 151–55; as oligarchy, 26, 245n29; Republic, 38–39, 72; oratory in (*see* Rome, rhetoric in); rhetoric in, 222, 265n95; and the Sabines, 93, 95–96; terror, 99, 146, 162–70; theater, 150–52, 156, 161–62, 197–98, 264n81; and tyranny (*see* Tyranny); violence in, 38–39, 42–43, 59, 78
Romulus, 93–97, 99

Sabine, George, 24–26
Sabines, 93, 95–97, 99–100
Sallust, 39, 91
Samnites, 129
Scaurus, Mamercus, 164
Scipio, Aemilianus, 43–45, 49
Scipio, Africanus, 43–45
"Scipio's Dream," 8–9, 40, 42–48, 59, 64–65, 76–77
Second Triumvirate, 78, 99
Sejanus, L. Aelius, 159, 166, 195
Seneca: and art, 205–16, 221; and authority, 188–95, 204–16; care of the self in, 11, 205–16; and citizenship, 182, 204–205; and Claudius, 180–81; and culture, 207–10, 215–16; and despotism, 11, 185, 188–204, 210, 212–13, 216; and duty, 189–91; and ethics, 205–207, 214, 216; and fame, 195–99; and honor, 190, 195–99; and jurisdiction, 187–95, 208–10, 216, 222; and law, 189–95, 275–76n31, 276n35; and liberty, 201–202, 215, 221–22; and madness, 180–81, 189–204, 220–22; and medicine, 140; and monuments, 214; and nature,186–88, 274n13; and Nero, 25, 180–82, 197–98; *oikeiôsis* in, 186–88, 275n20; oratory (*see* Seneca, speech in); political psychology of, 180–81, 186–88, 212–15; as political theorist, 185, 188, 226; rhetoric (*see* Seneca, speech in); role of philosophy, 204–22; role of sight, 197–99, 202–203, 207–10, 212–16; and Roman authority, 188–204, 275–76n31; self-fashioning in, 207–16; self as monument, 204–16; and spectacle, 202–203; speech in, 194, 221–22; theater, 150–51, 197–98; view by scholars of, 24–25, 35, 181–82
Servilius Vatia, 195, 199
Silanus, Gaius, 164
Smith, Munroe, 16

Socrates, 7, 48, 181, 196, 198, 205, 209
Solon, 110
Stoicism: care of the self in, 205–206; citizenship in, 64, 182; and fortune, 200; and nature, 55; *oikeiôsis* in, 186–88, 275n20; and philosophy, 55–56; political psychology of, 186–88; and reflection, 186–88; and rhetoric, 86
Strauss, Leo, 28, 34, 121
Sulla, 39, 99, 133, 142, 162
Syme, Ronald, 26, 36, 135

Tacitus: and the Britons, 139–46, 160; and *delatores*, 163–70; despotism in, 10–11, 132–38, 140–42, 150–51, 157, 162, 169–70, 174–79; and fortune, 199–204; and the Germans, 139–46, 150, 160; and liberty, 142, 151, 171–72; and madness, 132, 137–38, 142–46, 151–55, 157–70, 199; *maiestas* prosecutions in, 162–70; oratory in (*see* Tacitus, speech in); political psychology of, 136–46, 150, 164, 176–79, 257n15, 257n18; as political theorist, 176–79, 225; and primitive societies, 259n26; in the Renaissance, 133–34; rhetoric in (*see* Tacitus, speech in); role of historiography, 174–79; speech in, 153–55, 157–58, 175–79, 221–22; and the Tacitists, 134; and tyranny (*see* Tacitus, despotism)
Tarquinius, Sextus, 100–101, 113
Tarquinius Supurbus, 99–102
Tarquins, 98–104, 110–12
Terra incognita, 225
Terra recognita, 5–11
Tiberius, 132–35, 145–46, 149, 151, 154–57, 161–63, 166–69, 176, 192–93, 195
Tribunes. *See* Power, of the tribunes
Truman, David, 26
Tullia (daughter of Cicero). *See* Cicero, death of Tullia
Tullia (wife of Tarquinius Superbus), 99, 101
Tyranny: in Livy, 100–102, 110–15; in Machiavelli, 106, 110; in Rome, 100, 110–15, 132–38, 257n13, 259–60n31. *See also* Despotism

Valerius, Publius, 103–104
Vatia. *See* Servilius Vatia
Verginia, 112–14, 119
Verginius, 112–15
Voegelin, Eric, 27–28
Von Premerstein, Anton, 25
Von Ranke, Leopold, 15–16
Von Wilamowitz-Moellendorff, Ulrich, 15–16, 21

Willoughby, W. W., 17–18
Wissenschaft, 21
Wolin, Sheldon, 6, 24, 34–35, 70, 72, 122, 182, 218, 226

Zeno, 238n29